Genocide and Gender in the Twentieth Century

Genocide and Gender in the Twentieth Century

A Comparative Survey

Edited by

Amy E. Randall

Bloomsbury Academic
An imprint of Bloomsbury Publishing Plc

B L O O M S B U R Y
LONDON · NEW DELHI · NEW YORK · SYDNEY

Bloomsbury Academic

An imprint of Bloomsbury Publishing Plc

50 Bedford Square	1385 Broadway
London	New York
WC1B 3DP	NY 10018
UK	USA

www.bloomsbury.com

BLOOMSBURY and the Diana logo are trademarks of Bloomsbury Publishing Plc

First published 2015

British Library Cataloguing-in-Publication Data
A catalogue record for this book is available from the British Library.

ISBN: HB: 978-1-4725-0567-5
PB: 978-1-4725-0708-2
ePDF: 978-1-4725-0646-7
ePub: 978-1-4725-0980-2

Library of Congress Cataloging-in-Publication Data
Genocide and gender in the twentieth century: a comparative survey/edited by Amy E. Randall.
pages cm
ISBN 978-1-4725-0567-5 (hbk) – ISBN 978-1-4725-0708-2 (pbk) 1. Genocide–History–20th
century. 2. Women–Violence against–History–20th century. 3. Rape as a weapon of
war–History–20th century. I. Randall, Amy E. (Amy Elise) 1967-
HV6322.7.G4475 2015
304.6′630810904–dc23
2015004255

Typeset by Deanta Global Publishing Services, Chennai, India
Printed and bound in India.

For Mathew Reed, as always,
and our children, Zeiler Robeson and Zaria
Jordan Randall-Reed,
who inspire me and give me hope.

In honor of Olga Lengyel, Holocaust survivor and
author of Five Chimneys: A Woman Survivor's
True Story of Auschwitz,
and the first generation of feminist scholars
of the Holocaust.

CONTENTS

NOTES ON
CONTRIBUTORS

Jennie E. Burnet is Associate Professor of Anthropology at the University of Louisville. Her research interests include gender, ethnicity, race, war, genocide, and reconciliation in postconflict societies in the African Great Lakes region. She has published articles in *African Affairs*, *African Studies Review*, *Politics and Gender*, and *Genocide Studies and Prevention* and chapters in several edited collections. Her award-winning book, *Genocide Lives in Us: Women, Memory and Silence in Rwanda*, was published in 2012 by the University of Wisconsin Press.

Doris Buss, Associate Professor of Law at Carleton University (Canada), teaches and researches in the areas of international law and human rights, women's rights, global social movements, and feminist theory. Over the last few years, her work has concentrated on international criminal prosecutions of sexual violence during or as part of armed conflict. More recently, Buss has been investigating gender equality mainstreaming in postconflict state-building and law reform projects on the African continent. Other new work examines the "measurement turn" in gender policy, both in Canada and internationally. Buss is the author (with Didi Herman) of *Globalizing Family Values: The International Politics of the Christian Right* (Minnesota Press, 2003), coeditor (with Ambreena Manji) of *International Law: Modern Feminist Approaches* (Hart, 2005), and coeditor (with Joanne Lebert, Blair Rutherford, and Donna Sharkey) of *Sexual Violence in Conflict and Post-Conflict Societies: International Agendas and African Contexts* (Routledge, 2014).

Mark A. Drumbl is the Class of 1975 Alumni Professor at Washington & Lee University, School of Law, where he also serves as Director of the Transnational Law Institute. He has held visiting appointments with a number of law faculties, including Oxford, Paris II (Pantheon-Assas), Trinity College–Dublin, Melbourne, Monash, and Ottawa. His scholarly interests include public international law, international criminal law (including specifically within the Rwandan context), and the role of masculinities and femininities in transitional justice. His books *Atrocity, Punishment and International Law* (Cambridge University Press, 2007) and *Reimagining Child Soldiers in International Law and Policy* (Oxford University Press, 2012) have been widely reviewed and have earned critical acclaim. He holds degrees in law and politics from McGill University, University of Toronto, and Columbia University.

Lerna Ekmekcioglu is McMillan-Stewart Career Development Assistant Professor of History at Massachusetts Institute of Technology, where she is also affiliated with the Women and Gender Studies Program. She received her BA in Sociology from Boğaziçi University (Istanbul) in 2002, her MA from New York University in 2004, and her PhD from NYU in 2010 in the joint program of the Department of History and the Department of Middle Eastern/Islamic Studies. She is the coeditor of the 2006 volume, *A Cry for Justice: Five Armenian Feminist Writers from the Ottoman Empire to the Turkish Republic (1862-1933)*(in Turkish), and is currently working on a monograph on Armenians in postgenocide Turkey, with particular attention to women and gender issues.

Elisa von Joeden-Forgey is Assistant Professor of Holocaust and Genocide Studies at the Richard Stockton College of New Jersey. Prior to this she was a visiting scholar and lecturer in the Department of History at the University of Pennsylvania, where she earned her PhD in modern German and African history. She teaches courses on the Holocaust, genocide, human rights, war, and imperialism. Her work on German imperial history has been published in several journals and collected volumes. Her current research on gender and genocide has appeared in the *Journal of Genocide Studies and Prevention*, the *Oxford Handbook on Genocide*, the collected volume *New Directions in Genocide Research*, *Genocide: A Bibliographic Review*, *Hidden Genocide: Power, Knowledge and Memory*, and the forthcoming collected volumes *Reconstructing Atrocity Prevention* and *Economic Aspects of Genocide, Mass Killing, and Their Prevention*. She is currently completing a book on gender and the prevention of genocide which will be published by the University of Pennsylvania Press.

Stephen Haynes is Professor of Religious Studies at Rhodes College in Memphis, TN. He is the author of several works on the Holocaust, including most recently *The Bonhoeffer Phenomenon: Portraits of a Protestant Saint* (Fortress Press, 2004), and the *Bonhoeffer Legacy: Post-Holocaust Perspectives* (Fortress Press, 2006). He has also written about the American South, slavery, and the civil rights movement, of which his most recent publication is *The Last Segregated Hour: The Memphis Kneel-Ins and the Campaign for Southern Church Desegregation* (Oxford University

Press, 2012). Haynes teaches courses on theology, the Holocaust, and religion and racism.

Nicole Hogg is an international lawyer, specializing in international humanitarian law and weapons law. In 2001, she conducted extensive research on women's role in the Rwandan genocide, including interviews with seventy-one female genocide suspects in Rwandan prisons. Since 2003 she has worked for the International Committee of the Red Cross in various positions in the field and in Geneva where she currently works as a legal adviser. She holds a Master of Laws from McGill University, Canada and a Bachelor of Laws and a BA from Melbourne University, Australia.

Anthonie Holslag is an independent researcher and anthropologist. He is the author of several works on the Armenian genocide and Armenian diaspora, including *In Het Gesteente van Ararat* (Aspekt, 2009); "Within the Acts of Violence: An Anthropological Exploration on the Meaning of Genocide as a Cultural Expression," in *The Crime of Genocide: Prevention, Condemnation, and Elimination of Consequences* (Yerevan: Ministry of Foreign Affairs of the Republic of Armenia, 2011); "Ik zag ze gaan: een analyse van de relatie tussen minderheidsgroepen en volkerenmoord in het Ottomaanse Rijk 1915-1917," *Leidschrift* 29:1 (2014); *Near the Foot of Mt. Ararat* (Taderon Press, forthcoming). Holslag has taught at the University of Amsterdam, the Center for Holocaust and Genocide Studies, and the Utrecht University.

Adam Jones is Professor of Political Science at the University of British Columbia in Kelowna, Canada. He is the author of *Gender Inclusive: Essays on Violence, Men, and Feminist International Relations* (Routledge, 2009) and author or editor of more than a dozen other books, including *Gendercide and Genocide* (Vanderbilt University Press, 2004). He serves as executive director of Gendercide Watch (www.gendercide.org), a web-based educational initiative that confronts gender-selective atrocities against men and women worldwide.

Selma Leydesdorff is Professor of Oral History and Culture at the University of Amsterdam. Most of her oral history publications are on the narratives of traumatized people, and her 2008 book on Srebrenica, *De leegte achter ons laten: Een geschiedenis van de vrouwen van Srebrenica*, was published in English in 2011. Leydesdorff has conducted numerous interviews with survivors of Auschwitz and Mauthausen. Her most recent work focuses on the life stories of survivors of the Sobibor extermination camp and those involved in the war crimes trial of John Demjanjuk in Munich. She is currently working on a biography of Aleksandr Pechersky, the leader of the Sobibor uprising of 1943.

Lisa Pine is Reader in History at London South Bank University. She studied International History at the London School of Economics and Political Science and obtained her PhD from there in 1996. Her main publications include *Education in Nazi Germany* (Bloomsbury Academic, 2010); *Hitler's "National Community": Society and Culture in Nazi Germany* (Bloomsbury Academic, 2007); and *Nazi Family Policy, 1933-1945* (Bloomsbury Academic, 1997). She is currently editing a new book, *Life and Times in Nazi Germany*, for publication by Bloomsbury Academic in 2016.

Amy E. Randall is Associate Professor of History at Santa Clara University in California. She is also a member of the teaching faculty for the Women's and Gender Studies Program. Randall is the author of *The Soviet Dream World of Retail Trade and Consumption in the 1930s* (Palgrave Macmillan, 2008). She has also published articles in *The Russian Review, The Journal of Social History, The Journal of Women's History*, and *Russian Studies in History*. Recent scholarship and publications have focused on gender and sexuality in the post-Stalin era, particularly Soviet masculinities. Randall teaches courses on the Soviet Union, gender and national identity in twentieth-century Eastern and Western Europe, the history of sexuality, and ethnic cleansing and genocide in the twentieth century.

Olivera Simić is Senior Lecturer at the Griffith University Law School, Queensland, Australia. Her research engages with transitional justice, international law, peacekeeping, gender, and crime from an interdisciplinary perspective. Simić has published numerous articles in journals such as *International Peacekeeping, Law Text Culture, Women's Studies International Forum, Journal of International Women Studies*, book chapters in various edited collections, and other writings. Her latest coedited collection, *The Arts of Transitional Justice: Culture, Activism, and Memory after Atrocity* (with Peter D. Rush), was published by *Springer* in 2013. Her latest monograph, *Surviving Peace: A Political Memoir*, was published by Spinifex in 2014.

Zoë Waxman is the author of *Writing the Holocaust: Identity, Testimony, Representation* (Oxford University Press, 2006) and the forthcoming *Anne Frank* (2015), as well as numerous articles on the Holocaust and other genocides. She teaches courses on the Holocaust, memory, and gender and genocide at the University of Oxford Centre for Hebrew and Jewish Studies and is currently completing *A Feminist of the Holocaust* for Oxford University Press.

Patricia Weitsman was Director of War and Peace Studies at the Center for International Studies and Professor of Political Science at Ohio University. Sadly, she passed away in 2014, after struggling with a long and difficult illness. Patricia coauthored *The Politics of Policy Making in Defense and Foreign Affairs* (1993) and co-edited *Towards A New Europe: Stops and Starts in Regional Integration* (1995) and *Enforcing Cooperation: "Risky" States and the Intergovernmental Management of Conflict* (1997). Her first book, *Dangerous Alliances: Proponents of Peace, Weapons of War* (Stanford University Press, 2004) was a finalist for several major book awards, and her second book, *Waging War: Alliances, Coalitions, and Institutions of Interstate Violence* (Stanford University Press, 2013), was completed even as Weitsman struggled with her health. Weitsman's work was published in numerous edited volumes as well as journals in the field. Weitsman was a talented professor and won several awards for her teaching. She was also a very active member of the International Security Studies Section of the International Studies Association, and served as its chair from 2011 to 2013.

Patricia (Patty) Weitsman was a wonderful scholar, teacher, and mentor as well as a loving wife, mother, daughter, sister, and friend, and she is missed by many.

ACKNOWLEDGMENTS

In the spring of 2009, I taught my upper-level seminar on ethnic cleansing and genocide in the twentieth century for the first time. As students in this initial class and in subsequent classes struggled with questions about the origins of genocide, the unfolding of genocidal processes, how ordinary people become mass murderers, the international community's responses to and accountability for genocide, and other related matters, they engaged in many difficult conversations with me and each other. It was out of this shared inquiry that the seeds for this book were sown. I am, therefore, grateful to my students in all of these classes for contributing to my thinking about genocide and for giving me the opportunity to become more deeply immersed in existing scholarship on this important topic.

Santa Clara University (SCU) has generously supported this project. I owe a special thanks to the Provost's Office for awarding me a course release in the academic year of 2013/14 as part of the Faculty Research Course Release Initiative Pilot Program to support my book project on genocide and gender. The one-course reduction in my teaching load, as well as the grant that accompanied the course release, allowed me to make significant headway on the edited collection. I am also thankful to the Provost's and Dean's offices for awarding subvention grants to cover copyright permission and indexing fees.

Cynthia Bradley and Carolee Bird, the manager and supervisor (respectively) of SCU's Interlibrary Loan Office, provided significant assistance with this project. Their consistent professionalism and their ability to make articles and books appear, almost magically, in a very short time are much appreciated. I am extremely grateful to two undergraduate students at SCU who helped move this project to completion. Brennah Kelly provided excellent assistance with the bibliography and endnotes. Michaela Ahlstrom spent countless hours helping to copyedit and proofread almost all of the volume's chapters; her outstanding work and good humor were invaluable. Thanks also to Yasmeen Wanees for providing preliminary assistance with one of the volume's chapters. I also wish to thank Judy Gillette for her help.

I am indebted to Naomi Andrews and Matthew Newsom-Kerr, two of my colleagues in the Department of History at SCU, for reading my introduction closely and offering important feedback. Their insights and suggestions helped to improve the final product. Naomi Andrews was also instrumental in encouraging me to pursue this publication in the first place; I cannot thank her enough for her faith in me and my intellectual goals, and for her friendship more broadly. Thanks also to Sharmila Lodhia for being a writing buddy during this project and for offering general encouragement.

I want to thank Rhodri Mogford at Bloomsbury for helping to make this book possible. After a lengthy exchange with him on my perceived need for the publication of an edited collection on genocide and gender, and more comparative genocide scholarship, Rhodri encouraged me to submit a book proposal. That I did so was an unexpected turn in my intellectual and professional journey, and I am most glad that I decided to move along this new path. I am grateful to the anonymous reviewers for their constructive criticism as well as their belief in the value of this book. Emma Goode and the production team at Bloomsbury, especially Ian Buck and Grishma Fredric, also deserve thanks for bringing this project to publication.

Finally, I would like to express my sincere thanks to my family and friends. I am particularly grateful to my mother and stepfather, who taught me by example at an early age to take an active stand against hatred and intolerance of others—because of their "differences"—and to speak out for the rights and dignity of all people. I would also like to express my appreciation to Pat Hofrichter for spending many hours looking after my children; knowing that they were under her loving care proved to be critical in allowing me to complete this book. My deepest gratitude goes to my life partner and closest friend, Mathew Reed, and our two children, Zeiler and Zaria. Their love sustains me. They also remind me on a daily basis that despite all the ugliness and violence in the world, which this work on genocide and gender has underscored again and again, there is also great beauty, kindness, and joy.

* * *

I am grateful to the following authors and publishers for permission to reproduce, in part or in whole, earlier published versions of three of the volume's chapters:

Chapter 7, "Ordinary Masculinity: Gender Analysis and Holocaust Scholarship," by Stephen Haynes, first appeared in *Journal of Men's Studies* 10:2 (Winter 2001). It is reprinted by permission from Men's Studies Press, LLC, © 2013.

Chapter 9, "The Biopolitics of 'Rescue': Women and the Politics of Inclusion after the Armenian Genocide," by Lerna Ekmekcioglu, is an abridged version of "A Climate for Abduction, A Climate for Redemption: The Politics of Inclusion during and after the Armenian Genocide," *Comparative Studies in Society and History* 55 (2013), © Society for

Comparative Study of Society and History. It is reproduced with permission from Cambridge University Press.

Chapter 13, "Gender and the Future of Genocide Studies and Prevention," by Elisa von Joeden-Forgey, originally appeared in *Genocide Studies and Prevention* 7:1 (2012), © Genocide Studies and Prevention. It is reprinted with permission from the University of Toronto Press (www.utpjournals.com).

Introduction: Gendering Genocide Studies

Amy E. Randall

When it comes to understanding genocide, gender matters. This has not always been evident, and even today there are critics and skeptics. Indeed, when feminist scholars in Holocaust studies first began examining women's experiences and gender questions, their scholarship was ignored or met with hostility by many academics and others, including some survivors. Opponents expressed various concerns, including the idea that gender research and analysis would "trivialize" or "politicize" the Holocaust, de-emphasize the centrality of anti-Semitism and racism to Nazi persecution,[1] and promote "comparative victimhood or creat[e] unequal victims."[2]

Studying the gendered dimensions of genocide, however, does not trivialize the enormity of the crime. Nor does it minimize the importance of real and imagined ideas about ethnic, national, racial, and religious difference in explaining the victimization, destruction, and mass killing of certain groups. The fear that gender analysis will lead to a hierarchy of victims is also misplaced. Gender scholarship does not argue that women had it better or worse than men; rather, it acknowledges differences in women's and men's experiences and examines how the unfolding of genocide has involved "events that specifically affect men as men and women as women."[3] More generally, the purpose of this scholarship is to use gender as a lens for better comprehending the seemingly incomprehensible crime of genocide.

As this volume makes clear, an examination of gender and genocide allows us to hear the voices and stories of women that are often overlooked and to read men's voices and stories in a more nuanced way. By considering both women and men as gendered subjects, this research sheds light on how discourses of femininity and masculinity, gender norms, and understandings of female and male identities contribute to victims' experiences and responses. Such analysis highlights, for example, how Jewish men became demoralized in Nazi Germany, not merely because of the marginalization and increasingly alarming situation of Jews, but also because they could not fulfill their traditional male gender roles as providers for and protectors of their families. Moreover, this feeling of manly "failure" was then compounded by the utter inability of Jewish husbands, fathers, and brothers in concentration/death camps to protect their loved ones.[4]

Historically, the leaders and perpetrators of genocide have promoted deliberately gendered genocidal strategies and processes, which, not surprisingly, have then produced gender-specific traumas or "gendered harms." Investigating these strategies and processes provides a window not only on victims' experiences, but also on genocidal ideologies and discourses, the intentions of perpetrator regimes, the motivations of perpetrators, and the significance of genocidal propaganda. Gender analysis demonstrates, for example, how by raping women *en masse*, often in front of their families and communities, or by forcing family and community members to rape their own, perpetrators intend not merely to devastate the victims and their families but to destroy the targeted group by tearing family and community ties asunder.[5]

The study of sexual violence in the context of genocide shows how it can be used as a genocidal weapon, and scholarship that employs this framework has usefully complicated older narratives about women, war, and rape, in which rape was depicted as a by-product of war, as something incidental.[6] An investigation of genocidal sexual violence also discloses how constructions of ethnic, national, racial, or religious identity are gendered. This research reveals, for example, how certain beliefs about gender, gender roles, and ethnic, national, or racial identity can inspire the leaders and perpetrators of genocide to promote campaigns of mass rape and forced impregnation or, alternatively, to promote forced abortion and forced sterilization.[7] In addition, this research shows how pregenocidal gender dynamics, cultural practices, and political economies can inform the motivations for and forms of genocidal sexual violence. For instance, an analysis of women and gender in pregenocidal Rwanda highlights how rape during the Rwandan genocide was used not only as a symbolic and psychosocial weapon but also as an economic weapon; men claimed the women and girls they raped as war booty so that they could acquire their land and property in forced "marriages."[8] By shedding light on forms of sexual violence, such as forced marriages, and on "invisible" victims who do not fit into existing categories of victimhood, such as male victims or others, the study of genocidal sexual violence can also call attention to issues that have been largely ignored by policymakers and others.[9]

Gender analysis is valuable too in helping us to understand the complexity of human behavior in genocidal circumstances. Why do perpetrators commit atrocities? How do ordinary people become mass murderers, or at least complicit in the processes of genocide? Why do so many people remain bystanders in the face of terrible crimes? How is it that some people decide to resist and undermine genocidal tactics, and sometimes actively aid victims? What role does gender play in shaping individual and group attitudes and conduct during genocide? While gender is only one variable among many in explaining human behavior, it is nonetheless important. As chapters in this volume demonstrate, for instance, discourses of masculinity have contributed to the transformation of ordinary boys and men into active killers.[10]

Using gender as a lens to examine the aftermaths of genocide can also be useful, for even after mass atrocities and mass killings stop, and genocide has officially "ended," the effects of genocide persist in the lives of victims and their communities. How do the targeted groups transition to a postgenocidal society? How do international bodies (including nongovernmental organizations), domestic institutions, and local groups negotiate postgenocidal problems, such as the emotional and physical trauma, and the pragmatic needs, of victims or encourage the reconciliation and the rebuilding of societies? Scholarship suggests that gendered norms and beliefs—as well as the interconnectedness of gender, race, ethnicity, nationality, religion, and sexuality—can inform perceptions of, and responses to, postgenocidal issues. For example, after the Armenian genocide ended, local Armenian organizations temporarily suspended long-established ideas about paternal lineage and women's sexual purity and honor to promote the reintegration of "dishonored" women and of children fathered by the "enemy."[11] In postgenocidal Bosnia-Herzegovina, by contrast, the persistence of the belief that a child's ethnic identity was determined by his or her father's identity, beyond the mother's biological contribution or the child's socialization in the mother's ethnic community, led to the marginalization and abuse of "children born of rape."[12] Considering the gendered effects of trauma underscores how female survivors of sexual violence are often subject to additional violence, such as sexual exploitation or HIV, and male survivors are denied important resources. Looking into and "seeing" the continuation of gendered harms after genocide can result in new and more effective efforts to help survivors.

Analyzing the gendered dimensions of genocide "justice" in its various forms raises questions about the value and limits of such justice. How have international criminal courts, for example, recognized and obscured gendered forms of genocidal violence? In recognizing rape as an instrument of genocide, the Rwanda and Yugoslavia tribunals have enabled violence against women to be foregrounded and taken seriously, including in efforts to punish perpetrators. Yet, as groundbreaking as this has been, the conceptualization of rape as genocide has simultaneously had limiting effects; in focusing on mass rape, for example, international criminal prosecutions have downplayed or ignored other acts of violence, such as "forced marriages."[13] Research on women's testimonies in international criminal prosecutions has also shown how court proceedings have both valorized *and* silenced women, leading to distortions in their narratives in the courtroom and in later accounts of their experiences.[14]

Another topic worth considering is how gender plays a role in memory and commemoration. Memorial culture, which produces official representations of genocidal events, is not gender-neutral. How does gender inform the construction of collective memories, historical spaces, and ritual or national remembrance? In what ways are the motifs and tropes of traumatic memorialization gendered? How can the public imagery of gender-specific atrocities—such as the sexual abuse of women—contribute to voyeurism and the sexual objectification of female victims? How do representations of genocidal violence reinforce gender stereotypes and, in the process, render invisible the complexity of men's and women's unofficial memories and trauma?[15]

A gender perspective can also contribute to genocide prevention. As scholars, human rights activists, and policymakers grapple with the challenges of how to stop genocidal violence before it starts or when it is happening, and how to discern if genocide is unfolding in the midst of violent conflict, a focus on gender-specific actions and patterns might yield insights. Scholars have pointed out how there is a high correlation between certain types of gendered violence and genocide. For instance, in many genocides, mass violence has been directed first at "battle-aged" boys and men, followed by "root-and-branch" killings that aim for the wholesale annihilation of the targeted group. This insight is just one example of how analyzing the gendered harms in violent conflict could contribute to the identification of genocide as well as preventative efforts.[16] In present-day conflicts if the gender-selective slaughter of a specific ethnic/racial/national group of male civilians occurs, it could be a warning that the more generalized destruction and mass murder of that population might soon follow.

As this short discussion has suggested, gender analysis can complicate and enrich our understanding of genocide and its processes, effects, and aftermaths. It is also the case that the study of genocide can complicate and enrich our understanding of gender. Scholarship on genocide and gender underscores the lack of fixity to gender; it shows how genocide, like other historically and culturally specific phenomena, can destabilize and redefine gender norms and identities. In addition, this scholarship highlights how social constructions of gender intersect with constructions of ethnicity, nationality, race, religion, and sexuality.

Although scholarship on gender and genocide is still relatively new, debates about the definition of genocide are not. The first part of this introduction examines the invention of the word "genocide" and the problematic definition of genocide adopted by the international community when it decided to criminalize the practice. The introduction then turns to the emergence and evolution of genocide studies. The third section focuses on the development of scholarship on gender and genocide. The last part of the introduction, which discusses the framework for this book and how I came to this project, also summarizes the individual chapters' scholarly contributions.

Gender and the Definition of Genocide

As many scholars have pointed out, although the term "genocide" is relatively new, the practices and events associated with genocide are age-old phenomena. There is no shortage of historical examples of the widespread destruction and mass murder of particular groups of people. Moreover, many of the violent practices from earlier cases have been deployed in more recent episodes. Despite some continuity between older and more recent genocides, however, some scholars have argued that there is "something very new" about twentieth-century genocides.[17] According to this perspective, these genocides are distinct because they are a product of "modernity's defining features, the combined force of new technologies of warfare, new administrative techniques that [have] enhanced state powers of surveillance, and new ideologies that [have] made populations the choice objects of state policies and that [have] categorized people along strict lines of nation and race."[18] Moreover, these "modern" genocides have been marked by (1) "the seizure of state power by revolutionary movements"[19] that seek to create a "better, and radically, different society," a society shorn of human "weeds" who are considered "irrelevant" and/or a "danger" to this end goal[20]; and (2) the mass mobilization and participation of ordinary civilians in the brutalities against and killing of targeted groups.[21]

One of the modern manifestations of twentieth-century genocides, I would add, is the mass targeting of women as victims as well as the mass mobilization of women as indirect and direct participants. In earlier examples of genocide, of course, women have not been immune from great violence, including rape, and undoubtedly some women have acted as indirect participants as well as more violent aggressors. But in the context of the twentieth century, which was marked by mass politics, mass culture, and total war, women began to be recognized as fuller members of polities and, as such, were expected to aid in nation-building as well as the defense of the nation. One way that women were encouraged to contribute to nation-building and national defense was by becoming mothers: pre-First World War fears about population decline, in conjunction with First World War loss of life, transformed motherhood from one of a gendered expectation for individual women to that of a national duty, a civic obligation: women became "mothers" of the nation. Women were also mobilized to fulfill their responsibilities by supporting mass violence and/or engaging *actively* in atrocities. Another hallmark of modernity—the biologization of ethnicity, nationality, and race—combined with the construction of women as mothers of a national/ethnic/racial collectivity to make women more central to genocidal violence.[22]

Whatever scholarly debates there are about the continuities and discontinuities between older and more recent "modern" genocides, academics can easily agree that the term "genocide" is a twentieth-century modern invention. Raphael Lemkin, a Polish-Jewish lawyer and scholar,

conceived of the word genocide in 1943, in the context of the Second World
War and Nazi efforts to annihilate the Jews and other racially undesirable
groups in Western and Eastern Europe. Even before the Holocaust, however,
Lemkin was concerned about mass atrocities committed against groups *as
groups*—particularly the mass murder of Armenians under the Ottoman
Empire during the First World War. Indeed, in 1933, he had appealed to
his colleagues at the Fifth International Conference for the Unification of
Criminal Law (sponsored by the League of Nations) to criminalize "Acts of
Barbarity," the brutalities and acts of extermination against "national, racial,
religious and social collectivities," and "Acts of Vandalism," the "destruction
of works of art and culture" of such targeted groups.[23] After continuing
in the 1930s to push for the criminalization of these acts, and then fleeing
Nazi-occupied Poland in 1939, Lemkin combined his earlier concepts in the
neologism "genocide," which he produced from the Greek "genos" (race
or tribe) and the Latin "cide" (killing).[24] Lemkin sought a word that could
describe the Nazi methods of destruction and mass murder, a word that
"could not be used in other contexts (as 'barbarity' and 'vandalism' could),"
a word that would connote moral judgment.[25]

Lemkin formally introduced the term genocide in his 1944 book, *Axis
Rule in Occupied Europe: Laws of Occupation, Analysis of Government—
Proposals for Redress*. Although the text focused largely on specific German
and Axis practices, laws, and decrees in "incorporated" and occupied
territories, it contained a short chapter on "The Legal Status of Jews"
that highlighted the "special status" accorded to Jews in every occupied
country and a chapter on "Genocide," which detailed a range of German
techniques—political, social, economic, biological, physical, religious, and
moral—that were being used to destroy "national groups" throughout
occupied Europe. Although Lemkin acknowledged that the Germans
targeted Jews and other racially "undesired" groups in particular, including
Poles and Russians, his chapter made it clear that German occupation was
accompanied by genocidal processes that affected a wide array of people.[26]

Significantly, Lemkin produced a broad definition of genocide—one that
could include but was not reduced to mass murder. He explained:

> Generally speaking, genocide does not necessarily mean the immediate
> destruction of a nation, except when accomplished by mass killings of all
> members of a nation. It is intended rather to signify a coordinated plan
> of different actions *aiming at the destruction of essential foundations
> of the life of national groups, with the aim of annihilating the groups
> themselves* [my emphasis]. The objectives of such a plan would be
> disintegration of the political and social institutions, of culture, language,
> national feelings, religion, and the economic existence of national groups,
> and the destruction of the personal security, liberty, health, dignity, and
> even the lives of the individuals belonging to such groups. Genocide is
> directed against the national group as an entity, and the actions involved

are directed against individuals, not in their individual capacity, but as members of the national group.[27]

In Lemkin's view, nonlethal techniques of destruction, such as culturally destructive acts, could be genocidal, insofar as they were part of a broader "coordinated plan" aimed at eradicating a national group.[28] The distinction that Lemkin drew between mass murder and genocide was conceptually significant. Moreover, this distinction, and Lemkin's emphasis on genocide as the "*destruction of essential foundations of the life of national groups,*" suggests the importance of gender analysis in examining genocidal processes. To take one example, consider the role that sexual violence plays in destroying the "essential foundations of the life" of groups. Because women are seen as contributing not only to the biological but also to the cultural reproduction of ethnic, national, racial, and religious groups, sexual violence against women—in its myriad forms—can be an effective strategy for devastating not only individual female members of a group but also group reproduction (in part by having damaging effects on families and communities). The rape and sexual torture of men can similarly impede their ability to promote the biological and social continuance of groups.

Although Lemkin did not explicitly make the case that gendered strategies were used to advance genocide, he repeatedly argued that genocide needed to be recognized as an international crime, and his unflagging efforts to convince others ultimately resulted in action. In 1946, the General Assembly of the United Nations (UN) officially declared genocide an international crime, and in 1948, it adopted the UN Convention on the Prevention and Punishment of the Crime of Genocide. The UN Convention not only defined genocide but also mandated that contracting parties "undertake to prevent and punish" it.[29]

The UN definition of genocide was fraught from the outset. According to the UN, "acts committed with intent to destroy, in whole or in part, a national, ethnical, racial or religious group" constituted genocide. These genocidal acts included: "(a) killing members of the group; (b) causing serious bodily or mental harm to members of the group; (c) deliberately inflicting on the group conditions of life calculated to bring about its physical destruction in whole or in part; (d) imposing measures intended to prevent births within the group; and (e) forcibly transferring children of the group to another group."[30] To the dismay of many at the time (and since), acts aimed at the physical, biological, and reproductive destruction of a group were specified, whereas cultural techniques of destruction, which Lemkin had included in his broader formulation of genocide, were excluded, although "vestiges" of the cultural remained.[31] The subjective and elusive nature of "intent" was also of concern; what was evidence of "acts committed with intent to destroy?" Interpretive difficulties existed as well in connection with the clause "in whole, or in part"; how was "in part" to be determined? What yardstick should be used?

One of the major problems with the legal definition adopted by the United Nations Communications Group (UNCG) in 1948 was its omission of political and social groups. Although these groups had been acknowledged as potential targets of genocide in the UN resolution of 1946 and in earlier drafts of the UN definition of genocide to be used in the Convention, they were ultimately excluded for two main reasons: (1) behind-the-scenes political maneuvering and (2) the idea that membership in political and social groups was "transient and unstable" and, moreover, often voluntary, and hence different from other groups for which membership was inevitable or virtually so.[32] Significantly, given the topic of this book, the destruction of groups defined by gender or sexuality was excluded as well. Moreover, sexual violence was not recognized as an act of genocide. As some of the chapters in this volume note, international criminal tribunals in the 1990s addressed the initial failure to include rape and sexual violence as genocidal acts by arguing that they could be used to cause "serious bodily or mental harm to members of the group" and by convicting *génocidaires* of this type of genocidal violence.[33] Under international law today, rape and sexual violence can constitute genocide if they are "committed with the specific intent to destroy, in whole or in part, a national, ethnical, racial or religious group."[34]

The limits of the UNCG's definition of genocide contributed to limits on the UNCG's promise to prevent and punish genocide. When, after all, was murderous violence not merely a terrible by-product of war but a result of an intentional plan to exterminate members of a populace? What counted as evidence of an intentional plan? Again and again, the UN and contracting parties turned a blind eye to mass brutalities and genocides in the post–Second World War Cold War era. To be sure, various factors other than definitional challenges, such as the Convention's ineffective procedures for activating "prevention," contributed to this lack of international response. One of the main problems was governments' pursuit of *realpolitik* in international relations in the context of the Cold War.[35]

Silence and the Emergence and Evolution of Genocide Studies

Although the term "genocide" was adopted by the UN and publicized in the media in the 1940s, the academic field of genocide studies developed only in the late 1970s and 1980s, after "Holocaust studies" emerged in the 1960s and 1970s. Indeed, this new field was "part offspring of, part uneasy junior partner to" Holocaust studies.[36]

Academic examination of the Nazi extermination of the Jews began in the wake of the Second World War but did not generate much scholarship until the

1960s.[37] Moreover, although in the late 1940s and 1950s presses published some memoirs and institutions began to collect valuable materials about the destruction of the Jews, public discussion about, and commemoration of, the great crimes that had been committed was very limited, in Israel as well as in the United States and Eastern and Western Europe.[38] In the face of this relative silence, prominent Israelis became concerned that the "Holocaust was being forgotten" and decided to use the Israeli capture, and 1961 trial of, Adolf Eichmann—the Nazi leader responsible for organizing the mass deportation of Jews to their deaths—to publicize this tragic history to "Israeli youngsters" and the world.[39] Given that Israel was surrounded by a sea of hostility from its Middle Eastern neighbors, reminding the world of the Holocaust was also useful for legitimizing the nation's right to exist.

The Eichmann trial played a huge role in the development of Holocaust studies, as did other factors, especially the publication in the early 1960s of historian Raul Hilberg's seminal work, *The Destruction of the Jews*, which was a masterful accounting of the crimes committed against Jews; Hannah Arendt's controversial analysis, *Eichmann in Jerusalem: A Report on the Banality of Evil*, and the Frankfurt-Auschwitz trials from 1963 to 1965.[40] In addition to new scholarship and new trials, the broader political context of the 1960s was significant. A "new political consciousness" emerged in West Germany, which resulted in calls for greater openness about the country's Nazi past.[41] Meanwhile, the rise of the "New Left" in West Germany, France, the United States, and elsewhere; the ongoing civil rights movement in the United States; American violence in the Vietnam War (including massacres of innocent civilians); and the end of European colonial empires that had been justified through ideas of racial and civilizational superiority fostered academic and nonacademic discussions about and comparisons between historical and present-day examples of what some saw as the "mass cruelty and mass human destruction perpetrated by state authorities," including the Nazi brutalization and extermination of the Jews.[42]

Growing popular interest in the Holocaust also provided support for academic studies. As Holocaust memorialization expanded in the 1970s and 1980s, memorial sites, museums, and commemorative plaques in the West began to proliferate.[43] The introduction of educational initiatives in schools as well as artistic productions about the Holocaust—such as television series and films that focused on the Nazi annihilation of the Jews—also raised public awareness about the Holocaust.[44] Not surprisingly, the institutionalization of Holocaust memory fueled the growth of "Holocaust studies" in many colleges and universities.

As was the case with the Holocaust, academic interest in the Armenian genocide developed after a period of relative silence. Despite widespread media coverage and popular uproar about the "Armenian massacres" in the Ottoman Empire during the First World War – as well as short-lived Turkish and international efforts in the immediate postwar period to punish some of the main perpetrators, and the publication of various memoirs and document collections in the years thereafter – international and public attention to the "Armenian question" subsided during the interwar era and the following decades. The Turkish government's downplaying of wartime events and its denial of charges of genocide converged with Western geopolitical interests to foster silence or misinformation about the mass crime carried out against Armenians.[45] This silence was largely reproduced in the Western academic world, where there was little scholarship on the Armenian genocide until the 1970s and 1980s.[46]

In the face of this continued silence, Armenian activists organized a day of commemoration on the fiftieth anniversary of the genocide in 1965, and this activism contributed to the development of Armenian genocide studies. In Yerevan, Soviet Armenia, and in many other cities and countries, Armenians "took to the streets" and called attention to the deportations and mass killings of the Armenians during the First World War in the Ottoman Empire. Activists not only demanded that the Turkish government admit "the wrongs of its Ottoman and Young Turk predecessors," but also pressed for "an end to world indifference." Some Armenians also insisted upon "the return of Armenian lands under Turkish occupation."[47] Nonviolent calls for the recognition of the mass violence carried out against the Ottoman Armenians were accompanied in the 1970s and 1980s by more violent calls that led to the assassination of dozens of Turkish diplomats and the death of many others.[48] As public awareness about the annihilation of the Armenians grew, and the Turkish government countered by promoting a vociferous "campaign of denial," scholarly attention to the genocide increased.[49] Richard Hovannisian, one of the pioneers in Armenian genocide studies, explains, "It was the reprehensible action of a government to wipe clean the slate of history, just as its predecessor had wiped clean an entire people, that aroused in me a sense of moral indignation and a commitment to engage in the struggle of memory against forgetting despite the unfavorable odds."[50] International recognition in the 1980s of the Ottoman crimes committed against Armenians during the First World War as genocide lent further support to Armenian genocide studies.[51]

Holocaust studies also played a role in the development of Armenian genocide studies. Some scholars who initially examined the Holocaust later turned to the study of the Armenian genocide.[52] Meanwhile, some academics who examined the mass destruction of Armenians under the Ottoman Empire became interested in comparing this tragedy with the Nazi destruction of Jews, to uncover similarities and differences, and to demonstrate that what happened to the Armenians was indeed genocide. The idea that the Armenian genocide was the prototype of modern genocides emerged in this context.[53]

As Holocaust studies and Armenian genocide studies emerged, contemporaneous examples of mass atrocities and acts of extermination against specific groups of people occurred in a variety of different countries and contexts. In 1971, for example, the West Pakistani regime committed what is now considered genocide in East Pakistan/Bangladesh during the Bangladesh War of Independence. The Pakistani army and militias engaged in mass rape and murdered over one million Hindus and Bengalis, if not more (some scholars estimate the number of deaths was close to three million).[54] From 1975 to 1979, between 1.5 million and 3 million people in Cambodia died under the communist Khmer Rouge regime. Genocide was the result of the regime's radical efforts to pursue a total reorganization of society and the economy—via forced de-urbanization, forced collectivization of agriculture, forced labor, torture, mass executions, and other policies. Although the vast majority of victims were ethnic Khmer, many of whom were murdered for being "oppositionists" (including intellectuals, professionals, religious leaders and enthusiasts, and others), minority groups such as the ethnic Vietnamese and ethnic Chinese were also targeted.[55]

Genocide studies began to cohere as ongoing instances of genocidal violence—along with the growing scholarly literature on particular genocides—began to foster greater academic interest in other cases of genocide as well as the processes of genocide more broadly. For some scholars, the current examples of mass destruction and murder in the world demanded activism in the form of research and teaching about genocide. An expert on the Armenian genocide, Robert Melson, discusses the connection between the terrible violence perpetrated against the Igbo ethnic group in the second half of the 1960s and his growing interest in genocide studies:

> As a child I survived the Holocaust, and as a young adult I witnessed the beginnings of the Biafran war that led to mass death in Nigeria. Both of these events, in different ways, started me on the intellectual and emotional journey to study genocide with the hope of understanding and preventing it.[56]

Henry Huttenbach, another early genocide studies scholar, explains that his existing commitment to contextualize the Holocaust in his teaching in the 1970s was boosted in part by the massive bloodshed in Cambodia, leading to a new course on twentieth-century genocide (and not just the Holocaust) and new comparative scholarship on the Holocaust.[57]

Early genocide scholarship included not only individual case studies, but also comparative analysis. Leo Kuper's foundational text for genocide studies in 1981 is a good example of this; although it contained a more detailed analysis of the "Turkish genocide against Armenians" and "German genocide against the Jews," it nonetheless discussed genocides and "genocidal massacres" elsewhere—those linked to colonization, decolonization, and ethnic and religious conflicts in postcolonial successor states.[58] In his preface, Kuper acknowledged the criticism that could be leveled against his approach. He noted: "The very act of comparison is an affront. Should not 'each human evil be understood in its own terms'?" Nonetheless, Kuper asserted, "even in the particular case," understanding was difficult, for "genocide seems to defy understanding." Moreover, because genocides were "all too common in our day," comparative study was necessary; identifying commonalities among genocides (as well as their particularities) would aid in the prevention of genocide.[59] Scholars offering a comparative perspective during early genocide studies asked such questions as "which forms of social organization" make it more or "less likely for a massive genocide to occur?"[60] They also sought to provide a conceptual framework for better understanding the crime by focusing on definitions, classifications, and typologies of genocide, raising questions, for example, about the problems and consequences of the UN definition and classifying genocides—for example, ideological, retributive, utilitarian—to distinguish different historical examples. Whereas many of these comparative scholars examined the types of leaders, ideologies, political structures, and social institutions that could make mass atrocities and murder possible, others investigated the importance of social group dynamics and individual human behavior. One of the founding texts along these lines is Israel Charny's book, *How Can We Commit the Unthinkable? Genocide: The Human Cancer*. As Charny explained,

> This book is not about the holocaust of the Jewish people, nor is it about any one or another specific instance of genocide. Rather, it is a search for the underlying rhythms, patterns, and meanings within the human mind, individually and collectively, that make it possible for us human beings to be drawn to the worst possible side of ourselves.[61]

Some of the earliest advocates of comparative genocide studies were scholars and teachers who had previously focused on the Holocaust, as well as Jewish survivors or escapees from the Nazi genocide who became academics. Moreover, many Holocaust studies scholars welcomed the development of this new approach.[62] (As already mentioned, some of this early work focused on the Holocaust and the Armenian genocide). Enthusiasm for comparative analysis, however, was countered by significant opposition to it from those who argued that the Holocaust was a singular event in history, a horror so different from other historical examples of mass murder that it could not be compared to them. In Stephen Katz's view: "The Holocaust, that is, the intentional murder of European Jewry during World War II, is historically and phenomenologically unique." For many critics, the inclusion of the Holocaust in comparative analyses of genocide was intellectually and morally wrong; it would diminish the enormity of the Nazi crime against Jews, and it would lead to a de-emphasis on the anti-Jewish essence and totalizing nature of the Holocaust, in which the Nazi state intended to annihilate all Jews throughout Europe.[63] For those who favored comparative analysis, the point was not to downplay the specific features of the Holocaust—such as the Nazi regime's anti-Semitic ideology, domestic political structures, and social processes—or the scope and methods of mass murder.[64] Instead, the point was to better comprehend the Holocaust and other genocides by examining commonalities as well as differences, discerning patterns (e.g., of dehumanization and humiliation), and contextualizing genocides in broader world processes (e.g., world war or colonialism). For some proponents of comparative studies, this approach was a moral issue. In the face of "more and more examples [of genocide] tragically and contemporarily coming to the fore," one scholar explained, "The 'success' of Holocaust studies in increasing our awareness of that which humanity is capable of doing to itself ethically mandate[d] a broader understanding of its repetitive, if not paralleling, behavior."[65] Comparative analysis was also a moral issue because it was linked to prevention. Was it possible to identify regimes, factors, or conditions that enhanced the likelihood of genocide? Could genocide be anticipated? And if so, could it be prevented?

The interdisciplinary field of genocide studies has developed significantly in the last twenty to twenty-five years. The mass atrocities and mass slaughter that occurred in the former Yugoslavia in the 1990s and in Rwanda in 1994 shocked the world and demonstrated not only that "genocide was not a thing of the past" but also that "the West could still host the crime."[66] These cases of immense violence increased academic and public interest in the origins and mechanisms of genocide and fueled new scholarship in genocide studies, both in the area of individual genocides and in comparative analysis.[67] Another major geopolitical event, the end of the Cold War and the collapse of Communism in Eastern Europe and the Soviet Union, played a role too in the growth of genocide studies. As Dan Stone notes, "Since the end of the Cold War far more documents have been discovered than historians would have believed possible at the end of the Nuremberg Trial."[68] The availability of new research materials has resulted in many new studies—for example, on the local dimensions and microprocesses of the Holocaust in formerly communist Eastern Europe countries, the complicity of ordinary civilians in genocidal events, and religious leaders' and institutions' collaboration with the Nazis— that have contributed to broader and comparative interest in topics such as civilian complicity.[69] The end of the bipolar division of the world, combined with the murderous violence in Bosnia-Herzegovina and Rwanda, also fostered a new moral context for trying to prevent genocides, intervening actively once they had begun, punishing perpetrators, and assisting survivors with their trauma and needs in the aftermath of genocide. The focus on these goals by policymakers, human rights activists, international and local nongovernmental organizations, women's groups, legal bodies, and other individuals and institutions has contributed to new scholarly works on genocide.

As the field has developed, the disciplinary boundaries of genocide studies have broadened. Whereas much of the early genocide scholarship was produced by historians and social scientists, more recent scholarship has emerged from scholars in cultural studies, legal studies, indigenous studies, gender studies, and many other disciplines and fields. This work has raised important new questions and issues in genocide studies, such as whether or not the forced removal of indigenous children from their families, communities, and culture constitutes genocide, or how states and nonstates can perpetrate genocide "by attrition" by denying human rights, such as health care and/or food, to members of groups.[70] Since the 1990s, the geographic and temporal range of genocide studies has also expanded, and academic inquiries into pre-modern and colonial genocides and lesser-known instances (such as those in Guatemala in the 1980s or in German South West Africa in 1904) increasingly accompany genocide scholarship on what some call the "twentieth-century" core.[71]

Gender and Genocide

Scholarship on gender and genocide is a relatively new phenomenon. Although it began to gain momentum in the mid- to late 1990s, partly because of the widespread sexual humiliation and mass rape of women in the Rwandan and Bosnian genocides, it started with the study of women and the Holocaust, which feminist scholars initiated in the early 1980s. As was the case with Holocaust studies and Armenian genocide studies, concerns about the silencing of victims' and survivors' voices and experiences—in this case, female victims and survivors—played a critical role in the development of this scholarly focus. According to Joan Ringelheim, one of the pioneers of women's Holocaust studies, the impetus for studying women and the Holocaust was twofold: "the experiences and perceptions of Jewish women ha[d] been obscured or absorbed into descriptions of men's lives," and studying women and the Holocaust would presumably "yield new questions and data."[72] Sybil Milton, another pioneer of the study of women and the Holocaust, noted that it was not merely that women's "gender-specific experiences" had been left out of the scholarly record, but that "recent literature, based mostly on the experiences of male perpetrators, male victims, and male survivors," had promulgated inaccurate and "misleading" information about women's experiences.[73] In Lisa Pine's view, this new field of study was a product of three developments in the 1970s: increased scholarship on the Holocaust more generally; the emergence of a "second wave of feminism" and women's studies (which, among other things, aimed to end the silencing of women's stories); and the vast expansion of published Holocaust memoirs and testimonies.[74]

Despite resistance to the study of women and the Holocaust (noted earlier), the study of this topic began to grow. In 1983 the Institute for Research in History sponsored the conference, "Women Surviving the Holocaust," at Stern College. Although proceedings from the first conference ever to focus on women and the Holocaust were subsequently published, and then followed by some related scholarly articles, chapters, and books, it was only in the 1990s that scholarship on women and the Holocaust started to expand significantly.[75] Importantly, this work did not merely "add women" into narratives of the Holocaust (although this was valuable), it also discussed the importance of gender—that is, the cultural ideas and social prescriptions about femininity and masculinity assigned to "female" and "male" sexed bodies. The increased scholarship was reflective of the growing legitimacy of gender studies and was accompanied by the study of women and Nazism as well as women and fascism more broadly. New academic studies on women and the Holocaust also appear to have been partly inspired by the institutionalization of Holocaust memory and its limitations. As Joan Ringelheim has suggested, the failure of the four-day opening conference of the United States Holocaust Memorial Museum in 1993 to have any panels on women or gender, and the initial failure of the museum to have any conceptualization of gender, underscored the need for greater attention to gender and the Holocaust, including on survivor memories and the "construction of collective memory in both national and community settings."[76] Reports in the 1990s about the widespread sexual violence perpetrated against non-Serbian women in the Balkans and Tutsi women in Rwanda fueled greater interest in the study of sexual violence during the Holocaust, perpetrated by both Germans and non-Germans against Jewish as well as non-Jewish women, which has resulted in a prodigious amount of new scholarship on this topic in the last ten to fifteen years.[77]

The study of gender and the Armenian genocide emerged even later than the study of gender and the Holocaust. Although some women's memoirs and autobiographies—and biographies about Armenian female victims—were published in the 1980s and 1990s, most gender analyses emerged after 2000. The turn to gender was a product of several factors, including the mass rape of women in the former Yugoslavia and Rwanda in the 1990s, which confirmed the legitimacy of examining gender-based distinctions in mass violence and increased scholarly interest in analyzing gender and genocide comparatively. Recently, greater openness in Turkey about discussing the fate of Islamized Armenian women in Turkish families and their descendants and "the keen interest of third-generation Armenians in the experience of their grandmothers" (and, I would add, interest on the part of Turks who "discovered" their grandmothers' past) have also fostered new scholarship.[78]

Gender analyses of the Rwandan and Bosnian genocides began to appear as the atrocities and destruction unfolded, and stories about the sexual violence perpetrated against women began to be publicized. As the feminist Slavenka Drakulic notes about the carnage in the former Yugoslavia: "It was all there, on the television screens"—"shells, bombs, slaughter, rape, blood, destruction—the entire war unfolded in front of [Europeans'] eyes. Everybody knew what was going on."[79] In the view of many, the media accounts of Serbian policies of mass rape, including the use of rape camps, and the news about the mass rape of Tutsi women, often accompanied by sexual mutilation and then followed by killing, demanded scholarly, legal, and humanitarian attention as well as international intervention.

Inclusions and Exclusions in the Volume

In addition to being a gender studies scholar, I am a historian of the Soviet Union, and, as such, it might seem surprising that this volume does not include a chapter on gender and the terrible mass crimes that Stalin spearheaded, which resulted in the imprisonment, deportation, and death of millions.[80] As Nicholas Werth and others have argued, the mass crimes perpetrated against the Soviet people were not discrete events; they were part of a larger project, a "radical, murderous form of *social* engineering" on behalf of a "transformative vision of Utopia"—the utopia of Soviet socialism.[81] Moreover, some scholars claim that the mass crimes are evidence of the "genocidal character" of the Stalinist regime, which "killed systematically rather than episodically."[82] Although there is scholarly consensus that the great violence perpetrated under Stalin's rule was horrific and destroyed countless lives, there is no scholarly consensus on how to conceptualize this violence.

Whether or not these mass crimes should be understood as genocidal or as evidence of "Stalin's genocides," they are not included in this volume for three main reasons. First, as I conceptualized this book, I decided it should concentrate on just a few examples of genocide in the twentieth century, so that it could offer a more detailed examination of these cases. That is, I opted for depth and not breadth. As a result, the book focuses primarily on the Armenian genocide and Holocaust in the first half of the twentieth century and the genocides in Bosnia-Herzegovina and Rwanda in the second half. The chapters by Adam Jones and Elisa von Joeden-Forgey are the exceptions, in that they consider not only one or more of these four core cases but other examples of genocide as well. (Jones examines genocide in Rwanda *and* the Democratic Republic of the Congo [DRC], and Joeden-Forgey's analysis includes discussion of Argentina and Darfur.) It should be noted, as well, that this volume focuses on Nazi efforts to exterminate the Jews of Europe and not on the victims of the Holocaust more broadly, even though the Nazis also attempted to annihilate groups other than the Jews for racial reasons, especially "Gypsies" (Roma and Sinti), gay men, and mentally and physically "handicapped" people. This focus on the Jewish victims of the Nazis has to do with the content of individual contributions to the volume and not with any belief on my part that these other groups are somehow less important victims of the Nazi regime's murderous actions.[83]

One reason for the book's focus on these four cases is that they more or less fit the legal definition of genocide adopted by the UN Convention, which provides a useful framework for comparison, despite the limits of the definition. Like many others, I consider the definition problematic, not least of all because it excludes cases of genocide in which groups of people have been (or could be) targeted because of real and imagined gender, sexual, social, political, and other differences. An additional reason for focusing on these four cases is the growing scholarship on *gender* and these particular genocides. Although some academic attention has been paid to the plight of women in the Bangladesh genocide of 1971 and in the more recent Darfur genocide, gender scholarship on most other examples of twentieth-century genocidal violence is limited.[84]

Contributions to this Volume

In Part One of this volume, both authors demonstrate the importance of examining women as well as men as gendered victims of genocide. After reviewing some of the main scholarly developments and issues in the study of gender and the Holocaust, Lisa Pine's chapter examines Jewish men's and women's responses not only to Nazi persecution in the 1930s but also to Auschwitz-Birkenau, the largest of the Nazi death camps. Pine's analysis provides insight into how gender norms and social constructions of male and female identities informed victims' experiences as well as their testimonies and memories about this past. Pine also explores a subject that is often glossed over—how some men and women "deviated" from expected gender and sexual norms in the context of the camps. Pine focuses in particular on women's "deviation" and describes, for example, how many women traded sexual favors for food and other items. Pine's discussion provides a window on how women and men at Auschwitz-Birkenau faced difficult moral choices and physical situations that challenged their previous sense of self.

In Chapter 2, Adam Jones examines masculine vulnerabilities in the Rwandan and Congolese genocides, upsetting the standard framing in studies of mass violence of men as perpetrators and women as victims. He details how in both the Rwandan and Congolese cases (and in the ongoing violence in the DRC), men and boys—particularly those of "battle age"— were specifically targeted for direct killings and sexual violence because they were male. In addition, Jones explores how "gendercidal" military conscription and forced (*corvée*) labor have historically resulted in the victimization of men, including in the unfolding of tragic events in Rwanda and the DRC. Jones argues that it is imperative "from a humanitarian-intervention viewpoint" to recognize and address the forced mobilization of and gender-selective atrocities against males.

Although sexual violence was addressed briefly in Pine's and Jones's chapters on the gendered experiences and gendered harms that men and women have faced in different genocidal contexts, Part Two provides an in-depth exploration of sexual violence against girls and women in the four cases of genocide that are the focus of this volume. The chapters analyze a wide variety of forms of sexual violence, including forced concubinage, marriage, and enslavement of women and children; forced assimilation; rape; sexual torture; and "degenderization" (the destruction of genitals and secondary sex characteristics). Together, they provide an important comparative perspective on sexual atrocities during genocide and underscore how different ideologies and different historical and cultural contexts have shaped this type of violence.

Anthonie Holslag, in Chapter 3, utilizes ideas from anthropologist Gerd Baumann about the dialectic process of "Othering" and "Selfing" in identity formation to explore the unfolding of violence, particularly sexual violence, during the Armenian genocide. He argues that sexual violence played a key role in the Ottoman Empire's leaders' efforts to construct a new Ottoman Self based on Turkishness, which, in the context of the First World War, came to rely not merely on the marginalization but also on the elimination of Armenians, who had been constructed as the "Other." Holslag explores how perpetrators sought to destroy the very essence and reproduction of Armenian identity by committing acts of "gendercide" and rape, sexual torture, and "degenderization," and by exposing the intimate parts of the bodies of the dead. Holslag also examines how the forced assimilation and enslavement of women and young boys served not only to subordinate but also to eliminate Armenianness.

In Chapter 4, Zoë Waxman analyzes sexual violence against Jewish women in the Holocaust. Waxman acknowledges that the Nazi persecution of Jews included various forms of sexual violence, such as forced abortion and sterilization as well as the sexual humiliation and violation of women upon first examination and registration at camps. In comparing these forms of sexual violence to similar sexual aggression in more recent cases of mass destruction and murder, she argues that the Holocaust was distinctive. Whereas rape was an integral and widespread instrument of genocide in Bosnia-Herzegovina and Rwanda, the rape of Jewish women was not a systematic or organized part of Nazi genocidal policy because of Nazi racial ideology.

Patricia Weitsman's chapter examines the Serbian policies of mass rape, forced impregnation, and forced maternity against Bosniak women in the Bosnian War. In the process, she illuminates how particular conceptions of gender in the former Yugoslavia informed constructions of ethnic identity to produce these specific forms of sexual violence. The popular perception that women were mere vessels for paternal identity, and that their maternal biological connection and role in a child's upbringing did not contribute to a child's ethnic identity, allowed the Serbs to claim that forced impregnation would result in more "Serbian" babies. Weitsman also discusses how this gendered notion of ethnic identity resulted in tragic consequences for the children born of rape.

In Chapter 6, Burnet explores the mass rape of women during the Rwandan genocide. Her chapter adds to the existing scholarship on this subject by examining in particular how the political economy of everyday gender violence and notions of sexual consent and gender roles in pregenocidal Rwanda—all of which subordinated women to men—heightened "women and girls' vulnerability to sexual violence" during the genocide, affected the ways this mass violence unfolded, and shaped the postgenocidal repercussions of this aggression on survivors, their families, and local communities (e.g., reactions to children born of rape). By discussing the perpetrators and survivors who did not fit into the "Hutu-perpetrator/Tutsi-victim dyad," and by raising the question of women's "sexual agency" and militarized sex, Burnet complicates traditional narratives of sexual violence in Rwanda and sheds light on the silenced victims of this violence.

Part Three of this volume contains two chapters that use gender as a lens for better understanding complicity and participation in genocidal violence.[85] Although in the 1980s and 1990s, important scholarship raised the question of German women's relationship to and support for the Nazi regime and its anti-Semitic and racist policies, and in the last decade there has been greater attention paid to women perpetrators in the Holocaust, there has been relatively little work on masculinity and male perpetrators.[86] Stephen Haynes's chapter, which was first published in 2002 in the *Journal of Men's Studies*, thus remains groundbreaking. The introduction to this chapter is a bit dated because, as Haynes notes, there was virtually no scholarly interest in applying gender analysis to the study of men in the Holocaust at the time of his writing. Since then, the field of masculinity studies has burgeoned, and there has been increased—albeit still limited—academic inquiry into male experiences and discourses of masculinity in the Holocaust.[87] Haynes explores how discourses of masculinity contributed to male Holocaust perpetrators' genocidal conduct and "verbal self-justifications" for their behavior. In addition to analyzing the experiences and testimonies of more elite and Nazified men—death camp commandants, SS men, and *Einsatzgruppe* officers—Haynes investigates "ordinary men/ordinary Germans," that is, the reserve police forces that have been the subject of so much scholarly debate. His analysis of both groups underscores the need for genocide scholarship to investigate men as gendered beings and sheds light on how notions of ideal German masculinity played a part in shaping men's actions.

Nicole Hogg and Mark Drumbl's chapter examines the mass participation of "ordinary" women and female leaders in the Rwandan genocide. Although the vast majority of those engaged directly in killings were male, many women did kill Tutsis. Moreover, they actively contributed to genocidal processes by exposing victims to the killers and engaging in the looting of victims' property. Some ordinary women, however, tried to save Tutsis. Hogg and Drumbl explore the importance of gender roles and gender dynamics in determining ordinary women's actions as bystanders, active participants, and rescuers. They also investigate the gendered discourses that were deployed against and by women perpetrators in leadership positions who faced prosecution after the genocide.[88]

The chapters in Part Four focus on postgenocidal trauma and memory. How do the victims of genocide recover after the violence has ended? How do communities try to rebuild? How do ideas about gender affect recovery efforts and survivor resources? How does memory operate? What are the effects of particular gendered narratives and collective memories about genocidal violence?

Lerna Ekmekcioglu's chapter examines the complexities of Armenians' postgenocidal and post-First World War rescue efforts to track down, "emancipate," and reintegrate into their own communities the children and women who had been taken into Muslim households and orphanages during the wartime genocide. Ekmekcioglu explores how differences between Ottoman and Armenian authorities about how to deal with married female abductees, resistance to reintegration among some Armenian children and women, Ottoman fears that "true Muslim" children were being taken in Armenian rescue efforts, and a broader Turkish-Armenian dispute over territory in eastern Turkey (which was connected to demographics) led to a fierce battle about ethnoreligious identity and "who belonged to whom." In order to repopulate the Armenian community and strengthen Armenian land claims, Armenian leaders promoted a pronatalist campaign and temporarily altered lineage rules as well as gender and sexual norms. In the process, maternity trumped paternity in determining a baby's identity, and women who had been forcibly married or had served as sexual concubines, and children of Muslim fatherhood, could be reclaimed as "Armenian."

In Chapter 10, Olivera Simić investigates the sexual violence experienced by men during the Bosnian War, the silence surrounding these male victims, and the consequences of this silencing for male survivors. During the war, hundreds of men were subjected to various forms of sexual abuse: rape, sexual torture, genital mutilation (including castrations), and forced incest. These male victims have been virtually ignored, by both the international community and local bodies, partly because of their shame and reluctance to speak out about their experiences and partly because of a gendered narrative about the Bosnian War, which has underscored the great sexual violence that Bosniak women were subjected to but has rendered male victims invisible. Moreover, gender norms and stereotypes have made it difficult for men to be seen as victims of sexual violence. The result, Simić argues, is that male survivors of sexual violence have not received counseling or other forms of assistance, nor have they seen the prosecution of their perpetrators, all of which could have helped with healing from their great trauma. Moreover, the lack of scholarly attention to these male victims has hindered understandings of wartime and genocidal violence. As Simić explicates, male perpetrators who sexually abuse "enemy" men not only disempower and feminize them, but also humiliate these men's ethnic group and assert their own dominant masculinity.[89]

Selma Leydesdorff, in Chapter 11, considers the great difficulty women survivors of Srebrenica have in conveying what happened to themselves and others during the genocide. She also examines how the lack of recognition afforded to these women in the international arena of the International Criminal Tribunal for the former Yugoslavia (ICTY), and the failure of the courts to really listen to these female survivors, has led to the distortion of their narratives. In the ICTY and other legal proceedings, women's complex stories of great sadness and pain and incomprehension have been transformed by juridical language into simpler testimonies of denunciation and self-defense. This has not only resulted in a new kind of violence against survivors, Leydesdorff suggests, but it has also undermined an opportunity to better comprehend how deeply Bosniak women's lives were disrupted by the Bosnian tragedy.

The last part of the volume considers how international law has shaped understandings of genocide and how the study of gender and genocide is central to realizing genuine genocide prevention. Doris Buss's chapter examines the role of international law in recognizing gendered forms of genocidal violence. In particular, she contextualizes how the international tribunals for Rwanda and the former Yugoslavia came to see rape as a crime of genocide, worthy of prosecution and punishment. The courts' framing of rape and sexual violence as a product of elite-orchestrated ethnic conflict, she argues, was linked to a broader effort to make sense of violence in Rwanda and Yugoslavia by reframing these conflicts as a product of elite manipulation of ethnic identities, rather than as a product of old tribal hatreds and "atavistic animosities." Although this narrative of sexual violence can be seen as an improvement over older narratives about war and its effects, in which the sexual victimization of women was ignored or considered incidental, Buss points out how this legal framework has nonetheless been limiting. Similarly to Leydesdorff, Buss maintains that particular types of juridical framing have discouraged a more complex analysis of sexual violence and have obscured other forms of gendered harms that accompany genocide as well as victims and perpetrators of sexual violence who do not "fit" into this framework.

The last chapter in the volume argues that gender research can aid in the determination of mass violence as genocidal and in efforts to prevent it. In Joeden-Forgey's view, when gendered violence and "life force atrocities" accompany violent conflict, they are a strong indicator of genocidal intent. This is because "ritualized atrocities that target the life force of a group" by destroying familial and community bonds, ties to the land, symbols of group cohesion, and the social and biological reproduction of a group are common to genocides, despite local and cultural variations. Instead of reading the crime of genocide in the numbers of bodies and massacres, genocide can thus be read from the "bottom up"—through examples of gendered and life force atrocities. If in monitoring violent conflict, human rights organizations, government agencies, or other groups identified the existence of these types of crimes, this information could then potentially serve as a red flag for the unfolding of genocidal violence.

* * *

As a historian of the Soviet Union, I never expected to edit a book or write on the topic of genocide. Before 2008, I also never expected to teach a course on twentieth-century genocides. So how did I get here? As with many scholars and teachers of genocide studies, I came to this project through intellectual and personal avenues. My intellectual journey is connected to my pursuit of gender and sexuality studies in graduate school at Princeton as well as my teaching of the Holocaust and gender history in my first academic job and ever since. Indeed, it was in these early years that I discovered Olga Lengyel's memoir, *Five Chimneys: A Woman Survivor's True Story of Auschwitz*, in my search for a text that undergraduates were unlikely to have read in other college-level classes, high school, or on their own. This memoir fueled my interest in gender and genocide. Lengyel's description of complicity and resistance in Auschwitz, including among women, and the gendered dimensions of her and other women's experience of the camp, raised important questions for me about gender and the Holocaust. My interest in this topic was not merely intellectual, however. As a child I became interested in the unequal status, discriminatory treatment, and abuse of girls and women in our society; one of my stronger middle-school memories is being chased by boys who mocked me for being a "women's libber" and for getting in trouble by fighting back (in a very unladylike way). As a young woman, I became increasingly aware of how I and other women in our society were subjected to disdain, mistreatment, marginalization, and violence because of sexism, gendered beliefs, gender norms, and, in some cases, misogyny. And yet, I was also aware of how fortunate I was to be female in the United States, because despite significant similarities in the abuse that females suffer the world over—such as domestic violence and rape—it was clear to me that in some other countries, girls and women suffered from additional forms of abuse and aggression, such as honor killings and genital mutilation. Anti-Semitism too was personal; although I grew up in a community with a significant Jewish population and few overt expressions of anti-Semitism, I was to some extent aware as a ten-year-old in the 1970s that my stepfather's Jewish identity was part of the reason why he was so disliked by the Boston political establishment. It was only years later that I came to fully understand how central anti-Semitism was to the unfolding of his fate as Chief Justice of the Superior Court of Massachusetts and to the personal history of our family.[90] This experience of anti-Semitism contributed to my interest in historical cases of anti-Semitism, which was reinforced by my Hebrew Sunday School discussions of pogroms against Jews in Imperial Russia and two units in my K-8 school about the Holocaust. As a teenager and young adult, I also began to learn and think more about the history and persistence of racism (both in our society and elsewhere) as well as the marginalization and hatred of the "Other"— including the racial, religious, female, and sexual Other. This knowledge, along with my activism as an undergraduate in the antiapartheid divestment movement and in efforts to raise awareness about sexual violence against women, contributed to my intellectual and moral development and has led to a lifelong concern about the violation of people's rights and dignity and the violence—economic, political, psychological, sexual, and physical—that frequently accompanies it. As a professor, I have tried to be an activist by teaching about these issues. Indeed, this edited collection on genocide and gender is a result of my decision to teach a course on genocide and ethnic cleansing in the twentieth century at Santa Clara University.

Notes

1 Joan Ringelheim, "Thoughts about Women and the Holocaust," and Myrna Goldenberg, "Different Horrors, Same Hell: Women Remembering the Holocaust," in *Thinking the Unthinkable: Meanings of the Holocaust*, ed. R. Gottlieb (New York, NY: Paulist Press, 1990), pp. 144–5, and 152, respectively.

2 Helene Sinnriech, "Women and the Holocaust," in *Plight and Fate of Women During and Following Genocide*, ed. Samuel Totten (London, UK and New Brunswick, NJ: Transaction Publishers, 2009), p. 27.

3 Raul Hilberg, *Perpetrators Victims Bystanders: The Jewish Catastrophe, 1933–1945* (London, UK: Secker and Warburg), p. 126.

4 See Lisa Pine's chapter in this volume.

5 See Elisa von Joeden-Forgey's chapter in this volume.

6 See Doris Buss's chapter in this volume.

7 See Patricia Weitsman's chapter in this volume.

8 See Jennie Burnet's chapter in this volume.

9 See the chapters in this volume by Anthonie Holslag, Adam Jones, Jennie Burnet, and Olivera Simić.

10 See the chapters by Adam Jones and Stephen Haynes in this volume.

11 See Lerna Ekmekcioglu's chapter in this volume.

12 See Patricia Weitsman's chapter in this volume.

13 See Doris Buss's chapter in this volume.

14 See Selma Leydesdorff's chapter in this volume.

15 Janet Jacobs, *Memorializing the Holocaust: Gender, Genocide, and Collective Memory* (London, UK and New York, NY: I. B. Tauris, 2010).

16 See Elisa von Joeden-Forgey's chapter in this volume.

17 Robert Gellately and Ben Kiernan, "The Study of Mass Murder and Genocide," in *The Specter of Genocide: Mass Murder in Historical Perspective*, ed. Robert Gellately and Ben Kiernan (Cambridge, UK: Cambridge University Press, 2003), p. 9. For an early example of this scholarship, see Roger Smith, "Human Destructiveness and Politics: The Twentieth Century in an Age of Genocide," in *Genocide and the Modern Age: Etiology and Case Studies of Mass Death*, ed. Isidor Wallimann and Michael N. Dobkowski (Westport, CT: Greenwood Press, 1987), pp. 21–39.

18 Eric Weitz, "The Modernity of Genocides: War, Race, and Revolution in the Twentieth Century," in *The Specter of Genocide*, p. 54.

19 Weitz, p. 56.

20 Zygmunt Bauman, *Modernity and the Holocaust* (Cambridge, UK: Polity Press, 1989), pp. 91–3.

21 Marie Fleming, "Genocide and the Body Politic in the Time of Modernity," in *The Specter of Genocide*, p. 98. Some scholars criticize this emphasis on the distinctiveness of twentieth-century genocides, because they argue that it underplays or ignores the "colonial essence of modernity." Or to put it another way, the "revolutionary social logic" of modern genocides in the twentieth century "was inherently colonial." For more on this critique, see Dirk Moses, "Genocide and Modernity," in *The Historiography of Genocide*, ed. Dirk Moses (Basingstoke, UK: Palgrave Macmillan, 2008), p. 179; and Richard King and Dan Stone, eds., *Hannah Arendt and the Uses of History: Imperialism, Nation, Race, and Empire* (New York, NY and London, UK: Berghan Books, 2007). Hannah Arendt argued that there were important continuities between the colonialism/imperialism of the nineteenth century and Nazi totalitarianism and the Holocaust; the former promoted ways of thinking (about race) and practices for domination and exploitation (bureaucracy) that helped to foster the possibility "for a totalitarian government on the basis of racism." See Hannah Arendt, *Origins of Totalitarianism* (Cleveland, OH: World Publishing Company, 1958), part II, here p. 185.

22 Although scientific racism and negative eugenics largely ceased to have scholarly credibility in the second half of the twentieth century, after their murderous use by the Nazis, the biologization of race still has popular currency, and science is still mobilized to propagate racist ideas.

23 Ana Filipa Vrdoljak, "Human Rights and Genocide: The Work of Lauterpacht and Lemkin in Modern International Law," *The European Journal of International Law* 20:4 (2010), p. 1176; Samantha Power, *"A Problem from Hell:" America and the Age of Genocide* (New York, NY: Basic Books, 2002), p. 21.

24 For more on Lemkin's efforts to convince the international community that certain acts violated international law and were therefore international crimes, see Vrdoljak, "Human Rights and Genocide," pp. 1163–93.

25 Power, *"A Problem from Hell,"* p. 42.

26 Raphael Lemkin, *Axis Rule in Occupied Europe: Laws of Occupation, Analysis of Government—Proposals for Redress* (New York, NY: Howard Fertig, 1973 [1944]), chapters 8 and 9.

27 Ibid., p. 79.

28 For more on Lemkin's book and his understanding of genocide, see Dirk Moses, "The Holocaust and Genocide," in *The Historiography of the Holocaust*, pp. 537–40.

29 "The United Nations Convention on the Prevention and Punishment of the Crime of Genocide," in *The Genocide Studies Reader*, ed. Samuel Totten and Paul Bartrop (London, UK and New York, NY: Routledge, 2009), p. 31.

30 Ibid.

31 Kuper argued that "vestiges" of cultural genocide remained in two main ways; ethnical groups (that is, "groups with distinctive culture of language") were

included as groups to be protected against genocide, and "forcibly transferring children of the group to another group" constituted an act of genocide. Leo Kuper, *Genocide: Its Political Use in the Twentieth Century* (New Haven, CT: Yale University Press, 1981), p. 31.

32 Kuper addresses these complexities and controversies regarding the UN definition in pp. 22–35, here 26. Also see Samuel Totten, ed., *Teaching about Genocide: Issues, Approaches, and Resources* (Greenwich, CT: Information Age Publishing, 2004), especially chapters 3 and 4. In addition to already mentioned concerns about the definition—for example, about how it excludes political and social groups as targets of and hence deserving protection from genocide—there is another problem; as Alexander Hinton notes, this legal definition reifies the idea of race as "immutable," which belies the fact that race itself is a social construction that historically has been highly mutable. Alexander Hinton, "Critical Genocide Studies," in *Genocide Matters: Ongoing Issues and Emerging Perspectives*, ed. Joyce Apsel and Ernesto Verdeja (Oxon, UK and New York, NY: Routledge, 2013), p. 50.

33 For more on the prosecution of sexual violence as an act of genocide, including significant limitations regarding what is viewed as sexual violence, see Anne-Marie de Brouwer, *Sexual Violence as an Act of Genocide: Supranational Criminal Prosecution of Sexual Violence: The ICC and the Practice of the ICTY and the ICTR* (Antwerp, Belgium and Oxford, UK: Intersentia, 2005). Helen Fein has argued that sexual violence could also be considered an act of genocide because it falls "within several of the five acts defined by the UNCG as genocide"—that is, acts C and D (and not only B). For more on her view, see Roger Smith, "Genocide and the Politics of Rape: Historical and Psychological Perspectives," in *Genocide Matters*, p. 98.

34 Smith, "Genocide and the Politics of Rape," in *Genocide Matters*, p. 99.

35 Paul Bartrop and Samuel Totten, "The History of Genocide: An Overview," in *Teaching about Genocide*, pp. 45–6. For a more detailed discussion of the failures of the international community, see Power, "*A Problem from Hell*," and Karen E. Smith, *Genocide and the Europeans* (Cambridge, UK: Cambridge University Press, 2010). For problems with prevention, see Samuel Totten, *Impediments to the Prevention and Intervention of Genocide* (New Brunswick, NJ and London, UK: Transaction Publishers, 2013).

36 Donald Bloxham and A. Dirk Moses, eds., *The Oxford Handbook of Genocide Studies* (Oxford, UK: Oxford University Press, 2010), p. 3.

37 As Michael Marrus notes, up until the Eichmann trial in 1961, there was "relatively little discussion of the massacre of European Jewry" in academic circles and the wider public, and when academics did mention it, they usually "did so in passing as one more atrocity in a particularly cruel war." Michael Marrus, *The Holocaust in History* (Hanover, NH and London, UK: University Press of New England, 1987), pp. 4–5. For some of the earliest academic literature on the Holocaust, see Raul Hilberg, *The Destruction of the European Jews* (New York, NY: Holmes & Meier, 1961); Hannah Arendt, *Eichmann in Jerusalem: A Report on the Banality of Evil* (New York, NY: The Viking Press, 1965); Lucy Dawidowicz, *The War against the Jews, 1939-1945* (New York, NY: Holt, Rinehart, & Winston, 1975); Helen Fein, *Accounting*

for *Genocide: National Responses and Jewish Victimization during the Holocaust* (New York, NY: Free Press, 1979); Henry Friedlander and Sybil Milton, eds., *The Holocaust: Ideology, Bureaucracy, and Genocide* (Millwood and New York, NY: Kraus International Publications, 1980); Yehuda Bauer, *A History of the Holocaust* (New York, NY: Franklin Watts, 1982).

38 For more on why awareness about and commemoration of the Holocaust was initially so limited and then began to expand, see Dan Stone, "Memory, Memorials, and Museums," in *The Historiography of the Holocaust*, pp. 512–15; Jacobs, *Memorializing the Holocaust*, pp. xvii–xviii; Eliezer Don-Yehiya, "Memory and Political Culture: Israeli Society and the Holocaust," *Studies in Contemporary Jewry* 9 (1993), pp. 139–61; Idith Zertal, *Israel's Holocaust and the Politics of Nationhood* (Cambridge, UK: Cambridge University Press, 2005); Peter Novick, *The Holocaust in American Life* (New York, NY: Houghton Mifflin Company: 1999); Alan Mintz, *Popular Culture and the Shaping of Holocaust Memory* (Seattle, WA: University of Washington Press, 2001).

39 Marrus, *The Holocaust in History*, pp. 4–5.

40 Ian Kershaw, *The Nazi Dictatorship: Problems and Perspectives of Interpretation* (London, UK: Edward Arnold, 1985), pp. 83–4.

41 This new political consciousness, which resulted in calls for greater openness about the country's past and its perpetration of terrible crimes against Jews in the Second World War, was particularly prominent among younger West Germans. See Jacobs, *Memorializing the Holocaust*, p. xvii.

42 Henry R. Huttenbach, "Vita Felix, Via Dolorosa: An Academic Journey towards Genocide," in *Pioneers of Genocide Studies*, ed. Samuel Totten and Steven Leonard Jacobs (London, UK and New Brunswick, NJ: Transaction Publishers, 2002), p. 51. For more on the links between politics of the 1960s and the Nazi past, including the historical rhetoric used by critics to delegitimize various state actions, see Harold Marcuse, "The Revival of Holocaust Awareness in West Germany, Israel, and the United States," in *1968: The World Transformed*, ed. Carole Fink, Philipp Gassert, and Detlev Junker (Cambridge, UK: Cambridge University Press, 1998), pp. 421–38.

43 Stone, "Memory, Memorials, and Museums," pp. 512–15; Gellately and Kiernan, "The Study of Mass Murder and Genocide," p. 6; Jacobs, *Memorializing the Holocaust*, p. xvii. For an interesting discussion of the United States Holocaust Memorial Museum, which President Carter commissioned in 1979 and which finally opened in 1993, see Alison Landsberg, "America, the Holocaust, and the Mass Culture of Memory: Toward a Radical Politics of Empathy," *New German Critique* 71 (1997), pp. 63–86.

44 Kershaw argues that German "popular consciousness was reached only through the showing of the American filmed 'soap-opera' dramatization of the Holocaust on Western German television in 1979." Kershaw, *The Nazi Dictatorship*, 83.

45 For Turkish narratives, including scholarship, on the Armenian deaths and massacres, see Donald Bloxham and Fatma Müge Göçeck, "The Armenian Genocide," in *The Historiography of Genocide*, pp. 346–52. For geopolitical reasons, the West legitimized the new state, the Republic of Turkey, which

succeeded the Ottoman Empire after its collapse in 1918. This included
"Western abandonment of the Armenians" in the final postwar peace treaties
and Western complicity in the cover-up in subsequent decades. As Richard
Hovannisian notes, Turkish leaders secured this complicity by "playing upon"
Turkey's importance as "a bulwark against communism" and an international
trade and commerce partner. See Hovannisian, "The Armenian Genocide,"
in *Genocide: A Critical Bibliographic Review*, ed. Israel Charny (New York,
NY: Facts on File Publications, 1988), pp. 97–8; "Confronting the Armenian
Genocide," in *Pioneers of Genocide Studies*, p. 32, respectively.

46 Some of the early works include: Richard Hovannisian, *The Armenian
Holocaust (A Bibliography Relating to the Deportation, Massacres, and
Dispersion of the Armenian People, 1915-1923)* (Cambridge, MA: Armenian
Heritage Press, 1980); Richard Hovannisian, ed., *The Armenian Genocide in
Perspective* (New Brunswick, NJ: Transaction Books, 1986); Yves Ternon, *Les
Arméniens, histoire d'un génocide* (Paris, France: 1977); Gerard Chaliand and
Yves Ternon, *The Armenians; From Genocide to Resistance*, trans. Tony Berret
(London, UK: Zed Press, 1983); Vahakn Dadrian, "The Role of the Turkish
Physicians in the World War I Genocide of the Armenians," *Holocaust and
Genocide Studies* 1:2 (1986), pp. 169–92.

47 Rubina Peroomian, "Historical Memory: Threading the Contemporary
Literature of Armenia," in *The Armenian Genocide: Cultural and Ethical
Legacies*, ed. Richard Hovannisian (New Brunswick, NJ: Transaction
Publishers, 2007), p. 107; Richard Hovannisian, "The Armenian Genocide and
Patterns of Denial," in *The Armenian Genocide in Perspective*, pp. 121–2.

48 Radical international groups, such as the Justice Commandos of the Armenian
Genocide and the Armenian Secret Army for the Liberation of Armenia, used
violent attacks and assassinations to spread the same message and to demand
apologies and reparations from the Turkish government.

49 In 1982, this growing academic interest in the Armenian genocide was
reflected in the founding of the Zoryan Institute for Contemporary Armenian
Research and Documentation, which explicitly promoted genocide research
and documentation. In addition to serving as an international scholarly center,
the institute has organized international conferences as well hundreds of
seminars and lectures in conjunction with academic institutions. By launching
an oral history project in 1983, which recorded 700 survivors' testimonies,
and collecting a vast array of archival materials, the institute has also become
an important research repository. K. M. (Greg) Sarkissian, *The Making of a
National Research Centre: The Zoryan Institute* (The Zoryan Institute, 2004).

50 Hovannisian, "Confronting the Armenian Genocide," in *Pioneers of Genocide
Studies*, p. 33. Among other things, the Turkish government produced a flood
of denial literature that it then sent to Western libraries and schools. It also
pressured NATO allies to collude in the silencing of what really happened—for
example, by not lending support to commemorations or conferences about the
Armenian genocide. For more on this topic, see Hovannisian, "The Armenian
Genocide," in *Genocide: A Bibliographic Review*, pp. 100–1 and "Genocide
and Denial: The Armenian Case," in *Toward the Understanding and Prevention
of Genocide: Proceedings of the Proceedings of the International Conference
on the Holocaust and Genocide* (Boulder, CO; Westview Press, 1984).

51 People's Tribunal at Sorbonne, 1985, United Nations Commission on Human Rights, 1985, European Parliament after that (see Dadrian, *History of the Armenian Genocide*, p. xix).

52 Irving Louis Horowitz, "Gauging Genocide: Social Sciences Dimensions," in *Pioneers of Genocide Studies*, p. 263.

53 Some of the comparative scholarship includes: Vahakn Dadrian, "The Convergent Aspects of the Armenian and Jewish cases of Genocide," *Holocaust and Genocide Studies* 3:2 (1988), pp. 151–69; Robert Melson, *Revolution and Genocide: On the Origins of the Armenian Genocide and the Holocaust* (Chicago, IL: University of Chicago Press, 1996); Robert Melson, "Revolution, War, and Genocide: The Armenian Genocide and the Holocaust Compared," in *Encyclopedia of Genocide*, vol. 2, ed. Israel W. Charny (Denver, CO: ABC Clio, 1999).

54 For some early academic work on Bangladesh, see Kalyn Chaudhuri, *Genocide in Bangladesh* (Telangana, India: Orient Longman, 1972); Abul Hasanat, *Bangladesh, Sufferings, Survival: Let Humanity Not Forget the Ugliest Genocide in History* (New York, NY: Muktadhara, 1978). Although there was some Western media coverage of and some early non-Western scholarship on the genocide in Bangladesh, most academics in the West paid little attention to it in the following two decades. Donald W. Beachler, "The Politics of Genocide Scholarship: The Case of Bangladesh," *Patterns of Prejudice* 41:5 (December 2007), pp. 467–92. One of the earlier Western academics to focus on the Cambodian genocide, Ben Kiernan, provides an excellent overview of it in *The Pol Pot Regime: Race, Power and Genocide in Cambodia under the Khmer Rouge, 1975–1979* (New Haven, CT: Yale University Press, 1996).

55 Although there was Western media coverage in the late 1970s and early 1980s about the mass atrocities and deaths in Cambodia, geopolitical factors played a role on how these events were explained. Because of the US alliance with China against the Soviet Union and the Vietnamese, for example, most American politicians did not acknowledge the Khmer Rouge's murderous policies and mass killings—both during the height of the carnage and in the 1980s. Moreover, some explained the mass deaths by promoting the narrative that the Vietnamese invasion in 1979 had led to "genocide by starvation." US diplomatic support for the Khmer Rouge continued until 1991. For more on how politics shaped recognition of and attention to the genocides in Bangladesh and Cambodia, see Donald W. Beachler, *The Genocide Debate: Politicians, Academics, and Victims* (Basingstoke, UK and New York, NY: Palgrave Macmillan, 2011).

56 Robert Melson, "My Journey in the Study of Genocide," in *Pioneers of Genocide Studies*, p. 139.

57 Huttenbach, "Vita Felix, Via Dolorosa," p. 54.

58 Kuper, *Genocide*. Other examples of early scholarship in genocide studies include: Richard Arens, ed., *Genocide in Paraguay* (Philadelphia, PA: Temple University Press, 1976); Irving Louis Horowitz, *Taking Lives: Genocide and State Power* (New Brunswick, NJ: Transactions Books, 1976); Leo Kuper, *The Prevention of Genocide* (New Haven, CT: Yale University Press, 1985); Frank Chalk and Kurt Jonassohn, *The History and Sociology of Genocide: Analyses*

and Case Studies (New Haven, CT: Yale University Press, 1990). In their book, Chalk and Jonassohn explicitly adopted a comparative approach to "attempt to identify the social conditions and situations in which genocide [was] likely to occur" (p. 4). This book discusses genocides in many different historical contexts and places, including ancient Carthage, New England in the 1630s (Puritans' destruction of the Pequots), twentieth-century Bangladesh, Burundi, Indonesia, Cambodia, and so on.

59 Kuper, *Genocide*, pp. 9–10.

60 Isidor Wallimann and Michael N. Dobrowski, eds., "Introduction," in *Genocide and the Modern Age*, pp. xxiii.

61 Israel Charny, *How Can We Commit the Unthinkable? Genocide: The Human Cancer* (Boulder, CO: Westview Press, 1982), p. 4.

62 This openness and interest of some Holocaust studies scholars led to the first international conference on the Holocaust and genocide in 1982 in Israel. See Israel Charny, ed., *Toward the Understanding and Prevention of Genocide: Proceedings of the International Conference on the Holocaust and Genocide* (Boulder, CO; Westview Press, 1984).

63 For more on the uniqueness debate, see Alan Rosenbaum, ed., *Is the Holocaust Unique: Perspectives on Comparative Genocide* (Boulder, CO: Westview Press, 1996).

64 Donald Bloxham, *The Final Solution: A Genocide* (Oxford, UK: Oxford University Press, 2009), p. 7.

65 Steven Leonard Jacobs, "From Holocaust to Genocide: The Journey Continues," in *Pioneers of Genocide Studies*, p. 515.

66 Donald Bloxham and A. Dirk Moses, "Editors Introduction: Changing Themes in the Study of Genocide," in *Oxford Handbook of Genocide Studies*, ed. Donald Bloxham and A. Dirk Moses (Oxford, UK and New York, NY: Oxford University Press, 2010), p. 2.

67 Some of these comparative works include: Mark Levene, *Genocide in the Age of the Nation State* (vols. 1 and 2) (London, UK: I. B. Tauris, 2005); Gellately and Kiernan, eds., *The Specter of Genocide*; Benjamin Valentino, *Final Solutions: Mass Killing and Genocide in the 20th Century* (Ithaca, NY: Cornell University Press, 2005); Samuel Totten, William S. Parsons, and Israel Charney, eds., *Genocide in the Twentieth Century: Critical Essays and Eyewitness Testimony* (New York, NY: Garland Publishing, 1995).

68 Dan Stone, "The Holocaust and its Historiography," in *The Historiography of Genocide*, p. 374.

69 For example, see Olaf Jensen and Claus-Christian W. Szejnmann, eds., *Ordinary People as Mass Murderers: Perpetrators in Comparative Perspectives* (Basingstoke, UK: Palgrave Macmillan, 2008).

70 For example, see Sheri Rosenberg and Everita Silina, "Genocide by Attrition: Silent and Efficient," in *Genocide Matters*, p. 107.

71 Hinton, "Critical Genocide Studies," pp. 54–5.

72 Joan Ringelheim, "Women and the Holocaust: A Reconsideration of Research," *Signs* 10:4 (1985), pp. 741–2.

73 Sybil Milton, "Women and the Holocaust: The Case of German and German-Jewish Women," in *When Biology Became Destiny: Women in Weimar and Nazi Germany*, ed. Renate Bridenthal, Atina Grossman, and Marion Kaplan (New York, NY: Monthly Review Press, 1984), p. 297.

74 Lisa Pine, "Gender and the Family," in *The Historiography of the Holocaust*, p. 364.

75 Esther Katz and Joan Ringelheim, eds., *Proceedings of the Conference, Women Surviving the Holocaust* (New York, NY: Institute for Research in History, 1983). Some of the earlier scholarship from the 1980s and early 1990s included: Marlene Heinemann, *Gender and Destiny: Women Writers and the Holocaust* (New York: Greenwood Press, 1986); Joan Ringelheim, "Thoughts about Women and the Holocaust," and Myrna Goldenberg, "Different Horrors, Same Hell: Women Remembering the Holocaust," in *Thinking the Unthinkable: Meanings of the Holocaust*, ed. R. Gottlieb (New York, NY: Paulist Press, 1990), pp. 141–9, and 150–66, respectively; C. Rittner and J. Roth, eds., *Different Voices: Women and the Holocaust* (New York, NY: Paragon, 1993). For some (but by no means all) of the more recent scholarship on gender and the Holocaust, see the following books: Judith Baumel, *Double Jeopardy: Gender and the Holocaust* (London, UK: Valentine Mitchell, 1998); Rochelle Saidel, *The Jewish Women of Ravensbruck Concentration Camp* (Madison, WI: University of Wisconsin Press, 2004); Nechama Tec, *Resilience and Courage: Women, Men, and the Holocaust* (New Haven, CT: Yale University Press, 2003); Elizabeth R. Baer and Myrna Goldenberg, eds., *Experience and Expression: Women, the Nazis, and the Holocaust* (Detroit, MI: Wayne State University Press, 2003).

76 Joan Ringelheim, "The Split between Gender and the Holocaust," pp. 346–7; quote from Jacobs, *Memorializing the Holocaust*, pp. xxiii.

77 For the connection between sexual violence and these genocides and the study of sexual violence during the Holocaust, see Waxman chapter in this volume. Also see Catherine MacKinnon, "Turning Rape into Pornography: Postmodern Genocide," *Ms. Magazine* 4:1 (1993). For some of this new academic work, see Sonja M. Hedgpeth and Rochelle G. Saidel, *Sexual Violence against Women during the Holocaust* (Waltham, MA: Brandeis University Press, 2010); Robert Sommer, "Camp Brothels: Forced Sex Labour in Nazi Concentration Camps," Regina Mühlhäuser, "Between 'Racial Awareness' and Fantasies of Potency: Nazi Sexual Politics in the Occupied Territories of the Soviet Union, 1942-1945," and Na'ama Shik, "Sexual Abuse of Jewish Women in Auschwitz-Birkenau," in *Brutality and Desire: War and Sexuality in Europe's Twentieth Century*, ed. D. Herzog (Basingstoke, UK: Palgrave Macmillan, 2009, 2011), pp. 168–196, 197–220, 221–47, respectively. In addition to studying sexual violence, some scholars have begun to investigate the significance of sexuality, more generally, for understanding Nazism and the Holocaust. For an overview of this scholarship and its importance, see Elizabeth Heineman, "Sexuality and Nazism: The Doubly Unspeakable," in *Sexuality and German Fascism*, ed. Dagmar Herzog (Oxford and New York: Berghahn Books, 2005), pp. 22–66. See the chapters in this same book for some of this new scholarship.

78 A few of the earlier works include Isabel Kaprielian-Churchill, "Armenian Refugee Women: The Picture Brides 1920–1930," *Journal of American Ethnic*

History 12:3 (1993), pp. 3–29; Donald Miller and Lorna Touryan Miller, "The Experience of Women and Children," *Survivors: An Oral History of the Armenian Genocide* (Berkeley and Los Angeles, CA and London, UK: University of California Press, 1993). Scholarship in the last fifteen years includes but is not limited to A. Sarafian, "The Absorption of Armenian Women and Children into Muslim Households as a Structural Component of the Armenian Genocide," in *In God's Name: Genocide and Religion in the Twentieth Century*, ed. O. Bartov and P. Mack (New York, NY and Oxford, UK: Berghahn Books, 2001), pp. 209–21; Vahram Shemmassian, "The League of Nations and the Reclamation of Armenian Genocide Survivors," in *Looking Backward, Moving Forward: Confronting the Armenian Genocide*, ed. Richard Hovannisian (New Brunswick, NJ: Transaction Publishers, 2003); Katharine Derderian, "Common Fate, Different Experience: Gender-Specific Aspects of the Armenian Genocide, 1915-1917," *Holocaust and Genocide Studies* 19:1 (Spring 2005), pp. 1–25; Vahé Tachjian, "Gender, Nationalism, Exclusion: The Reintegration Process of Female Survivors of the Armenian Genocide," *Nations and Nationalism* 15: 1 (2009): 60–80; Matthias Bjornlund, "'A Fate Worse Than Dying;' Sexual Violence During the Armenian Genocide," in *Brutality and Desire*, pp. 16–58; Rubina Peroomian, "Women and the Armenian Genocide: The Victim, the Living Martyr," in *Plight and Fate of Women*, pp. 7–24; Ayse Gul Altinay, Fethiye Cetin, *The Hidden Legacy of "Lost" Armenians in Turkey*, trans. Maureen Freely (New Brunswick, NJ: Transaction Publishers, 2014); Fethiye Çetin and Maureen Freely, *My Grandmother: A Memoir*, trans. Maureen Freely (London, UK: Verso, 2008); Arlene Voski Avakian, "Surviving the Survivors of the Armenian Genocide: Daughters and Granddaughters," in *Voices of Armenian Women*, ed. Barbara Mergeurian and Joy Renjilian-Burgy (Belmont, MA: AIWA Press, 2000); Arlene Voski Avakian, "A Different Future? Armenian Identity through the Prism of Trauma, Nationalism and Gender," *New Perspectives on Turkey* 42 (Spring 2010), pp. 203–14.

79 Slavenka Drakulic, *Café Europa: Life After Communism* (London, UK and New York, NY: Penguin Books, 1996), p. 213.

80 These crimes included forced collectivization and *dekulakization*, which resulted in terrible famine and the mass deportation and death of millions of peasants; the purges of 1936-7, which led to the execution of hundreds of thousands (if not more) and imprisonment in the Gulag of millions of so-called enemies of the people (political and national "enemies" as well as alleged intellectual, economic, and military opponents); the mass operations of 1937–8, which entailed the mass repression of millions of "socially harmful elements" (e.g., petty criminals, hooligans, and prostitutes), "former people" (e.g., former members of non-Bolshevik political parties and former Whites), and nationally suspect peoples (who had "foreign contacts" or lived in the borderlands); the execution of over 20,000 Polish army officers in the Katyn massacre of 1940; and the forced deportations of Chechens, Crimean Tatars, and other "punished peoples" in 1944. There is a vast and excellent literature on these topics. For some recent examples, see Paul Hagenloh, *Stalin's Police: Public Order and Mass Repression in the USSR, 1926-1941* (Baltimore, MD; Johns Hopkins University Press, 2009); Wendy Z. Goldman, *Terror and Democracy in the Age of Stalin: The Social Dynamics of Repression* (Cambridge, UK: Cambridge

University Press, 2007); Lynne Viola, *The Unknown Gulag: The Lost World of Stalin's Special Settlements* (Oxford, UK: Oxford University Press, 2007); Oleg Khlevniuk, *The History of the Gulag: From Collectivization to the Great Terror*, trans. Vadim Staklo (New Haven, CT: Yale University Press, 2004); J. Arch Getty and Oleg V. Naumov, *The Road to Terror: Stalin and the Self-Destruction of the Bolsheviks, 1932-1939* (New Haven, CT: Yale University Press, 1999); David Shearer, *Policing Stalin's Socialism: Repression and Social Order in the Soviet Union, 1924-1953* (New Haven, CT: Yale University Press, 2009).

81 Nicholas Werth, "The Mechanism of a Mass Crime: The Great Terror in the Soviet Union, 1937-1938," in *The Specter of Genocide*, p. 238; Norman Naimark, *Stalin's Genocides* (Princeton, NJ: Princeton University Press, 2010), p. 137, respectively.

82 Naimark, *Stalin's Genocides*, pp. 3, 14.

83 For the Holocaust and Roma and Sinti women, see Sybil Milton, "Hidden Lives: Sinta and Roma Women," in *Experience and Expression*, pp. 53–75. For more on the Romani experience in general, see Gabrielle Tyrnauer, "The Fate of the Gypsies During the Holocaust" and Ian Hancock, "Gypsy History in Germany and Neighbouring Lands: A Chronology Leading to the Holocaust and Beyond," in *The Gypsies of Eastern Europe*, ed. David Crowe and John Kolsti (Armonk, NY: M. E. Sharpe, 1991); Ian Hancock, "Romanies and the Holocaust: A Reevaluation and an Overview," in *The Historiography of the Holocaust*, pp. 383–96; Janos Barsony and Agnes Daroczi, *Pharrajimos: The Fate of the Roma during the Holocaust* (Budapest, Hungary: Central European University Press, 2008). Scholarship on the Nazi persecution of gay men and lesbians includes, but is not limited to, Richard Plant, *The Pink Triangle: The Nazi War against Homosexuals* (New York, NY: Holt, 1986); Gunter Grau, ed., *Hidden Holocaust? Gay and Lesbian Persecution in Germany, 1933-1945*, trans. Patrick Camiller (Chicago, IL: Fitzroy Dearborn, 1995); Claudia Schoppmann, "National Socialist Policies towards Female Homosexuality," in *Gender Relations in German History: Power, Agency and Experience from the Sixteenth to the Twentieth Century*, ed. Lynn Abrams and Elizabeth Harvey (Durham, NC: Duke University Press, 1996); Stefan Micheler, "Homophobic Propaganda and the Denunciation of Same-Sex Desiring Men under National Socialism," and Erik Jensen, "The Pink Triangle and Political Consciousness: Gays, Lesbians, and the Memory of Nazi Persecution," *Journal of the History of Sexuality* 11:1 and 2 (2002), pp. 105–30, and 319–49, respectively.

84 For Bangladesh, see Anthony Mascarenhas, *The Rape of Bangladesh* (New Delhi, India: Vikas Publications, 1971); Yasmin Saikia, "Overcoming the Silent Archive in Bangladesh: Women Bearing Witness to Violence in the 1971 'Liberation' War," in *Women and the Contested State*, ed. M. Skidmore and P. Lawrence (Notre Dame, IN: University of Notre Dame Press, 2007); Yasmin Saikia, *Women, War, and the Making of Bangladesh: Remembering 1971* (Durham, NC: Duke University Press, 2011); Nayanika Mookherjee, *The Spectral Wound: Sexual Violence, Public Memories and the Bangladesh War of 1971* (Durham, NC: Duke University Press, 2012), and "The Bangladesh Genocide: The Plight of Women," in *Plight and Fate of Women during and*

Following Genocide, ed. Samuel Totten (London, UK and New Brunswick, NY: Transaction Publishers, 2009), pp. 47–66. For more on women and the Darfur genocide, see "The Darfur Genocide: The Mass Rape of Black African Girls and Women," in *Plight and Fate of Women*, pp. 137–68; Kelly Dawn Askin, "Prosecuting Gender Crimes Committed in Darfur: Holding Leaders Accountable for Sexual Violence," in *Genocide in Darfur: Investigating the Atrocities in the Sudan*, ed. Samuel Totten and Eric Markusen (New York, NY: Routledge, 2006), pp. 141–60. For more on women and the Cambodian genocide, see Judy Ledgerwood, "Death, Shattered Families, and Living as Widows in Cambodia," in *Plight and Fate of Women,* pp. 67–81. Ledgerwood maintains that "the specific plight of women in this period [the Khmer Rouge Revolution and genocide] has not been the focus of research" (p. 67). As of now, more research exists on women after the Cambodian genocide.

85 Originally a chapter on masculinity and violence in the former Yugoslavia was supposed to be included in this section of the edited collection, but in the end, this did not come to pass. For some scholarship on this topic, see Euan Hague, "Rape, Power and Masculinity: The Construction of Gender and National Identities in the War in Bosnia-Herzegovina," in *Gender and Catastrophe*, ed. Ronit Lentin (London, UK: Zed Books, 1997), pp. 50–63; Aleksandra Milićević, "Joining the War: Masculinity, Nationalism and War Participation in the Balkans War of Secession, 1991–1995," *Nationalities Papers* 34: 3 (1996), pp. 265–87; Dubravka Zarkov, "The Body of the Other Man: Sexual Violence and the Construction of Masculinity, Sexuality and Ethnicity in Croatian Media," in *Victims, Perpetrators or Actors? Gender, Armed Conflict and Political Violence*, ed. Caroline O. N. Moser and Fiona C. Clark (London, UK: Zed Books, 2001).

86 For example: Claudia Koonz, *Mothers in the Fatherland: Women, the Family and Nazi Politics* (New York, NY: St. Martin's Press, 1987); Gisela Bock, "Racism and Sexism in Nazi Germany: Motherhood, Compulsory Sterilization, and the State," in *When Biology Became Destiny*, ed. Renate Bridenthal, Atina Grossman, and Marion Kaplan (New York, NY: Monthly Review Press, 1984), pp. 271–96; Gisela Bock, "Ordinary Women in Nazi Germany: Perpetrators, Victims, Followers and Bystanders," in *Women in the Holocaust*, pp. 85–100. For more recent work, see E. Harvey, *Women and the Nazi East: Agents and Witnesses of Germanization* (New Haven, CT: Yale University Press, 2003); S. Heschel, "Does Atrocity Have a Gender? Feminist Interpretations of Women in the SS," in *Lessons and Legacies: New Currents in Holocaust Research, Vol. IV.*, ed. Diefendorf (Evanston, IL; Northwestern University Press, 2004), pp. 300–21; Wendy Adele-Marie Sarti, *Women and Nazis: Perpetrators of Genocide* (Palo Alto, CA: Academica Press, 2012); Irmtraud Heike, "Female Concentration Camp Guards as Perpetrators: Three Case Studies," in *Ordinary People as Mass Murderers*, pp. 120–42; Wendy Lower, *Hitler's Furies: German Women in the Nazi Killing Fields* (New York, NY: Houghton Mifflin, 2013).

87 For example, see Zoë Waxman, "Towards an Integrated History of the Holocaust: Masculinity, Femininity, and Genocide," in *Years of Persecution, Years of Extermination: Saul Friedlander and the Future of Holocaust Studies*, ed. Christian Wiese and Paul Betts (London, UK: Continuum, 2010);

Jane Caplan, "Gender and the Concentration Camps," in *Concentration Camps in Nazi Germany: The New Histories*, ed. Jane Caplan and Nikolaus Wachsmann (London and New York: Routledge, 2010), pp. 82–107; Jacobs, *Memorializing the Holocaust*; Nechama Tec, *Resilience and Courage: Women, the Men, and the Holocaust* (New Haven, CT and London, NY: Yale University Press, 2003).

88 For more on women's complicity, see Lisa Sharlach, "Gender and Genocide in Rwanda: Women as Agents and Objects of Genocide," *Journal of Genocide Research* 1:3 (1999), pp. 387–99; and the other sources listed in Hogg and Drumbl's chapter in this volume.

89 For more analyses of the male-on-male sexual violence in the Bosnian conflict, see Simić's endnotes as well as Elysia Ruvinsky, "*My Heart Bleeds, But Where To Take My Grief Is Not There:*" *Wartime Sexual Violence Against Men in the Balkan and Great Lakes Regions* (Thesis, University of Amsterdam, 2012).

90 This anti-Semitism, in conjunction with antiliberalism, homophobia, and misogyny, created a toxic political environment, which contributed to the political downfall of my stepfather. For more on this, see James Aloisi, *The Vidal Lecture: Sex and Politics in Massachusetts and the Persecution of Chief Justice Robert Bonin* (Cambridge, MA: Chillmark/Ashburton Hill, 2011).

PART ONE

Gendered Experiences of Genocide

1

Gender and the Holocaust: Male and Female Experiences of Auschwitz

Lisa Pine

Introduction

The lens of gender has been applied comparatively recently both to the Holocaust, in particular, and to genocide studies, more widely. Research on gender and genocide has expanded considerably over recent years.[1] Gender-based distinctions provide a useful analytical tool in the discussion of genocides. As Adam Jones has noted, the perspective of gender allows us to define how men and women are targeted during episodes of genocidal violence.[2] Moreover, Stephen Haynes, writing on "ordinary masculinity" in Chapter 7 of this book, underlines how a greater recognition of the gendered character of male experiences can enhance our understanding of the Holocaust. Haynes's chapter is concerned with perpetrators, but a discussion of male attributes in Holocaust victims and the behavioral norms expected of Holocaust victims as men is also highly significant. Much of the writing on gender to date has been on women and their experiences. This chapter examines both male and female experiences, and both as particular to their gender, rather than as *universal* experiences. Femininity and masculinity are both about the social construction of particular kinds of identities and behavioral expectations, and this chapter will explore how this related to women and men during the extreme and extraordinary circumstances of the Holocaust.

This chapter begins with an analysis of the main developments in the historiography of the Holocaust in relation to gender. This is an important starting point, as the implications and knowledge from this research are very significant to our understanding of the Holocaust. Having established the parameters of the existing research in this area of scholarship, the chapter turns to a discussion of the concepts of gender and gendered expectations in relation to Holocaust victims. The social construction of male and female identities and roles was important in the history of the Holocaust. This chapter examines, first, the structural sources of gender difference in relation to Nazi persecution before the war and then the distinctions between the ways in which Jewish men and women experienced the Holocaust, using significant examples from both male and female survivors' accounts to underline and illustrate the key points. In particular, it discusses gender-related experiences at Auschwitz. It considers both male behavior that reflected expected gender norms, such as egotism, strength, and identity through work, and male behavior that deviated from these expectations, such as social bonding to enhance chances of survival. It then examines female behavior that met with traditional gender norms, such as adaptation and coping mechanisms and social bonding among female victims. Lastly, it moves to a consideration of female behavior that differed from the expected female type. While this is an uncomfortable topic, it is nevertheless an important one. The literature has tended to overlook the desperate actions taken by Holocaust victims in order to survive under the appalling conditions in which they found themselves. But this does not mean that they did not occur. The purpose of such discussion is not to judge but to offer a more complete picture of Holocaust experiences and to try to establish a greater historical understanding of the subject.

Historiographical Developments

Raul Hilberg argued that "the road to annihilation was marked by events that specifically affected men as men and women as women."[3] Yet, the subject of gender was a relative newcomer in the wider field of Holocaust studies. Gender studies of the Holocaust emerged as a response to existing research and available sources within the broader fields of both Holocaust studies and women's studies. The term "gender" refers to the social and cultural construction of the roles of men and women in society. The application of a gendered perspective to comprehend the Holocaust has been an important development in the area of Holocaust studies since the 1980s.

Yehuda Bauer has suggested that "the problems facing women as women and men as men have a special poignancy in an extreme situation such as the Holocaust."[4] Dalia Ofer and Lenore Weitzman have emphasized that, rather than distracting us from the Nazi brutality against all Jews, a gendered approach enhances our understanding of it "by locating it in the specificity of individual experiences."[5] It expands our knowledge base and provides a greater and more differentiated understanding of the experiences of Holocaust victims. As Myrna Goldenberg has suggested, a separate examination of "the lives of women and of men" allows us "to determine the differences and the similarities in the way they were treated as well as the way they responded."[6] The situations faced by Jewish men and women under Nazi persecution meant that some aspects of their traditional gender roles were increased, while others were decreased. As Anna Reading has suggested, some "aspects of 'femininity' and 'masculinity' and their respective cultural scaffolding were disarticulated and dismantled."[7]

In addition, certain aspects of life and experiences have been taboo subjects in the writing on the Holocaust. Joan Ringelheim has referred to the "sexual" vulnerability of women: sexual humiliation, rape, sexual exchange, pregnancy, abortion, and vulnerability through their children. Women expressed feelings of "sexual vulnerability as women, not only about mortal danger as Jews."[8] These were concerns that men either described differently or did not describe at all. Stories about sexual abuse are infrequently told, as Ringelheim has noted: "Some think it inappropriate to talk about these matters; discussions about sexuality desecrate the memories of the dead, or the living, or the Holocaust itself. For others, it is simply too difficult and painful. Still others think it may be a trivial issue."[9] Moreover, as Anna Hardman has noted, the tendency in historical writing has been to define Jewish women "with a very particular notion of what constitutes female behavior"—as mothers, sisters, and nurturers.[10] Testimonies that homogenize women's experiences and identities can be misleading.[11] Sara Horowitz challenges the type of interpretation that "erases the actual experiences of women and, to an extent, domesticates the events of the Holocaust."[12] Zoë Waxman argues that assumptions that women only had motherly and caregiving roles "obscure the diversity of women's Holocaust experiences."[13] She states that "the collectivization of Holocaust memory has led to a homogenization of Holocaust comprehension that eschews difficult testimony or stories that fall outside accepted narratives."[14]

Pascale Bos, too, has examined the place of gender in the study of Holocaust victims and survivors.[15] She has called for a more critical approach to the evidence of gender distinctions in Holocaust narratives, emphasizing the discursive construction of the experience, memory, and representation of the past. Indeed, Bos argues that "precisely in acknowledging (and highlighting) the elements of choice and subversive power in the creation of (gendered) personal narratives we can conceive of survivors' agency in compelling new ways."[16] The lens of gender enables readers to consider what is distinctive between the ways in which women and men have selected and constructed their narratives. As Bos argues, "Men and women experience, remember, and recount events differently," because of their socialization.[17] For example, in her testimony, Giuliana Tedeschi uses knitting, a traditionally feminine activity, as a metaphor to describe the significance of female bonding at Auschwitz.[18] This mode of narration is particular to a female voice. It is indicative of how women not only experienced their imprisonment differently to men, but also remembered and expressed their experiences in ways that were prompted by their gender. As Baer and Goldenberg have noted, "Gender-based experience influenced the way women survivors interpreted and transmitted their experiences."[19] This is also true about men's writings if we analyze them through the lens of gender, rather than simply accepting them as "universal."

Gendered Responses to
Nazi Persecution before 1939

In the early twentieth century, the dynamic of most Jewish families in Western Europe corresponded to the bourgeois model, in which the men were the breadwinners and the women were responsible for the spiritual essence and harmony of the family.[20] Their roles and responsibilities involved them in different experiences, social environments, and networks, which gave them different knowledge and skills with which to face the Nazi persecution and, subsequently, the "Final Solution." Their roles changed and their relationships transformed as living conditions for Jewish people in Germany deteriorated throughout the 1930s.[21] As Jewish shops and businesses were closed down and Jewish men became unemployed, they were no longer in the position to make all the important decisions. Women had to both run their households and keep up the morale of their family members. They comforted their husbands and children, who faced abuse and hostility outside the household.[22] They tried to maintain a semblance of normality in the home at a time of growing uncertainty and persecution outside the home. Many also undertook voluntary work for Jewish women's organizations.[23]

Jewish women were generally less assimilated into German society than Jewish men, who had non-Jewish business and professional contacts. They took refuge and solace in their familial duties such as cooking. They tried to retain their composure for the sake of their children.[24] A gendered analysis of the desire to emigrate highlights distinctions between men's and women's priorities and perceptions. Women were generally more keen than men to leave Germany, being "less status-conscious, less money-oriented . . . more confident of their ability to flourish on new turf," but in practice, as Marion Kaplan states, "fewer women than men left Germany," often because they ultimately chose to stay behind with elderly parents.[25]

In terms of anticipatory reactions to the Nazi regime, most Jews, especially at first, believed that the Germans were "civilized" and therefore, honoring traditional norms, would not harm women and children. (The reality, however, turned out to be exactly the opposite.) Hence, they formulated plans to save the men, whom they believed to be the most endangered. Jewish families generally decided that the men should have priority in their plans for emigration, hiding, or escape. Even in everyday activities, such as queuing for bread, expectations of German behavior dictated that women should go out because Jewish men, especially those in traditional garb, were easy to identify and harass. Their beards, sidelocks, and clothing made Orthodox Jewish men identifiable as such, and they were subjected to abuse because of these features. Many Jewish families believed that it was safer for the women to go out than for the men.

How did Jewish men and women differ in their responses to Nazi persecution? An analysis of testimonies demonstrates significant differences in the impact of Nazi persecution upon men and women. Much of the testimony given by men initially focused on feelings of being betrayed by their fatherland. Edwin Landau recalls his feelings on the day of the national boycott of Jewish shops and businesses on April 1, 1933:

> I was ashamed that I had once belonged to this people. I was ashamed of the trust I had given to so many who now revealed themselves as my enemies. . . And when, as always, I consecrated the Sabbath . . . [my] composure was at an end. The whole weight of the day's experiences struck me, and I broke down, just barely stammering the last words. . . This was my leave-taking from everything German, my inner separation from what had been my fatherland—a burial.[26]

This sense of betrayal and the feelings brought about by the situation in which he found himself were closely connected to gendered notions of both citizenship and men's place in the public sphere.

In contrast, the testimony of women often highlighted their unselfish feelings of concern and worry for the welfare of their children and husbands, particularly in cases of physical separation. As Hilberg has noted, this was an era in which "the newly isolated community consisted of men without power and women without support."[27] Both men and women recounted feelings of despair at the worsening situation and its impact upon their children, in particular. Men who lost their businesses and jobs, their financial security, and their ability to provide for their families experienced a corresponding loss in their status and dignity. They were unable to fulfill their traditional roles and became demoralized and depressed. On a psychological level, too, men felt damaged in their capacity to act as men, specifically as protectors of their wives and children. They could not fulfill this traditional gender role, and this was an assault upon their sense of manhood and their identity. Women shouldered an increased physical workload and psychological duty to compensate for these changes. They did not blame the men, but tried to help them. Women's testimonies have tended to relate in more detail the impact of the physical destruction of their homes. Margaret Czellitzer described the state of her house when she returned to it after the "Night of Broken Glass" (November 9–10, 1938):

> I found my radio broken at the garden door, my lovely china smashed all over the kitchen floor, the beds overturned, the mattresses cut into pieces, the paintings as well as all the other valuables stolen . . . . We were all heartbroken, but especially myself, who had discovered . . . that lovely place and built our little house according to my own ideas.[28]

After the war began, the Nazis' persecution of the Jews escalated rapidly, culminating in the construction of death camps in Poland where the "Final Solution" was carried out. The following sections of this chapter discuss the privations and experiences of male and female internees at Auschwitz, in particular.

Men at Auschwitz: Experiences and Behavior[29]

The terrible privations and circumstances of internment at Auschwitz included thirst and hunger, extremes of temperature, arduous physical labor, overcrowding, inadequate food and foul water, lengthy roll calls, exhaustion, illness, injury, and the constant fear of "selection" for the gas chambers. In terms of men's behavior, gendered expectations were centered on strength and hardness, toughness, and determination.[30] Signs of weakness fell short of normative behavior for men. Victor Frankl states that "it was necessary . . . to keep moments of weakness and furtive tears to a minimum."[31] Men did not wish to appear cowardly or weak. As a result of different social constructions of gender, men were less likely to discuss emotions or admit to weakness or the need for another person with whom to share their burden. Lagerway notes that "male survivors framed their narratives in order and coherence, and often de-emphasized emotions" and that they told of "personal isolation, personal survival at any cost, ruthless competition."[32] It appears that, because men had been socialized into being independent and autonomous, these characteristics were the ones most often portrayed in their narratives. Male and female survivor accounts also represent work as a means of survival very differently. Pride in work and its impact on their identities is much more common in male writings. By contrast, female accounts have tended to be much less specific about work and how it was conducted. This suggests that work was more central to men's experiences, in line with contemporaneous gendered norms.

While "food talk" among women at Auschwitz has been much written about (see the section on Women at Auschwitz: Experiences and Behavior), Victor Frankl also recounts men engaging in food talk. He states that the majority of prisoners, when they were working near each other and were not closely watched by guards, "would immediately start discussing food," asking each other about their favorite dishes. Frankl writes: "Then they would exchange recipes and plan the menu for the day when they would have a reunion—the day in a distant future when they would be liberated and return home."[33]

Male memoirs have tended to underplay bonds and relationships and instead to emphasize examples of individual valor, strength, or autonomy. Bruno Bettelheim has explained his view on the subject of survival in the camps as follows:

> Survival in the camps—this cannot be stressed enough—depended foremost on luck. . . . While nothing one could do could assure survival, and while chances for it at best were extremely slim, one could increase them through correctly assessing one's situation and taking advantage of opportunities; in short, through acting independently and with courage, decision, and conviction, all of which depended on the measure of autonomy one had managed to retain.[34]

Dutch survivor, Louis de Wijze, underlined the need for care of the self in his memoirs as well: "Everyone lives for himself. Our one and all-encompassing credo is: Survive! Between the outer limits of life and death, previous values and norms lose their meaning, and our spiritual baggage gradually erodes. The only norm that counts is 'I.'"[35]

It is important to note and add, however, that references to close relationships do appear in male narratives, and there are instances of male writing that show men behaving in ways that differed from expected male gender norms. Richard Glazar, who survived the Treblinka death camp, recalls:

> My friend Karl Unger and I were always together. We were like twins. In this camp you could not survive an hour without someone supporting you and vice versa. We knew that we were destined to die. . . . No individual could make it alone. . . . I and my friend Karl survived because we supported each other constantly. We divided absolutely everything, even a small piece of bread.[36]

Of course, such support groups in themselves could not avert death, but where they existed they were, in some ways, life promoting, as Glazar's experience shows. Primo Levi provides another example of this, telling of an Italian civilian worker, Lorenzo, who brought Levi "a piece of his bread and the remainder of his ration every day for six months."[37] Without Lorenzo, Levi believes that he would not have survived Auschwitz. He states that this was

> not so much for his material aid, as for his having constantly reminded me by his presence, by his natural and plain manner of being good, that

there still existed a just world outside our own, something and someone still pure and whole, not corrupt, not savage. . . . Lorenzo was a man; his humanity was pure and uncontaminated, he was outside this world of negation. Thanks to Lorenzo, I managed not to forget that I myself was a man.[38]

He later describes a "tight bond of alliance" with Alberto, another prisoner.[39] Hence, social bonding did apply to male experiences, not only to female ones.

Furthermore, the testimonies of other male survivors underline the importance of the father-son relationship to survival, when fathers and sons had managed to avoid separation and stay together. Henry Wermuth recalls: "The presence of my father was, without a doubt, a major factor in my survival; but it also meant that I did not have, nor was I in need of, any other social contacts."[40] This suggests that the father-son relationship was so strong and significant that it completely replaced the necessity for other bonds. On the death march from Auschwitz, Elie Wiesel recalls his momentary desire to fall out of line, to the edge of the road, and die: "My father's presence was the only thing that stopped me. . . . He was running at my side, out of breath, at the end of his strength, at his wit's end. I had no right to let myself die. What would he do without me? I was his only support."[41] Wiesel shows here the significance of his relationship with his father and their mutual support.

The death marches have been described in many memoirs and testimonies as driving Holocaust victims to increasingly desperate behavior. Hans Winterfeld recalls the death march from Auschwitz:

Normally, one could talk to the other prisoners, but when food was distributed, they began to look and act like lunatics: their eyes stared rigidly at the ladle or at the arm that distributed the bread. When they received their ration, they constantly watched other prisoners to check that nobody had been given more. It was completely irrelevant what kind of person it was: uneducated and primitive, or educated and intellectually superior. I often wondered how cultivated human beings could behave like animals.[42]

Indeed, Levi comments too on the aim of the Nazi camps to "reduce us to beasts." But, he writes, "we must not become beasts; that even in this place one can survive, and therefore one must want to survive, to tell the story, to bear witness; and that to survive we must force ourselves to save at least the skeleton, the scaffolding, the form of civilization."[43] His desire to survive was thus underpinned by his desire to bear witness. He was determined to defend his strength and dignity for this purpose. As Eva Kolinsky has noted, many other survivors defined their own personal code of behavior in a bid to maintain a sense of their own self-value.[44] In Levi's *Survival in Auschwitz*, for example, Steinlauf insisted on washing, even though washing did not get him clean, because it enabled him to keep his dignity and demonstrated his refusal to become a beast, thus undermining German goals. This type of behavior is also evident in the writings of female survivors.

Women at Auschwitz: Experiences and Behavior

Female prisoners at Auschwitz had to deal with a number of problems that affected them specifically as women. Their testimonies highlight the trauma of losing their sense of their physical selves. One significant aspect of this was the SS camp ritual of shaving the inmates on their arrival. Having their heads shaved was a much more traumatic and degrading experience for women than for men. While all prisoners were deeply shamed by this measure, for women this was a blow to their feelings of femininity and to their sexual identity. Livia Bitton-Jackson writes of newly arrived female prisoners having the hair shaved from their heads, under their arms, and in the pubic area: "The shaving of hair has a startling effect. The absence of hair transforms individual women into like bodies. Indistinguishable.... We become a monolithic mass."[45] Rena Gelissen describes the humiliation of being "naked in front of strangers" and of being shaved by male prisoners: "They shear our heads, arms; even our pubic hair is discarded just as quickly and cruelly as the rest of the hair on our bodies."[46] Another survivor, Isabelle Choko, in her memoir, also relates that at Auschwitz, "at the precise moment my head was shaved, I ceased to exist as a human being."[47] Rose Meth, who was deported to Auschwitz in August 1943, gives a similar account of her arrival: "I can't begin to describe the shock and the humiliation. We were sheltered children. They made us undress completely in front of the Nazi soldiers. We wanted to die. They shaved our heads. They shaved all our hair, everywhere. We were given numbers."[48]

The tattooing of their camp numbers was described by survivor Eva Schloss as "part of the process intended to strip me of my pride and identity. When I was marched away from Auschwitz railway station, I left the girlish Eva Geiringer and her dreams, behind."[49] Olga Lengyel describes the degrading and humiliating treatment of female inmates on their arrival: being made to undress and undergo physical examinations before being allowed to dress in camp clothes. Gelissen mentions the gynecological examination for new female prisoners as well. These gynecological examinations were invasive and humiliating; they were painful and traumatic experiences recounted with much horror by female survivors.

The distribution of random and ill-fitting clothes had a significant impact on women as new camp inmates. Their individuality and their sense of feminine identity were entirely removed by all of these actions. Gelissen recounts her feelings of despair when she noticed her "lovely white boots with their red trim" being worn by an SS woman.[50] Lengyel describes the "bizarre rags that were handed out for underwear" that were "not white or any other color, but worn out pieces of coarse dusting cloth."[51] In addition, tattered dresses were randomly distributed with no regard to size. In terms of the emotions these circumstances generated, Lengyel states: "In spite of the tragedy of our situation, we could not help but laugh as we saw others so ridiculously outfitted. After a while, it was a struggle to overcome the disgust we felt for our companions, and for ourselves."[52] A similar reaction to their "grey, sack-like dresses" is described by Bitton-Jackson, as she compares herself after her arrival at Auschwitz with inmates who had been there longer:

> The strange creatures we saw as we entered the camp, the shaven, grey-cloaked bunch who ran to the barbed wire to stare at us, we are them! We look exactly like them. Same bodies, same dresses, same blank stares. They, too, must have arrived from home recently. They, too, were ripe women and young girls, bewildered and bruised. They too longed for dignity and compassion. And they, too, were transformed into figures of contempt instead.[53]

After the initial shock and horror engendered by their new appearance, some women attempted to improve their outfits. In the space of twenty-four hours, they adjusted their ill-fitting garments to their bodies and sewed up the holes, "using needles made out of wooden splinters and threads pulled out of the one blanket allocated to them."[54] Isabelle Choko describes feeling a need to hide her shaved head and tie up her dress, which was much too large: "I ripped a piece from the bottom of my pale pink shirt to tie around my head like a turban and another piece to roll into a belt. My mother helped me since I had no mirror. . . . Other women, too, were trying to 'look human' again."[55]

Menstruation became a significant biological problem that women had to confront in Auschwitz. Bitton-Jackson describes a girl in front of her at roll call: "The blood simply flows down her legs."[56] When they menstruated, women and girls had no way of stopping the flow of blood, which was extremely difficult and humiliating. Gelissen recalls her first period at Auschwitz: "I scour the ground for anything that might help me hinder the flow. There is nothing."[57] Over time, in the abnormal circumstances in which they were living, women stopped menstruating. While this removed the problem of humiliation, the cessation of menstruation created other concerns for many women. Some felt a loss of their identity as women, while others feared they would never be able to have children. Lengyel attributes the ceasing of menstruation partly to "the constant anguish under which we lived," but she also suggests a "mysterious powder" or "substance" "mixed into all the food given to the inmates."[58] Gelissen writes similarly that "most of the girls and women in camp" lost their periods.[59] Female inmates, specifically, faced these biological and psychological issues relating to menstruation and its cessation.[60]

In addition, some girls and women were subjected to appalling violence, as well as sexual abuse and violations. In her desperation for some string to use as shoelaces, Gisella Perl hoped to exchange her bread ration for a piece of string from a Polish male prisoner:

> I stopped beside him, held out my bread and asked him, begged him to give me a piece of string in exchange for it. He looked me over from head to foot, carefully, then grabbed me by the shoulder and hissed in my ear: "I don't want your bread. . . . You can keep your bread. . . . I will give you a piece of string but first I want you. . . . you. . . ." For a second I didn't understand what he meant. . . . His hand, filthy with the human excrement he was working in, reached out for my womanhood, rudely, insistently. The next moment I was running, running away from that man, away from the indignity that had been inflicted on me, forgetting about the string, about the shoes, about everything but the sudden realization of how deeply I had sunk.[61]

After this shameful experience, she was determined to maintain her dignity in the face of every humiliation, every torture. Women's vulnerability, their fear of rape, and their reactions to humiliation are amply evident in the narratives of female survivors. For example, the fear of rape and the theme of humiliation run through the account of Judith Magyar Isaacson, a Hungarian Jew deported to Auschwitz in 1944.[62] Schloss too writes: "It seems hard to believe that the German SS guards would take a sexual interest in the starving, dirty, ragged women they were ruling over—but some of them did."[63] Hence, while rape was not official policy, because Nazi racial laws prohibited German sexual relations with Jewish women, there is evidence that at least some German guards and others, including Kapos (prisoner-supervisors) and other prisoners, raped Jewish women. Women and young girls were subjected to traumatic sexual abuse and violations.

In Liana Millu's first narrative in *Smoke over Birkenau*, a young inmate, Lili, was the victim of the cruelty of her Kapo, Mia, whose "frustration and impatience" turned to anger if her boyfriend was late or failed to turn up: "A violent shove sent my head slamming against the iron bar."[64] This was commonplace behavior on the part of the Kapo. Lili's position was invidious and fraught with tension. She was a pretty, young, and gracious girl, and because of this, she was favored by the Kapo, who gave her good work—sewing. However, Lili was in a very dangerous situation, as Mia's boyfriend liked her. On one occasion, Mia's boyfriend, who had drunk too much, began overtly flirting with Lili and kissing her, "his lips brushing her neck." This proved catastrophic for Lili, as Mia was furious and savagely attacked her, inflicting terrible injuries.[65] She called Lili "a whore" and subsequently ensured that she was selected for the gas chambers.[66]

In another of Millu's narratives, Zina, accused of being "a whore," was violently attacked by an old camp guard: "Raising his club, he began beating Zina furiously on the chest and shoulders. The blows were so fierce that in her frail state she collapsed instantly. He kept on beating her as she lay there on the ground."[67] Bitton-Jackson describes violence from the moment of her arrival at Auschwitz and numerous episodes of random punishments and beatings.[68] Lengyel similarly details the threat of violence from the outset and refers to many occasions on which she and other female inmates were subjected to violence and physical abuse.[69] Gelissen's writing too mentions many incidences of extreme violence and brutality directed against female prisoners.[70]

Apart from such examples of random punishment and brutality, Lengyel further describes "medical" experimentation on female inmates, including experiments in relation to menstruation, subjection to artificial insemination, injection with sex hormones, sterilization, and gynecological experiments.[71] Gelissen's narrative makes reference to such experiments as well.[72] Sterilization experiments on women at Auschwitz took place in Block 10, a place described by Robert Lifton as "quintessential Auschwitz."[73] The notorious Block 10 induced fear and terror in female victims.

At Auschwitz, women tried to adjust and adapt to their changing circumstances. They used resourcefulness, homemaking skills, and cleaning in order to establish some modicum of control over themselves and their space. For instance, they tried to clean themselves and to rid themselves of lice. Lengyel recounts how they "passed the single scrubbing brush to one another with a firm determination to resist the dirt and the lice. That was our only way of waging war against the parasites, against our jailers, and against every force that made us victims."[74] Gelissen too writes of how the women engaged in a "ritual cleansing" of lice.[75] Furthermore, there was a need for cooperation in extreme circumstances and self-preservation through mutual help, which has been highlighted, in particular, in many female survivor testimonies. At Auschwitz, women used different strategies to cope with their situation, such as the formation of *ersatz* families and "camp sister" relationships, as well as the sharing of recipes, cooking methods, and memories of Sabbath and Festival meals.

Millu writes of Gustine, a prisoner at Auschwitz from Holland, who talked about her home, "for hours on end," as a coping strategy: "The fire sparkling in the big blue tiled stove and her mother preparing the snacks for tea, the smell of fresh bread, the most comforting smell in the world, and the butter, the ruby-hued currant marmalade, the gaily colored curtains on the windows. Oh, beloved home, the most cherished place on earth!"[76] Gelissen recalls the Sunday morning picnics with cheese Danish pastries that she used to have with her sister Danka: "Around noon we open Mama's Danishes, still warm from the oven, or maybe the sun kept them warm, and eat them while languishing in the sun. . . . How I miss . . . eating Mama's homemade sweets."[77] Lengyel too talks of reminiscing and reciting poetry as coping strategies, "to escape the frightful present."[78] Furthermore, Gisella Perl recalls: "Later, as we came to know one another better, we invented games and recited poetry to keep our minds off the sordid present." Other evenings, Perl describes:

> We played another game, which spread from block to block until every woman in Auschwitz played it enthusiastically. We called the game "I am a lady." . . . I am a lady—I said one night—a lady doctor in Hungary. It is morning, a beautiful sunny morning and I feel too lazy to work. I ring for my assistant and tell her to send the patients away, for I am not going to my office today. . . . What should I do with myself? Go shopping? Go to the hairdresser? Meet my friends at the café? Maybe I'll do some shopping. I haven't had a new dress, a new hat in weeks. . . .[79]

The references in this game are clearly gender specific to the women's previous experiences and social construction.

Furthermore, kitchen memories reminded women of their former position in their families and communities and reaffirmed their own sense of value. Women used conversation as a distraction from their circumstances and talked about their "old" lives.[80] Women's exchanges with each other reminded them of their strengths as nurturers, homemakers, and cooks. Food preparation was part of the ritual of living in family, social, and community life, as well as Jewish festivals, and it defined the former status of many women. The sharing of recipes and cooking tips was significant for women psychologically, because it indicated a commitment to the future.[81] In addition, they fantasized about the future, a time when the war would be over, as a coping strategy.[82] These types of themes are common in female survivor testimonies and narratives. Furthermore, by describing the food they once cooked to another inmate, "they shared a familiar experience and connected to another person."[83]

Female narratives often describe how inmates shared food with each other. For example, Lili shared a "precious gift" of "some cabbage leaves" with two of her fellow prisoners.[84] Gelissen describes clandestinely sharing a packet of macaroni, procured from a nearby factory, between a few women in the laundry room: "Dividing the noodles evenly into their waiting bowls, I figure, accurately, that there are five tablespoons for each girl, then pour the hot water on top, making sure everyone gets some. Danka and I are served last. The rest wait until we are all served; then in silent unison we begin to eat the warm, nourishing macaroni."[85] On another occasion, she describes sharing another rare provision: sugar. Rena and Danka agreed to share a bag of sugar they procured with "twenty of our closest girlfriends . . . after everyone is asleep." Rena carefully leveled off each spoon, "making sure that everyone gets an equal amount."[86] Bitton-Jackson recalls smuggling potatoes and how her mother saved her own in order to use them in place of candles on Friday night:

> One evening while shoveling snow in the yard, we discover mounds in which potatoes are stored for the winter. We quickly dig them up and, hiding them under our dresses, smuggle enough potatoes into the camp to allow each inmate at least one potato. We wash them in the toilet and eagerly await our bedtime. . . . Noiselessly, with utmost care, so as not to attract the attention of the guard on patrol we bite into the hard, delightful skin of the raw potato. But Mummy saves her potato. "For Sabbath lights" she says. Friday at sunset Mummy kindles her Sabbath lights in the carved-out potato halves using oil smuggled from the factory and threads from our blankets for wicks.[87]

This example illustrates not only the resourcefulness of these women, but also the determination of Bitton-Jackson's mother to try to continue her tradition of lighting candles for the Sabbath. She was caught but not punished on this occasion. Bitton-Jackson goes on to relate how they subsequently saved "potatoes for a Hanukkah celebration with lights." With care and secrecy, they lit "Hannukah oil lamps in carved-out potato halves" and succeeded in kindling the lights for eight nights without being caught.[88] Millu writes of maintaining rituals and the celebration of Hannukah as well.[89] These attempts by women to uphold religious traditions were valuable coping strategies.

Family relationships were of great significance where mothers and daughters, or sisters, could stay together, as illustrated by Gelissen's account. She was fiercely protective of her sister, Danka, and tried to shield her as much as possible. Rena's promise, after all, was to protect and look after her sister—indeed, her determination to bring her sister back alive was her *raison d'être* and motivation for survival:

> My one great feat in life, my fate, is to survive this thing and return triumphant with my sister to our parents' house. . . . I will succeed because I have no other choice. Failure does not even occur to me. We may die in the interim—death cannot be avoided here—but even that will not dissuade me from my sole purpose in life. Nothing else matters but these four things: be with Danka, be invisible, be alert, be numb.[90]

She looked after Danka when she had scabies and procured lotion to treat it, and she cared for her sister when she became ill with malaria.[91] In Danka, Rena found her "reason and will to live."[92] Gelissen kept up her sister's spirits when she lost the will to go on and swore to her that if Danka was ever selected for the gas chambers, Gelissen would accompany her.[93] Ultimately, they both survived. Millu's writing also notes the strength of feeling between sisters in the camp and observes that most of them loved each other "with an almost morbid attachment."[94]

Moreover, even in *ersatz* family relationships, such as those of "camp sisters," social bonding, in groups of two or more, helped women to keep up their struggle to survive. Meth describes her *ersatz* camp sister: "Estusia and I were like sisters. People never knew that we were not really sisters. As soon as all my real sisters were taken away from me and Estusia saw my condition, she helped me a lot morally. She told me I must be strong and survive."[95] Such surrogate families cared for each other and improved women's chances of survival. Lucie Adelsberger describes her camp family in which her "daughters" provided her with clothing and food whenever they could. She states that members of such families often put their own lives at risk and that even for those who did not survive "the friendship and love of a camp family eased the horror of their miserable end."[96] This kind of bonding was not exclusive to women, but it appears to have been much more prevalent among women and has been expressed in many testimonies written by women, including those of Isabella Leitner and Charlotte Delbo.[97] Female prisoners offered each other support, comfort, and solidarity. Women were able to "transform their habits of raising children or their experience of nurturing into the care of the nonbiological family."[98] As the isolation and separation of families was deliberately imposed by the camp system, the creation of new "families" helped inmates by giving them a system of mutual support and a source of material and psychological strength in place of their real families.[99] For example, Tedeschi recounts "a small, warm hand, modest and patient, which held mine in the evening, which pulled up the blankets around my shoulders, while a calm, motherly voice whispered in my ear, 'Good night, dear—I have a daughter your age!'"[100] She goes on to describe how this *ersatz* mother, Zilly, comforted her when she felt desperate. Such relationships gave prisoners the courage to live a little longer.

Behavior Outside Female Gendered Norms

There has been a taboo on considering women whose behavior did not match perceived gender norms and expectations that largely reflects a reluctance to deal with a painful and difficult subject. Yet, examples of such behavior in female narratives do exist. Fanya Gottesfeld Heller states in her memoirs that "the unrelenting fear of death and gnawing pain of hunger led to acts of desperation among many who survived; some stole, others lied and schemed. Still others took comfort in intimate relationships that might be considered illicit or misguided in ordinary times. It was not all pure and righteous, but it happened."[101] Gendered norms about expected types of female conduct such as social bonding and nurturing were contradicted by examples of spiteful and hateful behavior. Millu describes how physical hardship and deprivation produced competitive, self-interested behavior— women who were "ready to pummel and trample over the others in order to get in first and grab a good place."[102] Lengyel relates how women, "who formerly would not have taken a hairpin, became utterly hardened thieves and never suffered the slightest feeling of remorse."[103] Millu also refers to inmates stealing food from others: "It's so awful to sleep with a thief. You can't ever relax. Just last night she nibbled up a piece of bread someone had left over for the morning. A regular rat!"[104] Schloss too states that "if you kept some of your ration to eat later, another starving inmate would usually steal it from you."[105] Gelissen, who shared everything with her sister, was dismayed to see a teenage girl eating a whole lemon without sharing it with her mother, who begged for a bite: "I do not understand the selfishness before me."[106] Bitton-Jackson details an episode when a bed collapsed onto her very weak mother. The other inmates did not care or help, as they were awaiting the distribution of food—"They laugh at my alarm. . . . Not one of them pays attention to my frantic pleas."[107] Millu describes the "morbid curiosity" of the women at Birkenau at the selections for the gas chambers. They craned their necks to see "like spectators at a sports match."[108] Such behavior was at variance with gendered norms about women's conduct.

Millu depicts the transformative and destructive effect of Birkenau on the identity and behavior of its prisoners over time. The inmates taunted and abused each other. She writes: "I recoiled in shame from their weary eyes gleaming with malice and their pinched mouths spewing out vulgarities, sick at the sight of what our misery had made of us. . . . Soon I would be a true daughter of the *Lager* [camp]. . . . I would be no different from the old-timers."[109] Lengyel too states that "it seemed as though the Germans constantly sought to pit us against each other, to make us competitive, spiteful and hateful" and notes how even "the most peaceful souls were occasionally seized with a desire to strangle their neighbors" in the overcrowded conditions in the bunks, through exasperation at their circumstances.[110]

Lesbianism was a taboo form of behavior, and references to it are uncommon in survivor narratives; however, in the context of Auschwitz, sexual identity and behavior that differed from traditional gender norms emerged, and there is some mention of lesbianism. Lengyel distinguishes between "three categories" of lesbians: the first group, who were "lesbians by instinct"; the second group, who "because of the abnormal conditions, suffered changes in their sexual viewpoint" and often "yielded under the pressure of necessity"; and the third group, who "discovered their lesbian predilections through an association with corruption." She goes on to describe lesbian "orgies."[111] In Millu's book, there is a reference to a "most evil Kapo" with a "black triangle" on her shirt, portrayed as "fat and sturdy."[112] There is an implicit connection drawn between her appearance, her lesbianism, and her "evil" character. There is reference to another lesbian Kapo, the "Kapo of the dressmakers renowned for her lesbian predilections."[113] The "heavy, resounding footsteps" of the "formidable" Frau Gotti could be heard every morning as "she came to wake her lover with a long kiss as well as a little snack." The suggestion here is not only of lesbian stereotyping but also of sexual favors granted for food. Gelissen too details an occasion on which Erika, a Kapo, asked her to spend the night with her, although Gelissen did not understand her meaning: "Erika laughs. 'You go back to your block. You're not ready for this.' She leads me toward the door. 'Here.' She slips me an extra portion of bread. I take it quickly, not understanding why she would offer me such a nicety, not comprehending anything that has just happened."[114]

The fight for survival also affected women's sexual conduct. Survivor narratives refer to the granting of sexual favors by some girls and women in exchange for food, other items, or "camp luxuries." This was commonplace and formed a significant aspect of what women found to be so humiliating and degrading about the camp experience. Lengyel describes an episode when Tadek, a carpenter who came to mend the bunks, was friendly and attentive to her. She describes him as handsome, tall, and smiling. He gave her food, but then he made it clear that he expected sexual favors in return.[115] Some women adopted the survival strategies of flirting, bantering, or acting coy with men and performing sexual favors as a way of gaining extra food or luxuries. The final chapter in Millu's book tells the story of Lise, who, although married and devoted to her husband, ended up submitting to the foreman's demands for sexual favors in exchange for food and a harmonica. The story particularly focuses on how Lise grappled with her dilemma and offers an insight into her motivations for making her choice. Lise was upset at the suggestion that she was getting "prettied up" for Sergio, "the foreman with the harmonica."[116] Her distress intensified later on, as she had to decide whether or not to grant him sexual favors; her dilemma is constructed in terms of a choice between chastity and death. Yet Lise applied different standards to other women. She was not "like those little tarts who for a slice of bread spread themselves out for half the camp."[117] She was "a respectable woman who loved her husband." In the end, she submitted to Sergio's demand for sexual favors. Her predicament was that she felt forced into a contradiction: "If I deceive my husband, it's because I love him."[118] Lise's capitulation to Sergio's demands makes a statement about the nature of existence at Auschwitz and the types of choices it might have been necessary to make. Sergio had a predatory, callous demeanor and made it clear that he expected sexual favors from Lise in return for allowing her to play his harmonica. He made cruel remarks about Lise's husband and was physically aggressive toward her, yet ultimately she acquiesced to his sexual demands.

The impact of the existence of the *Puffkommando* (brothel) on different women was significant. There was a marked difference of attitude between those women inside the brothel and those outside. On one level, there was the moral stance of rejection of a woman for prostituting herself, yet on another level, there was some jealousy and resentment about the "luxuries" that life in the brothel afforded. References to this type of prostitution are difficult to find, but they do demonstrate behavior that deviated from perceived attitudes and conceptions about the appropriate conduct of women. Indeed, in the historiography of women's experiences of the Third Reich and the camps in general, brothels have been mentioned only comparatively recently as these fields have developed to encompass them.[119]

Pregnancies had to be concealed at Auschwitz, because all pregnant women were sent immediately to the gas chamber. Pregnant women hid their condition for as long as possible, for "the camp was no maternity ward."[120] Despite the attempts of German officers to trick women into revealing their pregnancies, Lengyel writes: "Incredible as it may seem, some succeeded in concealing their conditions to the last moment, and the deliveries took place secretly in the barracks."[121] At the infirmary at Auschwitz, as soon as a baby was born, both mother and infant were sent to the gas chambers. Lengyel describes how, to save the lives of the mothers, newborn infants were killed: "And so, the Germans succeeded in making murderers of us. . . . The only meager consolation is that by these murders we saved the mothers."[122]

Gisella Perl, a Jewish doctor, also recounts killing newborn children "to save the life of the mother."[123] "It was up to me to save the life of the mothers, if there was no other way, than by destroying the life of their unborn children." She recalls that the procedure took place "in the dark, always hurried, in the midst of filth and dirt. After the child had been delivered, I quickly bandaged the mother's abdomen and sent her back to work." She states:

> I delivered women pregnant in the eighth, seventh, sixth, fifth month, always in a hurry, always with my five fingers, in the dark, under terrible conditions.
>   No one will ever know what it meant to me to destroy these babies. After years and years of medical practice, childbirth was still to me the most beautiful, the greatest miracle of nature. I loved those newborn babies not as a doctor but as a mother and it was again and again my own child whom I killed to save the life of a woman . . . and if I had not done it, both mother and child would have been cruelly murdered.[124]

Conclusion

The lens of gender provides a useful tool for interpreting the behavior and experiences of Holocaust victims. Gender is a characteristic of all human experience. Both masculinity and femininity have been socially constructed and shaped by historical circumstances and expectations. Moving away from universal interpretations, both women's experiences as specifically female and men's experiences as specifically male are significant to our understanding of the Holocaust. The field of Holocaust studies that was gender-neutral until the 1980s now includes a substantial body of literature on gender. Furthermore, a comparatively recent yet substantial output of memoirs and testimonies by female Holocaust survivors has ensured that women's voices are no longer unheard. These developments in the historiography have meant that scholars are now in a much better position to comprehend the diversity and complexity of the experiences of Holocaust victims.

Both male and female survivors state that luck played a large part in their survival. For example, Eva Schloss, with a similar view to that of Bruno Bettelheim, writes: "A large part of my survival was down to pure luck."[125] Emerging gender analyses that include discussions of men as men and of masculinity shed light on the differences in, and similarities of, male and female Holocaust experiences. For example, men's traditional role as protectors of women and children entirely turned on its head during the Holocaust, as Jewish male victims were unable to fulfill this role, and Nazi perpetrators in the death camps dispensed with women and children with alacrity.

In the face of experiences at Auschwitz, it is important to note not only the distinctions in how men and women have written their testimonies but also that not all female and not all male behavior in the camp was homogenous. The formation of surrogate families was life-sustaining when families were separated. While this is mentioned more widely in female writings, it is also evident in male writings. Sharing recipes, reminiscing, and forming social bonds were important survival strategies and coping mechanisms that many women utilized. In some ways, although women had more severe circumstances, this was balanced by the additional support from and solidarity with other female prisoners, in close bonds or *ersatz* families. However, the situation in which women found themselves at Auschwitz led some to behave in desperate ways. Some women lied, schemed, and stole. Some granted sexual favors to men (and women) who were in a position to ameliorate their circumstances in some way in return. A reluctance to treat subjects such as lesbianism, prostitution, indifference, or cruelty—that is, modes of being or behavior that did not fit into broad traditional gendered expectations— has led to the creation of an incomplete picture in much of the historical literature. Previously unknown and unheard voices have begun to find their place in our knowledge and understanding of Holocaust experiences.

Moral choice has gendered implications too—not only did women have to make choices that men did not have to make, but also they were judged (and indeed judged themselves) by a double moral standard that was harsher. This often engendered a sense of shame and guilt. At times, women were forced to make very difficult moral decisions. Langer's term "choiceless choices" refers not to "options between life and death, but between one form of abnormal response and another, both imposed by a situation that was in no way of the victims' own choosing." Some women worked as prostitutes in the camp brothel. Other women had to make extremely difficult decisions in relation to pregnancy and childbirth, as Jewish newborn infants, babies, and young children were completely expendable to the Nazi rulers, and so too were their mothers.

In many ways, women were placed in a position of "double jeopardy"—
they were in a position of blame not only for behaving in a particular
manner or for carrying out an act or deed but also because, by so doing,
they contravened the social construction of femininity whereby they should
not prostitute themselves or kill their babies in order to survive. Women
were placed in moral and physical situations that men did not have to face.
During their imprisonment at Auschwitz they had to opt for agency and
make choices in a variety of ways that were distinct from those made by
men. Frankl notes that for men, too, the "choice of action" existed even
in the face of the terrible privations they endured at Auschwitz.[126] In the
end, all Jews were equally destined for death, but there were differences
on the road to that destination for men and women. Women's and men's
experiences of the Holocaust were not identical, but, as Goldenberg has
suggested, they were "different horrors" within the "same hell."[127] Hence, an
analysis of gender-based distinctions in Holocaust experiences and the ways
in which they have been narrated by men and women adds an important
angle to our knowledge and understanding of this dark chapter in modern
history.

Notes

1 Mary Anne Warren, *Gendercide: The Implications of Sex Selection* (Totowa,
   NJ: Rowman and Allanheld, 1985); Adam Jones, *Gendercide and Genocide*
   (Nashville, TN: Vanderbilt University Press, 2004); Helen Fein, "Genocide
   and Gender: The Uses of Woman and Group Destiny," *Journal of Genocide
   Research* 1:1 (1999), pp. 43–63; Roger Smith, "Women and Genocide: Notes
   on an Unwritten History," *Holocaust and Genocide Studies* 8:3 (1994),
   pp. 315–34.

2 Jones, *Gendercide and Genocide*, p. 264.

3 Raul Hilberg, *Perpetrators, Victims, Bystanders: The Jewish Catastrophe, 1933
   to 1945* (London, UK: HarperCollins, 1993), p. 126.

4 Yehuda Bauer, *Rethinking the Holocaust* (New Haven, CT: Yale University
   Press, 2001), p. 167.

5 Lenore Weitzman and Dalia Ofer, eds., "The Role of Gender in the Holocaust,"
   in *Women in the Holocaust* (New Haven, CT: Yale University Press, 1998), p. 13.

6 Myrna Goldenberg, "Different Horrors, Same Hell: Women Remembering
   the Holocaust," in *Thinking the Unthinkable: Meanings of the Holocaust*,
   ed. R. Gottlieb (New York, NY: Paulist Press, 1991), p. 152.

7 Anna Reading, "Scarlet Lips in Belsen: Culture, Gender and Ethnicity in the
   Policies of the Holocaust," *Media, Culture and Society* 21 (1999), p. 496.

8 Joan Ringelheim, "Women and the Holocaust: A Reconsideration of
   Research," in *Different Voices: Women and the Holocaust*, ed. C. Rittner and
   J. Roth (New York: Paragon House, 1993), p. 376.

9 Ringelheim, "Women and the Holocaust: A Reconsideration of Research," p. 377.

10 Anna Hardmann, "Women and the Holocaust," *Holocaust Educational Trust*, Research Papers, 1:3 (London, UK: Holocaust Educational Trust, 2000), p. 12.

11 Brana Gurewitsch, *Mothers, Sisters, Resisters: Oral Histories of Women Who Survived the Holocaust* (Tuscaloosa, AL: University of Alabama Press, 1998).

12 Sara Horowitz, "Memory and Testimony of Women Survivors of Nazi Germany," in *Women of the Word: Jewish Women and Jewish Writing*, ed. J. Baskin (Detroit, MI: Wayne State University Press, 1994), p. 265.

13 Zoë Waxman, "Unheard Stories: Reading Women's Holocaust Testimonies," *The Jewish Quarterly* 47:177 (2000), p. 53.

14 Zoë Waxman, *Writing the Holocaust: Identity, Testimony, Representation* (Oxford, UK: Oxford University Press, 2006), p. 186.

15 Pascale Bos, "Women and the Holocaust: Analysing Gender Difference," in *Experience and Expression: Women, the Nazis and the Holocaust*, ed. E. Baer and M. Goldenberg (Detroit, MI: Wayne State University Press, 2003), pp. 23–50.

16 Ibid., p. 25.

17 Ibid., p. 33.

18 Giuliana Tedeschi, *There is a Place on Earth: A Woman in Birkenau* (New York, NY: Pantheon Books, 1992), p. 124.

19 Elizabeth Baer and Myrna Goldenberg, *Experience and Expression: Women, the Nazis and the Holocaust*, p. xiv.

20 Michael Mitterauer and Reinhard Sieder, *The European Family* (Oxford, UK: Blackwell, 1981), pp. 129–30; Lynn Abrams, *The Making of Modern Woman* (London, UK: Longman, 2002), pp. 127–9.

21 Marion Kaplan, *Between Dignity and Despair: Jewish Life in Nazi Germany* (Oxford, UK: Oxford University Press, 1998), pp. 59–62.

22 Marion Kaplan, "Keeping Calm and Weathering the Storm: Jewish Women's Responses to Daily Life in Nazi Germany," in *Women in the Holocaust*, ed. Ofer and Weitzman, p. 43.

23 Marion Kaplan, "Jewish Women in Nazi Germany: Daily Life, Daily Struggles, 1933–1939," *Feminist Studies* 16 (Fall 1990), pp. 579–606.

24 Kaplan, "Keeping Calm and Weathering the Storm," pp. 44–5.

25 Ibid., p. 48.

26 Monika Richarz, *Jewish Life in Germany: Memoirs from Three Centuries* (Indianapolis, IN: Indiana University Press, 1991), pp. 311–12.

27 Hilberg, *Perpetrators*, p. 127.

28 Lisa Pine, *Nazi Family Policy 1933-1945* (Oxford, UK: Berg, 1997), p. 162.

29 Sybille Steinmacher, *Auschwitz: A History* (London, UK: Penguin Books, 2005); Deborah Dwork and Robert Jan van Pelt, *Auschwitz: 1270 to the Present* (New York, NY: W. W. Norton, 1996).

30   Maurice Berger, Brian Wallis and Simon Watson, *Constructing Masculinity* (New York, NY: Routledge, 1995).

31   Viktor Frankl, *Man's Search for Meaning* (London, UK: Simon & Schuster, 2004), p. 86.

32   Mary Lagerway, *Reading Auschwitz* (London, UK: Sage, 1998), p. 75.

33   Frankl, *Man's Search for Meaning*, p. 41.

34   Bruno Bettelheim, *Surviving the Holocaust* (London, UK: Fontana Paperbacks, 1986), pp. 100–1.

35   Louis de Wijze, *Only My Life: A Survivor's Story* (New York, NY: St. Martin's Press, 1997), p. 67.

36   Nechama Tec, *Resilience and Courage: Women, Men and the Holocaust* (New Haven, CT: Yale University Press, 2004), pp. 188–9.

37   Primo Levi, *If This is a Man*, trans. Stuart Wolff (London, UK: Abacus Books, 1987), p. 148.

38   Ibid., p. 150.

39   Ibid., p. 168.

40   Henry Wermuth, *Breathe Deeply My Son* (London, UK: Vallentine Mitchell, 1993), p. 139.

41   Elie Wiesel, *Night: with Connections* (London, UK: Holt, Rinehart and Winston, 1988), pp. 92–3.

42   Eva Kolinsky, *After the Holocaust: Jewish Survivors in Germany after 1945* (London, UK: Pimlico, 2004), p. 27.

43   Levi, *If This is a Man*, p. 58.

44   Kolinsky, *After the Holocaust*, p. 14.

45   Livia Bitton-Jackson, *I Have Lived a Thousand Years* (London, UK: Simon & Schuster, 1999), p. 75.

46   Rena Gelissen, *Rena's Promise: A Story of Sisters in Auschwitz* (London, UK: Weidenfeld and Nicolson, 1996), p. 139.

47   I. Choko, F. Irwin, L. Kahana-Aufleger, M. Kalina, and J. Lipski, *Stolen Youth: Five Women's Survival in the Holocaust* (New York, NY and Jerusalem, Israel: Yad Vashem, 2005), p. 42.

48   Carol Rittner and John Roth, *Different Voices* (New York, NY: Paragon House, 1993), p. 136.

49   Eva Schloss, *After Auschwitz* (London, UK: Hodder and Stoughton, 2013), p. 114

50   Gelissen, *Rena's Promise*, p. 67.

51   Olga Lengyel, *Five Chimneys: The Story of Auschwitz* (Chicago, IL: Academy Chicago Publishers, 1995), p. 29.

52   Ibid., p. 30.

53   Bitton-Jackson, *I Have Lived a Thousand Years*, p. 77.

54   Ruth Bondy, "Women in Theresienstadt and the Family Camp in Birkenau," in *Women in the Holocaust*, ed. Ofer and Weitzman, p. 323.

55   Choko, *Stolen Youth*, pp. 48–9.

56 Bitton-Jackson, *I Have Lived a Thousand Years*, p. 92.

57 Gelissen, *Rena's Promise*, p. 81.

58 Lengyel, *Five Chimneys*, pp. 98–9.

59 Gelissen, *Rena's Promise*, p. 139.

60 Tec, *Resilience and Courage*, pp. 168–9.

61 Rittner and Roth, *Different Voices*, p. 109.

62 Judith Isaacson, *Seed of Sarah* (Chicago, IL: University of Illinois Press, 1991).

63 Schloss, *After Auschwitz*, pp. 127–8.

64 Liana Millu, *Smoke over Birkenau* (Evanston, IL: Northwestern University Press, 1997), pp. 22–3.

65 Ibid., pp. 39–41.

66 Ibid., p. 47.

67 Ibid., p. 138.

68 Bitton-Jackson, *I Have Lived a Thousand Years*, pp. 73, 99, 127, 140.

69 Lengyel, *Five Chimneys*, pp. 26, 108, 131 and 156.

70 Gelissen, *Rena's Promise*, pp. 75, 83, 90–1, 115, 144–5, 166–7 and 172.

71 Lengyel, *Five Chimneys*, pp. 199 and 186–93.

72 Gelissen, *Rena's Promise*, pp. 148 and 183.

73 Robert Jay Lifton, *The Nazi Doctors: Medical Killing and the Psychology of Genocide* (London, UK: Macmillan, 1986), p. 270.

74 Lengyel, *Five Chimneys*, p. 135.

75 Gelissen, *Rena's Promise*, p. 80.

76 Millu, *Smoke over Birkenau*, p. 155.

77 Gelissen, *Rena's Promise*, p. 225.

78 Lengyel, *Five Chimneys*, p. 72.

79 Rittner and Roth, *Different Voices*, p. 109.

80 Millu, *Smoke over Birkenau*, pp. 26–7.

81 Myrna Goldenberg, "Memoirs of Auschwitz Survivors: The Burden of Gender," in *Women in the Holocaust*, ed. Ofer and Weitzman, p. 335. See also, Michael Berenbaum, "Introduction," in *Memory's Kitchen: Recipes from Terezin*, ed. Cara de Silva (Northvale, NJ and London, UK: Rowman & Littlefield, 1996).

82 Goldenberg, "Memoirs of Auschwitz Survivors: The Burden of Gender," pp. 62–3, 122, 148.

83 Myrna Goldenberg, "Food Talk: Gendered Responses to Hunger in the Concentration Camps," in *Experience and Expression*, ed. Baer and Goldenberg, p. 171.

84 Millu, *Smoke over Birkenau*, p. 29. On sharing food, see also p. 57.

85 Gelissen, *Rena's Promise*, p. 207.

86 Ibid., p. 213.

87 Bitton-Jackson, *I Have Lived a Thousand Years*, p. 153.

88 Ibid., p. 154.

89 Millu, *Smoke over Birkenau*, pp. 68–9.

90 Gelissen, *Rena's Promise*, p. 101.

91 Ibid., pp. 127–8 and pp. 154–62.

92 Ibid., p. 71. On this, see also pp. 52, 72, 73, 75, 99, and 101.

93 Ibid., pp. 124–5.

94 Millu, *Smoke over Birkenau*, p. 151.

95 Rittner and Roth, *Different Voices*, p. 140.

96 Lucie Adelsberger, *Auschwitz: A Doctor's Story* (Boston, MA: Northeastern University Press, 1996), pp. 98–100.

97 Isabella Leitner, *Fragments of Isabella: A Memoir of Auschwitz* (New York, NY: Dell Publishing Company, 1978), p. 44; Charlotte Delbo, *Auschwitz and After* (New York, NY: Yale University Press, 1995), pp. 63, 66, 103.

98 Joan Ringelheim, "Women and the Holocaust: A Reconsideration of Research," *Signs: Journal of Women in Culture and Society* 10 (1985), p. 747.

99 Pine, *Nazi Family Policy*, p. 178.

100 Tedeschi, *There is a Place on Earth*, pp. 9–10.

101 Fanya Gottesfeld Heller, *Love in a World of Sorrow: A Teenage Girl's Holocaust Memoirs* (New York, NY: Devora Publishing Company, 2005), p. 10.

102 Millu, *Smoke over Birkenau*, p. 52.

103 Lengyel, *Five Chimneys*, p. 56.

104 Millu, *Smoke over Birkenau*, p. 104.

105 Schloss, *After Auschwitz*, p. 127.

106 Gelissen, *Rena's Promise*, p. 190.

107 Bitton-Jackson, *I Have Lived a Thousand Years*, p. 121.

108 Millu, *Smoke over Birkenau*, pp. 46–7.

109 Millu, *Smoke over Birkenau*, p. 58. See also p. 65, where Millu uses the metaphor of smoke to describe how the camp transformed prisoners over time.

110 Lengyel, *Five Chimneys*, pp. 36, 40.

111 Ibid., pp. 197–9.

112 Millu, *Smoke over Birkenau*, p. 173.

113 Ibid., p. 192.

114 Gelissen, *Rena's Promise*, p. 88.

115 Lengyel, *Five Chimneys*, pp. 60–2.

116 Millu, *Smoke over Birkenau*, p. 187.

117 Ibid., p. 181.

118 Ibid., p. 191.

119 Dagmar Herzog, *Sexuality and German Fascism* (New York, NY and Oxford, UK: Berghahn, 2005).

120 Lengyel, *Five Chimneys*, p. 116.

121 Ibid., p. 115.

122 Ibid., p. 114.

123 Rittner and Roth, *Different Voices*, p. 114.

124 Ibid., pp. 113–14.

125 Schloss, *After Auschwitz*, p. 116.

126 Frankl, *Man's Search for Meaning*, pp. 74–5.

127 Goldenberg, "Different Horrors, Same Hell: Women Remembering the Holocaust," p. 152.

2

Masculinities and Vulnerabilities in the Rwandan and Congolese Genocides

Adam Jones

Introduction: Genocide and Gender

"The word [genocide] is new, the concept is ancient," wrote Leo Kuper in a field-defining 1982 volume.[1] Much the same can be said of the concept of male and masculine vulnerabilities in genocide and crimes against humanity. On some level, most people *know* that the phenomenon of selectively targeting males *en masse* for slaughter and other atrocities extends back to the dawn of history, and surely to prehistory as well. We find glimpses of it in the Old Testament, in Homer, and in Thucydides.[2] Moreover, genocide has always been inseparably bound to warfare: the two institutions are the "Siamese twins" of mass atrocity.[3] We likewise *know* that war has traditionally been a hellish experience for men, who are usually the ones forced and conscripted (as well as those who eagerly volunteer) to kill and be killed.

Yet the concept of specifically masculine vulnerabilities in genocide is also quite new. The designation of men and masculinity as the human standard, captured in the use of the universal "he," has tended to obscure the distinctively male/masculine component. As Harry Brod wrote,

> While *seemingly* about men, traditional scholarship's treatment of generic man as the human norm in fact systematically excludes from consideration what is unique to men *qua* men. The overgeneralization from male to generic human experience not only distorts our understanding of what, if anything, is truly generic to humanity but also precludes the study

of masculinity as a *specific male* experience, rather than a universal paradigm for *human* experience.[4]

Of course, until the midpoint of the twentieth century, we effectively lacked a meaningful gender framing of human experience at all, until Simone de Beauvoir and her indispensable successors laid the foundations of contemporary feminist inquiry. But, while greatly heightening awareness of female and feminine vulnerabilities and liabilities to violence and persecution, feminist framings created obstacles of their own to comprehending male and masculine experience. Feminist studies of violence tended to cast men and masculinities in the role of perpetrator and victimizer, a trend that perhaps intensified with the extension of feminist frameworks beyond the Western world. The key concept of "gender-based violence," popularized in the 1990s, is still constructed almost exclusively in terms of female victims/survivors and male perpetrators. The notion that men and boys are also gendered beings with specifically gendered vulnerabilities has barely begun to be articulated.

In this chapter, I want to explore male/masculine vulnerabilities in the genocides in Rwanda in 1994 and the Democratic Republic of the Congo (DRC) from 1996 to the present.[5] I place these case studies in a global-historical context, with references to other twentieth- and twenty-first-century genocides. My main themes are the selective ("gendercidal") killing of males; the little-studied theme of rape and sexual violence; and the "gendercidal institutions" of military conscription and forced labor. In the closing section of the chapter, I explore the implications of my findings for a gendered approach to humanitarian intervention and a gendered discourse of human rights.

I have always stressed, and reiterate here, that while my critique challenges certain feminist framings of gender and violence/mass conflict, it would be inconceivable without them. The objective is not to obscure women's specific vulnerabilities to genocide and mass atrocity, which are amply represented in this volume and acknowledged at various points in this chapter. Rather, I want to explore an alternative and still little-studied side of the gender-and-genocide equation, one that is intimately linked to female experiences—and is of great concern to the female victims and survivors of genocide, who often call for greater attention to be paid to *their* men's vulnerabilities.[6]

Male/Masculine Vulnerabilities in the Rwandan and Congolese Genocides

Gendercidal Killing

The term "gendercide" was coined by the US feminist Mary Anne Warren in her 1985 book, *Gendercide: The Implications of Sex Selection*. Warren's focus was on females and femininities targeted (especially) for structural and institutional forms of violence, such as female infanticide and sex-selective abortion. She nonetheless provided, in her framing chapter, a defense of the concept that makes clear its utility for examining male and masculine vulnerabilities as well:

> By analogy [with genocide], gendercide would be the deliberate extermination of persons of a particular sex (or gender). Other terms, such as "gynocide" and "femicide," have been used to refer to the wrongful killing of girls and women. But "gendercide" is a sex-neutral term, in that the victims may be either male or female. There is a need for such a sex-neutral term, since sexually discriminatory killing is just as wrong when the victims happen to be male. The term also calls attention to the fact that gender roles have often had lethal consequences, and that these are in important respects analogous to the lethal consequences of racial, religious, and class prejudice.[7]

In my own work, I have proposed a division of genocides into two broad categories: *gendercides*, in which the dimension of mass killing is overwhelmingly limited to one gender, virtually always males;[8] and "*root-and-branch*" *genocides*, in which the slaughter extends to all demographic sectors of the targeted population.[9] Examples of the former would be the Congolese "rubber terror" under Belgian King Leopold; Stalin's purges and other mass killings in the USSR; genocidal killing in Bosnia-Herzegovina in 1992–5 (aside from the sieges of Sarajevo and other cities); and Kosovo in 1999. In cases where root-and-branch genocide has resulted—the most infamous twentieth-century examples being the Ottoman genocide of Christian minorities, the Jewish *Shoah*, and the Rwandan genocide of 1994—a *progression* is typically evident from gendercidal to root-and-branch killings. Thus, in the genocides of the Christians, Ottoman forces typically rounded up both male elites and those of "fighting age"; these cohorts were murdered before the genocide was extended *en masse* to the remaining women, elderly, children, and handicapped of the targeted groups. Much the same dynamic was evident in the Jewish Holocaust. It was presaged by the roundup, detention, and brutal mistreatment of 20,000 Jewish *men* in the aftermath of the *Kristallnacht* in November 1938 and continued with the separation for mass slaughter of Jewish males during the first weeks of the "Holocaust by Bullets" in summer 1941, before full-scale "root-and-branch" Holocaust descended.

The prevalence of this pattern in the 1994 Rwandan genocide is somewhat open to question, as I pointed out in a detailed 2002 treatment of the subject:

> To enter into a discussion of the gendering of the holocaust's victims is both a painful and a difficult exercise. The pain and difficulty alike arise from the widespread accounts of massacres in April 1994 that were both gargantuan in scale and largely indiscriminate in targeting Tutsi men,

children, and women. One of these massacres, in fact, may qualify as the worst ground-level slaughter of the twentieth century, with another not far behind. "On April 20, at the Parish of Karama in Butare, between thirty-five and forty-three thousand people died in less than six hours"— a higher death toll than the Nazis' two-day slaughter of some 33,000 Jews at Babi Yar in September 1941, and higher than the highest single-day extermination spree in the gas chambers of Auschwitz-Birkenau. An even greater toll was exacted, though over a much longer period, in the weeks-long carnage on Bisesero mountain in southwestern Rwanda, where "more than fifty thousand people . . . lost their lives" amid heroic scenes of resistance. A number of other massacres, particularly in Cyahinda prefecture, claimed "ten thousand or more at one time." In nearly all cases, the carnage seems to have been utterly indiscriminate— save, of course, for the overriding ethnic variable. ("They encircled the whole hill," recalled one survivor of Bisesero. "They shot and shot and shot. There was no distinction. Everyone died—adult men and women, young men and women and children.")[10]

In contrast with the Ottoman Christian and Jewish cases, the worst and most gender-indiscriminate massacres in Rwanda occurred in the first weeks of the genocide, in April and early May 1994. Nonetheless, there is a wealth of evidence that during this period, and subsequently, Tutsi males were also targeted as such—a strategy that may account for the demographic gender disparity that was widely noted in the genocide's aftermath. Consider the account rendered by African Rights in its immensely detailed report, *Rwanda: Death, Despair and Defiance*:

> The primary target of the hunt [for survivors of the opening massacres] were Tutsi men, particularly what extremist propaganda portrayed as the "ultimate" enemy—rich men, men between their twenties and forties, especially if they were well-educated professionals or students. Most hated of all were well-educated Tutsi men who had studied in Uganda (and to a lesser extent Tanzania and Kenya) who were immediately suspected of being members or supporters of the RPF [Rwandan Patriotic Front]. Within days, entire communities were without their men; tens of thousands of women were widowed, tens of thousands of children were orphaned.[11]

Male children were also selectively targeted: "The extremists were determined to seek out and murder Tutsi boys in particular. They examined very young infants, even newborns, to see if they were boys or girls. Little boys were executed on the spot. Sometimes they ordered mothers to kill their children."[12]

As these accounts suggest—and a great many more are cited in my 2002 article—gender is often tied, empirically and in the *génocidaires*' interpretation, to variables of *economic status and community prominence*. Accordingly, it is unwise to draw too artificial a distinction between the gender variable and that of social-economic-political elite status. In that males of an imputed "fighting age" (roughly eighteen to fifty-five years of age) are depicted by *génocidaires* as constituting another societal elite— defined by age, physical strength, and presumed military capacity—they are also typically swept up in genocidal killing, particularly during its early stages (when the perceived need to "decapitate" the target group of both its leadership and its militarily capable members is felt most intensely by the killers). We are not, therefore, talking about a generalized hatred and fear of men (misandry) as alone fueling the gender-selective slaughter, although it is probably a more important factor than is usually appreciated. Instead, gender combines with other variables, as multiple variables *always* combine, to produce genocidal outcomes.[13]

My study of the Rwandan genocide also pointed out that the forces of the RPF—whose leader, Paul Kagame, now rules Rwanda—inflicted mass atrocities against Hutu civilians in the late stages of the genocide that displayed a gender configuration similar to the mass slaughters of Tutsis. The gendercidal component carried over to the postgenocide period. Seth Sendashonga, the ex-minister of the Interior in the RPF government, told documentary filmmakers from the Canadian National Film Board in 1997 that "the RPF wanted to establish its supremacy, and to do so they had to eliminate any potential rival. In many cases the Army came for men, ages 18 to 55, and took them away by night, never to be seen again. . . . The general pattern was to select youth and men who were still active, as well as leaders, teachers, farming instructors—anyone who played a role, any community leader was particularly singled out."[14]

Given that the Rwandan government and army bear responsibility for much of the direct and indirect killing in the DRC from 1996 onward, what can be said about the gendering of this violence? While much remains unclear, some observations can be hazarded.

The first again takes the form of a caveat. By all accounts, the vast majority of the killing that has occurred in the DRC since 1996 has been *indirect* in character, resulting from disease, malnutrition, and exhaustion—often a combination of all three. This by no means disqualifies it as "genocidal," or at least potentially so. The United Nations (UN) Convention on the Prevention and Punishment of the Crime of Genocide (1948) features, in its Article 3(c), an understanding that genocide can be perpetrated by "deliberately inflicting on the group conditions of life calculated to bring about its physical destruction in whole or in part."[15] The article, together with the almost identically framed offense of "extermination" as a crime against humanity under international law, points to those instances where populations are killed not by mass shooting or hacking or gas chambers but by imposing conditions intended/calculated to produce mass deaths. (Historical examples include German forces driving rebellious Hereros into the wastes of the Omaheke desert during the genocide of 1904–07; the Nazi imposition upon Jews of desperately crowded and unsanitary conditions in ghettos and death camps during the *Shoah*; the Khmer Rouge's starving of hundreds of thousands of Cambodians from 1975 to 1978; and the Indonesian government's contemporaneous infliction of mass deprivation on the population of East Timor.)

Because most of the mortality in the DRC has been inflicted indirectly, a persuasive case was made by Thomas Plümper and Eric Neumayer, in a 2006 study, that women and girls suffer disproportionately in such instances, because their average life expectancy declines more than men's. Plümper and Neumayer pointed to the economic and nutritional effects of war and social breakdown, contending that "women are likely to suffer more from an increase in food prices and famines," in part because of a physiological susceptibility "to vitamin and iron deficiencies in diets" and in part because "in male-dominated societies, males get priority in food distribution at the expense of girls and women." Likewise, "the decline in basic health care hits women more because of their specific reproductive roles. Damage caused to the health infrastructure reduces obstetrical care and increases the number of miscarriages as well as maternal and infant mortality." While acknowledging Philip Verwimp's findings of a gendered deficit of males in Rwandan households after the 1994 genocide, Plümper and Neumayer cited alternative data on life expectancy that suggested "a small decline in the gender gap: while life expectancy of [Rwandan] men declined from 45.1 to 41.1 years between 1993 and 1995, female life expectancy declined by 4.8 years from 47.2 to 42.4 years over the same period." In Congo, meanwhile, according to the Red Cross, "an extraordinarily high maternal mortality rate of 3 percent [prevailed] in the rebel-controlled areas" of the country. Likewise, women were especially afflicted by conditions in refugee camps and by an elevated incidence of sexual assault that is typical in conflict-ridden regions: "Particularly in sub-Saharan Africa, rape was used with the intention of spreading HIV/AIDS and other sexually transmitted diseases. Injuries to vaginal tissue is a common consequence of rape and renders affected women much more susceptible to sexually transmitted diseases."[16]

Plümper and Neumayer concluded: "The finding that, on average, conflicts lower the life expectancy of women more than that of men means that policymakers, nongovernmental organizations, and the academic community need to pay much closer attention to the hidden, indirect consequences of conflict, which are both 'profound' and 'underappreciated.' . . . Our findings suggest giving priority to women when it comes to the indirect and long-term effects of armed conflicts."[17] Their work is an important corrective to gendered framings of conflict that privilege more traditional understandings of "violence" over more structural and institutional manifestations.[18]

Turning to direct forms of mass atrocity, it is clear that, in keeping with the strategies pursued in the Rwandan genocide, much of the mass killing in the DRC since 1996 has been of the gender-indiscriminate, "root-and-branch" kind. Human Rights Watch's 2009 report "*You Will Be Punished:*" *Attacks on Civilians in Eastern Congo*, for example, cataloged mass slaughters by the Hutu rebel group, Forces Democratiques de Liberation du Rwanda a holdover from the "Hutu Power" regime in Rwanda. In a grotesquely gender-inclusive note left for the civilians of the community of Mihanda in South Kivu province, the group warned: "Be on guard. We are going to kill the pregnant women and open their stomachs and we are even going to kill the young girls. The men will be decapitated like the salted fish."[19] Typical of the atrocities that resulted was the FDLR's May 2009 attack on the town of Busurungi and adjacent villages:

> The FDLR combatants massacred at least 96 civilians, including 25 children, 23 women, and seven elderly men. . . . Nearly half of the victims were shot or hacked to death by machete. Some had been tied up and then had their throats slit. Others were deliberately locked in their homes and burned to death or killed as they tried to flee into the nearby forests for safety. A further 26 civilians were seriously injured, the vast majority women and children. Two later died of their injuries.[20]

Note that in this account—and in a trope that is common in media and human rights coverage of abuses worldwide—the victims "included" in the count consist of all major demographic categories *except* men of an imputed "fighting age." One must engage in a grim arithmetic to discern that forty-one of the ninety-six civilians murdered—that is, the preponderant category—were adult males in this age range. The systematic inattention to this class of victims often makes it difficult to establish the extent to which "battle-age" civilian men are specifically targeted.

Substantial evidence indeed suggests that along with "root-and-branch" massacres, the strategy of selectively slaughtering men and boys has spilled over from the Rwandan genocide to the DRC. In a careful sifting of the evidence available as of 2009, Paula Drumond found that "in the Congolese genocide, men and boys are . . . more frequently victimized by killings and summary executions." She pointed to a 2001 mortality report by the International Rescue Committee (IRC) focusing on eastern Congo, where most of the direct violence has been concentrated. It "showed that 61 per cent of those violently killed were adult males . . . . In another mortality survey conducted in 2004, the IRC indicated another increase in this figure, affirming that in eastern DRC, 'adult males aged 15 years and over were at great risk of being killed, constituting 72 per cent of all violent deaths, although women and children were not exempt.'"[21]

The most extensive and significant source on mass atrocity in the DRC for the 1993–2003 period, focusing on the First (1996–8) and Second (1998–2001) Congo Wars, is the Mapping Report prepared by the United Nations High Commissioner for Human Rights (UNHCHR).[22] The 566-page volume represents an extraordinary and laudable feat of human rights investigation.

But it also serves as another object example of the difficulties that confront the analyst who seeks to discern the gendering of direct acts of killing. The challenge lies in the complex and ambiguous discourse surrounding gender in the Mapping Report. When reference is made to mass killings of civilians, groups traditionally coded as "vulnerable," notably children and women, are specifically mentioned as such (most commonly via the phrases "including women and children," "including many women and children," and "including large numbers of women and children").[23] Of course, as noted above, large numbers of adult male civilians are also "included" in such massacres. But this gender element tends to pass unmentioned. In some cases, it is possible to adduce a large majority of adult male victims, as when the report refers to a massacre of "11 civilians, including a woman and child."[24] It must also be assumed that in many, possibly most, cases where massacre victims are described as "civilians" or "people" (without members of traditional "vulnerable" groups being specifically mentioned), adult males constitute the large majority or even the totality of victims. (Sometimes further clues are provided, such as references to victims' ex-combatant status, or their political/administrative role, or accusations that they were "traitors" or "infiltrators.")[25]

Beyond this, the Mapping Report makes a single general reference to a pattern of selective killing of males, in the context of mass killings by Laurent Kabila's Alliance of Democratic Forces for the Liberation of Congo-Zaire (AFDL) militia and its principal ally and sponsor, the Rwandan Patriotic Army (Armée Patriotique Rwandaise or APR in its French acronym). "Whilst in general the killings did not spare women and children," states the report, "it should be noted that in some places, particularly at the beginning of the first war in 1996, Hutu women and children were apparently separated from the men, and allegedly only the men were subsequently killed."[26] Relatively numerous instances of such gendercidal killing are cited throughout the report, as in an account from the village of Luberizi, where "on 29 October 1996, units of the AFDL/APR/FAB killed around 220 male refugees. . . . The soldiers separated the men from the rest of the group and shot them or killed them with bayonets. The bodies of the victims were buried in mass graves near the church."[27] As in the case of the Rwandan genocide, the relative prominence of such gendercidal killing versus "root-and-branch" extermination strategies will likely never be fully known.

Rape and Sexual Violence

Like gendercidal killing, the targeting of males for sexual violence is an ancient phenomenon.[28] In one of the earliest sustained treatments of the subject (2002), Augusta Del Zotto and I noted that "Ancient Persian murals show triumphant warriors marching along bearing plates piled high with their enemy's penises," while "for centuries, men and boys who were captured in, or as a result of, combat became the 'body servants' (sex slaves) of western warriors, or the 'brides' of warriors in Mesoamerica."[29] Recent, carefully documented studies by Sandesh Sivakumaran and Lara Stemple point to the prevalence, even pervasiveness, of such atrocities in contemporary instances of genocide and war-unto-genocide.[30] According to Stemple,

> An astonishing 76% of male political prisoners surveyed in El Salvador in the 1980s reported at least one instance of sexual torture. In the wake of another conflict, 21% of Sri Lankan Tamil males receiving service at a torture treatment center in London reported that they had experienced sexual abuse while in detention. The forms of abuse began with forced nudity, taunting, and verbal sexual threats, creating an experience of degradation and humiliation. Ultimately, the abuse included various forms of genital mutilation and forced sex acts. Most of those abused had not reported the incidents to authorities, explaining that they were too ashamed. . . . One study of 6,000 concentration camp inmates in Sarajevo Canton [in Bosnia and Herzegovina] found that 80% of males reported that they had been raped in detention. Accounts of abuse throughout the conflict were often quite graphic, including severe genital mutilation and forced incest. . . . Reports have emerged from southern Sudan that boys held as slaves have been subjected to sexual abuse at the hands of government soldiers, including violent gang rape.[31]

The mass rape of women and girls in the Rwandan and Congolese genocides has become an international *cause célèbre*. There has been precious little investigation, however, of the sexual violence also inflicted on Rwandan and Congolese men. Nonetheless, available evidence and testimony suggests widespread sexual attacks against males as well as females, and with like aims: to degrade and humiliate the victims, and bolster the self-image of the perpetrators[32]; to terrorize target communities into flight and fragmentation; and to alienate community members from each other, further undermining the targeted group's cohesion, identity, and solidarity.[33]

Elysia Ruvinsky has studied what she has called "male sexual violence" (MSV) in both the Balkans and African Great Lakes regions. During the Rwandan genocide of 1994, "the use of [such] sexual violence can be gleaned from victim statements and eyewitness reports." Ruvinsky describes male genocide "victims who had previously posed as Hutus, been more prosperous or whom the perpetrators [especially] disliked" being "stripped in the marketplace before they were hacked to death by machete." Tutsi boys were often at risk of rape, such as the "13-year-old . . . kidnapped by a Hutu woman, kept in her house and raped three times a day for three days until he escaped." "There were also reports of mutilation and subsequent public display of male genitalia," such as the testimony of Lt.-Gen. Roméo Dallaire, who "saw objects crushed or implanted in vaginas, breasts cut off, stomachs opened and the mutilated genitals of men."[34]

The prevalence of MSV during the Congolese genocide is likewise hard to gauge, but it has featured in one gender-inclusive report by Kirsten Johnson and her coresearchers, published in 2010 in the *Journal of the American Medical Association*. Of nearly one thousand individuals surveyed, Johnson and her team found that "39.7% . . . of women and 23.6% . . . of men were reported to have been exposed to sexual violence during their lifetime." "Conflict-associated sexual violence" accounted for the assaults suffered by 74.3 percent of female and 64.5 percent of male survivors, with both sexes reporting rape as the primary form of abuse they experienced. (Strikingly, the survey found that *41.1 percent of the perpetrators of sexual violence against women were themselves women*, while 90 percent of the assailants of men were themselves men. In both cases, the perpetrators were overwhelmingly combatants. The finding, as the authors noted, "challenges the myth that women do not have the capacity to commit [such] atrocities.")[35]

More personal insights into the sexual violence inflicted upon men and boys have been generated by the exemplary work of the Refugee Law Project based in Kampala, Uganda. The organization, headed by Dr. Chris Dolan, was the focus of journalist Will Storr's groundbreaking investigation, "The Rape of Men," published in the UK *Observer* in 2011.[36] Storr relayed accounts from workers not just of the systematic and widespread rape of males, but also of "other ways in which their clients have been made to suffer. Men aren't simply raped, they are forced to penetrate holes in banana trees that run with acidic sap, to sit with their genitals over a fire, to drag rocks tied to their penis, to give oral sex to queues of soldiers, to be penetrated with screwdrivers and sticks."[37]

A regular strategy of sexual violence against males, in the African Great Lakes region and around the world, is forcing men and boys to rape or otherwise sexually assault others, both men and women. In its major 2009 report on atrocities in eastern Congo, "*You Will Be Punished*," Human Rights Watch found that FDLR rebel forces had "in some cases . . . forced civilian men and boys to rape women or girls, sometimes their own family members." For example, "In February 2009 in Miriki, Lubero territory, the FDLR stopped a group of six young people and forced the three boys to rape the three girls in the group. On July 2, in Remeka, Masisi territory, the FDLR tried to force a man to rape his 28-year-old daughter-in-law, after she had already been raped in his presence by seven FDLR combatants. When he refused, they killed him."[38]

Gendercidal Institutions against Men and Boys

The concept of "gendercidal institutions"—structural forms of violence that produce gender-selective suffering and death, often on a massive scale—was introduced earlier in the discussion of female mortality in Rwanda, the DRC, and elsewhere. In developing the concept, however, I have also explored the forms in which gendercidal institutions may target males. Two such institutions are worth citing for our purposes: military conscription and forced (*corvée*) labor, which throughout history and around the world have overwhelmingly victimized men and boys. Neither of these institutions *necessarily* produces massive fatalities, of course. In this respect, they differ from female-specific institutions that are fatal by definition, such as female infanticide and maternal mortality. Nonetheless, at many times and in many places, the results of conscription and forced labor have been a vast wastage and debilitation of male lives, on a scale and of a character that qualifies as gendercidal.

In approaching military conscription in both the Rwandan and the Congolese genocides, a challenge is to determine the extent to which males (and sometimes females) have been forcibly conscripted into the various armed forces; the extent to which they have joined "willingly;" and how far even "willing" participation reflects a desperate lack of alternatives (as women will sometimes "choose" prostitution or sexual concubinage, when no other means of earning a livelihood is available, or no other means of protection from more generalized predation can be found).

In the Rwandan case, there is little doubt that the large majority of men who "served" in Rwandan government forces and militias did so voluntarily, even eagerly. There was no formalized military conscription in pregenocide Rwanda. Indeed, the incipient threat of a downsizing of the Rwandan army (*Forces armées rwandaises*, FAR) as part of the Arusha Accords peace process—with the loss of thousands of male jobs that it entailed— seems to have been one of the factors that promoted a genocidal *esprit de corps* among "Hutu Power" forces. As the *Interahamwe* and other militias mobilized thousands of ragtag affiliates once the genocide erupted, they likewise offered undreamed-of opportunities to marginalized males. This gendering is implicit in Gérard Prunier's vivid description of the *déclassés* formations that inflicted much of the savagery:

> [The] social aspect of the killings has often been overlooked. In Kigali the *Interahamwe* and *Impuzamugambi* [militia] had tended to recruit mostly among the poor. As soon as they went into action, they drew around them a cloud of even poorer people, a lumpenproletariat of street boys, rag-pickers, car-washers and homeless unemployed. For these people the genocide was the best thing that could ever happen to them. They had the blessings of a form of authority to take revenge on socially powerful people as long as these were on the wrong side of the political fence. They could steal, they could kill with minimum justification, they could rape and they could get drunk for free. This was wonderful. . . . They just went along, knowing it would not last.[39]

A separate, quite different dynamic was also evident with regard to ordinary Rwandan Hutu men co-opted into the genocidal enterprise. My study of the mobilization of masculinities and femininities in the Hutu genocide of Tutsis found that frequently, "men participated only reluctantly, as numerous accounts from the barricades make clear. Adolescent boys—sometimes even younger ones—were also coerced into killing." For example,

> A ten-year-old named Ndayambaje described being ordered by a local councillor to murder another young boy: "The councillor was holding a machete and a masu [nail-studded club]. He beat a boy with the flat part of the machete. Then he said to me, 'Either you kill him or you will fuck your mother.' Still, I did not understand what I would have to do. The person he was beating was a boy slightly older than me. He had already clobbered him and wanted me to finish him off. He gave me a masu and told me to kill him after insulting me."

Ndayambaje complied, and he was tried and convicted for his participation in the genocide.[40]

Doubtless, this witches' brew of eager "service," low-level genocide entrepreneurialism, and conscription/coercion has featured in the Congolese wars and genocides as well. But investigations of the subject are extremely scarce, in contrast with the global attention paid to Congolese women who have been conscripted and violated as sexual slaves. The one male cohort that has received significant notice is child soldiers—children, like women, being classed as a "vulnerable" group by definition. Here, the challenge of distinguishing voluntary from involuntary participation is arguably less relevant, given the minority age of the victims.

Available data makes clear that the forcible recruitment of children has been widespread in the DRC conflict. The UN Security Council Group of Experts report, published in January 2014, cited "the recruitment of 459 children by armed groups. . . . The children were between 9 and 17 years old; many were under the age of 15. Of the total, 403 were boys and 56 were girls." The organization also "confirmed other cases of child soldiers in the eastern DRC." Screening of Mai Mai rebels who surrendered in the town of Bweremana indicated that "of 1,211 combatants, . . . 27 [were] children between the ages of 15 and 17, of whom 3 were girls" (and twenty-four were boys, presumably).[41] It is worth noting that male conscription, particularly of boys, has often involved sexual servitude analogous to that experienced by women and girls. The findings of Johnson et al.'s DRC survey found that a slight majority of conscripted females (51.1 percent) cited sexual servitude as among the principal requirements of their "service." So, too, did 20.3 percent of males.[42]

Forced Labor

The territory known today as the DRC has long been associated with the murderous—indeed gendercidal—conscription of men and boys as forced laborers. During the "rubber terror" instigated by Belgian King Leopold in the late nineteenth and early twentieth centuries, millions of men were forced deep into the rainforest to harvest the precious new commodity of the industrial age. The immense death toll, combined with permanent injury/ debilitation and the protracted separation of the sexes, prompted one of the most dramatic population collapses on the human record—estimated by Adam Hochschild at around *ten million* between 1890 and 1920. The gendercidal character of the direct and indirect killing was established by the 1970s research of the Belgian anthropologist Daniel Vangroenweghe, who, as reported by Hochschild in his classic account, *King Leopold's Ghost,*

> found persuasive demographic evidence that large numbers of men had been worked to death as rubber slaves or killed in punitive raids. . . . No other explanation accounts for the curious pattern that threads through the village-by-village headcounts taken in the colony long before the first territorial census. These local headcounts consistently show far more women than men. At Inongo in 1907, for example, there were 309 children, 402 adult women, but only 275 adult men. . . . At nearby Iboko in 1908 there were 322 children, 543 adult women, but only 262 adult men. Statistics from numerous other villages show the same pattern.

In an unforgettable coda, Hochschild declared that "sifting such figures today is like sifting the ruins of an Auschwitz crematorium. They do not tell you precise death tolls, but they reek of mass murder."[43]

"Precise death tolls" are no easier to establish for the resurgent use of forced labor in the contemporary Congo wars. The evidence, however, suggests widespread abuse and atrocity. The trend of conscripting males, overwhelmingly, for these often deadly tasks—and abusing or murdering them when they prove "unfit"—persists, although again the gender dimension is downplayed in the available investigations. Human Rights Watch's report, "*You Will Be Punished,*" for example, avoids an explicit gender framing in its brief discussion of forced labor during the Congolese government's 2009 offensive against FDLR rebels—in stark contrast to the "women-and-girls" framing for the coverage of sexual violence. But it does not take much reading between the lines to discern who are the "civilians" being victimized:

> Since the start of military operations against the FDLR, Congolese army forces have pressed hundreds of civilians [*sic*] into forced labor to carry their supplies, ammunition, and other equipment to the frontlines. The journeys are long and difficult, and the loads often very heavy. At least two men died after collapsing under loads that were too heavy for them to carry and at least ten others were killed when they refused or were physically unable to lift the load assigned to them.

The report cited the testimony of one man conscripted for forced labor in March 2009: "The FARDC [Congolese army] . . . made us transport their baggage all the way from Kirundu to Busurungi and then to Kibua. It took three days. There were over 100 civilians, all men taken from villages along the way to transport their baggage. If you walked slowly, they beat you. They beat me badly several times, and that's why I'm still sick and can't walk well. Some beat me with the butt of their gun and others whipped me on my legs." Another male informant described soldiers "go[ing] in front of each house every morning to force all the men to transport their baggage. . . . If we said we were tired, they beat us and told us to walk faster. There were children among us—five kids from the primary school, some as young as eight, who had to carry the soldiers' children on their backs." The investigators acknowledged that "many civilians [sic] suffered serious and long-term injuries as a result of the physical beatings and the heavy loads."[44]

In recent years, the "conflict minerals" or "blood minerals" aspect of the Congolese conflicts has received sustained attention. Control over mining sites for gold, tungsten, coltan, and other valuable resources has become essential to the operation of the various armies and militias. Such operations tend to feature the same complex mixture of coerced and "voluntary" labor. Congolese men and women—and boys and girls—have flocked to the mines, which offer one of the few halfway viable livelihoods in the conflict-torn east of the country. Predictably, men's work has tended to concentrate on extraction and women's on the provision of services such as bar work and prostitution. Women and girls have been exposed to pervasive sexual predation and servitude. For men and boys, the physical toll of mining work has likewise been extreme. According to a 2011 investigation by the US-based organization Free the Slaves,

Miners work without basic equipment and suffer landslides, cave-ins of shafts, and asphyxiation. Malnutrition, exhaustion, physical trauma, poor sanitation, lack of medical treatment, and no clean water supply mean that public health concerns are equally high. Common injuries and ailments include: eye injuries; silicosis; conjunctivitis; bronchitis; tuberculosis; asthma; diarrhea; skin lesions; deformed muscle and bone in children due to heavy loads; regular dental problems including abscesses, cavities and lesions; tetanus; fractures and contortions; and contusions and severe bruising. Added to these are the impact of extensive drug use and sexually transmitted diseases. The intense crowding—enslaved miners are sometimes forced to sleep jammed together in the mine shafts—means that infectious diseases are rampant. . . . One informant stated that after four to five years working in the mines the body was "completely deteriorated"; he cited spinal column damage and lung damage, conditions worsened by the extreme pollution of air and water and exposure to toxic chemicals.[45]

Congolese army and militia formations have frequently forced men to work in the mines without compensation and on pain of death: "Villagers [are] rounded up at gunpoint by an armed group, brutalized, threatened, and put to work. No payment is offered, there is no freedom of movement or choice, and resistance is met with deadly force. The work may entail digging of minerals or hauling or processing of mineral ores."[46] The long-standing tradition of part-time *corvée* (known in Congo as *salongo*), institutionalized by the Belgians and retained after independence, has been revived for extraction purposes. Strategies of debt peonage are also frequent. "New workers are required to borrow money to purchase food, supplies, and the tools and equipment needed to keep them employed. The return on their work proves to be insufficient and borrowed money is exhausted as the worker struggles to pay for food and drink, lodging, medical expenses, and in some cases, school fees. Interest rates are usuriously high and engineered to make it impossible to pay off the debt."[47] Free the Slaves found that peonage was in fact "the most frequently found type of slavery, almost exclusively affecting males. . . . When unable to repay their debts, [men] are forced to work excruciatingly long hours, while often subjected to threats of and/or actual injury, arrest or detention precipitated by their lender."[48]

Humanitarian Intervention and the Rights Discourse

The exploration to this point has, I hope, contributed to an understanding that a nuanced and inclusive approach is required to the operations of gender in cases of genocide and mass conflict—as well as to structural and institutional forms of violence. As I argued in 2002, "Only when a gender-inclusive approach is adopted . . . can this important variable in mass killings worldwide be properly understood, and integrated into an overarching analysis of one of humanity's greatest and most enduring blights."[49] More than a decade later, such an approach is somewhat better represented in the academic literature. But it remains decidedly absent in international policymaking circles, both governmental and nongovernmental. There, the paradigm of gender-equals-women and male-equals-perpetrator has become suffocatingly institutionalized. As a result, "a great many males continue to suffer and die, unrecognized and unprotested by international organizations, as a result of precisely the[se] blinkered mindsets."[50]

One of the most urgent requirements from a humanitarian-intervention viewpoint is to appreciate how the gender-selective targeting of males—their detention, "disappearance," torture/persecution, and selective killing—serves as a harbinger or tripwire for more generalized campaigns of atrocity. The Rwandan genocide supplies a particularly trenchant example. The outbreak of full-scale genocide in April 1994 was preceded by *years* of smaller-scale atrocities by the nascent forces of "Hutu Power" against members of the Tutsi minority and Hutu opposition. Tutsis, for example, vividly recalled the October 1990 pogrom, which "had been a disaster for Tutsi men," in one survivor's recollection. "Thousands of them were arrested and thrown into prison. Some died."[51] At the outset of the 1994 genocide, Tutsi males understood that they were particularly vulnerable. "As soon as I heard that Habyarimana had been assassinated, I knew they would go for all Tutsis, especially Tutsi men," survivor Emmanuel Ngezahayo related.[52] "It was simply not safe for a Tutsi man to be visible," another survivor, William Rutarema, told African Rights investigators.[53] In general, there are few more reliable warning signs of impending genocidal outbreaks than these gender-selective strategies against males—and perhaps none to which the relevant authorities, both governmental and nongovernmental, are so willfully oblivious.

The manifest likelihood of males to be targeted first, and often worst, in outbreaks of mass violence ought urgently to lead to a reexamination of how "vulnerable" groups are constructed. It would be disastrous to dispense with the vital insights into women's and girls' specific vulnerabilities that feminist-informed criticism has generated. But it is discriminatory and inhumane to ignore how traditional patriarchal and feminist constructions of masculinity-as-power and male-as-perpetrator have blinded us to the vulnerabilities and disempowerment of males in conditions of war and genocide.

Intervention into male-specific "gendercidal institutions" is also required. It is again striking how inattentive international policymakers have been to these issues—*or even supportive of the institutions in question.* Consider the two gendercidal institutions examined in the previous section. With regard to forced labor, note that the leading international legal instrument, the International Labor Organization's Convention Concerning Forced or Compulsory Labor (1930), *does not ban* forced labor. Rather, its Article 11 limits the legal imposition of forced labor to one group alone: males between eighteen and forty-five years of age.[54] One can easily imagine the atmosphere of crisis and sustained activism that would prevail in our gender-sensitive age, if only females of a certain age were designated as legitimate targets of *corvée.*

The 1930 Convention also grants an exemption for a particular institution of forced labor, indeed quasi-slavery: that of military conscription and impressment. The forced recruitment of children, overwhelmingly boys, has become a prominent human rights cause (albeit with the gender dimension muted). Certainly, such initiatives against the recruitment and exploitation of children should continue and be amplified. However, R. Charli Carpenter has challenged the exclusive focus on the forced recruitment of minors. She notes that "the forced recruitment of adults, a practice largely targeted at lower-class males, is still considered legitimate and is neither condemned nor addressed by civilian protection organizations. . . . The right not to be subject to the denial of fundamental human rights implicit in military service itself remains a gap in international law."[55] The need to reassess this normalizing of male quasi-slavery as legitimate "service" is made starkly plain by the comments of a UN Children's Fund official whom Carpenter interviewed in 2002. "We don't protect men from forced conscription," the official blithely declared. "Forced conscription is not a human rights violation. Forced conscription of children is. We will advocate against the recruitment of children. But every government has a right to conscript men unless they have it in their laws that they shouldn't."[56]

Widespread sexual violence against men and boys also calls for attention and humanitarian intervention, including postassault care and counseling. Doctoral research by Augusta Del Zotto in the early 2000s found that of "4,076 nongovernmental groups that address war rape and other forms of political sexual violence . . . only 3% mention the experiences of males at all in their programs and informational literature," usually as a passing comment or afterthought. "About one quarter of the groups explicitly deny that male-on-male violence is a serious problem," while "the entire issue of PTSD [posttraumatic stress disorder] relating to war-related sexual violence omits men as victims and offers solutions/treatment programs focusing only on females."[57] Little has changed, in the estimation of researcher Lara Stemple, who describes a "constant drum beat that women are *the* rape victims," while males are considered a "monolithic perpetrator class":

> International human rights law leaves out men in nearly all instruments designed to address sexual violence. The UN Security Council Resolution 1325 in 2000 treats wartime sexual violence as something that only impacts on women and girls. . . . Ignoring male rape not only neglects men; it also harms women by reinforcing a viewpoint that equates "female" with "victim," thus hampering our ability to see women as strong and empowered. In the same way, silence about male victims reinforces unhealthy expectations about men and their supposed invulnerability.[58]

This leads, in closing, to consideration of whether a discourse of human rights and *gendered* rights is appropriate to address the patterns of male/masculine vulnerability outlined in this chapter. It will come as no surprise to readers that I believe it is.

Unfortunately, though not always unfairly, the extension of a rights-based discourse to male and masculine experience ("men's rights") tends to evoke images of macho breast-beating and reactionary backlash against women's rights and feminist causes. When a field of profeminist masculinity studies emerged in the 1980s, it was careful to avoid a human rights discourse for men, focusing instead on males as perpetrators of violence and oppression (with some space granted to self-destructive male behavior under patriarchy). Contrary offerings tended to be scorned by feminists and men's-studies exponents alike. Discussion in the intellectual/academic sphere has since become substantially more inclusive and empathetic. Change in the all-important policy sphere, however—among both governmental and nongovernmental organizations and initiatives—has been much slower to arrive, reflecting both blinkered mind-sets and well-entrenched interests.

Surely, a discourse of gendered rights and vulnerabilities need not be a zero-sum game. To undermine feminists' hard-won accomplishments in promoting women's rights worldwide would be profoundly illegitimate. Indeed, further such initiatives should be welcomed and supported. "But it would be equally destructive to maintain the present state of affairs, in which violations of men's human rights—and the very *idea* of men's human rights—are either callously ignored or openly ridiculed."[59]

Notes

1 Leo Kuper, *Genocide: Its Political Use in the Twentieth Century* (Harmondsworth, UK: Penguin, 1981), p. 9.

2 For an overview, see Adam Jones, "Gendercide and Genocide," *Journal of Genocide Research* 2:2 (2000), pp. 185–211. See also the case studies compiled on the Gendercide Watch website: http://www.gendercide.org.

3 Adam Jones, *Genocide: A Comprehensive Introduction*, 2nd edn (London, UK: Routledge, 2010), p. 81.

4 Harry Brod, "Introduction: Themes and Theses," in *The Making of Masculinities: The New Men's Studies*, ed. Harry Brod (Boston, MA: Unwin Hyman, 1987), p. 2.

5 My preferred definition of genocide slightly adapts that of Steven Katz: "The actualization of the intent, however successfully carried out, to murder in whole or in part any national, ethnic, racial, religious, political, social, gender or economic group, as these groups are defined by the perpetrator, by whatever means." See the discussion in Jones, *Genocide*, pp. 24–5. Crimes against humanity, according to the definition of the Rome Statute of the International Criminal Court (1998), comprise murder, extermination, torture, persecution, forced transfer of populations, rape and sexual violence, arbitrary imprisonment, and apartheid, when inflicted against civilian populations, as part of a "widespread or systematic" campaign of the same, when perpetrators are conscious of that wider campaign. For elucidation, see Adam Jones, *Crimes Against Humanity: A Beginner's Guide* (Oxford, UK: One World, 2008).

6 For example, women from the former Yugoslavia and Bosnia-Herzegovina, interviewed by the activist Marsha Jacobs, expressed "a general concern that the issue of rape [of women] not be stressed at the expense of the alleged Serbian campaign of slaughter and genocide against the civilian population of Bosnia-Herzegovina, male and female alike." According to Jacobs, "They didn't want in any way to let the rape overshadow the real problem, which is the extermination and execution of thousands and thousands of men and women"—overwhelmingly men. See Adam Jones, "Gender and Ethnic Conflict in ex-Yugoslavia," *Ethnic and Racial Studies* 17:1 (1994), p. 119.

7   Mary Anne Warren, *Gendercide: The Implications of Sex Selection* (Totowa, NJ: Rowman & Allanheld, 1985), p. 22.

8   A very rare case in which women (and the elderly and children) appear to have been killed, while adult males have been preserved, is worth citing. It shows that the "logic" of anti-male gendercide, so often cited as though it somehow excuses the crimes in question, can lead in an opposite direction. Shaka Zulu, leader of the expansionist Zulu kingdom in southern Africa in the nineteenth century, adopted a "novel" approach in "utterly demolishing" neighboring populations "as a separate tribal entity by incorporating all their manhood into his own clan or following." His military forces were thereby bolstered; but Shaka "usually destroyed women, infants, and old people," who were deemed of no military value. See Frank Chalk and Kurt Jonassohn, *The History and Sociology of Genocide: Analyses and Case Studies* (New Haven, CT: Yale University Press, 1990), pp. 224–5; also Michael R. Mahoney, "The Zulu Kingdom as a Genocidal and Post-Genocidal Society, c. 1810 to the Present," *Journal of Genocide Research* 5:2 (2003), pp. 251–68. A more contemporary example, which carries its own evil-gendered logic, is the practice often followed by Nazi mass murderers in the death camps, of consigning all women (especially pregnant women) immediately to the gas chambers, while some men were preserved alive for a time as presumably stronger and more efficient slave-laborers. Thus, the initial dynamic of the Jewish Holocaust, in which men were disproportionately the victims of the early phase of the "Holocaust by Bullets" on the Eastern Front (1941–3), was substantially offset by the disproportionate slaughter of females in its later stages.

9   See Jones, *Genocide*, p. 5. Note that the phrase "root-and-branch" is itself implicitly gendered, conveying that the killing has progressed beyond adult males to encompass women (the reproductive "root") and children (the "branch").

10 Adam Jones, "Gender and Genocide in Rwanda," *Journal of Genocide Research* 4:1 (2002), pp. 71–2. The quoted passages are drawn from reports by African Rights (see following note) and Human Rights Watch.

11 African Rights, *Rwanda: Death, Despair and Defiance*, rev. edn (London, UK: African Rights, 1995), pp. 597–8.

12 Ibid., p. 815.

13 See the discussion of "multiple and overlapping identities," in Jones, *Genocide*, pp. 34–6. Neither, it should it be noted, does misogyny *alone* underpin most of the gendered atrocities inflicted upon women and girls. Genocidal killers and rapists do not kill, rape, and enslave women of their own group in like fashion—indeed, the atrocities are often presented as a means of *protecting* "their" womenfolk from external threats. Structural violence against females, such as female infanticide/neonaticide, genital mutilation, and other crimes, is likewise often influenced by variables of age, social class, religious and ethnic affiliation, and so on.

14 Sendashonga quoted in *Chronicle of a Genocide Foretold*, Volume 3, Part 3 (Video production, Ottawa, Canada: National Film Board, 1997).

15 United Nations, "Convention on the Prevention and Punishment of the Crime of Genocide." Available online: http://www.preventgenocide.org/law/convention/text.htm (accessed December 9, 1948).

16 Thomas Plümper and Eric Neumayer, "The Unequal Burden of War: The Effect of Armed Conflict on the Gender Gap in Life Expectancy," *International Organization* 60:3 (Summer 2006), pp. 730–1, 732, 742.

17 Plümper and Neumayer, "The Unequal Burden of War," p. 748.

18 See Adam Jones, "Gendercidal Institutions against Women and Girls," in *Women in an Insecure World: Violence against Women: Facts, Figures and Analysis*, ed. Marie Vlachová and Lea Biason (Geneva, Switzerland: Centre for the Democratic Control of Armed Forces, 2005), pp. 15–24.

19 Human Rights Watch, "*You Will Be Punished": Atrocities in Eastern Congo* (New York, NY: Human Rights Watch, 2009), p. 54. Available online: http://www.hrw.org/sites/default/files/reports/drc1209webwcover2.pdf.

20 Ibid., p. 63.

21 Paula Drumond, "Invisible Males: A Critical Assessment of UN Gender Mainstreaming Policies in the Congolese Genocide," in *New Directions in Genocide Research*, ed. Adam Jones (London, UK: Routledge, 2012), pp. 100–2.

22 United Nations High Commissioner for Human Rights (UNHCHR), *Report of the Mapping Exercise Documenting the Most Serious Violations of Human Rights and International Humanitarian Law Committed within the Territory of the Democratic Republic of the Congo between March 1993 and June 2003*, August 2010. Available online: http://www.ohchr.org/Documents/Countries/ZR/DRC_MAPPING_REPORT_FINAL_EN.pdf.

23 For examples of these discursive strategies, see UNHCHR, *Report of the Mapping Exercise*, pp. 185, 209, 229, 230.

24 Ibid., p. 380.

25 See, for example, ibid., pp. 298, 299, 314.

26 Ibid., p. 32.

27 Ibid., p. 199. The acronym FAB refers to the Burundian Armed Forces, another key ally of Kabila's AFDL. For further examples of the gendercidal targeting of males for mass execution, see elsewhere in p. 199; also pp. 185, 218, 223, 275, 278, 320, 358, 375, 450, 451.

28 Sexual violence may be defined as "any physical or psychological violence carried out through sexual means or by targeting sexuality and included rape and attempted rape, molestation, sexual slavery, being forced to undress or being stripped of clothing, forced marriage, and insertion of foreign objects into the genital opening or anus, forcing individuals to perform sexual acts on one another or harm one another in a sexual manner, or mutilating a person's genitals." Kirsten Johnson et al., "Association of Sexual Violence and Human Rights Violations with Physical and Mental Health in Territories of the Eastern Democratic Republic of the Congo," *Journal of the American Medical Association (JAMA)* 304: 5 (August 2010), p. 555. I am indebted to Elysia Ruvinsky for this source.

29 Augusta Del Zotto and Adam Jones, "Male-on-Male Sexual Violence in Wartime: Human Rights' Last Taboo?," paper presented to the Annual Convention of the International Studies Association (ISA), New Orleans,

LA, March 23–27, 2002. Available online: http://adamjones.freeservers.com/malerape.htm.

30 Lara Stemple, "Male Rape and Human Rights," *Hastings Law Review* 60 (February 2009), pp. 605–46; Sandesh Sivakumaran, "Sexual Violence against Men in Armed Conflict," *European Journal of International Law* 18 (2007), pp. 253–76.

31 Stemple, "Male Rape and Human Rights," pp. 613–14.

32 A paradoxical aspect of much male-on-male rape in patriarchal and homophobic contexts is that the humiliation and imputed feminization attaches only to the male who is forcibly penetrated—*not* to his male rapist, who instead sees his masculine prowess bolstered by the assault. As Lynne Segal described it, under these circumstances, "A male who fucks another male is a double male." Segal quoted in Charlotte Hooper, *Manly States: Masculinity, International Relations, and Gender Politics* (New York, NY: Columbia University Press, 2001), p. 78. For a further exploration, see Adam Jones, ed., "Straight as a Rule: Heteronormativity, Gendercide, and the Non-Combatant Male," in *Gender Inclusive: Essays on Violence, Men, and Feminist International Relations* (London, UK: Routledge, 2009), pp. 292–308.

33 This dynamic is well understood in the case of women survivors of sexual violence who are ostracized by their communities and menfolk as "impure" or complicit in their own victimization. A similar dynamic operates in the case of male victims. Salome Atim, gender officer at the Refugee Law Project in Uganda, described the prevailing view in the African Great Lakes conflicts thus: "A man must be a leader and provide for the whole family. When he fails to reach that set standard, society perceives that there is something wrong." Wives who learned their husband had been raped often "decide to leave them. 'They ask me: "So now how am I going to live with him? As what? Is this [victim] still a husband? Is it a wife?" They ask, "If he can be raped, who is protecting me?"' There's one family I have been working closely with in which the husband has been raped twice. When his wife discovered this, she went home, packed her belongings, picked up their child and left. Of course that brought down this man's heart." Quoted in Will Storr, "The Rape of Men," *The Observer* July 17, 2011. Available online: http://www.theguardian.com/society/2011/jul/17/the-rape-of-men.

34 Elysia Ruvinsky, "*My Heart Bleeds, But Where To Take My Grief Is Not There*": Wartime Sexual Violence Against Men in the Balkan and Great Lakes Regions (Thesis, University of Amsterdam, 2012), pp. 53–4.

35 Johnson et al., "Association of Sexual Violence," pp. 558–9.

36 Storr, "The Rape of Men."

37 All quotes from Storr, "The Rape of Men."

38 Human Rights Watch, "*You Will Be Punished*," pp. 75–6. See also UNHCHR, *Report of the Mapping Exercise*, p. 636.

39 Gérard Prunier, *The Rwanda Crisis: History of a Genocide* (New York, NY: Columbia University Press, 1997), pp. 231–2.

40 Jones, "Gender and Genocide in Rwanda," p. 76. In the context of the historically unprecedented involvement of women as perpetrators at all levels

of the Rwandan genocide, I have suggested "that a greater proportion of women than men participated voluntarily in the killings, since it was men, almost exclusively, who were forcibly conscripted into the 'work' of the roadblock [and other] killings, and who were exposed to suspicion or violent retribution if they did not take part. Evading direct participation was probably much easier for Hutu women (and children) than for Hutu men" (p. 83).

41 United Nations, *Final Report of the Group of Experts on the Democratic Republic of the Congo* (S/2014/42), January 22, 2014, pp. 157, 159.

42 Johnson et al., "Association of Sexual Violence," p. 559.

43 Adam Hochschild, *King Leopold's Ghost* (Boston, MA: Houghton Mifflin, 1998), p. 232.

44 All quotes from Human Rights Watch, "*You Will Be Punished*," pp. 108–10.

45 Free the Slaves, *The Congo Report: Slavery in Conflict Minerals* (Washington, DC: Free the Slaves, June 2011), pp. 7–8. Available online: http://www. freetheslaves.net/document.doc?id=243. The UNHCHR's Mapping Report notes: "It has been estimated that several hundred miners died between 1993 and 2003, particularly following subsidence. The victims often included young children. According to experts, several thousand people [*sic*] are likely to have been exposed to radiation in the DRC's uranium mines." UNHCHR, *Report of the Mapping Exercise*, p. 764. The gender variable is all but invisible, except by inference, in the UNHCHR's survey of abuses and atrocities associated with mineral extraction.

46 Free the Slaves, *The Congo Report*, p. 12.

47 Ibid., p. 14.

48 Free the Slaves, *Congo's Mining Slaves: Enslavement at South Kivu Mining Sites* (Washington, DC: Free the Slaves, June 2013), pp. 10, 17. Available online: http://www.freetheslaves.net/document.doc?id=305.

49 Jones, "Gender and Genocide in Rwanda," p. 89.

50 Adam Jones, ed., "Preface: A Pilgrim's Progress," in *Gender Inclusive*, p. xix.

51 Quoted in African Rights, *Rwanda*, p. 385.

52 Ibid., p. 587.

53 Ibid., p. 646. As an example of how gendered vulnerabilities of males and females are regularly intertwined, men of "fighting age" often seek to flee genocidal attackers—understanding that they are at primary risk, and expecting or hoping that members of traditionally "vulnerable" groups will not be targeted. The twentieth-century record is replete with instances in which such actions led to the consequent "root-and-branch" slaughter of the children, women, and elderly who remained *in situ*.

54 See the discussion in Adam Jones, "Genocide and Humanitarian Intervention: Incorporating the Gender Variable," *Gender Inclusive*, p. 278. Available online: http://adamjones.freeservers.com/ags.htm.

55 R. Charli Carpenter, "Recognizing Gender-Based Violence against Men and Boys," *Security Dialogue* 37 (2006) p. 91. Carpenter adds (p. 93): "The uncritical assumption that adult men should be required to fight for their country when asked raises questions about conflict-prevention policies,

particularly in areas where the international community is attempting to prevent the violent outbreak of ethnic or civil war. If adult men are denied the right to remain in the civilian sector, they may have little choice but to join the armed forces. Moreover, if, as civilians, adult men are denied the protection afforded other demographic groups, they may reluctantly take up arms simply to protect themselves. Such policies are counterproductive to conflict-prevention strategies, which have a stake in reducing the number of individuals actively engaged in violent conflict."

56 Quoted in Carpenter, "Recognizing Gender-Based Violence," p. 91.

57 Augusta Del Zotto, "Quantitative Inventory of Informational Materials of 4,076 NGOs Addressing Sexual Violence and Warfare," cited in Del Zotto and Jones, "Male-on-Male Sexual Violence."

58 Stemple quoted in Storr, "The Rape of Men." In their survey of sexual assault in the Congolese conflict, Kirsten Johnson et al. noted that their "study is *unique* in that it evaluates the prevalence of sexual violence among men in the study area." They concluded: "There is a need for inclusion of men in sexual violence definitions and policies in addition to targeted programs to address their needs. *The protections of men and boys should be considered by the United Nations as it has with women and children*" (emphasis added), Johnson et al., "Association of Sexual Violence," p. 559. See also the critiques of United Nations policy discourses by Sandesh Sivakumaran and Paula Drumond: Sivakumaran, "Lost in Translation: UN Responses to Sexual Violence against Men and Boys in Situations of Armed Conflict," *International Review of the Red Cross* 92:877 (March 2010), pp. 259–77; Drumond, "Invisible Males."

59 Adam Jones, "Of Rights and Men: Toward a Minoritarian Framing of Male Experience," *Journal of Human Rights* 1:3 (September 2002), p. 399.

PART TWO

Sexual Violence and Mass Rape

3

Exposed Bodies: A Conceptual Approach to Sexual Violence during the Armenian Genocide

Anthonie Holslag

*[The corpses] were laid in such a position as to **expose** their persons **to the ridicule of passersby, and on the abdomen of each was cast a large stone. They had evidently been murdered there at the noon hour and then the brutal guards had stopped to leave behind them the signs not only of violence but of** mockery and insult*[1] (emphasis added).

Introduction

The above passage was written by an American missionary, Henry Riggs, who was an eyewitness during the First World War of the then-named "Armenian Catastrophe" in the Ottoman Empire.[2] Riggs's words underscore the brutality of the killing of Armenians and other Christian minorities and show how their bodies were used as a warning sign for passersby and how the violence against them was sexualized. Riggs's use of "their persons" is a euphemism to describe the Armenians' sexual organs exposed by the perpetrators. This act made a mockery of the Armenians' deaths by insulting their corpses and inflicting shame on the Armenian culture of "honor." The perpetrators used their victims' bodies as a vehicle for showing their dominance, including sexual dominance, over Armenians.

Sex crimes and genocide are intertwined in a complicated web. Genocide involves cultural and physical destruction, including mutilation and torture. The popular assumption that genocide is a crime of efficiency, a quick and effective way to annihilate a group of people, is fictitious when considering the sexual nature of genocidal crimes. It is not efficient to torture victims to death. It is not efficient to mutilate sexual organs; rape women, men, and children; and, in some cases, subject victims to forced assimilation and marriages. There is another driving force beyond the cultural and physical destruction of a people, and it is this driving force that is the focal point of this chapter.

Legal scholar Doris Buss and political scientist Elisabeth Jean Wood both argue that sexual violence—or, more accurately, the sexualization of violence—has been more prominent during ethnic cleansings and genocide than other forms of warfare.[3] Examples include atrocious sexual experiments during the Second World War; the mass rape of Tutsi females by the Hutu majority, who not only abused the women sexually but also cut open their wombs during the Rwandan genocide[4]; or the famous rape houses where Bosniak women were systematically abused during the Bosnian and Serbian conflict.[5] These situations illustrate that rape and sexual violence are an integral part of genocide.[6]

This chapter explores the nature of sexual violence in the context of genocide. By doing so, I demonstrate how rape and other sex crimes are not separate and isolated forms of violence within the genocidal machinery but rather an integrated part of the whole genocidal spectrum of violence. I argue that sexual violence is more than a violent expression of dominance; it is more than simple opportunity. Sexual violence has symbolic meaning in a genocidal continuum. Or, as social anthropologist Anton Blok once observed,

> To characterize violence as pointless or irrational is to abandon research at the point where it should start. . . . Violence as a cultural category or construction should be understood in the first place as a symbolic activity—not as meaningless, but as meaningful behavior.[7]

The main questions this chapter will address are: how can we situate sexual violence in the genocidal intent and process, and furthermore, how can we understand and analyze sexual violence as a physical expression of the perpetrators' social *imaginaire*?

Sexual Violence and Genocide: A Conceptual Approach

Political scientist Elisabeth Wood argues that the use of sexual violence is interconnected with the intent of the violence itself.[8] Or, to rephrase—sexual violence usually has either an opportunistic or a strategic purpose with a specific political and militaristic goal. For example, sexual violence occurs when "an armed group believes rape to be an *effective form* of terror against or *punishment* of a targeted group" (emphasis added).[9] Rape can be used to humiliate and demoralize a group of people; it is a weapon against an entire community. Since women are often seen or visualized as "symbolic representations" of a culture or nation, they "become the embodied boundaries of the nation-state."[10] In this context, the intent of rape is not only to shame the woman but also to demean an entire culture.[11] Nevertheless, intent can also restrain sexual violence. When a dominant group's goal is to marginalize a particular ethnic group while simultaneously seeking the group's cooperation (which is often the case in the first phases of ethnic cleansing and genocide), the dominant group refrains from sexual acts.[12] However, and this is seemingly a paradox, sexual violence increases as the genocidal process unravels.

Why does sexual violence, in the late phases of genocide, assume such a central place? To answer this question, it is important to understand that sexual violence during genocide is more complex and varied than is often represented or understood. Sexual violence conjures up images of rape, forced prostitution, and other forms of abuse against women. Yet sexual violence also includes forced marriages and assimilation and, in its most brutal form, sexual torture and the genital reconfiguration of victims, both men and women, who are "degenderized." These acts should not be placed outside the symbolism, intent, context, and complexity of genocidal violence. Rather, we should study sexual violence as *one* form of violence in a barrage of violence that is often referred to as "genocide."

Genocide is a specific form of warfare that is highly symbolic. Genocide is not about conquering a country, gaining access to resources, repressing a population, or meeting specific political or militaristic goals, even though these elements are present during genocide. Genocide is first and foremost the destruction of an *identity* that occurs under the *cloak* of warfare. To comprehend this, we have to consider the perpetrators' mind-set, or what sociologist and political scientist Jacques Semelin considers their "imaginary constructs," based on "identity," "purity," and "safety."[13] It is through a process of destroying a group's identity and purifying the body politic (as defined by the perpetrators) that sexual violence gains a specific meaning, and this is where the analysis of sexual violence should start. By studying sexual violence within this continuum of destruction and placing it in the dialectic process of Othering, we can employ a new analytical point of view where even the most incomprehensible violent and sexual acts gain cultural meaning.[14]

This essay focuses on the Armenian genocide to illustrate the above-mentioned processes of identity destruction, purification, and self-reconstruction. It demonstrates how sexual violence acquires meaning in a particular historical and cultural context and how it is an interwoven part of genocidal intent and a genocidal continuum of destruction. Sexual violence is not a senseless and irrational act but, rather, a form of violence that is planned, sophisticated, and highly symbolic and is intertwined with a pathological fixation on identity by the perpetrators.

The Decline of the Ottoman Empire and the Struggle for Identity

The Ottoman Empire established in the fourteenth century was from the outset multiethnic, multinational, multicultural, and multilingual. The driving force behind the empire was the *Ghazi* (warrior) tradition based on a pan-Islam ideology. This ideology placed the world in two "houses": the House of Islam and the House of War. The House of Islam was inhabited by the true believers, the upright Muslims, who in an ideal future would coexist harmoniously in a large Islamic Empire. Nonbelievers occupied the House of War and were subordinated.[15] According to this ideology, the Ghazis were justified in conquering nonbelievers' land, thereby expanding both the House of Islam and the empire's boundaries through military expeditions.[16] At its height, around 1566, the empire included parts of present-day Hungary, Austria, and Egypt and extended to the Red Sea. In the sixteenth century, the empire was the dominant political and naval power in the region.[17]

The Ottoman Empire's political interior was central, hierarchal, and patriarchal. The system was composed of several *millets,* groups of religious people with their own representatives who were given *aman* (mercy) by the Islamic elite. On one hand, the millets were subordinated; on the other hand, since the millets practiced a monolithic religion, they were given some privileges within their own community. These privileges were extended to minority groups, like the Armenians, who could exercise limited political influence on both the state and community levels. Thus, various groups coexisted for centuries within the empire. At the top of this hierarchal system were the sultan and the Islamic elite.

Although the Ghazi tradition and pan-Islam ideology constituted the main economic driving force of the Ottoman Empire, the state declined from the seventeenth century onward. The size and enormity of the empire made central governance of all provinces extremely difficult. Another reason for the decline was that other imperial powers in Europe—including France, Great Britain, Russia, and the Habsburg Empire, and the Persian dynasties in the Middle East—were competing with the geographical and political aspirations of the Ottomans. The diverse Ottoman Empire included Armenian, Assyrian, and Orthodox Greek Christian minorities, who in earlier times had been governed by the Persian Empire. These groups had specific ethnic identities based on religion, kinship, and trade relations. Their identity, since they were encapsulated by different empires, was not national. It is important to remember this in the genocidal processes in the nineteenth and twentieth centuries, when these groups, out of nationalistic motives, were branded as "enemies" within.

The Ottoman Empire did not have a single national, cultural, or ethnic identity. Instead, there were several identities operating within its boundaries. This diversity posed challenges, especially in the nineteenth century, when the Ottoman Empire operated under constant international threat from the other superpowers in Europe and the Middle East. From 1807 to 1829, the Ottoman Empire lost the regions of Abkhazia and Bessarabia to Russia. Between 1830 and 1878, the Ottoman Empire lost parts of Moldavia, Romania, and Bosnia-Herzegovina to Austria-Hungary. Thus, the Ottoman Empire was in a rapid state of decline and was depicted in European and Russian newspapers as the "old sick man of Europe," especially in the run-up to the Crimean War in 1853.

The waning power of the Ottoman Empire fostered anxiety and fear among top political leaders and others about the empire's self-identity and future as a great power. This is significant, because as social psychologist Ervin Staub explains, fear can provide a breeding ground for a pathological fixation on identity and therefore offers insight into how genocides can develop.[18] He claims that genocide does not start with hatred, as is popularly argued, but rather with fear of what he considers the "self-concept":

All human beings strive for a coherent and positive self-concept, a self-definition that provides continuity and guides one's life. Difficult conditions threaten the self-concept as people cannot care for themselves and their families or control the circumstances of their lives.[19]

Political scientist Robert Melson emphasizes that genocide occurs during moments of crisis and is, in essence, *reactionary* in nature.[20] In the early twentieth century, the Ottoman Empire continued to decline as it lost more territory and grappled with economic and financial failure. Young intellectuals, called the "Young Turks," sought answers in the national and democratic movements in Europe and staged a coup in 1908, when the Committee of Union and Progress (CUP) was founded. Intellectuals, including Ziya Gökalp (one of the major identity entrepreneurs of the Young Turks movement and committee), were seeking answers to the Ottoman Empire's political and social challenges.[21] According to Gökalp and other Young Turks, the challenges the empire faced were *not* to be answered by reconfiguring the borders or halting its expansionist policies. Instead, the answers were sought within.

During this time, the pan-Islam ideology slowly became obsolete. An influential article in 1904 by Yusuf Akçura, "Three Types of Policies," contrasted Islamism with Turkism and argued that Islamism and the Ghazi tradition were doomed to failure.[22] Gökalp adopted these ideas and went a step further. Influenced by the national and secular movements in Europe and by Durkheim's social scientific ideas of social cohesion, Gökalp maintained that if Turkey were to survive, a new national identity and a new pan ideology had to be constructed. He envisioned a pan-Turkish identity, not one built on the pillars of Islam but rather a "Turan" or "Turkish" identity based on the pillars of the Turkish culture.[23] It was not only necessary to abandon pan-Islam, as Akçura had argued, but was also necessary to reconfigure the

Ottoman Empire and socially engineer it as an explicitly Turkish and *not* multiethnic entity. Doing this, so the argument went, would make it possible to restore the Ottoman Empire to its former glory.

It is important to understand the enormous social changes that these ideas implied. Abandoning the Ghazi tradition and the accompanying pan-Islam ideology was in fact abandoning the millet system and the multicultural and multiethnic character of the old Ottoman Empire. A new image of the "Self" had to be created. The Ottoman Empire had to become a monocultural and monoethnic nation-state. In this process of change and questioning of old beliefs, an "Other" had to be created—an "Other" that separated the old Ottoman elite from the new elite from 1908 onward. This is one of the key factors of the genocidal process—what the anthropologist Alexander Hinton considers "Othering."[24] Othering is a process by which a specific group within society is attached with negative connotations to differentiate the inner circle (e.g., the new political elite) from the outer circle (the outsiders). The purpose of Othering is to solidify the identity of the inner circle. In many cases, historically, these negative connotations have been attached first to the old governing elites, then to foreign powers and the external threat that they appeared to pose, and finally to the imagined "internal enemies." In each step of this dialectic process, the Self is being established and solidified. Or, as the anthropologist P. Geschiere suggested; "To establish an identity, so it seems, smaller circles have to be drawn to seek out an 'enemy within.'"[25] Thus, in the Ottoman Empire the blame for the economic and political decline slowly shifted from the old Ottoman elite and the sultan to outside foreign forces and then to internal specified minorities. Significantly, these minorities posed not a physical threat but a psychological and imagined threat of the self-concept; an identity imagined to be endangered.

This perceived threat to the self-concept allows the perpetrators of genocide to act on a sense of victimhood. (This is also why the process of Othering is considered to be "pathological"; it is based not on a positive self-image but on a negative and fragile self-image.) The perpetrators imagine that they are the victims of a crisis and promote a narrative of victimization that justifies their actions. For example, Hitler repeatedly emphasized that the National Socialist German Workers' Party, and later the German people, were victimized first by the politicians of the Weimar Republic, next by the European superpowers, and later by the intangible and imagined "Jewish conspiracy." Similar processes were at work in the former Yugoslavia, when Milosovic emphasized Serbian victimhood over the *poturice* (Muslim "turn-coats" and "traitors"),[26] and in Rwanda when the Hutus imagined themselves to be the slow-witted victims of the *hamite,* the intellectual invaders (Tutsis).[27]

This Othering also has another dimension that anthropologist Gerd Baumann considers "Selfing." To Baumann, Othering is a dialectic process— a process of "reverse mirroring" where not only an "Other" but, more importantly, a new "Self" is created.[28] Each time we attach a negative connotation to the "Other," we are, in essence and implicitly, creating an imaginary positive "Self." For example, if we perceive the "Other" as "backwards," "conniving," or "greedy," we implicitly consider ourselves to be "progressive," "technologically advanced," "honest," and "self-sacrificing." We ascribe positive connotations to ourselves by degrading the other. Or, as Staub puts it: "Devaluation of a subgroup helps to raise low self-esteem."[29]

Baumann considers this process of Othering and Selfing to be "normal," a constituent part of day-to-day identification processes where a sense of collective identity is created. It is during genocidal processes, however, where Othering and Selfing are taken to a negative and pathological extreme. To Bauman, Othering is the most basic or primordial form of identification.[30] When a state is politically and economically unstable, and the self-concept is conceived to be in danger, the Other becomes increasingly essentialized.[31] At this point, the process of Othering, which starts in the *social imaginaire* of the new elite, becomes physical and tangible. For the Self to be constructed, the Other has to be solidified. The Other cannot only exist in what Semelin considers a "mental construct"[32]; it has to become visible and tangible in day-to-day interactions. As a result, the first phases of genocide begin by isolating and stigmatizing the out-group.[33]

This process is apparent at the onset of the Armenian genocide. After the CUP assumed power in 1908, the Ottoman Empire continued to decline. Defeat in the Balkan Wars in 1912 and 1913 was the epitome of loss and failure. Some political leaders and opinion makers considered the Balkan War to be a punishment from Allah for not uniting the country and for failing to create a mononational and monoethnic or monoreligious society.[34] Although the CUP was a secular and multiethnic political movement at first, by the end of the second revolution in 1913, it became a dictatorship largely run by three prominent individuals: Mehmet Talaat (interior minister), Ishmail Enver (war minister), and Ahmed Jemal (military general). At this time, other ethnic groups, Assyrians and secular Armenians, were excluded from the party, and the CUP's Turkification program gained full momentum. Othering became a visible state policy. Armenians' names had to be changed to Turkish names, properties were confiscated, all business transactions had to happen formally in the Turkish language, and all Armenians had to turn in their personal weapons. From 1913 onward, Christian traditions were forbidden in public life, and the only language allowed in schools was Turkish.[35] These were major changes, especially in small towns in southeast Anatolia, where the Christian population was often a majority.

It is important to emphasize that the Othering that occurred during this time was no longer an imagined or intellectual exercise in the mind-set of the new political elite. Rather, this Othering was a political and physical exercise where a specific targeted group was no longer seen as part of the larger polity. As the newly constructed Ottoman Self was increasingly threatened, or perceived to be threatened, it used more and more extreme measures to protect itself. Ideas of social engineering took a new and prominent place in government policies. As stated before, genocide is not only a physical form of warfare or the destruction of a specific group; rather, it is the destruction of an *identity* in *all its forms*. That is why genocide includes a wide variety of violence—some physical and some symbolic. In the Ottoman Empire, languages were destroyed, identity indicators were destroyed, institutions were destroyed, churches were destroyed, Armenian businesses were destroyed, and so on. From the perspective of the perpetrators, the country had to be purified and cleansed of all foreign and cultural influences in order for the in-group to *exist*.[36] The start of the First World War only heightened tensions in the Ottoman Empire. The battle of identity became a battle of existence; as Gökalp stated in an article on the outset of the war, "only a State consisting of one nation can exist."[37] In the spring of 1915, Interior Minister Talaat spoke to a correspondent after he had received telegrams about the violence against Armenians in Erzurum:

> I received many telegrams about the Armenians and became agitated. I could not sleep all night. This is something that a human heart cannot bear. But if we hadn't done it, they *would have done it to us*. Of course we started first, that is *the fight for national existence* (emphasis added).[38]

Not surprisingly, it was during the First World War—when the Ottoman self-concept was in even more danger—that social engineering policies gained full momentum, and genocidal processes unfolded. The Ottoman Empire had to be literally cleansed: the "Others" had to disappear both from the civic and the political body as well as from the public space. In 1914, Orthodox Greeks were forcibly deported. In 1915, the millet system was dismantled and prominent Armenians were captured and murdered on April 24.[39] In May 1915, the first deportation orders for Christian minorities reached the southeast district of Van.[40] In the summer of 1915, the first death marches of Armenians and Assyrians commenced.

The Symbolism of Sexual Violence during Genocide

In the dialectic process of "Othering," sexual violence plays a key role. Sexual violence allows the newly constructed Self to assert its identity over the Other; it allows the dominant group to express its "superiority"—in a very intimate way—over the targeted group. Moreover, this sexual violence enables the dominant group to attack the reproduction of the "Other's" identity at its very core.

According to Buss, as mentioned before, women are often seen or visualized as "symbolic representations" of a community. Raping women, and sometimes men, and penetrating a victim's body is the aggressor's ultimate act of physical dominance. Rape also degrades women and, by extension, their communities. In the framework of Othering, rape is a way to differentiate the dominant cultural group from the outsider.[41]

Rape, however, is only one horrific form of genocidal sexual violence. How do we explain other forms, such as torture, removal of genitals, or disregard of dead bodies with their most private and intimate parts exposed? What is the symbolism in these acts? In these instances, anthropologist Arjun Appadurai may give us insight.[42] In his article, "Dead Certainty," he observes that violence is a symbolic representation of the Self and ideas of the nation-state and that the death of the Other actually solidifies the existence of the Self. The perpetrator not only eliminates the ethnic or national Other, but also "establish[es] the parameters of this *otherness*, by taking the body apart, so to speak, to divine the enemy within" (emphasis added).[43]

Abstract notions of "Othering" are therefore translated into literal and physical acts *during the violence*. The Other is not only "constructed" and "deconstructed" in the imagination of the perpetrator, but also physically constructed and deconstructed. The Other is subordinated, changed, stripped, and eventually killed. At each step the Self is established and further solidified, in flesh almost, as an entity.

Perpetrators show their supreme dominance over the social body, national body, geographic body, and even sexual body, or what Foucault considers the ultimate form of power over people—the power over body politics through violence.[44] Killing is an act where "constructed" identities demand the brutal "creation" of real identities.[45] The dominant group's members safeguard and protect their "psychological selves" and, to achieve this, real people need to die: "Violent action can become one means of satisfying one's sense of one's categorical self."[46]

In the context of genocide, therefore, the driving force behind sexual violence is not *only* to shame, dominate, repress, humiliate, or engage in "root-and-branch extermination" of a specific targeted group; nor is it only a result of opportunity, greed, or sexual and animalistic desires.[47] The primordial aim of sexual violence, I argue, is to destroy the Other for the Self to exist. From this perspective, all sexual acts of violence—gendercide, rape, torture, and the removal of genitals—gain specific meaning if placed in the framework of genocidal intent. This is why sexual violence is more prominent and present during genocides and ethnic cleansings. Perpetrators engage in it to obliterate an identity, first by shaming and humiliating the targeted group and second by controlling and destroying reproduction.

In the following paragraphs, I show examples of how these various forms of violence—gendercide, forced marriages, assimilation, sexual torture, and degenderization—occurred during what is now known as the first modern genocide, which was also a prototype of genocides to come, in the twentieth century.[48]

Gendercide and Rape

In the many eyewitness accounts, we see forms of what we now consider gendercide: the killing of one specific gender within the genocidal process. In most cases these were battle-aged young men, as the following narrative shows:

> Then the order came: "Men above the age of seventeen stand separately. Our country is in danger; it's no time to walk with women," repeated the gendarmes. Father kissed us in the morning, and together with my brother, Hovhannnes, went to join the men. Early morning the men moved in one direction, and after a while our caravan moved forward.[49]

What is noticeable about this eyewitness account is that Armenian men and women were separated at the early stages of the death marches. Indeed, in some cases, every male older than nine was taken away and killed on a nearby farm or hill, out of the females' sight. The above account is also striking because of the implicit logic behind the order to separate the men, especially if we consider it in the context of the First World War and the perceived and increased threat of the "self-concept." The statement, "Our country is in danger; it's no time to walk with women," underscores how, during this time of war, the enemy was not merely the Russians or the other European forces the Ottomans were battling; the enemy was also the Armenian population within. From the perspective of the aggressors, battle-aged Armenian men were enemies who had to be cleansed for the Self to survive. Killing them, moreover, would safeguard the Ottoman Self not only in the short term, but also in the long term. By removing sexually active men from women, the perpetrators damaged the Armenian community's reproductive capabilities.

After the Armenian males over nine years of age were killed, the women and children were at the mercy of the gendarmes and/or the specialized paramilitary unit (the Shotas), composed mainly of criminals and Kurds whose sole aim was to attack and kill the Armenians in the caravans. Females were often targeted for their femininity, as the following eyewitness account shows:

> They drove us all: women, girls and children and forced us into the Armenian Church. They chose the pretty girls and took them away, in spite of the fact that the girls had rubbed mud on their faces. Then they brought petroleum tins and lined them up. My grandmother said: "For God's sake, don't burn us," but they did not listen to that.[50]

This behavior was also a form of gendercide. The place where the perpetrators chose to perform the killings, an Armenian church, was extremely symbolic.

The Armenians were Orthodox Christians. By selecting the "prettiest girls" (therefore considered the most sexually attractive girls) to be killed in the face of their Christian beliefs, the perpetrators committed an act of aggression not only against the Armenian populace, but also against the Armenian religion. The act was meant to convey the message: "Armenian Christianity will not survive." Ottoman forces acted to prevent the religious and biological reproduction of the Armenian community.

The killings by the Shotas were organized, planned, and ritualized. The violence also had a high level of sexual connotation. According to Ottoman Lieutenant Sayied Ahmed Moukhtar Baas:

> When the first batches of the deported Armenians arrived at Gumush-Khana, all able-bodied men were sorted out with the excuse that they were going to be given work. The women and children were sent ahead under escort with the assurance by the Turkish authorities that their final destination was Mosul and that no harm will befall them. The men kept behind were taken out of town in batches of 15 or 20, lined up on the edge of ditches prepared beforehand, shot and thrown into the ditches. Hundreds of men were shot every day in a similar manner. The women and children were attacked on their way by the ("Shotas") the armed bands organised by the Turkish Government who attacked them and seized a certain number. After plundering and committing the most dastardly outrages on the women and children, they massacred them in cold blood. These attacks were a daily occurrence until every woman and child had been got rid of. The military escorts had strict orders not to interfere with the "Shotas."[51]

The comment about "the most dastardly outrages" being committed "on the women and children" likely refers to the act of rape. It also refers to the second wave of gendercide; where first the men were targeted, now the females became targets. By not only killing but also raping women in this second wave, the perpetrators asserted their control over the reproduction, and hence the identity, of the Armenians.

Gender, Enslavement, and Forced Assimilation

Whereas the Holocaust was a genocide based on racial ideologies, the Armenian genocide was based on national ideologies. This difference shaped the acts of violence carried out against the targeted groups. Because the Ottoman authorities did not imagine Armenians' "Otherness" to be in their blood, but rather in their ethnicity and culture, they used forced assimilation and enslavement as strategies for cleansing the empire of foreign "Armenian" elements. The gendered nature of forced assimilation and slavery is apparent in the following testimony:

> At midnight the wild gendarmes invaded our village. They proposed that they would "adopt" the boys from 9-13 and the women would be taken to serve in the houses of the Turkish beys [chieftains], which would be similar to the life of a harem.[52]

While the "adopted" Armenian boys were used for labor and often forced to convert to Islam,[53] females were often used as sex slaves and distributed to local populations in a wide network of "markets." Outside of Mezreh, for instance, Armenian women and children were driven into a camp that also served as a slave market. Local Muslims bought the most appealing women (e.g., those from wealthier families) after doctors had examined them for diseases. If an Armenian female tried to resist her new fate, local authorities held her until she accepted her new "owner."[54] And, because Turks valued Armenian virgins more than nonvirgins, some doctors checked if the girls were virgins so that their sales price could be raised.[55]

The fact that females were sold and virgins were more desirable shows once again the importance of subordinating both the sexual and cultural reproduction of the Armenian populace. Virgins were young and considered influential and malleable. Females were seen as gatekeepers, mothers, and cultural representatives. Forcing the Armenian females to reproduce with the Turks was a way not only to subordinate but also to eliminate the Armenian culture through sexual acts. The goal was to cleanse the Ottoman political, national, and civic body as well as the public space of Armenian culture, *and* to cleanse the Armenian populace of its Armenianness from within.

There is another, and more fundamental, symbolism at work in the selling of female Armenians: the symbolism of the dehumanization and commercialization of the victimized group. We see this in other genocides. During the Holocaust, human hair was used for the war industry, and during the Rwandan genocide, victims' bones were sold and resold. By commercializing victims and using them literally as a product, perpetrators transformed victims from humans into nonhumans. Victims essentially became cattle, whose bodies (or body parts) could be used in a variety of ways.

Maria Jacobsen, an eyewitness to the Armenian genocide, speaks of this dehumanization when she described the following scene: "These poor people did not look like humans any more, not even animals could be found in this state, people would be merciful and kill them."[56] Another eyewitness account noted—and here we also see the commercialization of the violence—how female Armenian deportees at temporary camps were examined before rape and abduction and compared this action with butchers examining animals before slaughtering them.[57]

Slavery and forced assimilation were gender-based. The Armenian boys who were taken into Turkish households were often considered "young enough" to still be converted to Islam, while Armenian females were often, but not always, used as sex slaves. "Conversion" and "assimilation" were, however, the central themes. Armenians could only survive if they subordinated themselves completely to the will of the dominant culture group, which reaffirmed the supremacy of the Turkish identity. The cleansing had to be complete. Not only were the subjects forced into strange households, they were forced to become Turkified, and in many cases this Turkification process involved sexual subordination. Christian names were obliterated, conversion to Islam was forced, and children and parents were separated. Everything that made a victim an "Armenian" had to be stripped away. Sometimes, as the following eyewitness account shows, fictitious familial relationships were created: "The other man took my sister, Varsenik, by the arm and said: 'Pretty girl, I'll take you to my house: you'll become our daughter.'"[58]

Sexualized Killings

One of the most horrific, and most understudied, sides of sexualized violence is torture and genital removal, which I term "sexualized killings." Of course, these violent actions are related to gender-based killings and have many similarities with gendercide. The only exception is that the sexual organs are specifically targeted within the violence of sexualized killings, as the following eyewitness account shows:

> In Dilman there is also the same amount of murdered Armenians, whose martyrdom was carried out in the most horrific manner. They cut off the feet of living people with saws, they cut their wrists in the same way, they cut noses, cheeks, and lips off with scissors. They burned those parts of the body which are more sensitive. Both the elderly and the young were killed by frightful tortures, without regard to gender. We saw the traces of boundless brutality, glowing skewers were run through genitals of both women and men, and they were put to death this way.[59]

Skewers were run through genitals, and everything that resembled Armenianness, including facial features, were cut off. The victims were not only made non-Armenian, but also degendered. We see this even more in the following eyewitness account:

> For a whole month [during the summer of 1915] corpses were observed floating down the river Euphrates nearly every day, often in batches of two to six corpses bound together. The male corpses are in many cases hideously mutilated (sexual organs cut off, and so on), the female corpses are ripped open.[60]

According to Appadurai, the ripping and cutting open of human bodies has a specific symbolic meaning. The physical body becomes the "theater of the body" for politics. Cutting open a body is a symbol for making the inward outward and for making the invisible visible so as to overtly show the enemy within.

Ottoman forces also degenderized the victims by removing their sexual organs. By making victim's bodies nongender-specific, perpetrators stripped the victims of their identity and made them appear asexual and less human. Sexual violence such as this was also interlinked with ideas of femininity and masculinity:

> The gendarmes caught my sister-in-law who was pregnant, and made a bet: "What is—girl or boy—inside this *gâvur's* belly?"[61] said one of them. The other cut open her belly with a sword before our eyes and replied: "*Gâvurs* do not bear boys, see!"[62]

What is noticeable about this eyewitness account is that masculinity is placed higher up the hierarchy in the mind of the perpetrator. *Gâvurs* (infidels), after all, do not "bear boys." They are incapable of doing so. Of course, boys symbolize the patriarchal character of the nation-state. Not being able to bear boys excludes females and their offspring from the political body; they are subordinated by the Ottomans, who can bear boys and thereby maintain the patriarchal structure and culture of the Turks.

If we analyze these eyewitness accounts, we see multiple forms of sexual killings, all with a similar aim. By cutting open pregnant women, the aggressors confirmed their dominant status. By cutting open bodies, the aggressors made public the enemy within. By degenderizing their victims, especially the males, the aggressors solidified their masculinity, and therefore the patriarchy of the dominant culture group. The Armenian victims became nonsexual nonhumans; they became objects to confirm a newly constructed Self—a newly established national Turkish identity.

Closing Remarks

For a topic of sexual violence, there is no "conclusion." A conclusion implies closure, an ending, to a topic that is ongoing both on the ground and in scholarly inquiry.

In this chapter, I have argued that the destruction of an identity plays a key role in the unfolding of genocidal violence, including sexual violence. Genocide, by definition, is aimed at obliterating an identity in the boundaries of (an imagined) nation-state or empire. The dominant culture group is faced with enormous political, social, and, often, economic crises wherein the identity of the dominant culture group is questioned. A new identity has to be established, and to do this the dominant culture uses "Othering" and "Selfing" to create a new sense of "we." In each step of the violence, which Staub considers the continuum of destruction,[63] a layer of identity—religious identity, economic identity, gender identity, and human identity—is stripped away from the victim group so that the identity of the dominant culture group can be solidified.

First, the obvious and primary identity markers, such as names (kinship), language, collective history, and religion, are destroyed. In the physical destruction that follows, the violence is highly symbolic: "The victims are concentrated, overpowered, de-gendered, penetrated, and in the end dehumanized and slaughtered like animals." This violence carries tacit and symbolic meaning as a cultural expression. As I have argued,

> By destroying the names of the victimized group, the perpetrators are confirming and solidifying their own kinship. By destroying the language of the out-group, the perpetrators are confirming the superiority of their own language. By making the collective history of the out-group subordinated to the nationalistic tale, the perpetrators are actually confirming their own history. By destroying the religion, the perpetrators are confirming the superiority of their own religion. Within each step of the violence, the pathological fixation on identity for the in-group is symbolically "resolved," ending with the most gruesome acts by which the in-group confirms its masculinity, [reproductive prowess] and humanity over the out-group.[64]

My argument is that Othering does not stop with mental constructions alone but rather is translated into physical and violent sexual acts. By raping victims, selling them as slaves, forcing assimilation, and removing genitals, the in-group is showing not only its dominance and masculinity, but also the power of the patriarchal nation-state or empire. The message is, "we control your lives" *and* "we control your identity." Further, "we control those most intimate parts of your life: your sexuality and in the end your sexual reproduction. You are no longer allowed to procreate. Only we—the dominant culture group—are allowed to exist." This message is the message of genocide—the intangible and symbolic battle of existence.

Notes

I would like to thank Matthias Bjørnlund for not only making this chapter possible, but also giving me access to Danish articles, quotes, and so on and showing me the first draft of his unpublished article, "A Fate Worse than Dying." Further, I would like to thank Julia Challinor for editing the first manuscript. Finally, I would like to thank Amy E. Randall for her close editing, constructive feedback, and enormous ability to go through every sentence.

1 H. H. Riggs, *Days of Tragedy in Armenia: Personal Experience in Harpoot* (Ann Arbor, MI: Gomidas Institute, 1997), pp. 57–8.

2 The word genocide was adapted in the 1948 UN Genocide Convention. Before this there was no word to describe the horrors that the Armenians experienced during the First World War. It is worth mentioning that Raphael Lemkin, who coined the term genocide in his book, *Axis Rule in Occupied Europe* (1944), used the Armenian Catastrophe as an example of genocide in his earlier (personal) writings in 1943. He also made comparisons between anti-Armenianism and anti-Semitism, as quoted in D. J. Schaller, "'La question arménienne n'existe plus:' Der Völkermord an den Armeniern während des Ersten Weltkriegs und seine Darstellung in der Historiographie," in *Völkermord und Kriegsverbrechen in der ersten Hälfte des 20. Jahrhunderts*, Fritz Bauer Institut (Hg) (Frankfurt, Germany and New York, NY: Campus Verlag, 2004), p. 113.

3 D. E. Buss, "Rethinking Rape as a Weapon," *Feminist Legal Studies* 17:2 (2009), p. 150; E. J. Wood, "Variation of Sexual Violence during War," *Politics and Society* 34:3 (2006), p. 327.

4 Adam Jones, ed., "Gender and Genocide in Rwanda," *Gendercide and Genocide* (Nashville, TN: Vanderbilt University Press, 2004), pp. 118–19. Rape was so extensive that the Trial Chamber at the International Criminal Tribunal for Rwanda extended the definition of rape as "a physical invasion of a sexual nature, committed on a person under circumstances which are coercive." Quoted in N. Pillay, "Sexual Violence in Times of Conflict: The Jurisprudence of the International Criminal Tribunal for Rwanda," in *Civilians in War*, ed. S. Chesterman (Boulder, CO: Lynne Rienner Publishers, 2001), p. 173.

5 Alexandra Stiglmayer, "The Rapes in Bosnia-Herzegovina," in *Mass Rape: The War Against Women in Bosnia-Herzegovina*, ed. A. Stiglmayer (Lincoln, NE: Nebraska Press, 1994).

6 This was performed to such an extent that it has even been taken into the legal definition of genocide, especially parts (d) and (e) of the adapted Article II of the 1948 United Nations Genocide Convention. In this article, it has been specified that (d) imposing measures intended to prevent births within the group and (e) forcibly transferring children of the group to another group are indeed (legal) genocidal acts.

7 A. Blok, "Zinloos en Zinvol Geweld," *Amsterdams Sociologisch Tijdschrift* 18:3 (1991), p. 203.

8 Wood, "Variation of Sexual Violence during War," pp. 325–7.

9 Ibid., p. 331.

10 Buss, "Rethinking Rape as a Weapon," p. 148. For further examination, see also V. Das, "Language and the Body: Transactions in the Construction of Pain," *Daedalus* 125:1 (1996), pp. 67–91; V. Das, "Violence, Gender and Subjectivity," *Annual Review of Anthropology* 37 (2008), pp. 283–99; A. Appadurai, "Dead Certainty: Ethnic Violence in the Era of Globalization," *Public Culture* 10:2 (1998), pp. 225–47.

11 S. Banerjee et al., "Engendering Violence: Boundaries, Histories, and the Everyday," *Cultural Dynamics* 16 (2004), p. 129.

12 Wood, "Variation of Sexual Violence during War," p. 332.

13 J. Sémelin, *Purify and Destroy: The Political Uses of Massacre and Genocide* (London, UK: Hurst and Co, 2007), p. 22.

14 The continuum of destruction involves psychological changes where more extreme forms of violence become acceptable: "Initial acts that cause limited harm result in psychological changes that make further destructive actions possible." E. Staub, *The Roots of Evil: The Origins of Genocide and Other Group Violence* (Cambridge, UK: Cambridge University Press, 1989), p. 17.

15 T. Zwaan, *Civilisering en Decivilisering: Studies over staatsvorming en geweld, nationalisme en vervolging* (Amsterdam, Netherlands: Boom, 2001), p. 210.

16 Even though the Ghazi tradition in the Ottoman Empire had a definite Islamic dimension, the warrior tradition of expanding boundaries through conquest was actually older than this. The Ghazi tradition started to have Islamic connotations after Islam was established. See also H. Y. Aboul-Enein and S. Zuhur, "Islamic Rulings on Warfare," *Strategic Studies Institute US Army War College* (2004), p. 6.

17 A. C. Hess, "The Ottoman Conquest of Egypt (1517) and the Beginning of the Sixteenth Century World War," *International Journal of Middle East Studies* 4 (1973), pp. 55–76.

18 Staub, *The Roots of Evil*; Staub, "The Origins of Genocide and Mass Killing: Core Concepts," in *The Genocide Studies Reader*, ed. S. Totten and P. R. Bartrop (New York, NY: Routledge, 2009).

19 Staub, *The Roots of Evil*, p. 15.

20 R. F. Melson, *Revolution and Genocide: On the Origins of the Armenian Genocide and the Holocaust* (Chicago, IL: University of Chicago Press, 1992), p. 63.

21 "Identity entrepreneurs" are often politicians, but also intellectuals, poets, and social scientists who reconstruct identities, often through mythology and a specific interpretation of history. See Sémelin, *Purify and Destroy*, pp. 16–21, 49.

22 D. Gaunt, *Massacres, Resistance, Protectors: Muslim-Christian Relations in Eastern Anatolia during World War I* (Piscataway, NJ: Gorgias Press, 2006), p. 50.

23 See the writing of Gökalp, in U. Heyd, *Foundations of Turkish Nationalism: The Life and Teachings of Ziya Gökalp* (London, UK: Luzac & Company and The Harvill Press, 1950).

24 A. L. Hinton claims: "Genocides are distinguished by a process of 'othering' in which the boundaries of an imagined community are reshaped in such a manner that a previously 'included' group (albeit often included only tangentially) is ideologically recast (almost always in dehumanizing rhetoric) as being outside the community, as a threatening and dangerous 'other'— whether racial, political, ethnic, religious, economic, and so on—that must be annihilated." Alexander Hinton, ed., "The Dark Side of Modernity: Toward an Anthropology of Genocide," in *Annihilating Difference: The Anthropology of Genocide*, ed. A. L. Hinton (Los Angeles and Berkeley, CA: University of California Press, 2002), p. 6.

25 P. Geschiere, *The Perils of Belonging: Autochthony, Citizenship, and Exclusion in Africa and Europe* (Chicago, IL: University of Chicago Press, 2009), p. 27.

26 T. Bringa, "Averted Gaze: Genocide in Bosnia-Herzegovina 1992-1995," in *Annihilating Difference: The Anthropology of Genocide*, ed. A. L. Hinton, p. 215.

27 C. C. Taylor, "The Cultural Face of Terror in the Rwandan Genocide of 1994," in *Annihilating Difference: The Anthropology of Genocide*, ed. A. L. Hinton.

28 G. Baumann, "Grammars of Identity/Alterity," in *Grammars of Identity/ Alterity: A Structural Approach*, ed. G. Baumann and A. Gingrich (Oxford, UK: Berghahn Books, 2004), p. 20.

29 Staub, "The Origins of Genocide and Mass Killing," p. 99.

30 This is also why he considers Othering a form of "baby-grammar." He considers three forms of grammar on how groups create identities. One is called "segmentation," inspired by the works of Evan-Pritchard; another is "encompassment"; and the third is the most basic and primordial: "baby-grammar." Baumann, "Grammars of Identity."

31 Hinton, "The Dark Side of Modernity."

32 Sémelin, *Purify and Destroy*, p. 9.

33 G. H. Stanton, "Eight Stages of Genocide," in *The Genocide Studies Reader*, ed. S. Totten and P. R. Bartrop.

34 See T. Akçam, *A Shameful Act: The Armenian Genocide and the Question of Turkish Responsibility* (New York, NY: Metropolitan Books, 2006), p. 84; and U. Ü. Üngör, "Seeing Like a Nation-State: Young Turk Social Engineering in Eastern Turkey, 1913–1950," *Journal of Genocide Research* 10:1 (2008), p. 20.

35 H. M. Chitjian, *A Hair's Breadth from Death: The Memoirs of Hampartzoum Mardiros Chitjian* (London, UK: Taderon Press, 2003), pp. 76, 100, 101.

36 See also Semelin, *Purify and Destroy*, pp. 38–9.

37 Heyd, *Foundations of Turkish Nationalism*, p. 131.

38 Gaunt, *Massacres, Resistance, Protectors*, p. 70.

39 The millet system was a political system where specific groups had a certain amount of autonomy. This exceptional position was only reserved for *dhimmis*, an ethnic group who professed a monotheistic religion, which was acknowledged as such by the prophet Muhammad. T. Zwaan, *Civilisering en Decivilisering*, p. 217.

40 N. Matossian, *Black Angel: A Life of Arshile Gorky* (London, UK: Pimlico, 2001), p. 60.

41 Banerjee et al., "Engendering Violence," p. 129.

42 Appadurai, "Dead Certainty."

43 Ibid., pp. 233–4.

44 M. Foucault, *The Will to Knowledge: The History of Sexuality 1* (London, UK: Penguin Books, 1978), p. 137.

45 Appadurai, "Dead Certainty," p. 242.

46 Ibid., p. 244.

47 A. Jones, "Gendercide and Genocide," *Journal of Genocide Research* 2:2 (2000), pp. 185, 193. Available online: http://www.gendercide.org/gendercide_and_genocide_2.html.

48 R. F. Melson considers the Armenian genocide a prototype of other genocides in the twentieth century. See also Melson, "The Armenian Genocide as Precursor and Prototype of Twentieth-Century Genocide," in *Is the Holocaust Unique*, ed. A. S. Rosenbaum (Boulder, CO: Westview Press, 2001).

49 Testimony by Ashkehn Hakob Poghikian in V. Svazlian, *The Armenian Genocide: Testimonies of the Eyewitness Survivors* (Yerevan, Armenia: Gitoutyoun Publishing House, 2011), p. 223.

50 Testimony by Dsirani Rafayel Matevossian, in Svazlian, *The Armenian Genocide*, p. 258.

51 Quoted in Matthias Bjørnlund, "'A Fate Worse than Dying': Sexual Violence during the Armenian Genocide," in *Brutality and Desire: War and Sexuality in Europe's Twentieth Century*, ed. Dagmar Herzog (Evanston, IL: Northwestern University Press, 2006), p. 20. As Bjørnlund notes, "The Shotas, or Chetes, were parts of the Special Organization, a secret organization created by the CUP leadership in order to wage guerilla warfare behind enemy lines, as well as to act as the main killer units massacring Armenians in Eastern Anatolia. The Chetes were usually made up of released convicts and/or Muslim tribesmen and refugees, and were led by officers or by CUP officials" (p. 45, note no. 27).

52 Testimony of Harutyun Zakar Martikian, in V. Svazlian, *The Armenian Genocide*, p. 257.

53 See also K. T. Watenpaugh, "'Are there Any Children for Sale?' Genocide and the Transfer of Armenian Children (1915–1922)," *Journal of Human Rights* 12:3 (2013), pp. 283–95.

54 A. Sarafian, "The Absorption of Armenian Women and Children into Muslim Households as a Structural Component of the Armenian Genocide," in *In God's Name: Genocide and Religion in the Twentieth Century*, ed. O. Bartov and P. Mack (New York, NY and Oxford, UK: Berghahn Books, 2001), p. 215. See also Matthias Bjørnlund, "A Fate Worse than Dying," p. 23.

55 S. H. Villa and M. K. Matossian, *Armenian Village Life Before 1914* (Detroit, MI: Wayne State University Press, 1982), p. 73; A. M. Benedictsen, *Armenien— Et folks Liv og Kamp Gennem to Aartusinder* (Copenhagen, Denmark: Gad, 1925), p. 254. For further information see Matthias Bjørnlund, "A Fate Worse than Dying."

56 M. Jacobsen, *Maria Jacobsen's Diary 1907–1919, Kharput–Turkey* (Antelias, Lebanon: Armenian Catholicosate, 1979), p. 270. For an English translation, see M. Jacobsen, *Diaries of a Danish Missionary: Harpoot, 1907-1919*, trans. Kristen Vind (Princeton, NJ and London, UK: Gomidas Institute, 2001). See also Matthias Bjørnlund, "A Fate Worse than Dying."

57 Khanum Palutian's [Palootzian] testimony, KMA, 10.360, Pk. 15, "*Armenier-Missionen, Diverse Skildringer vedr. Arminierne* [sic] 1906-1927."

58 Testimony by Ashkehn Hakob Poghikian, in Svazlian, *The Armenian Genocide*, p. 223.

59 Quoted from a contemporary Russian-Armenian newspaper article in
    E. G. Danielyan, *The Armenian Genocide of 1894-1922 and the Accountability
    of the Turkish State* (Yerevan, Armenia: Noyan Tapan, 2005), p. 32.

60 J. Bryce and A. Toynbee, *The Treatment of Armenians in the Ottoman Empire
    1915–1916*, ed. A. Sarafian, uncensored edn (Princeton, NJ: Taderon Press,
    2000), p. 67.

61 Gâvur could be translated as "infidel."

62 Testimony of Barouhi Silian, in Svazlian, *The Armenian Genocide*, p. 414.

63 Staub, *The Roots of Evil*, p. 17.

64 Anthonie Holslag, "Within the Acts of Violence: An Anthropological
    Exploration of the Meaning of Genocide as a Cultural Expression," in
    *The Crime of Genocide: Prevention, Condemnation, and Elimination of
    Consequences (Proceedings of International Conference, Yerevan, December
    14-15, 2010)* (Yerevan, Armenia: The Ministry of Foreign Affairs of the
    Republic of Armenia, 2011), p. 139.

4

An Exceptional Genocide? Sexual Violence in the Holocaust

Zoë Waxman

On February 22, 2001, the International Criminal Tribunal for the former Yugoslavia (ICTY) declared rape to be "a crime against humanity." Rape in this definition was not limited to forced penetration but was taken to cover sexual slavery, enforced prostitution, and any other form of sexual violence, including the forced undressing of women and parading them in public, humiliation, harassment (e.g., unwanted sexual comments or advances), and the intention to cause psychological harm. As we will see, sexual violence also includes forced impregnation and sterilization.[1] Although a report by Medécins sans Frontieres from 1993 concluded that "[in] Bosnia systematic rape was used as part of a strategy of ethnic cleansing,"[2] Judge Florence Mumba of the ICTY warned:

> It is to some extent misleading to say that systematic rape was employed as a weapon of war. This could be understood to mean a kind of concerted approach or an order given to the Bosnian Serb armed forces to rape Muslim women as part of their combat activities in the wider meaning. There is no sufficient evidence for such a finding before the Tribunal. What the evidence shows is that the rapes were used as an instrument of terror, an instrument they were given free rein to apply whenever and against whomsoever they wished.[3]

While Serbian soldiers may not have acted in accordance with a specific order to rape and sexually abuse their Bosniak (Bosnian Muslim) victims, they were nevertheless actively encouraged to use sexual violence to terrorize, humiliate, punish, and degrade the non-Serbian population. Rape was both legitimized and accommodated. What is more, the sexual violence was often used simultaneously with military action or attempts at ethnic cleansing. Sexual violence was widespread throughout all regions of Yugoslavia, especially in Croatia and Kosovo, but it appears to have been most prevalent in Bosnia-Herzegovina, where tens of thousands of women were raped. The existence of mass rape and the intense suffering of Bosnian Muslims was broadcast by the international media and reached the television sets of millions of people around the world.

By contrast, the mass rapes of the Rwandan genocide of 1994 attracted far less immediate attention. In the span of 100 days, the ethnic Hutu majority had raped between 100,000 and 200,000 Tutsi women.[4] Despite the rudimentary nature of the massacres—they were largely carried out by machete—it was the most rapid genocide in twentieth-century history. After the genocide ended, the United Nations Security Council (UNSC) Resolution 955 in November 1994 created the International Criminal Tribunal for Rwanda (ICTR). The ICTR not only explicitly defined the crime of rape in international law but found an individual guilty of rape not just as a crime against humanity but also as an act of genocide. The Hutu mayor, Gen. Jean-Paul Akayesu, was found guilty of nine of fifteen charges, including genocide, incitement to genocide, and rape. He was sentenced to fifteen years in prison.[5]

The cases of Bosnia and Rwanda raise troubling questions for the historian of genocide in general, and the Holocaust in particular. On the one hand it is clear that rape was committed, but on the other hand we do not know how intrinsic it was to the genocidal process. Discovering occurrences of rape, which is a problem even when studying genocides as well documented as those in Bosnia and Rwanda, becomes an almost insuperable difficulty when confronting the events of the Holocaust. For despite the work of three generations of scholars, it remains the case that rape in the Holocaust is both hard to find and hard to define. This short essay will counsel against reading rape back into the Holocaust, as though all genocides are the same and as though all genocides involve the same use of rape as a weapon of war. Instead, it will maintain the particularity of the Holocaust—not least, although not only—because rape, however conceptualized, appears to play such a limited role within it. In the Holocaust, rape was not absent but neither was it endemic, much less a key instrument of genocide.

In light of the visibility and scale of the sexual atrocities committed in Bosnia and Rwanda, many scholars have been prompted to revisit earlier acts of war and genocide to also look for sexual violence. Nonetheless, even though increased awareness of rape and sexual abuse as tools of genocide is a crucially important legacy from Bosnia and Rwanda, we have to be cautious about reading sexual abuse back into all genocides without sufficient documentary evidence or reliable sources. I myself, a historian of the Nazi Holocaust, became very interested in the question of sexual violence and the Holocaust and have published on the topic.[6] However, although I have used reports testifying to the existence of sexual abuse, I have found them to be mostly ad hoc and opportunistic. Moreover, uncovering rape and sexual violence so many years after the event presents serious methodological challenges to the historian. For the most part we have to rely on the memories of survivors to uncover the existence of rape and sexual violence.[7] Our reliance on survivors is made more problematic still, because experiences of rape and sexual abuse are mostly oblique or told through the lens of another person—a friend or a relative, for example. While these challenges mirror the difficulties of talking or writing about rape in civilian society, they nevertheless make it difficult to undertake a serious, considered analysis of rape and sexual abuse during the Holocaust.

The organized rape of Jewish women was certainly not part of the official German genocidal policy. For rape to be genocidal—to be an integral element of ethnic cleansing—it has to be calculated. Men—for it is mostly men (or boys coerced as child soldiers)—do not rape solely as individuals acting on individual desire but as members of a specific race, ethnicity, religion, or nationality.[8] They do not sexually abuse just individuals but members of a specific group.[9] Rape during genocide is characteristically brutal, disrupting notions of acceptable behavior, and is often done in full view of children or other family members. As Catharine MacKinnon has so powerfully written,

> This is not rape out of control. It is rape under control. It is also rape unto death, rape as massacre, rape to kill and to make the victims wish they were dead. It is rape to be seen and heard and watched and told to others: rape as spectacle. It is rape to drive a wedge through a community, to shatter a society, to destroy a people. It is rape as genocide.[10]

The problem of applying these notions of genocidal rape to the Holocaust in general—especially in Germany and German-controlled parts of Europe—begins with the Nazi prohibition on sexual relations between "Aryans" and Jews. "The Law for the Protection of German Blood and German Honor" passed on September 15, 1935, applied to both marriage and extramarital affairs as well as forced intercourse.[11] Far from encouraging rape as something "to be seen and heard and watched and told to others," this legislation in fact made any sexual contact—consensual or nonconsensual—a criminal offense, something to be concealed. Although it is difficult to gauge how completely individual soldiers, Nazis, and others adhered to this regulation as the Holocaust unfolded, there is little evidence to suggest that they transgressed in great numbers. To be sure, recent research has brought to light the fact that German soldiers serving on the Eastern Front did engage in sexual activity with local women—including some Jewish women—in both violent and consensual ways. Regina Mühläuser has uncovered documented cases of rape, gang rape, sexual torture—for example, the cutting off of a woman's breast—sexual enslavement, and military and civil prostitution among German men and "ethnically alien women" of all ages, a category that includes Jews as well as the majority Slav population, Gypsies, and other minorities.[12] Moreover, as Wendy Lower has argued, because actions on the periphery of the Nazi genocide were less scrutinized and therefore potentially more brutal, women were quite literally raped to death.[13] This was particularly the case when German soldiers were engaged in looting and under the influence of excessive alcohol consumption. Although some soldiers were court-martialed for such undisciplined behavior, this appears to have been the exception rather than the rule, which suggests that such actions were tolerated as an unavoidable by-product of warfare or normal heterosexual activity rather than actively encouraged.[14] Nonetheless, even this important analysis and scholarship is based on limited and sketchy sources. It remains the case that historians such as Mühläuser are unable—despite scrupulous research—to provide reliable data, and we simply do not know how many women suffered such a fate, much less whether Jewish women were disproportionately affected, much less whether they were raped despite being Jewish rather than because they were Jewish.

There is also evidence in the German satellites such as Croatia, Bulgaria, Hungary, Romania, Slovakia and Lithuania, and the Ukraine, where it was the local authorities rather than the Germans who took responsibility for the persecution and murder of the Jews, that Jewish women were subject to forced sex and to the sort of sexual violence that we might term rape.[15] However, in many of these places specific information about the fate of their Jewish populations was heavily censored, and historiography on the Holocaust is still in its relative infancy. This means that historians such as Anatoly Podolsky, trying to find material relating to the specific fate of Jewish women in the Ukraine during the Holocaust, mostly have to rely on the memoirs of the few Jewish women who survived the war in the Ukraine, and the recollections of non-Jewish witnesses who survived the Nazi occupation recorded after 1991.[16] This makes uncovering the rape and sexual abuse that Jewish women in occupied Ukraine suffered by both the Nazis and their Ukrainian collaborators extremely difficult. For example, in districts where there were no ghettos—such as the Kiev area, where Jewish men, women, and children were made to undress before being shot with submachine guns and flung into mass graves—eyewitnesses remember that some women were raped but are unable to supply specific details. It is extremely unlikely, of course, that any of the raped women survived. Again, we have to rely on the testimony of the few survivors. Women such as Dina Pronicheva, who survived the terrible massacre at Babi Yar in September 1941 by hiding herself amid the dead and dying, witnessed the rape of two young Jewish women by a group of German soldiers.[17] In the absence of further evidence, however, we cannot know how representative—or unrepresentative—her experience was. Thus, despite the importance of such testimony, it remains impossible to form any coherent analysis of the extent of sexual violence against Jewish women in the Ukraine and other areas of the *Generalgouvernment*.

The situation for women detained within the concentration camps was different again, though still governed by the Nazi race laws. In the camps if an SS man was found to be having sexual relations with a Jewish woman, he would most likely be sent to the Soviet front. This obviously served as a strong deterrent and makes it more probable that the SS would have made use of the concentration camp brothels and the non-Jewish women enslaved in them.[18] It also means that any woman who was raped by an SS guard is likely to have been killed to ensure the cover-up of the guard's violation of Nazi race laws. As such, very few accounts testifying to the rape of Jewish women by German guards exist. The testimony of Laura Varon, a Greek-Jewish woman, who testified that she and a friend were raped by three SS officers at Auschwitz, is one of the few exceptions.[19] Jewish women were far more likely to fall victim to sexualized violence perpetrated by the German civilians who ran the factories in which the prisoners worked or by so-called privileged prisoners, in particular by low-level prisoner functionaries such as the Kapos (leaders of work commandos). That other prisoners could be capable of such cruelty is not surprising. The brutality of the concentration camps and the extreme dehumanization that resulted diminished sensitivity to human suffering. The sense of fatality—of there being no chance of survival—encouraged the fulfillment of immediate gratification. The existence of this type of abuse, however, was neither systematic nor controlled but was indicative that extreme deprivation increased women's vulnerability.

While it seems probable that Jewish women were not raped in great numbers in the concentration camps, nearly every woman entering the camps did experience sexual humiliation. On entering the concentration camps all women—from the mature to the barely pubescent; from the orthodox to the secular; from the rich to the poor—were forced to undress in front of SS men making obscene comments and then to suffer the indignity of having to spread their legs as part of the shaving process, before being branded with tattooed numbers and drenched with delousing chemicals that burned the skin. For many women, the brutal removal of their hair was repeated as a means of punishment throughout their incarceration. They also had to undergo painful examinations of their oral, rectal, and vaginal cavities, supposedly to check for the lice that were endemic in the camps or even for concealed valuables. Women were also beaten on specifically targeted areas such as their buttocks, breasts, or pubic areas. However, again these are not necessarily examples of systematic, organized sexual violence but more of what the historian Doris Bergen has termed "horrific, taboo-breaking sexual violence,"[20] a toxic combination of what Dagmar Herzog has acutely observed as the boredom experienced by the concentration camp guards and the power they wielded over their prisoners.[21] The sexual violence women suffered may have amounted to rape—but it scarcely suggests that rape was intended to be an instrument of genocide. The sexual violence deployed by the Nazis was different from that used by the Hutus and Serbians.

In the concentration camps, the racism and sexism of the Nazis not only intensified the suffering of Jewish women, who occupied the lowest position in the hierarchy of prisoners and suffered particularly harsh conditions, but they also made these women especially vulnerable on account of their gender. The particular poverty of their conditions, with women housed in separate barracks and mostly prohibited from the better work commands, meant that they were susceptible to engaging in "sex for survival."[22] Without anything else at their disposal, dire necessity drove some women to exchange sex for better food, clothing, or anything that might increase their chances of survival. The extreme power imbalances that generated this type of sexual exchange mean that it could never be described as consensual; it was, by definition, coercive. Nonetheless, this sex is not evidence of sexual violence being used as a weapon of war.

It was in their reproductive capacity that thousands of women did experience targeted sexual violence during the Holocaust. As the World Health Organization states, forced abortion and sterilization are violent acts perpetrated against women as sexual beings.[23] Experiments in mass sterilization took place at both the Auschwitz and Ravensbrück concentration camps. While the majority of the victims of forced sterilization were Roma or Sinti women, Jewish men and women and children as young as twelve also suffered in this way as part of the Nazi commitment to prevent the birth of racially inferior children. X-rays, drugs, and surgery were all employed. Sometimes sterilization was achieved through a direct injection into the uterus. This was done without anesthesia, and many women died in agony. Other women were subjected to painful injections with sex hormones, which caused abscesses. Again, for many, these actions led to indescribably painful deaths.[24]

On arrival at the concentration camps, pregnant women were encouraged to identify themselves with the promise of better living conditions and additional food. Those who failed to succumb to this ruse were liable to be sent to the gas chambers when their pregnancy was inevitably discovered.[25] Alternatively, in Auschwitz, they were sent to the experiment block, as the infamous Nazi physician, Dr. Josef Mengele, was particularly interested in both pregnancy and birth. When he was satisfied that his observations were complete, both mother and newborn baby were sent to the gas chambers— sometimes within an hour of the birth. Women who were able to conceal their pregnancies had secret abortions with the help of prisoner physicians.

The Holocaust, then, presents serious problems for the historian of sexual violence in genocide. This is not just because of an absence of sources or the distance of time—although there is a notable absence of sources, which may partly be explained by the very different social mores of the mid-twentieth century. More than this and more importantly than this, the nature of the Holocaust as a state-sponsored assault on a particular racial group with whom sexual relations were strictly prohibited makes the Holocaust different in kind from the genocides in Bosnia or Rwanda.

Although at least some German soldiers and guards raped Jewish women and girls, it is therefore scarcely surprising that there are very few sources testifying to this.

This is in stark contrast to Bosnia, where corroborating documentary evidence from multiple investigations shows that both military and paramilitary units of the Serb and Bosnian Serb nationalist forces repeatedly raped non-Serbian women and girls in former cafés, hotels, barns, garages, schools, and other public buildings.[26] Muslim and Croat women interviewed by the UNSC were able to identify many of the men who detained and gang-raped them. Documented cases reveal that the victims of rape ranged from children as young as three years of age to women as old as eighty-four. Describing her experience in a "rape camp," a woman states: "I was one of 1,800 women kept as prisoners in Brocko. There were 600 women in my room. I was given a number—21. When they called your number you had to go."[27] Women have also testified that when they became pregnant they were refused abortions.[28] In other words, they were specifically raped with the goal of impregnation, although crucially the aim was not to produce Serbian children—as many have claimed—but to heap further shame on the raped women. In Bosnian society, where ethnicity is derived from the father, children born of rape are stigmatized as illegitimate.[29] In many cases women were imprisoned to be raped until they became pregnant. Some women induced their own abortions, while others were forced to make the choice of either abandoning or keeping their children. Young girls—assumed to be virgins—were especially targeted, as were particularly well-educated and prominent women. The aim was to destroy communities and to ensure that Muslims would leave and never return. Family members were made to witness the rape and murder of other family members. In addition, they were forced to rape each other. Evidence exists that some men were also subject to sexual violence; they were raped, compelled to perform fellatio, forcibly circumcised, and in some cases, castrated.[30] According to the Zagreb Medical Centre for Human Rights, approximately 4,000 Croat male prisoners were sexually tortured in Serbian detention camps.[31] The purpose of this widespread sexual violence was to obliterate non-Serbian ethnicity and replace it with a dominant ethnically homogenous Serbian state. For the men who took part in the mass rapes, it also served to reinforce their masculine identity. Lisa S. Price writes that for the perpetrator, the act of rape states: "I AM only to the extent that you are not—male because you are female, Serb because you are Muslim, soldier because you are civilian. Your absence makes, verifies my presence and your pain becomes my power."[32]

The impact of sexual violence cannot be overstated. Human Rights Watch believes that in Rwanda every woman who survived the genocide experienced sexual violence.[33] Girls as young as six years old were raped in front of their families. The perpetrators were ordinary men—fathers, husbands, and sons—who became implicated in the genocide: who became rapists as an instrument of war. Women had their breasts mutilated and their vaginas and pelvic regions penetrated with machetes, arrows and other weapons such as sticks, broken bottles, knives, and gun barrels, before being forced into sexual slavery by the Hutu militia—to be sold, traded, or proffered as a reward—or dragooned into domestic servitude. They also had physical features that were said to look particularly "Tutsi," such as long fingers or thin noses, disfigured or cut off. As in Bosnia, men and boys were also targets of sexual violence. In addition to suffering genital mutilation, they were forced to rape Tutsi women. While the vast majority of female victims were Tutsi, Hutu women married to Tutsi men, or those who tried to help their Tutsi neighbors, were not immune from sexual violence.[34] In Rwanda—as in Bosnia—women were quite literally raped to death. Other women were left to be raped by yet more men or shunned and killed because of their status as victims of rape. The women who survived rape continued to suffer not only the physical harm meted out to them,[35] but also unwanted pregnancies and the stigmatization that followed; sexually transmitted diseases, including HIV/AIDS; isolation; and all manner of mental health problems.[36] Crucially, however, despite their horrific ordeals, victims of rape in both Bosnia and Rwanda have nonetheless battled social stigma and come forward to report the sexual violence they were forced to endure.[37]

The evidence from the Rwandan genocide raises important—and troubling—questions for the historian of the Holocaust. That large numbers of rape victims in the former have testified, while very few in the latter recorded an experience of sexual violence, is surely noteworthy at the very least. More than this, it casts into doubt the reasoning of Holocaust scholars like Helene Sinnreich that the shame, fear, and embarrassment associated with rape has deterred serious research into the issue.[38] It can be argued that the Holocaust happened over half a century ago, and researchers are now much more open to hearing stories of rape and sexual abuse. The impact of shame as well as the influence of religious or cultural taboos on talking about these issues, however, must not be overstated. Indeed, many of the most candid discussions of rape, sexual abuse, and "sex for survival" were published in the immediate aftermath of the Holocaust. The Holocaust scholar Na'ama Shik argues that this is because survivors were not yet affected by the culture of "blaming the victim."[39] To some degree, this overlooks the extent to which women did encounter suspicion and unease at their very survival. Nonetheless, Sinnreich is right to highlight the importance of sociocultural factors in testifying to rape. For example, in societies such as Afghanistan and Iraq, women have been reluctant to reveal that sexual violence has taken place for fear of bringing shame on their entire family. Holocaust survivors—particularly those from an Orthodox Jewish community—might have shared similar concerns. A critical difference remains that most Holocaust survivors of sexual violence—unlike their Rwandan counterparts—did not have to live in close proximity to their abusers or their abusers' families, nor did they continue to be economically dependent on them, after the mass atrocities ended. This reality has affected Rwandan rape survivors and is reflected in the ambiguity surrounding the exact number of victims; although many Tutsi victims of rape have testified to sexual violence, many more have stayed silent because the costs of breaking this silence are high. This was not true for women victims of sexual violence who survived the Holocaust.

Crimes of sexual violence are rightly considered to be a key part of the genocides in both the former Yugoslavia and Rwanda. Importantly, the Rwandan and Yugoslav tribunals that followed the genocides made rape prosecutable under humanitarian law. It is clear that much work remains to be done in bringing justice—any kind of justice—to the victims. Nevertheless, it is essential that rape and sexualized violence should not be overstated and allowed to overshadow the myriad of other sufferings endured by women during war and genocide.[40] Strikingly, despite the appalling sexual violence endured by so many, women in the former Yugoslavia have complained that researchers are interested in their experiences only insofar as they testify to rape, forced impregnation, or prostitution and are not interested in hearing about the wider experiences of life as a refugee. Displaced women have to endure all manner of sufferings including forced exile, material losses, the loss of their husbands (and often the family breadwinner), the stress of waiting for the missing to return, and so on.[41] Although there is now the presumption of sexual violence in war-torn countries such as Darfur, the Democratic Republic of the Congo, and Syria, we do not really know how widespread it is. Despite the many human rights organizations and women's groups committed to compiling reports, in many instances we lack the crucial, hard documentary evidence needed to prove "genocidal rape." Indeed, rape in and of itself is difficult to prove, as victims are often unwilling or unable to report it.

What we *do* know, though, is that women—like children—are most certainly particularly vulnerable when it comes to war and genocide. In most cultures it is women who suffer disproportionately in times of austerity—for example, eschewing food so that others can eat. This affects not only their health but also their chances of survival. Their predicament worsens when their men are forced to flee, conscripted into armies, or killed, and women are left alone to look after not only the children but also the sick and the elderly. Forced displacement also means that women often lack the networks of support they have hitherto relied upon. In the Nazi ghettos, women were forced to engage in increasingly dangerous activities in order to support their families, including prostitution and smuggling. Reports from humanitarian camps following the latest wave of humanitarian and human-made disasters suggest that these survival strategies remain mostly unchanged. And, as recent history has demonstrated, the presence of peacekeeping troops and humanitarian agencies can be a double-edged sword. For example, in the former Yugoslavia it is now clear that both peacekeepers and aid workers exploited women by supporting prostitution and encouraging human trafficking. Prostitution exposes women not only to sexual violence but also to diseases such as HIV/AIDS.[42] Women in refugee camps are particularly vulnerable to infectious diseases as they often lack basic necessities such as clean water, nutritious food, and access to health care.

It is perhaps unsurprising that the genocides in the former Yugoslavia and Rwanda have encouraged more Holocaust survivors to come forward and tell their stories. Furthermore, some of these more recent testimonies talk about rape and sexual abuse—although rarely in the first person. To what extent this is due to increased awareness and understanding of sexual violence is difficult to say. Certainly, it is only in the last twenty years or so that the shaving and tattooing of new inmates in the Nazi concentration camps have specifically been recognized as examples of sexualized violence. However, we do have to be careful about reading rape *back* into genocide— of appropriating experiences as examples of sexual abuse when this was not the case. While historians have to be able to read between the lines—to identify gaps and silences in the historical record and to speak for women whose experiences are often regarded as unvoiceable—we need to be sure that we do not impose our own concerns and preoccupations. Although it is very clear that *some forms of sexual violence* and degradation as well as the dehumanization of women were an essential part of the Nazi persecution of the Jews, the actual physical act of raping Jewish women was not only not a specific genocidal policy; it was legislated against. Thus, any coherent analysis of sexual violence during the Holocaust remains elusive at best. Indeed, the Holocaust clearly remains one of the very few examples of war and genocide when rape was unequivocally not used as a deliberate strategy of warfare.

Notes

1   For a discussion of forced impregnation as an act of genocide, see Siobhán K. Fisher, "Occupation of the Womb: Forced Impregnation as Genocide," *Duke Law Journal* 46:1 (1996), pp. 91–133.

2   See Amnesty International, "Bosnia-Herzegovina, Rape and Sexual Abuse by Armed Forces" (1993). Available online: http://www.amnesty.org/en/library/info/EUR63/001/1993; Beverly Allen, *Rape Warfare: The Hidden Genocide in Bosnia-Herzegovina and Croatia* (Minneapolis, MN: University of Minnesota Press, 1996); Alexandra Stiglmayer, ed., *Mass Rape: The War Against Women in Bosnia-Herzegovina*, trans. Marion Faber (Lincoln, NE: University of Nebraska Press, 1994). For a feminist perspective on women's experiences of war in Bosnia-Herzegovina, see Sara Sharratt and Ellyn Kaschak, eds., *Assault on the Soul: Women in the Former Yugoslavia* (New York, NY: The Haworth Press, 1999).

3   Cited in Jacques Semelin, *Purify and Destroy: The Political Uses of Massacre and Genocide*, trans. Cynthia Schoch (London, UK: Hurst & Company, 2005).

See the International Criminal Tribunal for the former Yugoslavia website (judgment Kunarac et al.). Available online: http://www.un.org/icty.

4 For a thorough account of the genocide, see Alison Des Forges, "*Leave None to Tell the Story*": *Genocide in Rwanda* (New York, NY: Human Rights Watch, 1999). On the atrocities committed against Tutsi women during the genocide, see Binaifer Nowrojee, *Shattered Lives: Sexual Violence during the Rwandan Genocide and Its Aftermath* (New York, NY: Human Rights Watch, 1996). Available online: http://hrw.org/reports/1996/09/24/shattered-lives; and Elenor Richter-Lyonette, "Women After the Genocide in Rwanda," in *In the Aftermath of Rape: Women's Rights, War Crimes and Genocide*, ed. Elenor Richter-Lyonette (Givrins, Switzerland: Coordination of Women's Advocacy, 1997), pp. 119–23.

5 For a discussion of the case against Jean-Paul Akayesu, see Jessica A. Hubbard, "Justice for Women? Rape as Genocide and the International Criminal Tribunal for Rwanda," in *Rape: Weapon of War and Genocide*, ed. Carol Rittner and John K. Roth (St. Paul, MN: Paragon House, 2012), pp. 101–16.

6 See Zoë Waxman, "Testimony and Silence: Sexual Violence and the Holocaust," in *Feminism, Literature and Rape Narratives*, ed. Sorcha Gunne and Zoë Brigley Thompson (London, UK: Routledge, 2010), pp. 117–29; Zoë Waxman, "Rape and Sexual Abuse in Hiding," in *Sexual Violence Against Women during the Holocaust*, ed. Sonja M. Hedgpeth and Rochelle G. Saidel (Waltham, MA: Brandeis University Press, 2010), pp. 124–35.

7 See Annabelle Baldwin, "Sexual Violence and the Holocaust: Reflections on Memory and Witness Testimony," *Holocaust Studies: A Journal of Culture and History* 16:3 (2010), pp. 112–34.

8 In Rwanda, however, there are recorded cases of women inciting men to rape. For example, Pauline Nyiramasuhuko, former minister of the Family and Promotion of Women, was charged by the ICTR for complicity in rape as a crime against humanity. See African Rights, *Not So Innocent: When Women Become Killers* (London, UK: African Rights, 1995); cf. Tara McKelvey, ed., *One of the Guys: Women as Aggressors and Torturers* (Emeryville, CA: Seal Press, 2007); Lisa Sharlach, "Gender and Genocide in Rwanda: Women as Agents and Objects of Genocide," *Journal of Genocide Research* 1:3 (1999), pp. 387–99. More recently in Iraq, Guantánamo, and Afghanistan, US servicewomen were exposed as engaging in the sexual humiliation of prisoners. Private Lynndie England was famously photographed at the Baghdad Correctional Facility (Abu Ghraib) holding a naked Iraqi man on a leash. For more on this, see T. Osborn-Kaufman, "Gender Trouble at Abu Ghraib," *Politics and Gender* 1:4 (2005), pp. 597–619.

9 Convention on the Prevention and Punishment of the Crime of Genocide, December 9, 1949, 78 U.N.T.S. 277. Article 2 defines genocide as "any of the following acts committed with intent to destroy, in whole or in part, a national, ethnical, racial or religious group, as such: (a) killing members of the group; (b) causing serious bodily or mental harm to members of the group; (c) deliberately inflicting on the group conditions of life calculated to bring about is physical destruction in whole or in part; (d) imposing measures intended to prevent births within the group; (e) forcibly transferring children of the group to another group." See Catherine A. MacKinnon, *Are Women Human? And*

Other Dialogues (Cambridge, MA: Harvard University Press, 2006), p. 350; cf. Christine Chinkin, "Rape and Sexual Abuse of Women in International Law," *European Journal of International Law* 5:1 (1994), pp. 326–41; Christoph Schiessel, "An Element of Genocide: Rape, Total War, and International Law in the Twentieth Century," *Journal of Genocide Research* 4:2 (2010), pp. 197–210.

10 Catherine A. MacKinnon, "Rape, Genocide, and Women's Human Rights," *Harvard Women's Law Journal* 17 (1994), pp. 11–12.

11 See Raul Hilberg, *Destruction of the European Jews*, 2nd edn (New York, NY: Meier, 1985), pp. 190–1.

12 See Regina Mühläuser, *Eroberungen. Sexuelle Gewalttaten und intime Beziehungen deutscher Soldaten in der Sowjetunion 1941-1945* (Hamburg, Germany: Hamburger Edition, 2010).

13 Wendy Lower, "'Anticipatory Obedience' and the Nazi Implementation of the Holocaust in the Ukraine: A Case Study of Central and Peripheral Forces in the Generalbezirk Zhytomer, 1941–1944," *Holocaust and Genocide Studies* 16:1 (2002), p. 8.

14 Regina Mühläuser, "'Racial Awareness' and Fantasies of Potency," in *Brutality and Desire: War and Sexuality in Europe's Twentieth Century*, ed. Dagmar Herzog (New York, NY: Palgrave Macmillan, 2009), pp. 197–221.

15 Helen Fein, "Genocide and Gender: the Uses of Women and Group Destiny," *Journal of Genocide Research* 1:1 (1999), p. 53.

16 Anatoly Podolsky, "The Tragic Fate of Ukrainian Jewish Women during the Holocaust," in *Sexual Violence against Women during the Holocaust*, ed. Sonja M. Hedgpeth and Rochelle G. Saidel (Waltham, MA: Brandeis University Press, 2010), pp. 94–108.

17 Ibid., pp. 98–9.

18 There were official brothels in Auschwitz-Birkenau, Buchenwald, Mauthausen, Gusen, Dora-Mittelbau, Dachau, and Ravensbrück.

19 Cited in Helene J. Sinnreich, "The Rape of Jewish Women during the Holocaust," in *Sexual Violence against Jewish Women during the Holocaust*, ed. Hedgepeth and Saidel, p. 111.

20 Doris Bergen, "Sexual Violence in the Holocaust: Unique and Typical?" in *Lessons and Legacies VII: the Holocaust in International Context*, ed. Dagmar Herzog (Evanston, IL: Northwestern University Press, 2006), p. 188.

21 See Dagmar Herzog, "Sexual Violence against Men," in *Rape: Weapon of War and Genocide*, ed. Rittner and Roth, p. 39.

22 The term "sex for survival" comes from Myrna Goldenberg. See Myrna Goldberg, "Rape during the Holocaust," in *The Legacy of the Holocaust: Women and the Holocaust*, ed. Z. Mazur, J. T. Lees, A. Krammer, and W. Witalisz (Kraków, Poland: Jagiellonian University Press, 2005), pp. 159–69.

23 See World Health Organization, "Sexual Violence," in *World Report on Violence and Health* (Geneva, Switzerland: World Health Organization, 2002).

24 On this subject see, Ellen Ben-Sefer, "Forced Sterilization and Abortion as Sexual Abuse," in *Sexual Violence against Women during the Holocaust*, ed. Hedgpeth and Saidel, pp. 156–75.

25 See the testimony of inmate physician Gisella Perl, *I Was a Doctor in Auschwitz* (New York, NY: International Universities Press, 1984), pp. 80–2.

26 Euan Hague, "Rape, Power and Masculinity: The Construction of Gender and National Identities in the War in Bosnia-Herzegovina," in *Gender and Catastrophe*, ed. Ronit Lentin (London, UK: Zed Books, 1997), pp. 50–63; cf., Karen Engle, "Feminism and its (Dis)contents: Criminalizing Wartime Rape in Bosnia-Herzegovina," *The American Journal of International Law* 99:4 (2005), pp. 778–816; Cindy S. Snyder, Wesley J. Gabbard, Dean May and Nihada Zulćić, "On the Battleground of Women's Bodies: Mass Rape in Bosnia-Herzegovina," *Affilia* 21 (2006), pp. 184–95; Todd Salzman, "Rape Camps, Forced Impregnation, and Ethnic Cleansing," in *War's Dirty Secret: Rape, Prostitution, and Other Crimes Against Women*, ed. Anne Llewellyn Barstow (Cleveland, OH: Ohio University Press, 2000).

27 Grace Halsell, "Women's Bodies a Battlefield in War for 'Greater Serbia,'" *Washington Report on Middle East Affairs* 11:9 (1993), p. 9.

28 United Nations Security Council, "Rape and Sexual Assault," in *Final Report of the United Nations Commission of Experts Established Pursuant to Security Council Resolution 780* (1992), S/1994/674/Add. 2. Vol. V. (New York, NY: United Nations, 1994), annex IX, IC. For further testimonies, see Seada Vranic, *Breaking the Wall of Silence: The Voices of Raped Bosnia* (Zagreb, Croatia: Anti Barbarus, 1996).

29 Semelin, *Purify and Destroy*, p. 294.

30 See Mladen Lonçar, "Sexual Torture of Men in the War," in *War Violence, Trauma and the Coping Process: Armed Conflict in Europe and the Survivor Response*, ed. Libby Tata Arcel (Copenhagen, Denmark: University of Copenhagen Press, 1998), pp. 45–79; Pauline Oosterhoff, Prisca Zwanikken, and Evert Ketting, "Sexual Torture of Men in Croatia and Other Conflict Situations: An Open Secret," *Reproductive Health Matters* 12 (2004), pp. 68–77.

31 Cited in Janie L. Leatherman, *Sexual Violence and Armed Conflict* (Cambridge, UK: Polity Press, 2011), p. 46.

32 Lisa S. Price, "Finding the Man in the Soldier-Rapist: Some Reflections on Comprehension and Accountability," *Women's Studies International Forum* 24:2 (2001), p. 213.

33 Nowrojee, *Shattered Lives*.

34 Ibid.

35 For example, women who experience violent rape can be left with incontinence or "fistulas"—a rupture between the vagina, rectum, and bladder. Without complex reconstructive surgery some women are left permanently infertile.

36 It has been estimated that more than 67 percent of the women raped during the Rwandan genocide were infected with HIV/AIDS. Cited in Rittner and Roth, *Rape: Weapon of War and Genocide* (St. Paul, MN: Paragon House, 2012), p. x.

37 For testimonies of Rwandan survivors of sexual violence, see Anne-Marie de Brouwer and Sandra Ka Hon Chu, eds., *The Men Who Killed Me: Rwandan Survivors of Sexual Violence* (Vancouver, Canada: Douglas & McIntyre, 2009).

38 Sinnreich, "The Rape of Jewish Women during the Holocaust," p. 8; cf.,
    Sinnreich, "'And it was Something We Didn't Talk About': Rape of Jewish
    Women during the Holocaust," *Holocaust Studies: A Journal of Culture and
    History* 14:2 (2008), pp. 1–22; in a previous article, I too have argued: "The
    mostly female [Holocaust] victims of sexual violence were not only unlikely
    to have survived, but the few that did have largely stayed silent about their
    experiences. This stems from cultural taboos regarding public discussion of
    rape and sexual abuse, and also because such experiences are not considered
    to be part of the narrative of the Holocaust." See Waxman, "Testimony and
    Silence," p. 118.

39 Na'ama Shik, "Sexual Abuse of Jewish Women in Auschwitz-Birkenau," in
    Brutality and Desire: War and Sexuality in Europe's Twentieth Century, ed.
    Dagmar Herzog (New York, NY: Palgrave Macmillan, 2009), pp. 221–46; cf.,
    Ralph Segalman, "The Psychology of Jewish Displaced Persons," *Jewish Social
    Service Quarterly* 23:4 (1947), pp. 363–5.

40 On this subject, see Adam Jones, ed., *Gender and Genocide* (Nashville, TN:
    Vanderbilt University Press, 2004).

41 The Serbian antimilitarist feminist group, "Women in Black," has published
    a collection of testimonies from Serbian, Croatian, Bosnian, and Kosovar-
    Albanian women, which offers a wider account of women's wartime
    experiences. See Lina Vušković, and Zorica Trifunović, eds., *Women's Side of
    War* (Belgrade, Serbia: Women in Black, 2010).

42 See also Sarah Elizabeth Mendelson, *Barracks and Brothels: Peacekeepers and
    Human Trafficking in the Balkans* (Washington, DC: Centre for Strategic and
    International Studies, 2005).

5

Constructions of Identity and Sexual Violence in Wartime: The Case of Bosnia

Patricia A. Weitsman

Writing about birth in the face of mass death, or genocide, has an irony that should not be lost on anyone. In the face of mass slaughter, policies of sexual violence sometimes culminate in wide-scale rape as witnessed in Rwanda, Congo, and Bangladesh, to mention just a few examples. In the case of the wars in the former Yugoslavia, wholesale slaughter of identity groups went hand in hand with forced impregnation campaigns. These policies, undertaken for the purpose of actually eliminating, biologically, an ethnic or religious group, culminate in the proliferation of said group, because identity is not strictly paternally conveyed. So, while it is counterintuitive to have a chapter on war babies in a book on gender and genocide, frequently "genocidal campaigns" result in thousands of babies born of wartime—as many as 10,000 in Rwanda.[1] In Bosnia, during the Serbian assault in the 1990s, forced impregnation camps gave rise to uncounted thousands of children born of rape. The fate of these children is largely unknown, unspoken of, and relegated to an identity of shame.

Making sense of wartime sexual violence is predicated on an understanding of identity. While contrary perhaps to foundational beliefs about rape, rape in wartime is often seen not solely as violence of man against woman but as about one ethnic group against another. This chapter explores the notion of identity and its contextual nature and then applies this understanding to the case of Bosnia. I focus specifically on the Serb war against Bosnian Muslim women. I argue that, just as scholars advance the idea that ethnic conflict may occur as a consequence of ethnic identities, sexual violence in such situations arises not only from these identities but also from local understandings of masculinity, femininity, and the patriarchal nature of social and political organizations. Many ethnic identities contain within them understandings of matri- or patrilineal sources. This content is as important as the identities themselves in determining the nature and character of sexual violence in wartime.

Identity

The concept of identity is as malleable and contextual as are identities themselves. As James Fearon writes, "Our present idea of 'identity' is a fairly recent social construct, and a rather complicated one at that."[2] Despite the salience of identities and their power to produce action, sometimes violent, we are some distance from a universally accepted understanding of how we conceptualize and define them. Most definitions of identity assert a social category to which an individual may or may not belong.[3] As Fearon and David Laitin helpfully explain, identity refers to a social category, entailing groups of individuals who have labels, differentiated by two central characteristics:

> (1) rules of membership that decide who is and is not a member of the category; and (2) content, that is, sets of characteristics (such as beliefs, desires, moral commitments, and physical attributes) thought to be typical of members of the category, or behaviors expected or obliged of members in certain situations (roles). We would also include in content the social valuation of members of this category relative to others (contestation over which is often called "identity politics").[4]

Moreover, in regard to ethnic identities, Anthony Smith writes, "There can be no identity without memory."[5] In other words, identities are constructed by substance and narrative, with rules that determine if one fits or does not fit into a particular group.

The emphasis on identity and ethnic groups is important. Equally important, however, for understanding action is the content of those identities and the beliefs within them about social hierarchy and governance. In other words, we can delineate the identity of who is a Jew by examining the rules of who is and who is not a Jew—that is, the birth mother must be Jewish—and the substance of the beliefs in regard to being Jewish. What may be less obvious are the embedded beliefs about patriarchy and the value of women within the group's religious observances and practices, even while the role of gender in determining membership in this identity group is understood. While these are nearly impossible to refine into a snapshot of the identity practices, they become important in the context of the nature of campaigns of sexual violence in wartime and the way in which the identity of the children born of rape in wartime is viewed.

What is distinctive about the sexual violence campaigns in the wars in the former Yugoslavia is that they were undertaken with an eye to impregnating principally Bosnian Muslim women in order to force them to bear Serbian children.[6] Such campaigns can only result when there is a particular construct of identity and a particular understanding of how identity is derived. In other words, the Serbian government and militias believed that impregnating Bosnian women would lead these women to bear Serb children through forced "occupation of the womb."[7] These narratives obviate any maternal contribution to a child's identity. In contrast, the Nazis believed that any drop of impure blood would culminate in an impure child, irrespective of which parent the taint was derived from. The protagonists' beliefs about the biological roots of identity are essential for understanding state policies of sexual violence in wartime.[8]

Interestingly, there are voluminous literatures on identity and ethnic conflict and growing literatures on women and war and sexual violence in wartime. Yet there are many unanswered questions. For example, how beliefs about gender—in terms of social and political hierarchy and in regard to identity formation—are important causal mechanisms in the way that sexual violence manifests in wartime.[9]

How Gender Matters

When patriarchal beliefs about the role and status of women prevail in a nation under siege, rape during warfare culminates in shame, abandonment, and disenfranchisement for the women who have endured these assaults. Furthermore, children born of these rape campaigns are frequently shunned, abused, or abandoned.[10] What this means is that rape campaigns during wartime are a highly effective means of disrupting and punishing an enemy population. The woman is assaulted, victimizing her, but her family is also victimized because of the shame brought upon them by the assault and by any progeny that result.[11]

A central point here is that ethnic identity matters powerfully—but within those social groups, gender does as well. There are circumscribed roles and understandings that go along with those gender roles within a particular social or ethnic group identity. That is to say, an identity such as American Jew is a distinct social grouping and identity, but within that group there are designated roles specifically for men and for women. The *mikvah*, for example, may be an essential component and practice of an American Jewish woman but not (at least in the same way) for an American Jewish man. So, while the literature addresses ethnic identity and ethnic conflict, gender must be a part of these analyses, not only to understand those roles and their interplay, but also to understand how war campaigns are conceived and executed. Policies of sexual violence in wartime are predicated on these conceptions of gender roles within the larger context of ethnic identity. The degree to which such campaigns are effective in destroying and degrading the adversary, and the reasons such policies are crafted in the first place, are based on an understanding of ethnic identity as seen through the prism of gender roles and social hierarchies.

In the following sections of this chapter, I review the case of Bosnia in regard to identity, gender roles, the policies of sexual violence in the war, forced impregnation camps, the status of the children born of rape, and the human rights of the child.

The Case of Bosnia

The end of the Communist era in Eastern Europe brought turbulence and restructuring within the region that had been the "Eastern bloc" throughout the Cold War. The future of Yugoslavia, in particular, was uncertain and precarious. At the end of the Second World War, Josef Tito was instrumental in establishing the Yugoslav state. Under his governance, nationalism did not disappear, but it was tamped down so effectively that peaceful coexistence prevailed. With the death of Tito in 1980, no one capable of continuing this practice of unity came to the national fore. Instead, local parties vied for political power, many playing on nationalism and ethnic divisions to mobilize populations.[12] This triggered the breakdown of the Yugoslav state.

In July 1991, Slovenia and Croatia declared their independence, resulting in war between Croatia and the Yugoslav state and between Yugoslavia and Slovenia. By early 1992, a tenuous peace was forged, but shortly thereafter, Bosnia-Herzegovina declared independence. This brought about a civil war among Serbs, Croats, and Muslims in Bosnia that lasted for several years. Somewhere in the vicinity of 200,000 people died, two million people were left homeless, and tens of thousands of women and girls were raped. During the years of the civil war, there was no refuge—in the UN safe haven of Srebrenica alone, more than 8,000 men and boys were massacred.[13] Mass graves were uncovered for years after the violence ended. Bodies are still being exhumed, and efforts to identify the victims continue.[14]

Ethnicity, Identity, and Gender

The academic literature on the wars in the former Yugoslavia contests the "ancient hatreds" narrative that pervaded the media during the wars. This narrative stated that ethnic tension simmered beneath the surface and came to the fore with the death of Tito and the implosion of the Soviet Union.[15] However, the facts remain that the violence in former Yugoslavia was targeted against specific social groups, and within those groups, women were targeted with a particular brand of violence. Even if the struggle in the former Yugoslavia was for political and economic power, political actions utilized ethnicity to incite violence. The fault lines of conflict fell along ethnic cleavages, and given the distinct nature of sexual violence in the war that is the focus of this chapter—namely, forced impregnation camps—there is clearly a gendered aspect to the way these identities were experienced and perceived by others. The way in which those identities were understood and the way in which gender played into those identities are central to understanding the nature and form that this violence took.

The nexus of gender and identity is explored by Cynthia Cockburn, who writes of her research on the topic:

> As to *identity*, my hunch was quickly confirmed. The women were suffering a lot of what I came to think of as "identity hurt." The pain occurred where there was friction and disjuncture between a woman's sense of self and the identities with which she was labelled, that she was held to account for, or felt seduced by.[16]

As Cockburn asserts, the point of this chapter is to underscore the "connections between the oppression that is the ostensible cause of a conflict (ethnic or national oppression) in the light of another cross-cutting one: that of the gender regime."[17] Once uncovered, it becomes clear that societal views of gender and gender roles are instrumental in policy formation regarding strategies of sexual violence in wartime, but more globally as well in regard to citizenship, nationality, and belonging.[18]

In the former Yugoslavia, as in other patriarchal societies, ethnic identity was viewed as imparted largely by the father. In mixed marriages, the identity of the child was most often dictated by paternity. This became highly problematic once war came, as their mothers were viewed as traitors by their own ethnic group and were rejected by the ethnic group of their husbands.[19] Both groups similarly rejected the children of mixed heritage. Paradoxically, while women procreating to produce children in mixed marriages were marginalized, women were perceived as essential in bolstering the nation-state as mothers. As Julie Mostov underscores, state policy and edicts regarding a woman's place in society highlighted their centrality in national survival and the hazards of women being led astray from this crucial role of preserving and advancing the nation-state.[20]

Widespread patriarchal assumptions culminated in a perception that women were vessels for paternal identity. They also generated the view that women's identities were inherently dictated by their relationship to men: as daughters, wives, and mothers. Serb women in Bosnia married to Bosnian Muslim men were rejected by the Serbian state since they belonged to their husbands. These women faced repercussions from their own ethnic groups as well as the groups into which they married, even in the days leading up to the implosion.[21]

The malleability of identity and its manipulation by governmental and social forces are remarkable. This is well illustrated by an anecdote that R. Charli Carpenter relates. Carpenter writes of a social worker in Bosnia-Herzegovina who told the story of a woman who was raped in Bosnia, fled to Serbia, and tried to pass herself off as Serb. The woman gave birth to a child whom she left at an orphanage. The orphanage returned the child to the mother, saying the child could not stay because the child was not Serb. Upon returning to Bosnia, the baby was labeled a "*chetnik*" and rejected. The woman ultimately brought the child to another orphanage in Sarajevo. At this point, the child, likely around age three, had been in the mother's care and given up to orphanages twice.[22] A Serbian institution deems a child not Serb: a child conceived of wartime rape from a campaign designed to bring Serbian children into the world. His mother's community rejects the same child. And, ultimately, the mother rejects the child, demonstrating in a profound way the abnegation of the child's identity connection to his mother and the ambiguity of his identity.

So what is ethnic identity? Is it constituted in the social beliefs of a community? Is it enshrined in national policy of citizenship? Does it form the foundation of nationalism? I would argue that identity is all of these things but that it is experienced differently for women, men, and children. In the former Yugoslav case, the identity of women who had been raped was derived from both nationality and the view of women as vessels for paternal identity. For men, identity was derived from nationality and from being seen as the enemy. This is a classic wartime gender dichotomy—men as soldiers; women as mothers. The common identity of children born of rape was based on the circumstances of their conception; they were considered to be neither Bosnian Muslim nor Serb. Yet in reality, the offspring of the victim and perpetrator was both ethnicities, not neither ethnicity. This socially constructed understanding of identity makes generalizing about it across gender and across age groups problematic. Gender stereotypes make a dramatic difference in how wars are experienced. As summarized in the International Criminal Tribunal for the former Yugoslavia (ICTY) judgment against Kunarac et al., witnesses described what happened to the men after they were caught fleeing:

> The men, seven of them, were separated from the women. At some point, while they were being led away, the women were told to lie down and bursts of gunfire were heard coming from the place where the men had been detained. They later learnt that these men had been killed, and these witnesses never saw those men again.[23]

Men were massacred. Women were detained, often for long periods, and subjected to rape and, sometimes, forced impregnation and maternity.

Policies of Sexual Violence and Forced Impregnation and Maternity

There are a number of ways in which government "identity" policies became manifest during the Bosnian civil war. These policies generally entailed limiting the rights or civil liberties of some segment of the population, restricting their movement, or requiring them to bear some mark of their identity, either on their persons or on their identification papers.[24] In the case of Bosnian Muslims in the Foča municipality, for example, witnesses in the Kunarac et al. case at the ICTY testified that the:

> freedom of movement of Muslim citizens was increasingly restricted, their communication limited and their gatherings banned. Public announcements prohibiting gatherings and informing the Muslims that they were not free to move around their villages were made. Roadblocks were set up, Muslim villagers were prevented from moving around town, and were sometimes put under house arrest.[25]

During this time, an increasingly aggressive and hostile propaganda campaign was launched via the media.[26]

In addition to policies that serve to make explicit the differences between the "self" identity and the "other," government policies sometimes go further, by seeking to craft a national identity through invasive policies of social or genetic engineering. These efforts may include a policy of forced maternity: the production of new babies whose identities are connected to their fathers. Alternately, a government or military group may attempt to eradicate completely a group whose identity is constructed as the enemy. The two extremes in this regard were forced impregnation camps in the former Yugoslavia and forced sterilizations of impure women during the Nazi reign of terror alongside policies prohibiting sexual relationships between Aryan and non-Aryan populations. The way in which governments understand and manipulate identity culminates in dictates that have profound repercussions during war and its aftermath.

In the case of the wars in the former Yugoslavia, the Serb militias directed substantial violence against Bosnian Muslim women.[27] In August 1992, two reporters, Roy Gutman and Ed Vulliamy, were able to gain access to the Omarska camp, located in the north of Bosnia.[28] They emerged with stories of the atrocities being committed in the camp; of torture, rape, castrations, and more: atrocities committed often against people known to the perpetrators.[29] Extreme, and often fatal, beatings took place.[30] At this one camp alone, thousands perished in the four months in 1992 that the camp was open. Camps of this kind were established throughout Bosnia, where women were segregated, held, and repeatedly raped, day after day, for months.

Some camps were designated specifically as rape camps, such as the one at Foča, a small town in Bosnia. In the summer of 1992, dozens of women were held there. The camp procedure was to bring some of the women to a detention center, such as Buk Bijela, to be raped by soldiers. After this initial period, the women were then taken to one of the main rape camps, including the Foča High School, which served as a short-term detention facility, and the Partizan Sports Hall, which was a longer term holding camp. Once in these camps, the women were raped repeatedly until they were pregnant, the idea being that these women would then produce "Serb" babies. At least forty women in Partizan became pregnant.[31] Women were raped so many times by so many soldiers that they could not testify as to the exact number. One witness estimated that, during her forty-day detention at Foča High School and Partizan, she was raped approximately 150 times.[32]

Mass rape and forced maternity were critical elements of the war in the former Yugoslavia. According to the final report of the United Nations Commission of Experts established pursuant to Security Council Resolution 789 (1992), there were about 162 detention sites in the former Yugoslavia where people were sexually violated.[33] At rape camps across the country, Bosnian Muslim women were held, repeatedly raped by numerous men, and then either killed or detained for further sustained sexual torture. Some women were raped by as many as forty men in one night; some women were gang-raped in this way, day after day, for months at a time.[34]

Serb authorities dictated the policy of mass rape and forced impregnation. Rape camps were established in nearly identical ways—even down to the layout of the camps—throughout Bosnia-Herzegovina, and the patterns of rape were the same. The rapes occurred in noncontiguous sections of Bosnia simultaneously.[35] In the words of one survivor, Rasema, who identified her neighbor as one of the three men who raped her, "I said, 'Sasha, remember your mother. Remember your sister. Don't do it.' He said, 'I must. If I do not they will hurt me. Because they have ordered me to.'"[36]

During the onslaught, non-Serb men were beaten, frequently to death. Torture, particularly in ways that emasculated men, was widespread. For example, Serb paramilitary groups "cut off detainees' penises and ears and forced other prisoners to ingest them. If a prisoner did not do so, he was killed."[37]

Men who survived initial attacks were often detained and subsequently executed, or transferred to areas under control by the Bosnian government. The women and girls were held, then sent to rape camps where conditions were appalling. Soldiers were ordered and granted access to these centers, where they selected and took girls and women whom they raped and tortured. Some women were taken to different houses within Foča and often enslaved by Serb soldiers. Some of the women were sold and never seen again. Many of these women were detained, tortured, and raped daily for months on end. Some witnesses in the case against Kunarac et al. (IT-96-23&23/1) testified that they had been raped so frequently that they were unable to determine how many times they had been violated.[38]

The mass rapes of Bosnian Muslim men and women were undertaken with the intention of humiliating, degrading, and torturing the victims. They were also undertaken with the purpose of forcibly impregnating women and ensuring the children were carried to term. In her testimony against Serb leader Radovan Karadzic and General Ratko Mladic in July 1996, Irma Oosterman, a member of the prosecution investigation team, said, "The soldiers told often that they were forced to do it. They did not say who forced them to do it, but they were ordered do it." Her testimony continues: "They wanted to make Serb or Chetnik babies. The pattern was, yes, all over the same."[39]

Further evidence that forced impregnation and maternity were goals of the Serbian authorities is provided by survivors' accounts. Narratives given by hundreds of women held at camps around Bosnia suggest that women were repeatedly raped and, once impregnated, held until abortion was no longer an option. In the words of one survivor of the Doboj camp,

> They said that each woman had to serve at least ten men a day. . . .God, what horrible things they did. They just came in and humiliated us, raped us, and later they told you, "Come on now, if you could have Ustasha babies, then you can have a Chetnik baby, too." . . . Women who got pregnant, they had to stay there for seven or eight months so they could give birth to a Serbian kid. They had their gynecologists there to examine the women. The pregnant ones were separated off from us and had special privileges; they got meals, they were better off, they were protected. Only when a woman's in her seventh month, when she can't do anything about it anymore, then she's released. Then they usually take these women to Serbia. . . . They beat the women who didn't get pregnant, especially the younger women; they were supposed to confess what contraceptives they were using.[40]

These accounts were repeated by many survivors. One survivor of a rape camp at Kalinovik, where about 100 women were held and gang-raped, recounted that the rapists continually told the women "you are going to have our children—you are going to have our little Chetniks" and that the women who became pregnant were left alone.[41]

Serbian policies of forced impregnation were undertaken with the purpose of generating "Serbian" babies. Women detained and forced to endure repeated gang rapes with the intention of impregnating them were repeatedly told that they were being raped in order "plant the seed of Serbs in Bosnia," to give birth to little "chetniks," to deliver a Serb baby, and so forth.[42] The soldiers who participated in these rapes told their victims over and again that they would be forced to bear children of the enemy, that abortion would be denied to them, that they would be detained until termination of the pregnancy was out of the question, and that the soldiers were implementing these policies of forced impregnation and maternity on orders from their superiors.[43]

It is widely accepted by scholars and practitioners of international politics that the use of mass rape, forced impregnation, and forced maternity were policies implemented as part of the broader Serbian goal of ethnic cleansing and even genocide.[44] While policies of mass rape may be used to humiliate and degrade a population to such an extent that people leave en masse, thereby advancing the goal of ethnic cleansing, rape with the intent of forcing women to bear children cannot be similarly construed. To do so is tantamount to accepting the view of identity that is being perpetuated by the rapists—that it is paternally derived—and denying the cultural and genetic connection between mother and child. Forced impregnation and maternity is contrary to the ends of true genocide: eliminating the genus of a racial or ethnic group.

The critical questions in this context are what constitutes identity and under what assumptions about identity were the Serbs operating? The most important set of assumptions is that identity is biologically derived and that women are vessels for transmitting paternal identity. The belief that Bosnian Muslim women would give birth to little "chetniks" assumes away the maternal contribution to the child's biological makeup, as well as her role in the child's upbringing, should enforced maternity result, should the child survive, and should the child not be placed in an orphanage or abandoned. This gives rise to another assumption that pervades the thinking about the policy of forced impregnation and enforced maternity as well as the representations of the policies in the media and beyond—namely, that biology trumps culture: nature over nurture. While hard data are scarce, in at least some of the cases of forced maternity, the mother of the child raises him or her. However, the learning and culture associated with the mother's childrearing is allegedly negated by the biological fact of the child's paternity. In many, if not most, cases of forced maternity, the identity of the father is unknown, either because the woman did not know her victimizer or, more likely, because there were so many rapists that it is impossible to identify who was the source of the impregnation. In such cases, it would be logical to see the maternal connection as paramount in forging the identity of the child. Yet this is generally not the case—these children are represented in their own countries and by the media as "genocidal babies," little "chetniks," "children of hate," or "children of shame."[45] In other words, the identity of the children continues to be linked to their rapist fathers, even if the paternal identity is completely unknown, even if the child never meets the father, or even if the child is cared for and raised by the child's mother.

This is a powerful message about identity: how it is perceived, constructed, and imagined. The ethnic identity of the father and the shame surrounding the conception are paramount. This reveals an additional assumption about identity that underpins the policies of mass rape, forced impregnation, and maternity: that women's contributions to the makeup and raising of their children are rendered meaningless in the face of the act of sexual violation that took place at conception. The lifelong responsibilities of raising a child are, in essence, negated by the acts of violence that culminated in conception and by the identity of the mother as a victim. This degrades both the experiences of women as well as the legacies of the violence—the war babies. This gives rise to egregious infringements on the human rights of these children from birth throughout their entire lives.

These policies of enforced impregnation and maternity privilege biology; yet, the biological roots of identity that the policies are predicated on are actually socially constructed. Even if a child is born of and raised by a Bosnian Muslim, his or her identity, nevertheless, is linked inextricably to the biological father. Yet, racially, Bosnian Muslims and Serbs are both Slavs, and they have virtually no genetic or biological distinctions. So, in this case, even the construction of biological difference is social and not material.[46] Furthermore, both communities—those of the rapist father as well as the biological mother—rejected these children.[47]

The assumptions that underpin the policy of rape warfare, forced impregnation, and forced maternity are that women's worth derives from their relationships to men and that the shame of victimization is far worse than the perpetration of the crime. Many Bosnian Muslim women who were raped during the civil war, even if not impregnated, were shamed and cast out by their own families.[48] This has important implications not only for identity but for gender politics as well. Shaming the victims more than the perpetrators indicates that women's value derives from "purity"—in other words, her relationship to men to the extent that she has not engaged in sexual intercourse—and that in the event of violation, again, her value is inextricably linked to the interposing of a man's body onto her own. In essence, a woman's identity never really stands alone; it is always juxtaposed by her sexual relationships to men, whether coercive or consensual. These assumptions must be in place to support a policy of mass rape; if not, this policy loses its coercive power and may not be as successful in driving families apart or securing the goal of ethnic cleansing.

Finally, the assumptions that are inherent in the policies of forced impregnation and maternity witnessed in the wars in the former Yugoslavia have a grave effect on the human rights of the babies born of the violence. This can be seen in a number of ways. First, the grievous effect of the undermining of the human rights of these children can be witnessed in the large incidence of infanticide and the acceptance of it as a natural product of the savagery of conception.[49] Second, the language used to describe the children is all derogatory labels that are linked to the rapist fathers. These labels stay with the children throughout their lives—again, their identity is inextricably linked to their biological fathers. This means that a cloud of shame hangs over them by virtue of circumstances beyond their control. Third, in the aftermath of the civil war, the Bosnian government refused to allow these children to be adopted overseas since they were seen as an important means of repopulating the country.[50] In other words, escape from the stigma of their birth was impossible.

The assumptions that underpin policies of mass rape, forced impregnation, and forced maternity are important as they represent how identity is perceived and constructed. These assumptions also inform us about gender inequities and the ways in which the human rights of war babies are violated from the moment of their births.

Status of Children Born of Rape

In the postwar countries of the former Yugoslavia, extensive efforts have been made to exhume the dead, extract DNA from bones, and identify the bodies taken from mass graves in an effort to bring closure to the families who may still be searching for their loved ones who disappeared during the war and were never seen again.[51] Forensic investigations at exhumation sites have been undertaken by the Office of the Prosecutor of the ICTY.[52] Further, the International Commission on Missing Persons (ICMP) was created in 1996 with a mandate to locate and identify people who disappeared during armed conflict or as a consequence of human rights violations. By 2013, the ICMP operated the world's largest "high-throughput" DNA human identification facility and as developed:

> a database of 89,086 relatives of 29,109 missing people, with more than 36,000 bone samples taken from mortal remains exhumed from clandestine graves in the countries of former Yugoslavia. By matching DNA from blood and bone samples, ICMP has been able to identify 16,289 people who were missing from the conflicts and whose mortal remains were found in hidden graves.[53]

In addition to the dedicated efforts to exhuming and identifying war victim remains, the reburials of those remains have been a meaningful and sobering ritual. For example, on July 11, 2012, the seventeenth anniversary of the Srebrenica massacre, more than 500 newly identified victims of the massacre were reburied at the Potocari memorial center in Bosnia. Over 30,000 people came to the ceremonial reburial to heal from what has been called "the worst atrocity in Europe since the end of World War II."[54]

The extensive efforts to memorialize the dead stand in dramatic contrast with the neglect of the children born of rape, who have been sold on the black market, abandoned, illegally adopted, abused, and marginalized. Very little systematic work to document their whereabouts and well-being has occurred. The exception to this is Medica Zenica, a nongovernmental organization that provides support to women and children victims of war, including rape survivors and human trafficking victims.[55]

The memorialization of the dead and the tributes to the victims who perished during the campaigns of violence are meaningful and important. Yet they highlight the lack of attention to, or documentation of, the children born of sexual assault during war; that is, the lives that emerged from the devastation. These exhumations and reburials are important in healing and reconciliation. They honor the dead. The commemorations are symbolic. In the case of the children born of sexual violence in war, a concerted approach to tracking and assisting could have had material results, not merely symbolic ones. The marginalization of these children allowed the crimes of war to continue long after the fighting was done.

Human Rights of the Child

The view that a child born of rape is a mirror of the rapist and takes on the identity of the rapist is pervasive. Given this, it is not a surprise that the rights of the child once born are nonexistent. R. Charli Carpenter's pathbreaking book, *Forgetting Children Born of War*, delineates the marginalization of children born of war, particularly in Bosnia-Herzegovina. She puzzles that while there is an increasing number of organizations that tend to the children in war-torn areas, these networks do not concern themselves with children born of wartime rape. Instead, the focus is on child soldiers, children caught in the crossfire; that is, war-affected children broadly, but not children born of rape specifically. In regard to children born of rape, the focal advocacy point, as Carpenter calls it, is the victims of rape, that is, their mothers.[56]

Anecdotes regarding the fate of the children born of rape pepper media reports of the war in the former Yugoslavia. One mother threw her newborn child into the Sava river.[57] Another snapped her baby's neck.[58] Many babies were simply abandoned at the hospitals where they were born; others were left in orphanages.[59]

The children born of rape in Bosnia are labeled, among other things, "a generation of children of hate."[60] These children take on the identity based on the circumstances of their conception, and as a result, their quality of life, unless they are adopted out of the country, is severely compromised.

The marginalization, abuse, neglect, and death of these children represent clear violations to their human rights. And yet, because they are born as a consequence of a human rights violation to their mother, their rights are largely compromised. As the ultimate weak and vulnerable actors, these children have no say in the paths their lives take.[61]

According to the United Nations Children's Emergency Fund (UNICEF), children have:

the right to survival; to develop to the fullest; to protection from harmful influences, abuse and exploitation; and to participate fully in family, cultural and social life.

Further, UNICEF highlights the core principles of the Convention on the Rights of the Child:

> The four core principles of the Convention are non-discrimination; devotion to the best interests of the child; the right to life, survival and development; and respect for the views of the child. Every right spelled out in the Convention is inherent to the human dignity and harmonious development of every child. The Convention protects children's rights by setting standards in health care; education; and legal, civil and social services.[62]

Yet the challenges facing these children born of war go largely unaddressed. This is in large part a consequence of the fact that the crime of forced maternity has been framed and viewed as a crime against the victim of the rape; that is, the mother. The children are simply evidence of the atrocity.[63]

Postwar Pronatalism

The malleability of identity and gender politics is illuminated through the lens of the fate of children born of rape in wartime. The rape campaigns during the war were undertaken in order to produce more Serbs. Yet, in the aftermath of the war in the former Yugoslavia, international adoptions of children born of rape in Bosnia were highly restricted; these children were viewed by the state as a key means of repopulating the country.[64]

The view of women as vessels of the state was pervasive in the former Yugoslavia, with calls for women to bear as many children as possible in the postwar years. The media and religious leaders all undertook efforts and edicts to spur women on to bear more children.[65] While these rallying cries are well documented in Serbian and Croatian communities, it is worth noting that during and after the war in Bosnia-Herzegovina, Islamic clergy called for Bosnian Muslim women to produce more children and to legalize polygamy to increase the birth rate. Cash rewards were given to women for bearing their third and fourth children.[66] Although these campaigns were largely ineffective at actually producing an increase in the birthrate, the manipulations of identity and gender in this way are important to note. They represent how identity can best be understood through the lens of gender.

Conclusion

Eliminating the genus of a people—a complete destruction of an ethnic, racial, or social group—requires the destruction of life givers. And yet, in areas of mass slaughter and ethnic cleansing, we frequently see mass rape.

The outcome of these campaigns is the birth of hundreds if not thousands of children whose identities revolve around the circumstances of what gave them life. In cases such as the former Yugoslavia, one goal of Serb militias was to force Bosnian Muslim women to bear their children. Forced maternity cannot constitute genocide—seeing it as such negates the maternal contribution to the child. Given that the pervasive understanding of these rape campaigns is, in fact, as a tool of genocide, this tells us much about the implicit understandings of identity and gender in societies where such narratives resonate.

We see from the former Yugoslavia case that the experience of genocide is markedly different for women than for men. In areas of the world where strong views exist on the role that women and men play in society, those views will translate in times of conflict into particular policies of sexual violence. Tragically, this often results in grievous infringements on the human rights of not one but two principals: mother and child. It is a near universal belief that children born of rape assume the identity of the father. Eve Ensler, feminist activist and author of the *Vagina Monologues*, wrote, "When it is born it has the face of your rapist, the face of the person who has essentially destroyed your being and you will have to look at the face every day of your life and you will be judged harshly if you cannot love that face."[67] Thousands of women in the former Yugoslavia were forced to bear these children. Constructing their identity as one with their rapist father provides a permissive environment for egregious abuse. Most of these children in the former Yugoslavia are and will always be unaccounted for, as the DNA matching for identifying the dead in the uncovered mass graves continues.

Notes

1 Patricia A. Weitsman, "The Politics of Identity and Sexual Violence: A Review of Bosnia and Rwanda," *Human Rights Quarterly* 3 (2008), pp. 30, 573.

2 James D. Fearon, "What is Identity (as We Now Use the Word)?" Mimeo, Stanford University, November 1999, http://www.stanford.edu/~jfearon/papers/iden1v2.pdf.

3 Kanchan Chandra, "What is Ethnic Identity and Does it Matter?" *Annual Review of Political Science* 9 (2006), pp. 397–424.

4 Weitsman, "The Politics of Identity and Sexual Violence," pp. 561–78; James D. Fearon and David D. Laitin, "Violence and the Social Construction of Ethnic Identity," *International Organizations* 4 (2000), pp. 54, 848.

5 Anthony D. Smith, *The Ethnic Origins of Nations* (Oxford, UK: Basil Blackwell, 1988), p. 2.

6 Patricia A. Weitsman, "Children Born of War and the Politics of Identity," in *Born of War: Protecting Children of Sexual Violence Survivors in Conflict Zones*, ed. R. Charli Carpenter (Bloomfield, CT: Kumarian Press, 2007), pp. 110–27; Weitsman, "The Politics of Identity and Sexual Violence."

7   Siobhan K. Fischer, "Occupation of the Womb: Forced Impregnation as Genocide," *Duke Law Journal* 46:1 (1996), pp. 91-133.

8   Weitsman, "Children Born of War and the Politics of Identity"; Weitsman, "The Politics of Identity and Sexual Violence."

9   By gender I mean biological gender, female or male in regard to reproductive capacity. Clearly this is a simplification of gender—I myself am a bone marrow transplant recipient and carry the DNA of my male donor (any blood test will tell you I am male) despite being a female who has given birth to two children—but for my purposes here, I am simply invoking man or woman in regard to reproductive capacities.

10 Weitsman, "Children Born of War and the Politics of Identity"; Weitsman, "The Politics of Identity and Sexual Violence."

11 See, for example, Andrew Solomon, "The Legitimate Children of Rape," *The New Yorker Blogs*, August 29, 2012. Available online: http://www.newyorker. com/online/blogs/newsdesk/2012/08/the-legitimate-children-of-rape.html.

12 Sabrina Stein, "The UN and Genocide: A Comparative Analysis of Rwanda and the former Yugoslavia," in *The Politics and Policies of Relief, Aid, and Reconstruction: Contrasting Approaches to Disasters and Emergencies*, ed. Fulvio Attina (Basingstoke, UK: Palgrave Macmillan, 2012), p. 180.

13 Daniel McGrory, "Ten Years On, Sarajevo Mourns Forgotten Dead," *The Times* (London, UK), April 6, 2002.

14 Damir Arsenijević, "Gendering the Bone: The Politics of Memory in Bosnia Herzegovina," *Journal for Cultural Research* 15:2 (2011), pp. 193–205, 194.

15 See, for example, V. P. Gagnon Jr., *The Myth of Ethnic War: Serbia and Croatia in the 1990s* (Ithaca, NY: Cornell University Press, 2004), pp. 31–3.

16 Cynthia Cockburn, *The Space between Us: Negotiating Gender and National Identity in Conflict* (London, UK: Zed Books, 1998), pp. 9–10.

17 Ibid., p. 8.

18 Joyce P. Kaufman, and Kristen P. Williams, *Women, the State and War: A Comparative Perspective on Citizenship and Nationalism* (Lanham, MD: Lexington Books, 2007), pp. 17–18.

19 Ibid., pp. 97–9.

20 Julie Mostov, "Sexing the Nation/Desexing the Body Politics of National Identity in the Former Yugoslavia," in *Gender Ironies of Nationalism: Sexing the Nation*, ed. Tamar Mayer (London, UK: Routledge, 2000).

21 Kaufman and Williams, *Women, the State and War*, pp. 99–100.

22 R. Charli Carpenter, *Forgetting Children Born of War* (New York, NY: Columbia University Press, 2010), pp. 29–30.

23 International Criminal Tribunal for the former Yugoslavia Judgment: Prosecutor *v.* Dragoljub Kunarac Radomir Kovac and Zoran Vukovic (accessed May 20, 2013), p. 20.

24 For an overview of the Bosnian civil war and its contemporary ramifications, see Gerard Toal and Carl T. Dahlman, *Bosnia Remade: Ethnic Cleansing and its Reversal* (New York, NY: Oxford University Press, 2011).

25 Prosecutor *v.* Dragoljub Kunarac Radomir Kovac and Zoran Vukovic, pp. 16–17.

26 Ibid., pp. 17, 204.

27 It is important for me to note here that while my focus is on the rape and forced impregnation of Bosnian Muslim women, there were numerous rapes committed against women of other ethnic groups as well as rapes of men. The principal targets of the sexual violence were Bosnian Muslim women, but by no means were they the only victims.

28 Kelly D. Askin, "Omarska Camp, Bosnia: Broken Promises of 'Never Again,'" *Human Rights Magazine* (American Bar Association, 2003).

29 Ed Vulliamy, "Middle Managers of Genocide," *The Nation*, June 10, 1996.

30 Ray Gutman, *A Witness to Genocide: The 1993 Pulitzer Prize-Winning Dispatches on the "Ethnic Cleansing" of Bosnia* (New York, NY: Macmillan Publishing Company, 1993).

31 Joanne Barkan, "As Old as War Itself: Rape in Foca," *Dissent* 49:1 (2002), p. 61; Gutman, *A Witness to Genocide*, pp. 164–7.

32 Prosecutor *v.* Dragoljub Kunarac Radomir Kovac and Zoran Vukovic, p. 26.

33 Final report of the United Nations Commission of Experts established pursuant to Security Council Resolution 789 (1992), Annex IX Rape and sexual assault, under the direction of M. Cherif Bassiouni, chairman and rapporteur on the gathering and analysis of the facts, Commission of Experts, S/1994/674/Add.2 (Vol. V) December 28, 1994, pp. 4–5. This report details the sexual violence committed at fifty-seven counties across Bosnia-Herzegovina, nineteen counties in Croatia, and several in Serbia.

34 One woman who had been held at Bosanki Brod, a Croatian camp which held principally Serb women, described the experience of a woman who was raped by forty-one men before being shot in the head. Final report of the United Nations Commission of Experts, December 28, 1994, p. 13. It is also possible to read the narratives of the women who have testified at the ICTY. There were sixteen from Foča alone who testified in 2000. The documents and transcripts are available online at: http://www.un.org/icty (accessed May 20, 2013).

35 Lisa Sharlach, "Rape as Genocide: Bangladesh, the Former Yugoslavia, and Rwanda," *New Political Science* 22:1 (2000), p. 97. Even individuals who did not believe that the rapes were systematic became convinced, upon collecting statements from survivors, that it was indeed true; see "Mass Rape in Bosnia: Breaking the Wall of Silence, an Interview with Seada Vranic." Available online: http://www.barnsdle.demon.co.uk/bosnia/rapes.html (accessed July 7, 2008). See also Todd A. Salzman, "Rape Camps as Means to Ethnic Cleansing: Religious, Cultural, and Ethical Responses to Rape Victims in the Former Yugoslavia," *Human Rights Quarterly* 20:2 (1998), pp. 348–78; Jennifer Scott, "Systematic Rapes," *Reuters*, July 3, 1996; Deutsche Presse-Agentur, "Mass Rape in Bosnia Took Place on Orders from Above," July 2, 1996; Fischer, "Occupation of the Womb."

36 George Rodrigue, "Women: The Targets of Terror, Serbs Accused of Systematically Raping Muslims in Bosnia," *Dallas Morning News*, November 23, 1992.

37 International Criminal Tribunal for the former Yugoslavia: Trial Chamber Judgment Summary for Mićo Stanišić and Stojan Župljanin, The Hague, Netherlands (accessed May 20, 2013). See also the treatment and execution of Bosnian Muslim men in UNICTY, "Judgment Summary for Zdravko Tolimir," The Hague, Netherlands; December 12, 2012 (accessed May 20, 2013).

38 Matteo Fiori, "'The Foča Rape Camps:' A Dark Page Read through the ICTY's Jurisprudence," *The Hague Justice Portal* (December 19, 2007), pp. 2–3.

39 International Criminal Tribunal for the former Yugoslavia, Case No. IT-95-18-R61, Case No. IT-95-5-R61, Tuesday, July 2, 1996, p. 412.

40 Kadira quoted in Alexandra Stiglmayer, "The Rapes in Bosnia-Herzegovina," in *Mass Rape: The War Against Women in Bosnia-Herzegovina*, ed. Alexandra Stiglmayer (Lincoln, NE: The University of Nebraska Press, 1994), p. 119.

41 Robert Fisk, "Rape Victims Say Serb Troops 'Wanted Babies,'" *Toronto Star*, February 8, 1993; Fischer, "Occupation of the Womb," pp. 110–11.

42 Fischer, "Occupation of the Womb," p. 111.

43 Ibid., p. 133.

44 There is a voluminous literature that frames the issue in this way. See a discussion in Weitsman, "Children Born of War and the Politics of Identity," pp. 178–206. There are a number of scholars who object to this language, myself included. See especially R. Charli Carpenter, "Surfacing Children: Limitations of Genocidal Rape Discourse," *Human Rights Quarterly* 22:2 (2000), pp. 428–77.

45 Weitsman, "Children Born of War and the Politics of Identity," pp. 178–206.

46 Lynda E. Boose, "Crossing the River Drina: Bosnian Rape Camps, Turkish Impalement, and the Serb Cultural Memory," *Signs: Journal of Women in Culture and Society* 28:1 (2002), pp. 71–96. Boose's argument is extremely interesting: that ultimately, the Serbs linked Bosnian Muslim identity to the Turks despite the fact that in reality there is no connection. But the Serbs' constructed memory and association of the two culminated in the dreadful sexual violations witnessed in the war.

47 Carpenter, *Forgetting Children Born of War*, pp. 29–30.

48 This was true for Kosovar Muslims as well; see Carol J. Williams, "In Kosovo, Rape Seen as Awful as Death; Tradition-bound families shun victims, forcing women to suffer in silence or speak in euphemisms. For many, suicide or martyrdom in battle are the only alternatives," *Los Angeles Times*, May 27, 1999.

49 See Weitsman, "Children Born of War and the Politics of Identity," pp. 110–27.

50 Ibid., pp. 110–27.

51 See Arsenijević, "Gendering the Bone," pp. 193–205.

52 See, for example, International Criminal Tribunal for the former Yugoslavia, Office of the Prosecutor, Exhumations in Bosnia and Herzegovina (Netherlands: The Hague, 2000).

53 International Commission on Missing Persons, "About ICMP." Available online: http://www.ic-mp.org/about-icmp (accessed May 22, 2013).

54 "Srebrenica Victims Are Reburied," *BBC*, July 11, 2012, sec. Europe.
    Available online: http://www.bbc.co.uk/news/world-europe-18795203.
    On reburials, see Andrew A. G. Ross, *Mixed Emotions: Beyond Fear and
    Hatred in International Conflict* (Chicago, IL: University of Chicago Press,
    2014), pp. 101–6. See also proof of death database, missing persons, and
    the documentation of the dead in ICTY, IT-08-91-T Mićo Stanišić, Stojan
    Zupljanin 3 (2013), pp. 8–625.

55 Medica Zenica. Available online: http://medicazenica.org/uk/index.
    php?option=com_content&view=article&id=46&Itemid=28 (accessed May
    22, 2013). See Carpenter, *Forgetting Children Born of War*, p. 152.

56 Carpenter, *Forgetting Children Born of War*, p. 42.

57 Belma Bercebasic, "Invisible Casualties of War," *BCR 383, Institute for War
    and Peace Reporting* (2005). Available online: http://iwpr.net/report-news/
    invisible-casualties-war.

58 Helena Smith, "Rape Victims' Babies Pay the Price of War," *Observer*, April 16,
    2000.

59 Carpenter, *Forgetting Children Born of War*, p. 42.

60 Louise Branson, "A Generation of Children of Hate: The Unwanted Children
    Conceived in the Rapes of some 20,000 Women May be the Most Lasting Scar
    Left by Yugoslavia's Bitter Civil War," *Toronto Star*, January 29, 1993. She
    describes one mother who calls her child a chetnik baby.

61 Carpenter, *Forgetting Children Born of War*.

62 "UNICEF Convention on the Rights of the Child," UNICEF. Available online:
    http://www.unicef.org/crc/ (accessed May 21, 2013).

63 Carpenter, *Forgetting Children Born of War*, pp. 100–1, 108.

64 Carol J. Williams, "Bosnia's Orphans of Rape: Innocent Legacy of Hatred,"
    Los Angeles Times, July 24, 1993. This was true in Kosovo as well. See
    "Americans Offer to Adopt War Child Born of Rape: A Home Must be Sought
    in Kosovo First," *Ottawa Citizen*, May 11, 2000. See Weitsman, "Children
    Born of War and the Politics of Identity."

65 Mostov, "Sexing the Nation/Desexing the Body Politics."

66 Step Jansen and Elissa Helms, "The 'White Plague:' National-Demographic
    Rhetoric and its Gendered Resonance after the Post-Yugoslav Wars," in
    Gender Dynamics and Post-Conflict Reconstruction, ed. Christine Eifler and
    Ruth Seifert (Frankfurt, Germany: Peter Lang, 2009), pp. 223–5.

67 Eve Ensler, "Dear Mr. Akin, I Want You to Imagine . . ." *Huffington Post*,
    August 20, 2012. Available online at: http://www.huffingtonpost.com/eve-
    ensler/todd-akin-rape_b_1812930.html.

6

Rape as a Weapon of Genocide: Gender, Patriarchy, and Sexual Violence in Rwanda

Jennie E. Burnet

During the 1994 genocide in Rwanda, genocide planners and perpetrators used sexual torture, mutilation, and enslavement as weapons of genocide against Tutsi women and girls. An epidemiological survey of women in Rwanda in 1994 found that 49 percent of them had been raped.[1] The genocide (April 6 to July 4, 1994) was an intense episode of violence that occurred during a decade of violent conflict, beginning with the civil war (1990–4), continuing with the exile of more than two million Rwandans in refugee camps in eastern Zaire (now Democratic Republic of the Congo) and western Tanzania (1994–6), and ending with the insurgency in northwestern Rwanda (1997–2000). This decade was characterized by high rates of sexual violence and militarized sex, defined here as voluntary and coerced sexual relations between soldiers or members of paramilitary organizations and civilians, but the 1994 genocide constituted an abrupt break from social norms, especially in terms of sexual assault. Sexual violence in the genocide ranged beyond ethnic/racial dyads of Tutsi-victim and Hutu-perpetrator. Many Hutu women and girls also endured sexual violence in 1994, and an unknown number of women and girls of all ethnicities were pressured into sexual relationships with soldiers after they reached the safety of internally displaced persons camps in territory held by the Rwandan Patriotic Front (RPF). Focusing solely on sexual violence committed by Hutu perpetrators against Tutsi victims obscures the complexity of sexual violence, sexual agency, and militarized sex during conflict.

Research on sexual violence in Rwanda has emphasized rape and other forms of sexual violence as conscious strategies on the part of the perpetrators to terrorize and control women, girls, and other civilians.[2] Adding to these important contributions, this chapter explores how pregenocide social contexts and the political economy shaped sexual violence during the genocide and influenced the impact of sexual violence on survivors, families, and communities in the aftermath of the genocide. This chapter is based on ethnographic research conducted in urban and rural Rwanda between 1997 and 2013, including more than a hundred formal interviews with leaders and members of women's civil society organizations and several hundred ethnographic interviews with ordinary citizens in rural and urban Rwanda. This research focused broadly on changing gender roles in the aftermath of the 1994 genocide and did not focus exclusively on sexual violence or its legacies.[3]

The chapter is organized in five sections. In the first, I examine the political economy of everyday gender violence in Rwanda and the ways in which the decisions of women and girls have been shaped by, what Eric Wolf calls, "a social field of action" that makes some behaviors impossible and some behaviors more possible than others.[4] Then I examine how women in conflict zones exercise sexual agency in ways that challenge distinctions between consensual and nonconsensual sex on which international legal definitions of rape are based. Women's choices are limited—sometimes impossibly limited—but they still exercise their agency to survive and to pursue life goals, such as education or a career, marriage, or motherhood. In the third section, I describe how perpetrators used rape as a weapon of genocide and explain the ways that the local political economy, cultural symbolism, Rwandan notions of sexual consent, and gender roles shaped sexual violence during the 1994 genocide. Then I explore the short- and long-term impact of sexual violence on survivors, their families, and their communities. In the conclusion, I discuss the ways in which certain sexual violence survivors have either been silenced or have chosen to remain silent about their experiences of sexual assault.

The Political Economy of Everyday Gender Violence

In her groundbreaking study of Korean "comfort women," C. Sarah Soh highlighted the importance of situating sexual violence associated with war within the context of "everyday gender violence" and the "structural power" of the political economy.[5] Apart from Meredeth Turshen's comparative analysis of sexual violence in Rwanda and Mozambique, few works have situated the sexual violence of the 1994 genocide in this broader context.[6] And yet, long before the 1994 genocide, Rwandan women and girls faced a great deal of gender violence, including physical violence (such as domestic abuse and sexual assault) and structural violence (such as gender discrimination).

Patrilineage was the fundamental structuring element of society in precolonial Rwanda. Patrilineages operated as corporations that managed the economic and social well-being of its members, whether male or female. Widows, married women, and unmarried girls derived their social identities and rights to land from their male kin. A Rwandan proverb states "*Abagore ntibafite ubwoko*"—wives have no identity; meaning an unmarried girl has the same identity as her father or brothers, and a wife takes on the identity of her husband and his patrilineage.[7] In short, a woman's membership in a lineage defined who she was as a social person. During precolonial and colonial times, a woman after her marriage would be called by a name derived from her husband's name such as *Mukamanzi* (literally, "wife of Manzi") or some other anonymous kinship terms such as *umufasha* (literally, "helper," meaning wife) or *mama/nyoko/nyina* (literally, "my mother"/"your mother"/"his/her mother"). A woman's given name was rarely used—a literal, as well as symbolic, erasure of her individuated personhood. These practices were not necessarily based in patriarchy. Rather, they reflected a Rwandan notion of personhood whereby a person's kin relations, stage of life, and marital status constituted his or her social identity.

Female labor was central to Rwandan agricultural production in the precolonial and colonial periods. With the exception of a few regional ethnic groups and the ruling elite, most households, whether Hutu or Tutsi, subsisted primarily from agriculture, with livestock supplementing agricultural production. Up until the recent past, wives cultivated food for the household on land owned by their husbands or their husbands' families. Husbands produced cash crops, managed livestock, or migrated in search of paid labor. In the precolonial system, women and girls drew power from their productive and reproductive capacities and from the protection of their own patrilineage. In this system, women could carve out substantial spheres of power. Women also had land rights in their own lineages. A father could make gifts of land to a daughter; this land "remained the outright property of the woman and [was] inherited by her sons."[8] Should a woman never marry or should her marriage fail, she could return to her own patrilineage and be allocated a parcel of land.[9] Bridewealth marriages were key to this social configuration and helped ensure protection for married daughters. The colonial period wrought many changes in Rwandan gender roles, as the economy became monetized and the colonial state pushed husbands and men into the cash economy. These changes weakened the customary powers and rights of daughters and wives and increased the patriarchal nature of the Rwandan society.[10]

Although women gained some legal rights in the postcolonial period, they remained subordinated to men and largely excluded from nonagricultural, salaried work. The 1991 constitution guaranteed the equality of all people before the law regardless of race, color, origin, ethnicity, clan, sex, belief, religion, or social position, but numerous legal codes of the postcolonial period continued to subordinate women to men in the home and in the public sphere.[11] For example, Article 206 of Law no. 42/88 stated that "the husband is the head of the conjugal community made up of man, wife, and their children."[12] This provision was inspired, according to Jean-Marie Kamatali and Philippe Gafishi, "by custom, which defines the husband in reference to his physical strength and his duty to provide for the family's needs including their lodging."[13] At the time of the genocide in 1994, Rwandan women were, technically, legally emancipated. In practice, however, they were perceived as legal "minors [under] the guardianship of fathers, brothers, husbands or sons."[14] Banking, commercial, and land ownership laws limited women's ability to engage in the cash economy. Women told me in interviews that prior to 1994 they could not seek salaried work without the approval of their husbands, even though Rwandan law did not require employers to seek husbands' approval.[15] By law, women needed the signature of their husbands in order to open a bank account.[16] This legal requirement was intended to protect the conjugal household as a single economic unit. But, the provision made it easy for husbands to hide money from their wives or direct resources away from the conjugal household, since a husband did not require a wife's signature to open or close a bank account but a wife did require a husband's. While some women became successful entrepreneurs, their businesses were vulnerable to plunder by their husbands.[17]

Patriarchal ideas about the roles of women in society also led to an education system that limited girls' access to secondary school. According to World Bank Development Indicators, in 1990 the proportion of female to male primary enrollment was 96 percent for primary school, 71 percent for secondary school, and only 22 percent for tertiary school. When faced with limited household resources, families chose to educate their sons over daughters for two reasons. First, girl children provided significant labor in the household by fetching water, caring for young children, cooking, cleaning, and washing laundry. This time-intensive work required girls to miss school, whereas boys' labor, usually tending livestock or helping in the fields, could be accomplished outside school hours. Second, fathers often viewed educating daughters as "a waste," since these daughters would leave to join their husbands' patrilineage when they married. Thus, many institutional barriers prevented girls from achieving the levels of education necessary to secure salaried work in the private sector or in the government.

This history of everyday violence that subordinated women to men, combined with a political economy that strongly favored men for salaried employment, limited women and girls' choices. Despite laws that granted them individual rights and personhood, women and girls were viewed as dependent on men: as girls they were dependent on their fathers, uncles, and grandfathers and as women on their husbands, brothers-in-law, and adult male children. This systemic subordination increased women and girls' vulnerability to sexual violence in the genocide.

Women's Agency, Sexual Consent, and Conflict

In the Rwandan context, the issue of sexual consent is a particularly thorny problem, because Western legal definitions of consent are rarely appropriate.[18] According to Sophie Day, rape is commonly defined as "nonconsensual sex" or "nonconsensual sexual intercourse."[19] This definition raises some significant conceptual problems when used in Rwanda (and many other African countries) because women in these cultures usually do not give explicit, verbal consent to sexual intercourse. Modesty is a feminine ideal, and unmarried girls and women are expected to uphold a cultural model of the "modest virgin" devoid of any sexual knowledge or urges.[20] Because explicit expressions of sexual desire are considered immodest, females implicitly communicate their consent through nonverbal cues or "situational consent"; that is, a woman or girl's willingness to be in a particular place, at a particular time, with a particular person. For instance, a woman agrees to spend the night with a man in his home or a hotel. In the past, and even to a certain extent today, a married woman would also give subtle nonverbal cues to her husband to indicate her desire by cooking a special meal, wearing attractive clothing, attending to the husband's physical comfort, or lighting a pipe of tobacco for him at bedtime.[21] Rwandan cultural values precluded the notion of rape in marriage because a wife's consent became an irrevocable fact upon wedding.[22] Wives could refuse their husbands only due to illness or menstruation.[23] Thus the emic Rwandan cultural models of sexual consent do not coincide with the European and American models of consent. Research on socially acceptable forms of domestic violence in India[24] and on socially acceptable forms of domestic violence in the highlands of Peru suggest that many other cultures also reject a model of rape based on consent.[25]

Rwandan cultural models of sexuality and consent complicate investigations of sexual violence as a crime. For example, the lack of precise words for rape in Kinyarwanda (the local language) complicated research on sexual violence conducted in late 1994 and early 1995.[26] Article 360 of the 1977 Rwandan penal code defined rape as a crime punishable by five to ten years' imprisonment, but it did not delineate what behaviors constituted rape.[27] In unpublished research on child sexual assault conducted in 2002 for CARE-Rwanda, I found that Rwandans usually expressed the concept of rape as "*gufata ku ngufu* (to take by force)," which suggests that rape is conceived of as involving physical force. A former military policeman confirmed this when he explained to me in 2002 that he usually looked for signs of physical violence on an alleged victim's body in order to determine whether she had been raped. He said there was simply no other conclusive way to determine whether a woman alleging sexual assault was being truthful.

Historically, Rwandan cultural models of sexuality did not prescribe remedies for rape; rather, they addressed improper sexual relations such as adultery—a man having sexual intercourse with an unauthorized woman such as the wife of a different patrilineage or an unmarried girl. In these instances, the offending man's patrilineage would offer gifts such as beer and livestock to compensate the lineage to which the wife or unmarried girl belonged. A wife caught *en flagrant délit* with an unauthorized man was assumed to have consented to the sexual activity. Most likely she faced a severe beating at the hands of her husband, father-in-law, or brothers-in-law and risked being sent back to her own patrilineage without her children. For an unmarried girl, a marriage might be arranged, but if not she most likely faced a severe beating at the hands of her father or brothers for bringing shame to the family. Knowledge of her "mistake" would also lower the potential bridewealth that her lineage could seek during future marriage negotiations. All these instances assume the implicit consent of the women involved and preclude the possibility of rape defined as "nonconsensual sex." These data suggest that Rwandan cultural models for coping with sexual transgressions, including situations that were potentially rape, robbed women of their agency.

While a great deal of international attention has focused on sexual violence in conflict zones, few studies recognize that many different types of sexual encounters occur in war zones, including a great deal of consensual sex for pleasure and transactional sex that does not necessarily constitute harm.[28] Many of these encounters, to be sure, are conditioned by the circumstances of violent conflict and the political economy of war and are therefore hard to define as noncoercive. Many young women exercise their sexual agency in conflict zones and trade sexual access to their bodies for the means of survival: food, water, clothing, money. The degree to which these women are making a "choice" is highly contingent on the structural factors determined by the conflict, and often they must choose between several terrible options—what Begoña Aretxaga called "choiceless decisions."[29] In Rwanda, the lack of explicit consent further complicated these distinctions: how do women and girls refuse sexual intercourse when the means of survival are bound up with implicit signs of consent, such as accepting food, clothing, shelter, and protection? R. M. Hayden critiques assumptions by human rights researchers that Rwandan women who married men in exchange for protection during the genocide were victims of rape or forced marriage.[30] Indeed, it is plausible that some Rwandan women and girls exercised agency in the initiation of these relations, and it is highly likely that they have exercised agency in their continuation. Yet whether these relationships can be considered consensual or whether they constitute sexual harm is a much more difficult question to answer. If the only other option is death, is it really a choice at all?

Sexual Violence during the 1994 Genocide

Sexual assaults on women and girls increased dramatically after the advent of the civil war in 1990.[31] While it is almost certain that rape and sexual violence existed before then, they were not widely recognized as problems, and women's organizations did not mobilize on the issue. The civil war, the 1994 genocide, and their aftermath transformed aspects of Rwandan culture. In Rwanda in the 1990s, war became what Stephen Lubkemann called a "social condition," meaning war became the normal context of daily life rather than a disruption of normal social relations.[32] Before, during, and after the genocide, sexual violence was a common feature of a social landscape that already considered many forms of gender-based violence, such as wife-beating, normal.

As the general state of security in the country declined, members of the *Interahamwe* and *Impuzamugambi* militias, the Rwandan Armed Forces (*Forces armées rwandaises*, FAR), and others took advantage of the chaotic conditions to commit acts of sexual violence with impunity. Local government officials advised women to wear both shorts and underwear beneath their skirts as an impediment to rape rather than wearing nothing per custom.[33] While official reports of rape were almost nonexistent, Human Rights Watch reported in 1993, "Rwandan soldiers frequently rape women, but because they are never punished for the crime, victims rarely report the attacks. Women know that to accuse soldiers is futile and may well lead to further harassment or even death."[34] Many Rwandans, both male and female, told me that the FAR and the militias raped women during attacks on civilians in the civil war.

While sexual violence escalated during the civil war, its ferocity and intensity during the genocide from April 6 through July 4, 1994 constituted an abrupt break with social norms. Rape and sexual violence became weapons of genocide used to destroy the Tutsi ethnic group as well as "to terrorize the community and warn all people of the futility of resistance—those targeted as victims as well as those who might wish to protect the intended targets."[35] Women faced brutal acts of sexual violence: individual rape, gang rape, rape with objects, sexual slavery or "forced marriage," and sexual mutilation.[36] *Interahamwe* militiamen often raped or sexually tortured Tutsi women before killing them. Perpetrators sometimes mutilated women during the rapes or before killing them by cutting off their breasts, puncturing the vagina with sharp objects, or disfiguring body parts that looked "Tutsi," such as long fingers or thin noses.[37] In other cases, Tutsi women were gang-raped, sexually enslaved, or "married" by *Interahamwe* militiamen in exchange for having their lives saved.[38]

Although perpetrators in the 1994 genocide targeted victims based on ascribed identities, "age-old" ethnic hatred (or tribalism) was not the cause of the genocide.[39] Rather, the killings were the result of political strategizing and conscious choices by a political and economic elite who desired to maintain their hold on power. At the local level, community members usually knew the ethnicity of their neighbors. At roadblocks on main roads, policemen, soldiers, and militiamen used national identity cards, which indicated ethnicity, to select targets. During the genocide a man who presented an identity card marked "Tutsi" would be killed instantly, along with any children accompanying him. Women with Tutsi identity cards would usually be killed immediately or raped and then killed. Sometimes they might be spared according to the whims of their attackers, held as sexual slaves by soldiers or militiamen, or taken as "wives" by individual soldiers, militiamen, or civilian perpetrators. Individuals presenting identity cards marked "Hutu" or "Twa" would often be physically examined or interrogated for other clues to determine if the card was accurate. Many people had changed the ethnicity on their cards from Tutsi to Hutu during the Habyarimana regime because doing so was advantageous under the "ethnic equilibrium" policy, which reserved 90 percent of all posts in the government and in secondary schools or universities for Hutus. Thus, genocide perpetrators relied in many instances on stereotypical physical markers of "Tutsiness," which included a tall, slender frame; aquiline nose with small nostrils; long, narrow fingers or feet; dark gums in the mouth; and a tan skin tone on the palms of the hands or soles of the feet. For women, the rule of thumb was often beauty. Since colonial times, Tutsi (or Watussi) women were heralded as great beauties by European colonizers. Racist propaganda in the years leading up to the genocide further reinforced these stereotypes.[40] Beauty as a marker of Tutsiness was so strong in the popular imagination that Hutu women and girls who were considered beautiful risked being mistaken for Tutsi and raped, sexually enslaved or taken as "wives," sexually tortured, or killed.[41]

The International Criminal Tribunal for Rwanda (ICTR) established sexual violence as an explicit strategy of the genocide and yielded the first judgment of rape as a genocide crime in an international court. The ICTR convicted Jean-Paul Akayesu, burgomaster (mayor) of Taba commune, of using rape as a weapon of genocide even though he did not participate in sexual violence. Instead, he ordered others to rape and engage in sexual violence as part of the genocide.[42] Other leaders ordered militiamen and other community members to rape and also committed rape themselves.[43] In 2011, the ICTR found Pauline Nyiramasuhuko, a woman and minister of Women's Development in the interim government in power during the genocide, responsible for aiding and abetting rapes and ordering the rape of Tutsi women during the genocide.[44] Unfortunately, due to errors committed during the trial by the prosecutor's office, the court did not find her guilty of rape as a crime of genocide.[45]

Beyond physical brutality, sexual violence in the genocide consisted of symbolic and psychosocial violence. Perpetrators targeted the normally privileged role of Rwandan women as mothers. They disemboweled pregnant women while they were still alive and cut their fetuses out of their wombs.[46] They raped and sexually mutilated women and then told them bullets should not be "wasted" on them because they would "die of AIDS," presumably contracted during the rapes.[47] Extremist rhetoric targeted Tutsi beauty and desirability—militiamen were promised the opportunity for sexual intercourse with Tutsi women as a reward for their "work"; that is, killing Tutsis and others identified as enemies of the state. Survivors frequently reported that perpetrators said that they wanted "to see if Tutsi women were like Hutu women."[48] Many perpetrators raped Tutsi women as punishment for "their supposed arrogance," since Tutsi women were "said to scorn Hutu men."[49]

Rape during the genocide also became a political economic weapon. The Rwandan state sought to eliminate the Tutsi ethnic group through the destruction or systematic stripping of their assets, such as the looting and burning of Tutsi homes and businesses. Soldiers, militiamen, and civilian perpetrators were "rewarded" for their work with property taken from Tutsis, including Tutsi women and girls, who were often treated as war booty.[50] For example, Rwandan soldiers ordered the director of a nursing school to hand over female students and raped female employees of a Roman Catholic seminary as "a contribution to the war effort."[51] In some communities, local authorities worked to keep the Tutsi wives of Hutu men alive only because "depriving a man of the productive and reproductive capacities of his wife harmed his interests" and could diminish his willingness to support the genocide.[52] Women's land rights were sometimes part of the "reward" for militiamen. One survivor recounted how the head of the local militia gave her and her sisters to militiamen as "wives," and their father's land was split among the "husbands."[53] Women's and girls' greater survival rates can in part be explained through this use of women and girls as economic pawns to acquire land and property through so-called "marriage."

After the genocide, sexual violence remained a problem. For Rwandans in refugee camps in eastern Zaire or western Tanzania, the former FAR soldiers and *Interahamwe* militiamen who controlled the camps remained a constant threat. Rape was common, and perpetrators faced no consequences. Young, single women and adolescent girls remained vulnerable to becoming "wives" under coercive circumstances.[54] The FAR and *Interahamwe* in eastern Zaire organized incursions into Rwanda and attacked local communities, again using rape as a weapon.

The Rwandan Patriotic Army (RPA), the armed wing of the RPF that became the new national army following the RPF victory, was much more disciplined than the FAR had been. RPA soldiers did not engage in widespread rape, but two practices fall somewhere in the vicinity of coercive sex and definitely constitute militarized sex. In the internally displaced persons camps behind RPA lines, women and girls who had been saved by the RPA would often find themselves solicited by RPA soldiers for a "reward" (meaning sexual intercourse). This reward was often referred to as *kubohoza*, "to be liberated." While these women and girls may have consented to these sexual encounters, it is difficult to discern whether they felt as if they had a choice. In a second practice, RPA soldiers asked Tutsi women married to Hutu men to leave their husbands, "saying those marriages must have been the consequence of rape."[55] If the women refused, their husbands would be arrested on accusations of genocide and imprisoned—an almost certain death warrant between 1994 and 1997, given the abysmal prison conditions. The women were then forced to marry RPA soldiers, who acquired the woman's property.[56]

Little detailed information about sexual violence during the insurgency in northern and western Rwanda (1996–2001) is available, because researchers had little access to these communities at the time. Survivors of attacks against civilians, particularly those perpetrated by the RPA, were reluctant to testify for fear of reprisals from the government. For several years after the end of the insurgency, Rwandan women in northwestern Rwanda cited rape as a pressing social problem for women and girls.[57] These data suggest that sexual violence was a significant problem during the insurgency and in its aftermath. By 2009, women in the same community stated that local authorities had solved the problem by working closely with the population.[58]

The Aftermath of Sexual Violence

Human Rights Watch published the earliest, in-depth, examination of sexual violence during the 1994 genocide and its aftermath.[59] The report detailed the numerous economic, legal, and social problems faced by sexual violence survivors. Its analysis of the forms of sexual violence in the genocide helped establish that sexual violence was an intentional strategy of genocide. Research by Médecins sans Frontières also helped establish that sexual violence had been used as a weapon in the genocide.[60] As a result of this groundbreaking work, an international coalition of feminist human rights lawyers, scholars, and activists petitioned the ICTR's prosecutor's office to pursue prosecution of rape and sexual violence as genocide crimes and crimes against humanity.[61] Their advocacy and the amicus brief they filed led to the amendment of the charges against Jean-Paul Akayesu and the first successful prosecution of rape as a weapon of genocide under international law.

Ten years after its first report on sexual violence, Human Rights Watch revisited the situation of sexual violence survivors and the obstacles that prevented them from seeking justice.[62] The report acknowledged the important international legal precedents as well as improvements in national legal codes to protect civilians from sexual violence, but it made clear that numerous obstacles continued to prevent the prosecution of many cases of sexual violence. Several foreign and Rwandan scholars have collected testimony or life history narratives from sexual violence survivors.[63] These works have contributed to understanding some of the long-term consequences of sexual violence for survivors. Three significant themes that emerge from these studies are the psychosocial difficulties of raising children born of rape, the health consequences of living with HIV acquired through sexual violence, and the continuing economic struggles of rape survivors who are often living in poverty.

Many women and girls who were raped became pregnant. While abortion was illegal in Rwanda in 1994, in some hospitals and medical clinics nurses and physicians quietly offered an unknown number of these women abortions as treatment for their physical and psychological trauma.[64] Nonetheless, a significant number of women and girls gave birth to children who were commonly called "children of bad memories" in Kinyarwanda. Many of these women and girls faced extreme emotional difficulty. As one widow explained, "I can't look in this child's eyes."[65] Another woman, forced to marry an FAR soldier during the genocide and to accompany him into exile, explained, "I gave birth to a girl, but I hated her, because she was a constant reminder of what had happened to me. I didn't breastfeed her because of that."[66]

Some women left these children in orphanages, but thousands of others kept them. As Godelieve Mukasarasi, founder and coordinator of a Rwanda women's organization dedicated to helping sexual violence survivors and their children, explains, "Children born of rape are stigmatized, hated even by their own mothers or by their mother's kin."[67] These children remain as external embodied memories for their mothers who must face a lifetime of public shame because their kin and communities recognize the mother's defilement in the face of the child. Attempting to disguise children born of rape as illegitimate children offers these women little advantage, since having an illegitimate child drastically reduces the chance of a woman entering into a socially recognized marriage and social adulthood.[68] Thus, women impregnated through rape during the genocide, the civil war, or their aftermath found themselves with only terrible choices.

Despite these obstacles, children born of rape became central to some sexual violence survivors' agency: these survivors redefined themselves as mothers and made decisions to protect the well-being of their children. In Rwanda, as elsewhere in Africa, motherhood is the best light in which a woman can be seen. By reinventing themselves as mothers, albeit single mothers, these rape survivors recovered their dignity and reclaimed their agency.[69] The radically transformed social context wrought by the genocide made this option more practical. In the aftermath of the genocide, single motherhood became less stigmatized and parents became less willing to enforce customary sanctions, such as pregnant daughters' banishment or sending the infants to orphanages. In the years that followed the genocide, the increasing difficulty for Rwandan youth to achieve socially recognized marriages resulted in increasing numbers of single mothers in Rwanda.[70] Because families and communities had no other choice, they began to accommodate single mothers, including women raped in the genocide, by according them social adulthood. Nonetheless, sexual violence survivors impregnated through rape faced the additional challenge of learning to love children who embodied their physical and psychological trauma. As one rape survivor explained, "Learning to love the child of a killer is hard. . . . SEVOTA [a women's association] helped me learn to love him."[71] Not all women succeed in this endeavor. As one woman, who was only twelve years old at the time of her rape and sexual captivity during the genocide, explained, "I have never loved my daughter, who was born out of rape, and even though I try my hardest to love her, there is still a long way to go."[72]

Women and girls who contracted HIV/AIDS through sexual assault during the genocide were viewed, and continue to be viewed today, as tainted. During the genocide, men who knew they were infected with HIV raped women to inflict a delayed death.[73] Beyond the public shame of their rapes, these women faced the structural violence of living with a devastating illness in a resource-poor setting where treatment was unavailable in the critical years after the genocide. As African Rights reported, "Medical care for genocide rape victims in Rwanda can be summarized as 'too little, too late.'"[74] In the late 1990s through 2004, antiretroviral (ARV) treatments available to people living with HIV/AIDS in North America and Europe were only available to the very wealthy in Rwanda, as the medications' monthly cost exceeded $400 whereas the per capita gross national income in Rwanda was $730 per year (or $60 per month) in 2004.[75] The vast majority of people living with HIV/AIDS in Rwanda went untreated until the US President's Emergency Plan for AIDS Relief (PEPFAR) was created by President George W. Bush in 2003. Beginning in late 2004, ARV therapy began to be made accessible to poor Rwandans. Unfortunately, this treatment came too late for thousands of women who had already died of HIV/AIDS acquired through rape in the genocide. Nonetheless, in 2011 an estimated 61,900 Rwandans received ARV therapy, and 225,600 people living with HIV/AIDS received health care and other support through the PEPFAR initiative.[76]

Survivors of rape shared many of the same difficulties of genocide survivors in general: loneliness, social marginalization, depression, psychosocial trauma or posttraumatic stress disorder, and extreme poverty. In the aftermath of the genocide, survivors found themselves in a country whose infrastructure had been destroyed. Perpetrators had targeted the economic lives of Tutsis by destroying their homes, slaughtering their livestock, and stealing their belongings. Thus, genocide survivors faced restarting their lives from "less than nothing."[77] In this context, survivors of sexual violence found their suffering intensified by the dire economic circumstances and poverty they faced. While the new Rwandan government eventually came to the assistance of genocide survivors through the Genocide Survivors' Assistance Funds, known by their French acronym, FARG, survivors suffered for many years without basic necessities such as clothing, shelter, basic household tools, or farming implements necessary to survive. For sexual violence victims, many of whom suffered health problems as a result of their attacks, this poverty made it extremely difficult to access basic health care.

Despite these challenges, women survivors of sexual violence rebuilt their lives and began to seek meaning in their existence. M. Zraly and L. Nyirazinyoye found that some genocide-rape survivors in southern Rwanda joined associations and deployed a variety of coping mechanisms to continue living despite their horrific experiences during the genocide.[78] In my research with grassroots women's organizations in southern Rwandan and national women's organizations based in Kigali, I also found that joining women's associations brought solace to many genocide survivors, genocide widows, and other women whose husbands had died.[79]

Some sexual violence survivors sought to have children outside of marriage as another form of consolation and as a way to normalize their situation in the community. In 2013, one genocide survivor in the late stages of her battle with AIDS acquired through rape in the genocide explained, "I knew no man could take me like this. But I couldn't stand the idea of being alone in the world. So, I sought to have children through other means [than marriage]."[80] Other sexual violence survivors rejected the idea of marriage because of a lingering distaste for men.[81] These women sought to raise children as single mothers, either through adoption or through sexual encounters with men.[82]

Silenced Voices: Sexual Violence Survivors Omitted from the Public Discourse

Social interventions in postgenocide Rwanda focused mostly on Tutsi victims, leaving other rape survivors to cope on their own. Rape survivors who do not fit the Hutu-perpetrator/Tutsi-victim dyad remained mostly silent because their experiences did not fit the dominant paradigm of Rwandan history promoted by the RPF government.[83] Hutu women raped by FAR soldiers or *Interahamwe* militiamen during the civil war or genocide did not dare speak out publically because they risked not only disbelief (because Hutu women are not perceived as genocide targets) but also rejection by their husbands and families because of the "shame" of being raped. Tutsi women who were coerced into sex or forced into marriage with RPF soldiers had little or no access to social services for sexual violence survivors unless they adjusted their narratives and called the perpetrators "*Interahamwe*." Finally, an unknown number of (Hutu and Tutsi) women have remained in marriages that began as "forced" marriages. These women dare not talk about how their relationships began for fear of being cast off by their husbands or husbands' families. Like women in postpartition India and Pakistan, these women exercise their agency to remain in these marriages because they perceive it as the best option for themselves or their children.[84] In Punjab, Veena Das found that the social fiction of "practical kinship" allowed raped or forcibly married women to be incorporated into families and communities when the women's natal families and communities would have rejected them.[85] Hayden found that raped women in Bosnia exercised similar agency to find a socially acceptable place for themselves and their children in the aftermath of the conflict.[86]

Notwithstanding the individual and social silence surrounding these issues, silence should not be mistaken for secrecy. Even though many rape survivors and women in "forced marriages" remain silent about their experiences, family and community members often know about these women's and girls' sexual assaults. Given the public nature of genocide rapes and sexual enslavement during the genocide, community members are often aware that certain women were raped or held in sexual slavery or that some women's marriages began in questionable circumstances. Social silence on these matters helps preserve the women's dignity on the one hand and avoids reopening familial and community conflict on the other hand. Yet silence may also increase or prolong rape survivors' suffering.

The voices of sexual violence survivors who have not sought support through associational life have rarely been heard. Researchers use convenience samples drawn from associations whose membership is pre-identified as sexual violence survivors as a way to conquer the nearly insurmountable challenge of recruiting research participants into a study with numerous privacy, confidentiality, and psychological risks. Most studies conducted on sexual violence during the genocide in Rwanda relied on this strategy to recruit interviewees.[87] Despite its benefits, this recruitment strategy creates a sampling bias due to the de facto exclusion of sexual violence survivors who are *not* members of associations. In addition, it creates an artificial situation where interviewees may feel compelled to explain or justify their membership in these associations while giving their testimony.[88] In *The Men Who Killed Me*, Anne-Marie de Brouwer, Sandra Ka Hon Chu, and Samer Muscati's study, these kinds of assertions appear frequently in the published narratives.[89] While this theme can be identified as an artifact of their sampling strategy, it is impossible to detect other ways that the narratives or testimony of sexual violence survivors may have been influenced by a sampling bias or the research context.

Ethnographic research can sometimes overcome this obstacle. Some advantages of ethnography are the long-term presence of the researcher in the field and the more open-ended inductive research questions that can open doors to harder-to-detect phenomenon. In the course of fieldwork over a fifteen-year timespan, a handful of sexual violence survivors (or their families) shared their stories, or parts of their stories, with me. Most of these survivors do not belong to associations. Their experiences of sexual violence remained an individual (or family) secret. A striking common theme of their narratives is that they do not position themselves as a member of a group or groups; rather their individual stories serve as "a counter memory to official hegemonic history," as M. Hirsch and V. Smith describe some women's memory narratives.[90] These survivors' narratives emphasized sexual survivors' existence at the margins of social acceptability. Yet, rather than remain captives of a gendered social classification system that defines sexual violence survivors as morally tainted, these survivors refocused their lives and agency on their children, including those born of rape.

An ethnographic approach allows researchers to explore the ambiguity of sexual violence during conflict by uncovering survivors hidden by hegemonic public discourses about conflict and by gathering data on female sexual agency and consensual sexual activity in conflict zones. Since the majority of postgenocide interventions for sexual violence survivors in Rwanda assisted mostly Tutsi victims or Hutu genocide widows, many (perhaps even most) sexual violence survivors remained hidden by the public discourse on sexual violence, by their own shame, and by the cultural requirement for silence in matters of sexual violence. The assumption that European or North American models of sexual consent are relevant to other contexts ignores significant differences in the social construction of sexuality and marginalizes emic cultural models. As Dianne Otto asserts, conflating all forms of sex in conflict zones as harm undermines women's and children's rights because it reinforces "conservative hierarchies of gender and sexuality" and "diverts attention . . . from the searing poverty that characterizes transitional post-conflict societies."[91] Initiating sexual encounters can be a matter of rational choice—a coping strategy in the difficult economic circumstances that arise in the aftermath of violent conflict and genocide. Furthermore, it can be argued that the question of sexual consent and rape in Europe and North America still remains unresolved.[92] In conflict zones, some women and girls initiate sexual relationships out of sexual desire, as a means to secure their own or their families' survival, or because they face a choiceless decision whereby other options either do not exist or are less desirable. Finally, many of the dominant research methods on sexual violence during conflict detach the question of female sexual consent from the cultural historical context and political economy of poverty that structures women's agency and limits their options.

This case study points to the need for more open frameworks for confronting instances of sexual violence during violent conflict, ones that make it possible for more victims to come forward for medical, psychological, and social support. Furthermore, it points to the need to address the structural violence of wartime political economies that leave poor women and girls vulnerable to sexual exploitation and trafficking because they face choiceless decisions involving their or their families' survival. As Soh pointed out in the case of Japan's comfort stations during the Second World War, "The comfort system encompassed both commercial *and* criminal sex" (emphasis in original).[93] United Nations Security Council Resolution 1325 on gender-based and sexual violence in conflict zones as well as the UN Secretary-General's 2003 Bulletin on the sexual conduct of peacekeepers are important steps in the right direction.[94] Yet as Otto notes, the directives outlined in the secretary-general's bulletin rob women, as well as male peacekeepers, of their sexual agency.[95] Otto further argues there is a need to examine the real differences between women's "experiences of consensual and nonconsensual sexual conduct, no matter how fine those distinctions are."[96] Thus, human rights lawyers and academic researchers should investigate in a systematic fashion the degree to which all militarized sex encompasses this divide.

Acknowledgments

This essay draws from data collected during dissertation research in Rwanda between 1997 and 2001, during consultancies for CARE-Rwanda in 2002, and from research trips in 2007, 2009, and 2011. I would like to thank the Government of Rwanda and the Ministry of Gender and Women in Development for authorizing and facilitating my dissertation research and the Ministry of Health and Ministry of Education for authorizing more recent research. The research was funded by the University of Louisville, by the Joan B. Kroc Institute for International Peace Studies at the University of Notre Dame, by the University of North Carolina at Chapel Hill, by the United States Institute for Peace, by the United States Department of Education, and by the National Science Foundation.

Notes

1 Mary Fabri, Jianhong Lu, Agnes Binagwaho, Kathryn Anastos, Mardge Cohen, Davis Kashaka, and Henriette Kukayonga, "Chronic PTSD and HIV in Rwanda," paper presented at the Politics, Policy, & Public Health Conference (Washington, DC: APHA, 2007), p. 5.

2 See, for example, Catherine Bonnet, *Le viol comme arme de guerre au Rwanda: du silence à la reconnaissance* (Paris, France: Médecins Sans Frontières, 1995); Ariane Brunet and Isabelle Helal, "Monitoring the Prosecution of Gender-Related Crimes in Rwanda: A Brief Field Report," *Peace and Conflict: Journal of Peace Psychology* 4:4 (1998), pp. 393–7; Human Rights Watch, *Shattered Lives: Sexual Violence during the Rwandan Genocide and its Aftermath* (New York, NY: Human Rights Watch, 1996); Human Rights Watch, *Struggling to Survive: Barriers to Justice for Rape Victims in Rwanda* (New York, NY: Humans Right Watch, 2004); Donatilla Mukamana and Petra Brysiewicz,

"The Lived Experience of Genocide Rape Survivors in Rwanda," *Journal of Nursing Scholarship* 40:4 (2008), pp. 379–84; Françoise Nduwimana, *The Right to Survive: Sexual Violence, Women and HIV/AIDS* (Montreal, Canada: International Centre for Human Rights and Democratic Development, 2004); Christopher C. Taylor, *Sacrifice as Terror: The Rwandan Genocide of 1994* (London, UK: Berg Publishers, 1999); Meredeth Turshen, "The Political Economy of Rape: An Analysis of Systematic Rape and Sexual Abuse of Women during Armed Conflict in Africa," in *Victims, Perpetrators, or Actors?: Gender, Armed Conflict, and Political Violence*, ed. C. O. N. Moser and F. C. Clark (London, UK: Zed Books, 2001), pp. 55–68; Clotilde Twagiramariya and Meredeth Turshen, eds., "The Sexual Politics of Survival in Rwanda," in *What Women Do in Wartime: Gender and Conflict in Africa* (New York, NY: Zed Books, 1998), pp. 101–21; Maggie A. Zraly, "Bearing: Resilience Among Genocide-Rape Survivors in Rwanda" (PhD dissertation, Department of Anthropology, Case Western Reserve, 2008); and Maggie A. Zraly and Laetitia Nyirazinyoye, "Don't Let the Suffering Make You Fade Away: An Ethnographic Study of Resilience Among Survivors of Genocide-Rape in Southern Rwanda," *Social Science & Medicine* 70:10 (2010), pp. 1656–64.

3 This research was published as Jennie E. Burnet, *Genocide Lives in Us: Women, Memory, and Silence in Rwanda* (Madison, WI: University of Wisconsin Press, 2012). For detailed information on research methodology, see pp. 23–8.

4 Eric Wolf, "Facing Power: Old Insights, New Questions," in *Assessing Cultural Anthropology*, ed. Robert Borofsky (New York, NY: McGraw-Hill, 1994), p. 219.

5 C. Sarah Soh, *The Comfort Women: Sexual Violence and Postcolonial Memory in Korea and Japan* (Chicago, IL: University of Chicago Press, 2008), p. 3.

6 Turshen, "The Political Economy of Rape."

7 Today in Rwanda, the standard translation for this proverb is "wives have no ethnicity." The Kinyarwanda word translated here as "ethnicity," *ubwoko*, literally means "sort" or "type" and can be applied to monkeys, trees, or bananas as easily as to people. Before the 1950s, ethnicity was not the primary way that Rwandans classified each other. At that time, the term *ubwoko*, when referring to human beings, meant the combination of a person's social attributes and their relevance in a given context. Hence I translate *ubwoko* in this proverb as "identity."

8 Jennie E. Burnet and Rwanda Initiative for Sustainable Development, "Culture, Practice, and Law: Women's Access to Land in Rwanda," in *Women and Land in Africa: Culture: Religion, and Realizing Women's Rights*, ed. L. M. Wanyeki (New York, NY: Zed Books, 2003), pp. 176–206, 188.

9 Catherine Andre, "Terre Rwandaise, accès, politique et reforme foncières," *L'Afrique des Grands lacs annuaire* (1997–8), pp. 141–73; Danielle de Lame. *A Hill Among a Thousand: Transformations and Ruptures in Rural Rwanda (English Translation: Une colline entre mille, ou, le calme avant la tempête)* (Madison, WI: University of Wisconsin Press, 2005 [1994]).

10 Villia Jefremovas, "Loose Women, Virtuous Wives and Timid Virgins: Gender and Control of Resources in Rwanda," *Canadian Journal of African Studies*

25:3 (1991), pp. 378–95; Villia Jefremovas, *Brickyards to Graveyards: From Production to Genocide in Rwanda* (Albany and New York, NY: State University of New York Press, 2002).

11 Jean-Marie Kamatali and Philippe Gafishi, *Situation des enfants et des femmes du Rwanda: survie, développement et protection* (Kigali, Rwanda: Gouvernement de la République Rwandaise et UNICEF, 2000), p. 188.

12 Ibid., author's translation from the original French.

13 Ibid., p. 124, author's translation from the original French.

14 Turshen, "The Political Economy of Rape," p. 60.

15 Author interviews, 1997, 1998, 1999.

16 Kamatali and Gafishi, *Situation des enfants et des femmes du Rwanda*, p. 188.

17 Jefremovas, "Loose Women, Virtuous Wives and Timid Virgins," pp. 97–108.

18 For some other examples, see Sophie Day, "What Counts as Rape? Physical Assault and Broken Contracts: Contrasting Views of Rape among London Sex Workers," in *Sex and Violence: Issues in Representation and Experience*, ed. Penelope Harvey and Peter Gow (New York, NY: Routledge, 1994), p. 172; and Robert M. Hayden, "Rape and Rape Avoidance in Ethno-National Conflicts: Sexual Violence in Liminalized States," *American Anthropologist* 102:1 (2001), pp. 27–41.

19 Day, "What Counts as Rape?" p. 172.

20 Jefremovas, "Loose Women, Virtuous Wives and Timid Virgins"; Jefremovas, *Brickyards to Graveyards*.

21 Gaspard Musabyimana, *Pratiques et rites sexuels au Rwanda* (Paris, France: L'Harmattan, 2006), p. 79.

22 The Rwandan Parliament passed a gender-based violence law in 2008 that criminalized rape in marriage. Republic of Rwanda, "Law No 59/2008 of 10/09/2008 law on Prevention and Punishment of Gender-Based Violence," *Official Gazette of the Republic of Rwanda* 48:14 (2008), pp. 81–105.

23 Musabyimana, *Pratiques et rites sexuels au Rwanda*, p. 79.

24 Vivian F. Go, Sethulakshmi C. Johnson, Margaret E. Bentley, Sudha Sivaram, A. K. Srikrishnan, David D. Celentano, and Suniti Solomon, "Crossing the Threshold: Engendered Definitions of Socially Acceptable Domestic Violence in Chennai, India," *Culture, Health & Sexuality* 5:5 (2003), pp. 393–408.

25 Penelope Harvey, "Domestic Violence in the Peruvian Andes," in *Sex and Violence: Issues in Representation and Experience*, ed. Penelope Harvey and Peter Gow (New York, NY: Routledge, 1994), pp. 66–89.

26 Human Rights Watch, *Shattered Lives*, p. 39.

27 Ibid., p. 36.

28 For example, see Hayden, "Rape and Rape Avoidance in Ethno-National Conflicts;" Gretchen Borchelt, "Sexual Violence Against Women in War and Armed Conflict," in *The Handbook of Women, Psychology, and the Law*, ed. Andrea Barnes (Hoboken, NJ: John Wiley & Sons), pp. 293–327; Claudia Card, "Rape as a Weapon of War," *Hypatia* 11:4 (1996), p. 5; Veena Das, "National Honour and Practical Kinship: Of Unwanted Women

and Children," in *Critical Events: An Anthropological Perspective on Contemporary India*, ed. Veena Das (Oxford, UK: Oxford University Press, 1995), pp. 55–83; Veena Das, "Sexual Violence, Discursive Formations and the State," *Economic and Political Weekly* (1996), pp. 2411–23; Soh, *The Comfort Women;* Taylor, *Sacrifice as Terror*; Turshen, "The Political Economy of Rape;" Turshen and Twagiramariya, *What Women Do in Wartime.*

29 Begoña Aretxaga, *Shattering Silence: Women, Nationalism, and Political Subjectivity in Northern Ireland* (Princeton, NJ: Princeton University Press, 1997).

30 Hayden, "Rape and Rape Avoidance in Ethno-National Conflicts," p. 36.

31 This assessment is based on information gleaned during interviews with Rwandans conducted between 1995 and 2011. Official statistics of sexual assaults in Rwanda before 1994 are not available.

32 Stephen C. Lubkemann, *Culture in Chaos: An Anthropology of the Social Condition in War* (Chicago, IL: University of Chicago Press, 2008).

33 Interviews by author, 1998, 1999, 2002.

34 Human Rights Watch, *Beyond the Rhetoric: Continuing Human Rights Abuses in Rwanda* (New York, NY: Human Rights Watch, 1993), p. 11.

35 Turshen, "The Political Economy of Rape," p. 59.

36 Human Rights Watch, *Shattered Lives*, p. 39.

37 Alison L. Des Forges, *Leave None to Tell the Story: Genocide in Rwanda* (New York, NY: Human Rights Watch, 1999), p. 215.

38 Anne-Marie de Brouwer, Sandra Chu, and Samer Muscati, *The Men Who Killed Me: Rwandan Survivors of Sexual Violence* (Vancouver, Canada: Douglas & McIntyre, 2009); Human Rights Watch, *Shattered Lives.*

39 Scott Straus, *The Order of Genocide: Race, Power, and War in Rwanda* (Ithaca, NY: Cornell University Press, 2006).

40 Taylor, *Sacrifice as Terror*, pp. 170–1.

41 Interviews by author, 1997, 2001, 2002.

42 Christopher Mullins, "He Would Kill Me with his Penis': Genocidal Rape in Rwanda as a State Crime," *Critical Criminology* 17:1 (2009), pp. 15–33, 23–4.

43 Ibid., p. 24.

44 International Criminal Tribunal for Rwanda, Prosecutor *v.* Nyiramashukuko, Ntahobali, Nsamimana, Nteziryayo, Kanyabashi, Ndayambaje (ICTR, 2011) pp. 6–7.

45 Ibid., pp. 7–8.

46 Human Rights Watch, *Shattered Lives.*

47 Interviews by author, 1997, 2002; de Brouwer, Chu, and Muscati, *The Men Who Killed Me.*

48 Human Rights Watch, *Shattered Lives*, pp. 42–3; Lisa Sharlach, "Gender and Genocide in Rwanda: Women as Agents and Objects of Genocide," *Journal of Genocide Research* 1:3 (1999), pp. 387, 394.

49 Des Forges, *Leave None to Tell the Story*, p. 215; Human Rights Watch, *Shattered Lives*, p. 18; Sharlach, "Gender and Genocide in Rwanda," p. 394;

and Taylor, *Sacrifice as Terror:* where Taylor, an anthropologist, analyzes the symbolic discourse of sexual violence in extremist Hutu rhetoric leading up to the genocide and in certain practices of sexual violence during the genocide.

50 Turshen, "The Political Economy of Rape."

51 Des Forges, *Leave None to Tell the Story,* p. 494.

52 Ibid., p. 296.

53 Human Rights Watch, *Shattered Lives,* pp. 59–60.

54 Interview by author, 2009.

55 Turshen, "The Political Economy of Rape," p. 63.

56 Twagiramariya and Turshen, "The Sexual Politics of Survival in Rwanda," p. 112.

57 Interviews by author, 2000, 2001, 2002.

58 Interviews by author, North province, Rwanda, 2009.

59 Human Rights Watch, *Shattered Lives.*

60 Bonnet, *Le viol comme arme de guerre au Rwanda.*

61 Miriam Sapiro and Patricia V. Sellers, "Arriving at Rwanda: Extension of Sexual Assault Prosecution Under the Statutes of the ad hoc International Criminal Tribunals," *American Society of International Law, Proceedings* 90 (1996), pp. 605–11; J. Birenbaum, L. Wyndel et al., "Amicus Brief Respecting Amendment of the Indictment and Supplementation of the Evidence to Ensure the Prosecution of Rape and other Sexual Violence within the Competence of the International Criminal Tribunal for Rwanda in the Case of Prosecutor *v.* Jean-Paul Akayesu" (1996).

62 Human Rights Watch, *Struggling to Survive.*

63 Nduwimana, *The Right to Survive;* de Brouwer, Chu, and Muscati, *The Men Who Killed Me;* Zraly and Nyirazinyoye, "Don't Let the Suffering Make You Fade Away."

64 Author interviews, Kigali, Rwanda, 1998, 2000, 2013 and North Carolina, US, 2004.

65 "SEVOTA Imageclip visualizing the activities of the Rwandese women's rights NGO," Solidarity for the Development of Widows and Orphans to Promote Self-Sufficiency and Livelihoods (SEVOTA). Available online: http://vimeo.com/11660854 (accessed March 29, 2012). Author's translation from Kinyarwanda.

66 De Brouwer, Chu, and Muscati, *The Men Who Killed Me,* p. 122.

67 "SEVOTA Imageclip." Author's translation from Kinyarwanda.

68 Burnet, *Genocide Lives in Us,* pp. 42–3; Marc Sommers, *Stuck: Rwandan Youth and the Struggle for Adulthood* (Athens, GA: University of Georgia Press, 2012), p. 194.

69 De Lame, *A Hill Among a Thousand,* p. 385; David L. Schoenbrun, *A Green Place, A Good Place: Agrarian Change, Gender and Social Identity in the Great Lakes Region to the 15th Century* (Portsmouth, NH: Heinemann, 1998), pp. 151–4.

70   Sommers, *Stuck: Rwandan Youth and the Struggle for Adulthood.*

71   "SEVOTA Imageclip." Author's translation from Kinyarwanda.

72   De Brouwer, Chu, and Muscati, *The Men Who Killed Me,* p. 116.

73   Bonnet, *Le viol comme arme de guerre au Rwanda,* p. 20.

74   African Rights, *Rwanda—Broken Bodies, Torn Spirits: Living with Genocide, Rape, and HIV/AIDS* (Kigali, Rwanda: African Rights, April 2004), p. 51.

75   Data taken from the World Development Indicators in the World Bank's World DataBank. Available online: http://databank.worldbank.org/data/home.aspx (accessed December 12, 2013).

76   US President's Emergency Plan for AIDS Relief, "Partnership to Fight HIV/AIDS in Rwanda" (PEFAR, 2013). Available online: http://www.pepfar.gov/documents/organization/199598.pdf.

77   Burnet, *Genocide Lives in Us,* p. 76.

78   Zraly and Nyirazinyoye, "Don't Let the Suffering Make You Fade Away."

79   Burnet, *Genocide Lives in Us.*

80   Author interview, West Province, Rwanda, 2013.

81   African Rights, *Rwanda—Broken Bodies,* p. 75.

82   Ibid., pp. 75–6.

83   Jennie E. Burnet, "Whose Genocide? Whose Truth? Representations of Victim and Perpetrator in Rwanda," in *Genocide: Truth, Memory and Representation,* ed. A. L. Hinton and K. O'Neill (Durham, NC: Duke University Press, 2009), pp. 80–110.

84   Das, "National Honour and Practical Kinship"; Das, "Sexual Violence, Discursive Formations and the State."

85   Das, "National Honour and Practical Kinship."

86   Hayden, "Rape and Rape Avoidance."

87   Human Rights Watch, *Shattered Lives*; Human Rights Watch, *Struggling to Survive*; F. Nduwimana, *The Right to Survive*; de Brouwer, Chu, and Muscati, *The Men Who Killed Me*; Zraly and Nyirazinyoye, "Don't Let the Suffering Make You Fade Away."

88   This theme fits the model described by Hirsch and Smith in their critique of many studies of feminism and cultural memory: women's "stories . . . represent individual identity as shaped by members in one or several groups." Marianne Hirsch and Valerie Smith, "Feminism and Cultural Memory: An Introduction," *Signs: Journal of Women in Culture & Society* 28:1 (2002), pp. 1–19, 7.

89   De Brouwer, Chu, and Muscati, *The Men Who Killed Me.*

90   Hirsch and Smith, "Feminism and Cultural Memory," p. 7.

91   Dianne Otto, "The Sexual Tensions of UN Peace support Operations: A Plea for 'Sexual Positivity,'" *Finnish Yearbook of International Law* 18 (2007): 33–57, 38.

92 John F. Decker and Peter G. Baroni, "'No' Still Means 'Yes:' the Failure of the 'Non-Consent' Reform Movement in American Rape and Sexual Assault Law," *Journal of Criminal Law & Criminology* 101:4 (2011), pp. 1081–1169.

93 Soh, *The Comfort Women*, p. 108.

94 United Nations Secretary-General, "Special Measures for Protection from Sexual Exploitation and Sexual Abuse: What You Need to Know" published by Inter-Agency Standing Committee Task Force on Protection from Sexual Exploitation and Abuse, ST/SGB/2003/13. Available online: http://www.un.org (October 9, 2003).

95 Otto, "The Sexual Tensions of UN Peace Support Operations," p. 35.

96 Ibid., p. 34.

PART THREE

Gender and Complicity

7

Ordinary Masculinity: Gender Analysis and Holocaust Scholarship

Stephen R. Haynes

Gentlemen, if there is ever a generation after us so cowardly, so soft, that it would not understand our work as good and necessary, then, gentlemen, National Socialism will have been for nothing. On the contrary we should bury bronze tablets saying that it was we, we who had the courage to carry out this gigantic task.

–STATEMENT FROM NUREMBERG TRIAL OF A NAZI GUARD AT BELZEC

We were Germany's best and hardest. Every single one of us dedicated himself to the others. What held us together was an alliance of comradeship. Not even the bond of marriage can be stronger. It gave us the mental and physical strength to do what others were too weak to do.

–SS VETERAN WHO SERVED IN A NAZI CONCENTRATION CAMP

We men of the new Germany have to be very tough with ourselves even when we are forced by circumstances to be separated from our families for quite a long time.

–*GENDARMERIEPOSTENFÜHRER* FRITZ JACOB

*Ahrens called me a coward and a sissy, and the like . . . he ordered
me to stand guard right by the hole (mass grave) in order to harden
me up.*

–POLICE RESERVIST FROM THIRD POLICE BATTALION 91

At an academic conference on the Holocaust in 1997, I attended a panel
discussion concerned with "women's voices in the Holocaust." During
the question-and-answer period that followed, I asked the panelists, all of
whom were women, whether they saw their work as opening the way for a
consideration of men's experience in the Holocaust. I did not intend to be
radical or provocative. I knew, as the panelists did, that under the influence
of academic feminism, scholars in the humanities and social sciences have
emphasized the gendered character of all human experience. Nonetheless,
the women's responses indicated that they regarded my question as a threat,
as one more in a series of male attempts to silence or marginalize their
voices.

This anecdote is representative of a wider problem in the field of Holocaust
studies, one evident in journals, monographs, and textbooks[1] as well as in
conference presentations: scholars who study the Nazi "Final Solution"
professionally are ignorant of or reluctant to acknowledge insights from
the burgeoning discipline of men's studies. The relatively recent emergence
of men's studies in popular culture does not fully explain this phenomenon.
For masculinity has been a subject of scholarly analysis for nearly a
century.[2] It emerged in the theories of Sigmund Freud and his associates,
particularly Alfred Adler; and by the middle of the twentieth century,
considerable scholarly attention was being directed at the "male sex role"
and the prescriptive pressure it exerts upon male behavior. Furthermore,
contemporary interest in masculinity dates to the late 1970s, the very period
in which Holocaust studies became a discrete field of academic inquiry.

In recent years, the scholarly study of masculinity (sometimes called the
"new men's studies") has exploded among anthropologists, psychologists,
sociologists, and scholars of religion. Emphasis is placed on the social
construction of masculinity ("shaped by historical circumstances and
social discourses, and not primarily by random biology"),[3] on multiple
'masculinities' ("hegemonic" and "nonhegemonic," for example)[4] and
the dynamics among them, and on the relationship between maleness,
masculinity, and the exercise of social power.[5]

Of course, not all scholars concerned with gender have welcomed this new
emphasis on masculinity in scholarship and popular culture. Some express
concern that the new men's studies is only a kinder, gentler strategy for
reiterating male-biased scholarship and retaining male privilege. Advocates
counter that the contemporary study of masculinity is *new*, inasmuch as it
is rooted in an examination of men's experience as specifically male rather

than generically human. Following feminist scholars who observe that Western discourse treats male experience as universal and ungendered and that women's experience must be understood as departing from this putative "human" standard, scholars of masculinity argue that men's experience also fails to conform to the "male" universal. That is, masculinities are perceived not as generic norms, but as objects of study on a par with femininities. In an oft-cited formulation of this assumption, Harry Brod writes,

> Like women's studies, men's studies aims at the emasculation of patriarchal ideology's masquerade as knowledge. Men's studies argues that while women's studies corrects the exclusion of women from the traditional canon caused by androcentric scholarship's elevation of *man* as male to *man* as generic human, the implications of this fallacy for our understanding of men have gone largely unrecognized. While *seemingly* about men, traditional scholarship's treatment of generic man as the human norm in fact systematically excludes from consideration what is unique to *men* qua men.[6]

Thus, the argument goes, if women have been obscured from scholarly view by being relegated to the background of the Western imagination, men have been distorted by being thrust into the foreground.[7]

If this is the perspective animating "the new men's studies," it would appear to be quite compatible with—and a natural complement to—the gender scholarship that has made such a signal contribution to our understanding of women's experience in the Holocaust. Why, then, has the study of masculinity achieved so little scholarly recognition in the interdiscipline of Holocaust studies?

Men's Studies and the Holocaust

It must be kept in mind that feminist perspectives did not begin to affect mainstream Holocaust scholarship until the 1980s, and it was not until the 1990s that academic conferences regularly featured sessions devoted to "women's experience" in the Shoah. Yet now that the salience of gender analysis for interpreting female experience in the Holocaust has been established, it is curious that the door has not opened more widely to considerations of masculinity.[8] There remain several sources of indifference and resistance to the study of men's experience among scholars of the Holocaust.

First, unlike feminism, which promises to expose and liberate women from an oppressive patriarchy, the "liberation" offered by men's studies holds little appeal for many of the male scholars who dominate the discipline. Given their positions of relative power in society and the academy, just what are male scholars to be liberated from? In what sense have they been victimized by male gender roles? As the female panelists by whom I was rebuffed hastened to point out, scholarship—like most forms of public discourse—has always been about men, for men, and by men.

Second, Holocaust scholarship has been dominated—both numerically and in terms of professional clout—by historians. While they have much in common with scholars in other fields of the humanities, historians tend to be more traditional methodologically than practitioners in religion, sociology, anthropology, or literature. Generally speaking, they are more resistant to "postmodern" attacks on Enlightenment epistemology and less receptive to claims that their discipline is blind to crucial aspects of human existence. Because most historians pursue "scientific" objectivity (whether or not they believe it is attainable), and because "the guiding metaphors of scientific research . . . all stem from the social position of dominant men in a gendered world," historians (particularly male historians) tend to eschew methodologies that are implicitly critical of their privileged social location.[9] This may explain why recent scholarship on masculinity has emerged among sociologists, anthropologists, and scholars of religion and has not achieved the level of acceptance across the scholarly spectrum enjoyed by academic feminism.

Third, high-profile attempts to apply the study of masculinity to the Holocaust have had limited scholarly impact. An instructive example is Klaus Theweleit's two-volume *Männerphantasien* (1977, 1978; English translation *Male Fantasies* 1987, 1989). Theweleit's remarkable study of Weimar Freikorpsmen became an instant classic among feminists and neo-Freudians, but it has had little influence on mainstream Holocaust scholarship. In fact, one looks in vain for references to *Male Fantasies* in standard textbooks on the Final Solution. This is, in part, because the book has little to say about the Holocaust per se (focusing as it does on the German "soldier males" who were active between 1918 and 1923) and because it is so inaccessible (over 1,000 pages long in translation, the book must remain opaque to any who lack a thorough knowledge of psychoanalytic theory and familiarity with post-structuralism). But *Male Fantasies'* failure to affect Holocaust scholarship may also be related to its claim that a deep misogynist strain is constitutive of male subcultures.

The reasons for resistance to gender analysis in Holocaust studies remain obscure; but its applicability to interpreting men's experience in the Holocaust can be easily demonstrated. I will establish this applicability by approaching male Holocaust perpetrators with a series of assumptions that emerge from contemporary gender analysis: (1) all human beings are gendered, historical subjects as well as the scholars who study them; (2) men's experience is as gendered as women's, though in different ways; (3) masculinity and femininity are inherently relational concepts, which take on meaning only in reference to each other; (4) the behavior of male combatants during wartime represents an unparalleled laboratory for the analysis of masculinity, since "the socialization of the soldier is simply an exaggeration of typical masculine socialization in [a] society"[10]; (5) ignoring the role of gender in determining attitudes and behavior only enhances its capacity to structure and distort human interactions; and (6) although gender dynamics operate unconsciously, they can be traced through analyses of language.

Working from these assumptions, this essay develops a case for applying gender analysis to the behavior and verbal self-justifications of a variety of male Holocaust perpetrators—including death camp commandants, specially selected killing-unit personnel, members of the armed forces, and reservists. Analysis of gender clues in the testimony of the men who perpetrated crimes against Jews and others during the Third Reich will illumine a fundamental tenet of men's studies: in Western societies, masculinity is often constructed around images of strength, hardness, firmness, etc., and this has the effect of normalizing conformist, aggressive, and asocial behavior. We begin by examining the experiences of death camp supervisors, turn briefly to SS men and *Einsatzgruppe* officers, and conclude by discussing German reserve policemen.

The Elite: Camp Commandants

One of the earliest autobiographical accounts by a Holocaust perpetrator was *Commandant of Auschwitz: The Autobiography of Rudolf Höss*, first published in 1951 and appearing in English in 1959.[11] When read with an eye for gender, Höss's autobiography offers an illuminating introduction to the dynamics of masculinity among Nazi true believers who became perpetrators of genocide. Early in the autobiography, Höss characterizes his previous military experience as a rite of male passage: "The upshot of my army service [during the First World War] was that I had reached manhood, both physically and mentally, long before my years. . . . The frightened schoolboy who had escaped from his mother's care and fought his first action against the enemy had become a tough and hardened soldier."[12]

Here and throughout his autobiography, Höss narrates his path toward genocide as a process of replacing weakness with "hardness." One such passage concerns his stint as a guard at Dachau under Theodor Eicke, who taught him that:

> any show of sympathy [toward prisoners] would be regarded by the enemies of the state as weakness, which they would immediately exploit. Furthermore, it was unworthy of an SS man to feel pity for "enemies of the state." [Eicke] had no room for weaklings in his ranks, and if any man felt that way he should withdraw to a monastery as quickly as possible. Only tough and determined men were of any use to him. It was not for nothing that they wore the death's head badge and always kept their weapons loaded.[13]

In another passage, Höss describes Eicke's attitude toward guards who fraternized with prisoners: such emotions were "a sign of weakness and sentimentality," a "weak-kneed attitude" unbefitting men who were "unconditionally tough."[14] Interestingly, his Dachau experience led Höss to conclude that he was thoroughly unsuited for service in a concentration camp: "I did not want to make a laughingstock of myself," he writes. "I did not wish to reveal my weakness." On the other hand, he was unable to admit that he was "too soft" for an SS job.[15]

According to Höss's narrative, the line at Dachau separating acceptable from unacceptable models of masculinity—the demarcation between the regions of softness and hardness, emotion and performance—was extraordinarily clear: on one side were the "weak-kneed," "sentimentality," "sympathy," "pity," "soft[ness]," "weakness," "weaklings," and the "monastery"; on the other side were the "unconditionally tough," the "tough and determined men," who kept their "weapons loaded." By his own account, Höss gradually internalized this camp masculinity. For, despite overseeing the deaths of millions of Jews by 1945, he claimed never to have "personally hated" his victims, "the emotion of hatred" being foreign to his nature.[16]

Throughout his autobiography, Höss describes normative masculinity in the language of hardness while portraying its threats with images of softness and penetrability. As gender theorist James Nelson observes, these images are typical of the "erection mentality" men unconsciously project upon the world and what is valuable in it:

> Consider hardness. In the male world of achievement, hard facts mean more than soft data. Men listen more readily to data from the "hard sciences" than to the soft, seemingly mushy information and theories of the people sciences. . . . Consider upness. Computers are "up" when they are functioning "down" when they are in trouble.[17]

Höss invokes another image that is common in the writings of male Holocaust perpetrators when he places masculinity in dialectical relationship with family, particularly motherhood and childhood. Claudia Koonz elucidates this dialectic in her book *Mothers in the Fatherland,* where she notes that Nazi wives who wished to share in their husbands' work were rare. Quite typical, however, were spouses who helped sustain their husbands' psychological balance by maintaining a safe domestic world in which they found refuge emotionally, if not physically.[18] In Höss's story, as in the language of perpetrators at every level of the Final Solution, maleness is consistently defined over against what is soft and emotional. But while masculinity must eschew the maternal and the feminine, it cannot survive (or even be described) without them. As R. W. Connell notes, "Masculinity as an object of knowledge is always masculinity-in-relation."[19]

The complex relationship between masculinity and family in the lives of Holocaust perpetrators is foregrounded when Höss describes his days at *Vernichtungslager* ("extermination camp") Auschwitz. Though his wife and family are well provided for and happy there, Höss reports an enduring tension created by his identities as family man and death camp supervisor.[20] In one passage, he highlights the contradiction between his impassive commandant-self and his need to connect emotionally with his wife and children:

> I withdrew further and further into myself. I hedged myself in, became unapproachable, and visibly harder. My family, and especially my wife, suffered on account of this, since my behavior was often intolerable. I had eyes only for my work, my task. All human emotions were forced into the background. My wife was perpetually trying to draw me out of my seclusion. She invited old friends from outside the camp to visit us, as well as my comrades in the camp, hoping that I would be able to relax in their company. She arranged parties away from the camps with the same end in view.[21]

Despite his need for family members' acceptance, Höss remains acutely aware that softening his masculine shell could have fearful consequences: "I had to appear cold and indifferent to events that must have wrung the heart of anyone possessed of human feelings. I might not even look away when afraid lest my natural emotions get the upper hand. I had to watch coldly, while the mothers with laughing or crying children went into the gas chambers."[22] If Höss was "deeply affected" by some incident, he would not immediately return home, but mount his horse and ride, or "walk through the stables and seek relief among [his] beloved animals."[23]

To the very end of his life, Höss strove to maintain this barrier between his public deeds and his private world. Awaiting execution, he wrote: "Whatever use is made of what I have written, I beg that all those passages relating to my wife and my family, and all my tender emotions and secret doubts, shall not be made public."[24] In his final days, Höss confessed that he was "securely anchored" to his family and to the farm "that was to become their permanent home." His real aim in life, he concluded, was to provide his children a "stable home."[25]

Recorded twenty-five years later, the story of Franz Stangl, commandant of Sobibor and Treblinka, reveals the very same gender dynamics at work in Höss's autobiography. Journalist Gitta Sereny's biographical account in *Into That Darkness* elucidates how Stangl relied on his family for psychic balance during his stint as a death camp supervisor and how his wife and daughters sheltered him from the emotional consequences of the Final Solution following his postwar arrest. "Did you want your family to come visit you in Poland," Sereny asked Stangl in the early 1970s. "I was so glad to have them there," he replied. "I found rooms for us on an estate just a few kilometers from Sobibor camp, near the village."[26] But as much as he needed his family to shelter him from the reality of his work, the arrangement carried risks. When Frau Stangl learned from a German officer the true nature of her husband's job, Stangl feared that his happy domestic existence was at an end. But after a temporary emotional crisis, Frau Stangl allowed herself to be convinced that Franz's role at Sobibor was "purely administrative." Afterward she did not inquire too much about her husband's work and remained fiercely loyal to the end. Her role as shield from the actuality of Stangl's horrific acts remained intact through postwar accusations and legal proceedings. According to Sereny, although he refused to discuss with her the charges against him, Stangl desperately wanted his wife present during his internment and trial: "The only thing that mattered to him was her and his children's continued loyalty and love."[27]

The Middlemen: SS and *Einsatzgruppe* Personnel

What of male perpetrators who were not afforded the luxury of having families present to buffer them from the unpleasant reality of their professional lives? If the gender dynamics operating in the stories of Höss and Stangl were at work among the male perpetrators in the middle regions of the Nazi hierarchy, we would expect to see evidence of this in the letters, interviews, and court depositions that document their experiences. And indeed we do.

In a series of letters written during the fall of 1942 to his wife and children, *SS-Obersturmführer* Karl Kretschmer assures his family that, although hundreds of miles away, they remain "the very substance of [his] private life."[28] In this and other missives from the front, Kretschmer indicates that preserving his identity as an honorable father and husband is essential to rationalizing his participation in *Einsatzgruppe* murders. In one letter to his family, Kretschmer reveals the extent to which "camp masculinity" has come to inform his identity in the field:

> We have got to appear to be tough here or else we will lose the war. There is no room for pity of any kind. . . . I have already told you about the shooting—that I could not say "no" here either. . . . It is a weakness not to be able to stand the sight of dead people; the best way of overcoming it is to do it more often. Then it becomes a habit.[29]

Dozens of similar statements from members of Nazi killing squads indicate that within the ranks there prevailed a masculinity rooted in the opposition of courage/hardness/performance on one hand, and cowardice/softness/inability to perform on the other. "It's almost impossible to imagine what nerves of steel it took to carry out that dirty work down there . . . it was horrible," recalled one *Einsatzgruppe* member following the war. Another remembered his commanding officer warning his unit that they:

> would have to conquer [their] weaker selves and that what was needed were tough men who understood how to carry out orders. . . . Any officer who had declared that he was too weak to do such things [participate in shootings of Jews] would have been considered unfit to be an officer.[30]

Many SS men who in various ways helped execute the Nazi Final Solution later recorded self-justifications in which the language of hardened masculinity predominates:

> The officer shot the people himself as the others refused. He swore at us and said we were cowards.
>
> The reason I did not say to Leideritz that I could not take part in these things was that I was afraid that Leideritz and others would think I was a coward. I was worried that I would be affected adversely in some way in the future if I allowed myself to be seen as being too weak. I did not want Leideritz or other people to get the impression that I was not as hard as an SS man ought to have been.
>
> [Raschwitz] ordered me to go to the grave and to shoot Jews there with my pistol. I, however refused to comply with this order. . . . Raschwitz then hurled some abuse at me . . . he . . . used the term "coward" and other terms of abuse.[31]

The recurring images and themes in these passages communicate something fundamental about the parameters of masculine identity among Nazi perpetrators. But did the same conceptions of masculinity inform perpetrators who were less Nazified, who were neither true believers nor volunteered for actions' against Jewish civilians? In other words, do we find among the "ordinary men" who became killers largely by chance the same constructions of masculinity evident among those who were ideologically prepared for murder? Was conformity to the masculine ideal a source of motivation for male Holocaust perpetrators, no matter their experience, rank, or task?

Ordinary Men/Ordinary Germans: The Goldhagen-Browning Debate

To answer this question we will attend to seminal work by Daniel Goldhagen and Christopher Browning, scholars who have painstakingly studied the ordinary perpetrators who made the Nazi Final Solution a near reality. Goldhagen's *Hitler's Willing Executioners* has proved a magnet for attention and controversy since its publication in 1996, and the so-called Goldhagen debate turned out to be the affair of the decade in Holocaust studies. The participants in the "debate" were Goldhagen and his advocates, who claimed the book had effected a revolution in our understanding of German perpetrators and bystanders, and Goldhagen's detractors (led by the scholars whose work he summarily dismisses), who rarely overlooked an opportunity to attack *Hitler's Willing Executioners.*

Several years before the appearance of Goldhagen's book, Christopher Browning published an important study entitled *Ordinary Men* that focused exclusively on the wartime activities of Order Police Battalion 101. In part to refute Browning's interpretation of the battalion's career, Goldhagen dedicated a 100-page section of his book (*Police Battalions: Ordinary Germans, Willing Killers*) to reassessing the archival evidence. In two chapters devoted to the activities of Battalion 101 in Poland, Goldhagen fashioned a thorough repudiation of Browning's interpretation of these German perpetrators. Understandably, Browning did not concede defeat. In the revised edition of *Ordinary Men* and in shorter pieces published since the appearance of *Hitler's Willing Executioners,* Browning offered a spirited response to Goldhagen's reinterpretation of Battalion 101.

Despite their sharp differences, however, Goldhagen, Browning, and most other students of perpetrator behavior remain in implicit agreement on one thing: when interpreting the actions of "ordinary" German men who perpetrated crimes against Jewish civilians during the Holocaust, questions of gender are irrelevant. Is this assumption justified? Or is there evidence that the construction of gender played a role in the self-understanding and self-justification of these unlikely killers?

The Evidence for Gender

Browning's *Ordinary Men*, first published in 1992, is a detailed and compelling study of the composition, activities, and motivations of the men of Reserve Police Battalion 101 who operated in the Lublin District of Poland in 1942 and 1943. While Browning does not regard the social construction of masculinity as a fruitful field of interpretation, he cannot help but illuminate the role of gender in his subjects' behavior. For instance, on the very first page of *Ordinary Men*, Browning notes that at the time of their service in Poland his subjects were "middle-aged family men of working- and lower-middle-class background."[32] Yet while he makes much of the men's age, class, and occupation, Browning says very little of their identity as "family men."[33] This despite the fact that the designation "ordinary" is based in part on the men's identity as husbands and fathers. While Browning remarks that some of those who "stepped out" of the battalion's killing actions did so because they were "fathers with children and could not continue," he does not pursue the possible links between his subjects' identities as family men and their refusal to kill Jews.[34]

Browning notes in passing that one motivation for enlisting in the Order Police was the prospect of serving "closer to home," no doubt a reference to the psychic benefit of proximity to family and friends.[35] In fact, home and family recur throughout the study as sources of cognitive dissonance for the battalion's men, but Browning fails to note their significance. For instance, despite paying special attention to the moral reasoning of those who "stepped out" before or during battalion actions, Browning overlooks the fact that the men's justifications for inaction often featured references to women and children. Typical in this regard was Heinz Buchmann, who communicated to his commanding officer that he "would in no case participate in such an action, in which defenseless women and children are shot."[36] The prospect of killing children seemed a particularly strong deterrent for some of those who opted out of the killing operations. According to one eyewitness, "Almost tacitly everyone refrained from shooting infants and small children."[37] For instance, when confronted with a ten-year-old girl who had survived the Jozefow massacre, Major Wilhelm Trapp embraced her, promising "you shall remain alive."[38]

Browning's sources demonstrate that the men's perceived roles as protectors of women and children could play a paradoxical role in their thinking about murder. On one hand, Major Trapp sought to aid his men in overcoming their qualms about killing Jews by reminding them that "in Germany the bombs were falling on women and children."[39] On the other hand, psychic conflict between the duty to kill and respect for the sanctity of family was sometimes projected upon the battalion's Jewish victims. Browning quotes a letter asking that its author be spared "without fail from this police battalion," since "almost all [Jewish] families have been torn apart."[40]

In his analysis of individual decisions to comply with or resist killing orders, Browning records dozens of references to mastery, strength, and weakness, often setting them off with quotation marks to emphasize that the words are his subjects' own.[41] Browning does not perceive in this language any clues to the killers' state of mind. Read with an eye for gender, however, this language reveals that images of weakness proliferated in the testimony of men who refused to comply with killing orders. When a driver assigned to carry Jews to the forest during the Jozefow massacre asked to be relieved, he explained that "his nerves were not strong enough."[42] In order to forestall criticism from their comrades, nonshooters claimed they were "too weak" rather than too good to kill.[43] Finally, when battalion veterans attacked each other in postwar legal testimony, their aspersions trafficked in images of softness such as "weakling" and "shithead."

Browning does note the deterrent effect on moral courage of perceptions that a man was "too weak," was "cowardly," or might "lose face." He states that those who evaded action by intentionally misfiring risked being called "traitor and coward" if discovered.[44] He also reports that even after being warned to "become tougher," some men simply ignored orders to shoot Jewish women and children.[45] Furthermore, Browning observes that not everyone was strong enough to be considered weak and that conformity increased with the likelihood that weakness would be exposed. But Browning fails to appreciate the centrality of the strength/weakness dichotomy in the perpetrators' mental world and thus fails to recognize what this dichotomy indicates about the construction of masculinity among both shooters and nonshooters. The most obvious clue to these gender dynamics is the way participation in killing actions became a test of manhood that effectively bifurcated the battalion into the "tough" and the "weak." As one soldier put it, "No one ever approached me concerning these operations. For these actions the officers took 'men' with them, and in their eyes I was no 'man.'"[46]

According to Browning's own text, the physical and psychological reactions of the men who murdered civilians reveal a complex interplay of weakness and strength. At one point, in response to the constant need to display strength, Major Trapp wept "like a child."[47] Physical illness, another form of weakness, was common among the men, and often became an excuse for failure to participate in battalion "actions." Nausea, vomiting, and diarrhea were varieties of temporary weakness that spared the men from having to prove their "strength"; and, of course, the temporarily weak were further emasculated by the "strong." When a suspicious "irritable colon" put Captain Hoffmann out of action, his men began referring to him derisively as *Pimpf*, or "Hitler cub scout."[48] In response, Hoffmann desperately sought to reaffirm his manhood by invoking his "honor as an officer and soldier." Thus, in the construction of male behavior that held these perpetrators together, the "strong" masculine was consistently identified through negative evaluation of the "weak" nonmasculine (or feminine).[49]

Browning's book contains other clues that, in the context of a masculine fraternity competing to demonstrate strength, possess unmistakable gender connotations. First, like male sexuality, perpetrator masculinity was linked to performance; that is, it was established by taking part in battalion operations. Further, when Major Trapp announced that older men who were not "up to the task" of murder could step out of formation, we see how job performance and sexual virility are intimately connected in the battalion's vision of masculine behavior.[50] In fact, Trapp's offer to the older men who were not "up," taken in conjunction with Captain Hoffmann's reduction to the status of cub scout, indicate that in the battalion's collective psyche those who did not conform and perform were regarded as either too young or too old to be considered real men. Despite this proliferation of evidence for what theorists call "genitalization"—a thought pattern leading men to prize the qualities of hardness, upness, and linearity—Browning does not tell us whether impotence was a problem in the battalion, as it apparently was among other groups of male killers during the Holocaust.[51]

The strange case of Captain Wohlauf and his expectant wife is yet another aspect of Battalion 101's wartime career that cries out for gender analysis. According to Browning, the men of the battalion were appalled when Wohlauf's "young bride—four months pregnant, with a military coat draped over her shoulders and a peaked military cap on her head" climbed aboard one of the trucks headed for a killing action.[52] Browning surmises that the captain was seeking to impress his wife by demonstrating that he was a "master" over Polish Jewry, but also notes that Wohlauf's men reacted with "indignation and outrage that a woman was brought to witness the terrible things they were doing."[53] This reaction only intensified when Frau Wohlauf witnessed the deportation of Jews to Treblinka in August 1942. Because Goldhagen also emphasizes the men's reaction to Frau Wohlauf's presence with the battalion, we shall wait before commenting on its significance for gender analysis.

Finally, Browning records without comment several peculiarly male responses to the battalion's involvement in the murder of civilians. While the reservists performed guard duty around the Lodz ghetto, the company recreation room assumed a locker-room atmosphere: "A mark was made on the bar door for each Jew shot, and 'victory celebrations' were reportedly held on days when high scores were recorded."[54] Neither this masculine integration of alcohol and sport nor the association of the term "Jew-hunt" (*Judenjagd*) with an age-old male pastime receives any attention from the author.

In the final chapter of *Ordinary Men*, Browning considers a series of possible explanations for the behavior of the "ordinary men" of Battalion 101—wartime brutalization, racism, segmentation and routinization, special selection, careerism, obedience, deference to authority, ideological indoctrination, and conformity. While his analysis is impressive in its thoroughness, his conclusions would certainly be affected by acknowledgment of the gender clues that proliferate the evidence he reviews.[55] For one thing, Browning would be more reluctant to discount the role of ideological indoctrination in explaining the men's wartime behavior. According to Browning, Battalion 101's ideological training was brief and cursory, contained relatively little explicit anti-Semitism, and was utterly ineffective at "brainwashing" the men. But he underestimates the extent to which ideological education, even when it did not speak of killing Jews, could reinforce attitudes regarding strength and masculinity to which the men were already receptive. While their propaganda training did not *make* them kill, it no doubt encouraged would-be killers by applying masculine values to the war and their role in it. For the ideological literature they encountered trafficked in the very vocabulary of strength and mastery, which the men themselves relied on when describing their activities. Browning summarizes the message of one ideological pamphlet assigned to Order Police:

Shaped by a severe northern climate that ruthlessly eliminated weak elements, the Nordic race was superior to any other in the world, as could be seen from German cultural and military achievements. The German *Volk* faced a constant struggle for survival ordained by nature, according to whose laws "all weak and inferior are destroyed" and "only the strong and powerful continue to propagate."[56]

Another pamphlet delivered a similar message regarding partisans: "The incessant decision over life and death posed by the partisans and suspects is difficult even for the toughest soldier. But it must be done. He behaves correctly who, by setting aside all possible impulses of personal feeling, proceeds ruthlessly and mercilessly."[57] It is true, as Browning argues, that this literature did not include a call to eliminate racial enemies; but by serving to make the policemen "hardened killers" and encouraging them to segregate feeling from performance, it no doubt contributed to their fear of appearing "soft" or "weak" before their comrades.[58]

Commenting on the nonshooters' claim that it was weakness rather than moral superiority which led them to opt out of battalion killing actions, Browning comes close to elucidating the language of gender in which the behavior of his ordinary men is inscribed:

> Insidiously, therefore, most of those who did not shoot only reaffirmed the "macho" values of the majority—according to which it was positive quality to be "tough" enough to kill unarmed, noncombatant men, women and children—and tried not to rupture the bonds of comradeship that constituted their social world.... Only the very exceptional remained indifferent to taunts of "weakling" from their comrades and could live with the fact that they were considered to be "no man."[59]

Yet Browning fails to develop these insights, and near the end of *Ordinary Men*, he insists that "this story of ordinary men is not the story of all men."[60] However, much of the evidence he has cited suggests that it could well be the story of most men, at least where masculinity is similarly defined.

Goldhagen's Revision

In Chapters 7 and 8 of *Hitler's Willing Executioners*—"Police Battalion 101: The Men's Deeds" and "Police Battalion 101: Assessing the Men's Deeds," respectively—Daniel Goldhagen offers a major reconsideration of the behavior and motivations of Browning's ordinary men. Goldhagen places special emphasis on their willingness to comply with orders to kill—as evidenced by their "incessant volunteering," their "failure to avail themselves of opportunities to avoid killing," and the enthusiasm and brutality that accompanied their murderous deeds.[61] Goldhagen differs from Browning mainly in his explanation of these behaviors. For Goldhagen, the members of Battalion 101 are representative not of soldiers under the pressure of conformity but of Germans influenced by cultural anti-Semitism and Nazi propaganda. Accordingly, Goldhagen refers consistently to the men of Reserve Battalion 101 as "the Germans."[62]

But in his careful reassessment of the wartime career of Battalion 101, Goldhagen pays no attention to the gender clues that punctuate the men's testimony. In some cases, he passes by the same patterns of masculinity that are ignored in Browning's text.[63] For instance, Goldhagen notes that of those men for whom family information exists, 99 percent had wives and 75 percent had children. But he fails to relate this demographic data to the men's behavior or thought processes. For instance, in considering an episode in which Major Trapp assembled the battalion and asked his men "to think of our women and children in our homeland who had to endure aerial bombardments," Goldhagen writes that Trapp's justification was emblematic of "the Nazified German mind."[64] But he ignores the version of masculinity invoked by Trapp's words, in which maleness is judged in terms of one's ability to protect women.[65] Similarly, Goldhagen remarks that following the Jozefow massacre the men were sickened, vomited, and lost their appetites. But he overlooks these signs of temporary physical weakness, since "no one suffered any significant emotional difficulties" afterward.

At a few points, Goldhagen strains to find significance in testimony Browning has passed over. He observes, for instance, that the Germans in Battalion 101 "tellingly" referred to their search-and-destroy missions as "Jew hunts." He then writes:

> The Germans' use of the term "Jew-hunt" was not casual. It expressed the killers' conception of the nature of their activity and the attendant emotion. Theirs was the exterminatory pursuit of the remnants of a particularly pernicious species that needed to be destroyed in its entirety. Moreover, the word "*Jagd*" has a positive *Gefühlswert*, a positive emotional valence. Hunting is a pleasurable pursuit, rich in adventure, involving no danger to the hunter, and its reward is a record of animals slain—in the case of the men of this police battalion and other German "Jew-hunters," a record of Jews ferreted out and killed.[66]

This insightful paragraph is the kind that has made Goldhagen's book popular despite its length and density; but it misses the significance of the very language it seeks to illuminate. Yes, the men of Battalion 101 referred to their searches as "hunts"; yes, this term has a pleasurable connotation in cultures where one hunts for sport rather than survival. But even more important is the fact that in these same cultures, hunting is something men do with one another, away from family and society, in part to demonstrate their manhood.

Goldhagen makes much of the way German perpetrators sought to "master" their Polish victims, for instance by cutting off their beards.

But once again Goldhagen approaches an important gender clue only to misapprehend its significance. He writes that "the Jew, a grown man, had no choice but to stand by as another abridged his sovereignty over his own body by cutting away his beard, a symbol of his manhood."[67] He fails to imagine, however, why a group of *men* might develop this ritual of asserting mastery over other *men* before killing them. Goldhagen applies the dynamics of honor and shame to the encounter (citing Orlando Patterson's *Slavery and Social Death*) but ignores the fact that in most cultures honor is a gender-specific concept. Goldhagen is correct in his belief that removal of Jews' beards was fraught with symbolism. But rather than an emblem of the "limitless power" Germans wished to exercise over Jews, it was more likely a symbolic exercise in emasculation that allowed the killers to compensate for their own barely repressed impotence and fear.

The most glaring example of Goldhagen's failure to grasp the play of gender in the career of Battalion 101 comes in his discussion of the men's wives. Like Browning, Goldhagen comments specifically on the presence of Frau Wohlauf, who "stayed with the battalion for at least several weeks and several killing operations, and participated in one, if not two, of the large ones."[68] While in Poland, Vera Wohlauf and other women "got to observe firsthand how their men were purging the world of the putative Jewish menace." Goldhagen notes that this is how the pregnant Frau Wohlauf spent her honeymoon and, to illustrate the incongruity of her attendance at the battalion's killing actions, includes a photograph of the lovely Frau Wohlauf posing by the seaside.[69]

Also like Browning, Goldhagen observes that many of the men considered Vera Wohlauf's presence in the field inappropriate, particularly because she was pregnant. Their chief reaction, according to Goldhagen, was anger—at Frau Wohlauf and her husband alike. Goldhagen asks whether the men were concerned that Frau Wohlauf would discover the deeper nature of their activities. Hardly, he answers, since she had already accompanied her husband at some of the battalion's most brutal "actions." Goldhagen concludes thus:

> Their objections bespeak no shame at what they were dong, no desire to conceal from others their contribution to mass annihilation and torture, but rather a sense of chivalry and propriety that Frau Wohlauf's presence violated, particularly since this ghetto clearing was, even by their standards, unusually brutal and gruesome.[70]

Goldhagen's reference to chivalry is not so much inaccurate as it is misleading, for it ignores what the work of Claudia Koonz and other scholars sensitive to gender have made so clear: that the men of Battalion 101 were reacting to an impingement on their professional domain of the private domestic sphere in which male perpetrators desired their women to remain.

Goldhagen notes correctly that Frau Wohlauf's expectant state caused her to arouse the men's ire. Even Major Trapp complained before a large gathering of men and a few visiting wives that it was "outrageous that women who are in a state of pregnancy should witness" such things.[71] But Goldhagen mistakenly supposes that references to her pregnancy make it "clear that the men were agitated because of possible damage to her sensibilities and person."[72] Much more likely, her pregnancy and her extended stay with the battalion combined to make Frau Wohlauf a walking symbol of confusion between the public and domestic spheres that perpetrators desired so assiduously to keep apart. Goldhagen remarks on the irony that the men of Battalion 101 expressed more discomfort with the presence of women than they did with the heinous nature of their own deeds. But there is more to be gleaned from this fact than "the perpetrators' *obvious* approval of their own historic deeds."[73] Widespread outrage at the presence of an officer's pregnant wife is meaningful in itself, as it indicates the role "family" played in the men's efforts to maintain psychic equilibrium in the killing fields of Poland. Goldhagen himself notes that "during their time as genocidal killers, the men of Police Battalion 101 went home on furloughs, lasting weeks."[74] Yet the point to be noted about these furloughs is not that time "in the bosom of their families" should have allowed them to consider their horrendous deeds but that whoever granted these furloughs regarded them as a boon to the men's long-term performance.

Unknowingly, Goldhagen includes a variety of clues that indicate the importance of family in emotionally sustaining members of police battalions caught up in murder. For instance, in a chapter entitled "Police Battalions: Lives, Killings and Motives," he notes that policemen did not perform their duties in a social or cultural vacuum. He details the German cultural life that battalion members created for themselves in wartime Poland and places this in "stark, even jarring, contrast to their apocalyptic deeds."[75] Sanctioned cultural events included religious services, theater productions, opportunities for swimming and tennis, athletic events, musical afternoons, and "social evenings." But Goldhagen perceives in these activities nothing more than cruel irony and must conclude that the men's sensibilities did not "remotely approximate our own."[76] Yet the consistent provision of such diversions in the periods between genocidal killing sprees only confirms the role of domestic life—real or contrived—in maintaining the sanity of perpetrators. Obviously, the men in these battalions desperately needed the illusion of normalcy provided by the sorts of leisure activities they might pursue at home. They engaged in them not because they were unaffected by their murderous activities but precisely because they were. The fact that wives and children were encouraged to join their husbands in battalion-sponsored events suggests that those who planned them understood the importance of providing time and space for the men to express their private family selves—selves based in emotion rather than performance.[77]

Conclusion: Gender and Holocaust Scholarship

The issues raised in the Goldhagen-Browning debate continue to provoke discussion in Holocaust studies. In an article entitled "Ordinary Germans or Ordinary Men?: Another Look at the Perpetrators," Christopher Browning surveys the behavior of non-German perpetrators and confirms that "situational" rather than ideological or national factors best explain the conduct of the men in Battalion 101. Browning thus reasserts his original claim with regard to perpetrators in general. "In trying to understand the vast majority of perpetrators," he writes, "we are dealing not with 'ordinary Germans' but with 'ordinary men.'"[78]

Other scholars have joined the fray. Inga Clendinnen's *Reading the Holocaust* takes Goldhagen to task for his lack of curiosity ("He is not curious about these men and what they did, because he believes he already knows why") and applauds Browning's study as "more penetrating, more subtle, and more interesting both methodologically and morally."[79] But while such judgments point out Goldhagen's flaws, they also obscure those he shares with Browning, particularly the tacit assumption that the dynamics of masculinity possess no explanatory value for interpreting the behavior of Holocaust perpetrators. Thus Browning's response to Goldhagen—and Clendinnen's defense of Browning—only confirms the failure of all three to take into account the function of gender in the career of Battalion 101.

In terms of gender analysis, it is not necessary to take sides in the Goldhagen-Browning debate; for both scholars are right, and both are wrong. The men of Battalion 101 were "broadly representative" of German society, as Goldhagen maintains, and in this sense should be viewed as "ordinary Germans." And, as Browning reminds us, they were indicative both of other Holocaust perpetrators, regardless of nationality, and the perpetrators of other crimes—real and experimental. Yet both men fail to identify the various expressions of the perpetrators' identities as *men* that permeate the records they assess. How do we explain this failure of otherwise incisive students of human behavior to perceive the play of gender in the subjects they have analyzed so carefully?

It is not that they are unaware of recent scholarship or suffer from disciplinary tunnel vision. Goldhagen in particular represents an academic generation socialized since the advent of feminism, and his magnum opus is otherwise impressively interdisciplinary. Furthermore, he advocates a mode of analysis called "thick description," which seeks to create as rich as possible a background for interpretation by "setting down the meanings particular social actions have for the actors whose actions they are."[80] Yet despite his intention of attending as closely as possible to the perpetrators' own *Lebenswelt* ("life world"), Goldhagen, as inexplicably as Browning, overlooks the gender dynamics that animate the eyewitness accounts he painstakingly analyzes.

Nor are these scholars devoid of historical imagination. For instance, when discussing the men's willingness to murder Jewish children, Goldhagen imagines them walking "through the woods with their own children by their sides, marching gaily and inquisitively along."[81] Did they remember these walks as they accompanied young Jewish children to the killing sites, Goldhagen asks rhetorically? It is a powerful passage that gives the reader pause. But it also heightens our disappointment with the things the author cannot—or will not—imagine. Even Browning, whose style is more traditional, occasionally comments on the symbolic meaning of the language used by the perpetrators. He notes, for instance, that "the full weight" of one perpetrator's statement cannot be appreciated without the knowledge that *erlösen*, the German word for "release" (in the sense of releasing from suffering through murder) also means to "redeem." Browning is generally aware when repression and projection have distorted the language of the men whose testimonies he is reading. But he has no ear for gender.

An important factor appears to be the methodological assumptions of the scholars who study perpetrators. In addition to the notion that gender analysis has nothing to contribute to the study of Holocaust perpetrators, Browning, Goldhagen, and most of those who study the Holocaust share the view that the behavior of men like those in Battalion 101 resulted from the special circumstances in which these men found themselves. Browning and Goldhagen both emphasize that "environment" offers the key to understanding these ordinary perpetrators, though Browning refers to the various situational factors that came to bear upon them in Poland, while Goldhagen has in mind an anti-Jewish German culture. But in focusing on these environmental factors, these scholars unconsciously assume a univalent notion of masculinity—one that is heterosexual, misogynist, and hegemonic, one represented by the male who defines himself over and against women and is determined to prove his strength by dominating and, if necessary, eliminating others.

As Browning himself observes, "Other historians looking at the same materials would retell these events in somewhat different ways."[82] But gender consciousness—as opposed to gender theory—should not be regarded as a matter of style, methodology, or advocacy but as a kind of vision developed by interpreters of history, a way of seeing that emerges as men and women engage in conversation. This essay has sought to indicate the dynamics of masculinity in the experiences and testimonies of male perpetrators active at every level of the Nazi Final Solution, and in the process, to suggest how a wider recognition of the gendered character of male experience may enrich scholarly understanding of Holocaust perpetrators.

Notes

1   A recent collection of "interpretive essays from the field's leading scholars" provides compelling evidence of the problem. Editors Helen B. Mitchell and Joseph R. Mitchell address "gender" in a chapter dealing exclusively with women's experience in *The Holocaust: Readings and Interpretations*, ed. Helen

B. Mitchell and Joseph R. Mitchell (New York, NY: McGraw-Hill, 2001), ch. 7, pp. 363–409.

2   R. W. Connell writes that "in the course of the twentieth century there have been three main projects for a science of masculinity. One was based in the clinical knowledge acquired by therapists, and its leading ideas came from Freudian theory. The second was based in social psychology and centered on the enormously popular idea of 'sex role.' The third involves recent developments in anthropology, history and sociology." See R. W. Connell, *Masculinities* (Berkeley, CA: University of California Press, 1995), p. 7. For an excellent introduction to the historical development of this field, see Connell's chapter entitled "The Science of Masculinity," pp. 3–44.

3   Maurice Berger, Brian Wallis, and Simon Watson, eds., *Constructing Masculinity* (New York, NY: Routledge, 1995), p. 3.

4   "To recognize diversity in masculinities is not enough. We must also recognize the relations between the different kinds of masculinity: relations of alliance, dominance and subordination. These relationships are constructed through practices that exclude and include, that intimidate, exploit, and so on. There is a gender politics within masculinity" (Connell, *Masculinities*, p. 37).

5   "Gay theory and feminist theory share a perception of mainstream masculinity as being (in the advanced capitalist countries at least) fundamentally linked to power, organized for domination, and resistant to change because of power relations. In some formulations, masculinity is virtually equated with the exercise of power in its most naked forms" (Connell, *Masculinities*, p. 42).

6   Cited in Stephen B. Boyd, W. Merle Longwood, and Mark W. Muesse, *Redeeming Men: Religion and Masculinities* (Louisville, KY: Westminster/John Knox, 1996), p. xiv. See also James B. Nelson, *The Intimate Connection: Male Sexuality, Masculine Spirituality* (Philadelphia, PA: Westminster, 1988), p. 18.

7   Harry Brod, ed., "The Case for Men's Studies," in *The Making of Masculinities: The New Men's Studies* (Boston, MA: Allen and Unwin, 1987), pp. 40–1.

8   Among the major scholarly works that address the topic are Claudia Koonz, *Mothers in the Fatherland: Women, the Family and Nazi Politics* (New York, NY: St. Martin's, 1987); John K. Roth and Carol Rittner, eds., *Different Voices: Women and the Holocaust* (New York, NY: Continuum, 1993); Dalia Ofer and Lenore J. Weitzman, eds., *Women in the Holocaust* (New Haven, CT: Yale University Press, 1998).

9   Connell, *Masculinities*, p. 6. Connell does point out, however, that by the end of the 1970s some scholars were calling for a "men's history" analogous to "women's history."

10 Nelson, *The Intimate Connection*, p. 42. Nelson continues: "Steeling the recruit against his emotions, hardening his willingness to exercise violence and inflict death, works best on young men still unsure of their own identities. . . . During basic training, he is continually threatened by the awesome, intimidating drill instructor, who screams into his face epithets identifying him as homosexual or feminine, while he must remain utterly passive under threat of physical violence. When sexual identity is sufficiently threatened,

psychological control is achieved and the young man's sexuality is linked with military functions of aggression and dominance" (p. 71).

11 Rudolf Höss, *Commandant in Auschwitz,* trans. Constantine FitzGibbon (Cleveland, OH and New York, NY: The World Publishing Co., 1959).

12 Ibid., p. 42. In the Freikorps, Höss rediscovered the purpose of military life: "I found a home again and a sense of security in the comradeship of my fellows. Oddly enough it was I, the lone wolf, always keeping my thoughts and my feelings to myself, who felt continually drawn toward that comradeship which enables a man to rely on others in time of need and of danger" (p. 44).

13 Ibid., p. 73.

14 Ibid., p. 94.

15 Ibid., p. 87.

16 Ibid. Höss writes: "I must emphasize here that I have never personally hated the Jews. It is true that I looked upon them as the enemies of our people. But just because of this I saw no difference between them and the other prisoners, and I treated them all in the same way. I never drew any distinctions. In any case even the emotion of hatred is foreign to my nature" (p. 146).

17 Nelson, *The Intimate Connection,* p. 37.

18 Koonz, *Mothers in the Fatherland.*

19 Connell, *Masculinities,* p. 44.

20 "My family, to be sure, were well provided for in Auschwitz. Every wish that my wife or children expressed was granted them. The children could live a free and untrammeled life. My wife's garden was a paradise of flowers. The prisoners never missed an opportunity for doing some little act of kindness to my wife or children and thus attracting their attention" (Höss, *Commandant in Auschwitz,* p. 174).

21 Ibid., p. 124.

22 Ibid., p. 170.

23 Ibid., p. 172.

24 Ibid., p. 201.

25 Ibid., p. 200. "Since returning from the war to which I went as a youngster and from which I came back a man, I have had two lights to guide me: my fatherland and, later, my family. . . . My second worship was my family. To them I was securely anchored. My thoughts were always with their future, and our farm was to become their permanent home. In our children both my wife and I saw our aim in life. To bring them up so that they could play their part in the world, and to give them all a stable home, was our one task in life."

26 Roth and Rittner, eds., *Different Voices,* p. 278.

27 Ibid., p. 283.

28 Klee, Ernst, Willi Dressen, Volker Riess, and Hugh Trevor-Roper, eds., *The Good Old Days: The Holocaust as Seen through the Eyes of Perpetrators and Bystanders* (New York, NY: Free Press, 1994), p. 171.

29 Ibid.

30 A member of *Sonderkommando* 4a; a member of *Einsatzgruppe* A. In Klee et al., eds., *The Good Old Days*, pp. 62, 80.

31 *SS-Oberscharführer* Wilhelm Findeisen; an *SS-Scharführer* and *Kriminal-Assistant*; an *SS-Hauptscharführer* and *Kriminalangestellter*. In Klee et al., eds., *The Good Old Days*, pp. 67, 72, and 79.

32 Christopher Browning, *Ordinary Men: Reserve Police Battalion 101 and the Final Solution in Poland* (New York, NY: HarperCollins, 1992), p. 1. Page numbers hereafter refer to the first edition.

33 Ibid., pp. 47–8.

34 Ibid., pp. 62, 113.

35 Ibid., p. 5.

36 Ibid., p. 56.

37 Ibid., p. 59.

38 Ibid., p. 69.

39 Ibid., pp. 2, 73.

40 Carl to Kube, October 30, 1941 in Browning, *Ordinary Men*, p. 22. Recognition of the need to maintain psychic balance among the rank and file is suggested in a July 1941 directive from the Police Regiment Center, which stated that "the battalion and company commanders are especially to provide for the spiritual care of the men who participate in this [killing] action" (p. 14).

41 Browning, *Ordinary Men*, pp. 56, 72. One Order policemen described his breakdown during the Jozefow Massacre, saying "I thought I could master the situation . . ." (p. 72). When officers wished to pressure their underlings to conform, it was typically by calling them "cowards" (p. 56).

42 Christopher Browning, *Ordinary Men*, p. 63

43 Ibid., p. 185.

44 Ibid., p. 116.

45 Ibid., p. 130

46 Ibid., p. 129.

47 Ibid., p. 58.

48 Ibid., p. 118.

49 Nelson, *The Intimate Connection*, p. 42.

50 Browning, *Ordinary Men*, p. 57.

51 One SS officer reported that "a very common manifestation in members of these firing-squads was temporary impotence," and that "a number of SS officers and men were sent back to serve at home 'on account of their great weakness.'" Statement by *SS-Obersturmführer* (and Catholic priest) Albert Hartl. In Klee et al., eds., *The Good Old Days*, pp. 81–2.

52 Browning, *Ordinary Men*, p. 91.

53 Ibid., p. 93.

54 Ibid., p. 41.

55 In this section of the book, Browning does consider the role of self-interest and careerism among his ordinary men, particularly in officers such as Captain Hoffmann. He also notes the desire to appear "manly and tough" before one's peers (although in relation to subjects in the Milgram experiments, not to the men of Battalion 101).

56 Browning, *Ordinary Men*, p. 180.

57 Ibid., p. 183.

58 Ibid., p. 87.

59 Ibid., p. 185.

60 Ibid., p. 189.

61 Daniel Jonah Goldhagen, *Hitler's Willing Executioners: Ordinary Germans and the Holocaust* (New York, NY: Knopf, 1996), p. 250. Page numbers hereafter are to this edition. For critical responses to Goldhagen's book, see Franklin H. Littell, ed., *Hyping the Holocaust: Scholars Answer Goldhagen* (East Rockaway, NJ: Cummings & Hathaway, 1997); Norman G. Finkelstein and Ruth Bettina Birn, *A Nation on Trial: The Goldhagen Thesis and Historical Truth* (New York, NY: Holt, 1998); Robert R. Shandley, ed., *Unwilling Germans?: The Goldhagen Debate* (Minneapolis, MN: University of Minnesota Press, 1998); and Geoff Eley, *The Goldhagen Effect: History, Memory, Nazism—Facing the German Past* (Ann Arbor, MI: University of Michigan Press, 2000).

62 Goldhagen, *Hitler's Willing Executioners*, p. 206. Goldhagen stresses that very few (4 percent) of the men in battalion 101 were members of the SS and most were no more Nazified than the general German population. They hailed from an area (Hamburg) that was not a Nazi stronghold, and a few of them had even shown hostility to the regime. As relatively mature men with families and children, they were "the least likely to be martial in spirit and temperament."

63 Goldhagen uses the murder of one of the men by partisans in September 1942 and the retaliatory killings it provoked to emphasize how differently the "Nazified German mind" viewed the murder of Poles and Jews. But the language used to describe the incident—Major Trapp referred to it as a "cowardly murder" (*feige Mordtat*)—actually conforms to a gender-informed view of the battalion's activities.

64 Goldhagen, *Hitler's Willing Executioners*, p. 212

65 Goldhagen also quotes Trapp's offer of release to older battalion members who did not "feel up to it." Whether or not younger men believed they had been invited to step forward as well, as Goldhagen argues, it is significant that the invitation was couched in terms that made a concession to weakness in general and male impotence in particular.

66 Ibid., p. 238.

67 Ibid., p. 246.

68 Ibid., p. 241.

69 Ibid., p. 242.

70 Ibid., p. 242.

71 Ibid., p. 243.

72 Ibid., p. 242.

73 Ibid., p. 245.

74 Ibid., p. 254.

75 Ibid., p. 264.

76 Ibid., p. 269.

77 As Goldhagen writes, "Some significant number of perpetrators must have had their family members with them, as the invitation to the evening with the theater troupe suggests, by explicitly stating that families were welcome" (p. 267).

78 In Donald G. Schilling, ed., *Lessons and Legacies, Volume II: Teaching the Holocaust in a Changing World* (Evanston, IL: Northwestern University Press, 1998), p. 54.

79 Inga Clendinnen, *Reading the Holocaust* (Cambridge, UK: Cambridge University Press, 1999), pp. 118, 119.

80 Ibid., p. 117.

81 Goldhagen, *Hitler's Willing Executioners*, p. 218.

82 Browning, *Ordinary Men*, p. xix.

8

Women as Perpetrators: Agency and Authority in Genocidal Rwanda

Nicole Hogg and Mark Drumbl

Introduction

Although much of the literature on gender and armed conflict focuses, appropriately, on women as victims of violence, women also act as agents of violence in armed conflicts and mass atrocities. During the 1994 Rwandan genocide, women participated both at the local level and through leadership roles. Sometimes they directly joined in the killings, but more often women incited others to violence, denounced victims to the killers, and pillaged their dead neighbors' property. In these ways, women helped feed the genocidal machine, while largely (but not always) conforming to gender expectations.

The reality of women's experiences is, of course, diverse and complex— as, no doubt, is men's. As this chapter will discuss, female perpetrators also sometimes rescued individuals, while some extraordinary "ordinary" women were among the heroes who stridently opposed the genocide. While the vast majority of Rwandan women probably neither actively participated in the killings nor actively resisted them, ignoring, overstating, or minimizing their roles in the genocide does a disservice both to history and to efforts to prevent mass atrocities in the future.[1]

This chapter considers two broad categories of women. The first section explores the involvement of "ordinary" women in the genocide, which, consistent with distinctions made under Rwandan law, broadly encompasses all those who were not in positions of authority and leadership at the time.[2] This section discusses women's roles in killing, exposing Tutsis to the killers, and looting, but also considers their capacities for resistance, either within the family or on a wider scale. The second section discusses the roles of women in positions of authority, leadership, and influence. In the face of a purportedly "genderless" criminal justice system, the deeply gendered discourse surrounding the prosecutions and trials of many of these women, as well the accused's own portrayals of themselves, is a recurring theme.

By way of background, it is important to note that at least four different levels of criminal justice processes have been mobilized to prosecute individuals in relation to the Rwandan genocide. The first of these, and by far the most widely known outside Rwanda, is the International Criminal Tribunal for Rwanda (ICTR), which was established by the United Nations (UN) in 1994. The ICTR has targeted the alleged ringleaders of the genocide. Although it has completed only seventy-five cases, its work has served as an important benchmark. Second, a small number of trials have taken place domestically in various countries against Rwandan nationals who fled Rwanda after the genocide and who have often sought asylum abroad. In Rwanda, criminal trials have proceeded in the national courts, including for the planners, organizers, and leaders of the genocide who were not pursued by the ICTR. In light of the enormous caseload faced by the national courts, a local neotraditional system of justice called *gacaca* has also prosecuted over one million suspects for genocide-related crimes, while aiming to achieve justice and reconciliation.[3] In this chapter, we explore the intersection of women perpetrators with each of these four levels of legal process.

Women as "Ordinary" Perpetrators

(a) Female Killers

The difference is that men killed, women didn't.[4]

Women represent 6 to 7 percent of persons prosecuted for serious genocide-related crimes in Rwanda.[5] With important exceptions, women are more likely to have acted as accomplices rather than as principal offenders.[6] The low rate of women's direct involvement in the genocide, relative to men, at a time when "participation in the genocide had become the dominant social norm" can be primarily attributed to the persistence of traditional gender roles, even during the atrocities.[7] As noted by Donna Maier, "Women in Rwandan society . . . as in other traditional societies [were] expected to be submissive, subservient to men, compliant, and hard-working farmers and homemakers, not warriors."[8] In line with these traditions, it has been observed that "men wanted women to stay at home and not to participate in the killings."[9]

For a variety of reasons, some "ordinary" Rwandan women nevertheless did directly participate. For example, in August 2009, twenty-seven Rwandan women were convicted by a *gacaca* court and sentenced for between nineteen and thirty years for having stoned Tutsis to death in a parish in the Cyangugu prefecture.[10] The *gacaca* courts have also heard cases of women's involvement in acts of rape and sexual torture, including a group of women who raped a priest before his death.[11]

In 2001, researcher Nicole Hogg interviewed a number of women who had been either personally involved in individual killings or complicit in larger-scale massacres. At one extreme was a young woman whose brother was a local *Interahamwe* (militia) leader.[12] Fifteen years old at the time of the genocide, she said she participated in "countless killings," because "it was fun, like playing a game."[13] After she had a child of her own, this woman began to deeply regret her role in killing other children. She returned to Rwanda from the Democratic Republic of the Congo (DRC) specifically to confess and face her punishment. At the other extreme was a woman who poisoned her own four children. Although she was Hutu, her children were deemed to be Tutsi on account of their father's ethnicity.[14] After Hutu relatives had consistently refused to protect the children, and fearing the *Interahamwe* would otherwise kill them with a machete, she felt she had no choice but to kill them herself in a more kindly way. This woman also took poison herself but survived. She admitted: "I know I am a sinner but I also loved my children. I did not want to kill them. . . . I cannot sleep at night."[15]

Between these two extremes, several other interviewed women had confessed to clubbing Tutsi neighbors to death or taking people to be killed. Such active participation was often motivated by the genocidal propaganda, which pitted Hutu against Tutsi and Hutu women specifically against Tutsi women.[16] As one female detainee commented,

> The leaders told us that the Tutsis had prepared graves to put the Hutus in and that we had to kill the Tutsis first before they killed us. We believed them because they were educated people. . . . I believed them, and that is why I killed that woman.[17]

At least in some cases, therefore, the effect of the propaganda overrode traditional gender expectations and created new behavioral norms, which induced women to kill. In other cases, women killed under pressure from the *Interahamwe* or from other family members, often due to their special relationship with the victim. Thus, the wife of a Tutsi man who "finished off" her sister-in-law with a hoe handle under pressure from three *Interahamwe* claimed, "I was only a woman and they were three men so I had no power over them. And I wasn't myself by then. My whole family had been killed. . . . I wasn't scared. I was just being used."[18]

Another young woman charged with killing nine people, including three babies, admitted to her involvement in one incident. She said she took an old woman to be killed by the *Interahamwe* after being threatened by one of its members that if she did not do so he would murder two girls she was protecting in her home. She decided that the life of an "old woman, who was already sick and might not have survived anyway" should be sacrificed, as she "wanted to protect the two girls, and besides, I couldn't protect all the Tutsis around."[19] She later said,

> I regret a lot what happened, what we did to that old woman. Even if she was an old woman, she was still God's creation, and even if I couldn't have saved her, I shouldn't have accompanied [him] to kill her. If he had then killed the two girls, at least it wouldn't have been my responsibility.[20]

This very brief overview demonstrates that just as "women" are not a homogenous group, the reasons why they killed cannot always be neatly categorized. As Cohn has noted, gender is one important system that influences women's behavior, including during armed conflicts (and mass atrocities), but it is not the only one. Women's actions are also shaped by an array of factors such as age, economic class, social position, ethnicity, religion, culture, and personal relationships.[21] While gender expectations largely discouraged "ordinary" women's direct involvement in the killings, the given examples confirm that individual circumstances were also critical to determining the choices women made.

Another observation—which needs to be tested on a broader sample—is that where women did participate directly in the killings, it appears that they rarely, if ever, used a machete, despite this being the principal weapon of the Rwandan genocide.[22] Rather, female killers used clubs, hoes, blocks of wood, stones, and poison. Since almost all rural households owned at least one machete,[23] and others were distributed to the *Interahamwe* in the lead-up to the genocide,[24] this suggests either that the machetes remained primarily in the hands of men throughout the violence or that killing by machete was more abhorrent to women than by other means.[25]

(b) Exposing Victims to the Killers

Women knew a lot. Their eyes were open.[26]

If the genocidal killings were predominately a male affair, anecdotal evidence suggests that women were often complicit in them by exposing Tutsis to the killers. As explained by one female detainee, "It is true that it was mostly men who killed, but women who were out in the fields and saw Tutsis hiding called out their hiding spots."[27] Bernadette Kanzayire, a Rwandan lawyer, similarly contended that "some women played an active role . . . but the majority played a passive role, in refusing to hide their neighbors, and in particular, in showing the hiding places of Tutsis."[28]

"Refusing to hide their neighbors" has not been deemed a punishable offense in the aftermath of the genocide, despite the existence of the crime under Rwandan law of failing to assist a person in danger.[29] According to the *National Service of Gacaca Courts*, the reason for this is that "it would be unjust to punish an ordinary citizen for not daring to step forward, under risk of death, and attempt to stop acts that were planned and put into action by the government."[30] However, people who showed the hiding places of Tutsis are, at least in theory, punishable as accomplices to genocide and subject to the same punishment as principal offenders.

The *Gacaca Law* contains a broad definition of accomplice as "the person who has, by any means, provided assistance to commit offenses. . . ."[31] Yet, this provision has proven difficult to implement in practice. On the one hand, the *gacaca* courts have sometimes interpreted it too expansively—in one case convicting a woman to twenty-five years' imprisonment for having given food to the *Interahamwe*.[32] On the other hand, the relatively small number of women prosecuted for genocide, compared with the common view that women were regularly involved in exposing the victims to the killers, suggests that a large number of cases have not been pursued.

Significantly, no woman that Hogg met in the Rwandan prisons in 2001 admitted to having *willingly* committed such crimes.[33] One reason is that female detainees attached little moral responsibility to (merely) revealing the hiding places of Tutsis to the killers. As one woman commented, "Women have this feeling that they did not kill because they only called out,"[34] while another specifically concluded that "women did not carry machetes so they were not as involved as men."[35] A strong social aversion to accepting that women can be killers[36] has also apparently encouraged both denials of criminal responsibility on the part of women who were complicit in the genocide and acts of "chivalry" on the part of male prosecutors and judges toward women.[37] Combined with the difficulty of prosecuting "indirect" crimes, these factors may have resulted in the underrepresentation of women before the Rwandan courts.

Some women have confessed to exposing Tutsis to the killers, but claim to have acted out of fear. One woman, for example, recounted:

> I tried to stop them, by telling them not to take her, to let me keep her, but they threatened to throw a grenade at me. My husband was dead, my son was in France, so I couldn't do anything to stop them.[38]

Another woman said that she told two ringleaders of the *Interahamwe* where a boy was hiding after "they took out their machetes," because:

> these were very violent men. . . . They had been killing people and telling us in the community to kill as well. They had also been saying that if they

found anyone hiding a Tutsi they would kill him [*sic*]. So, I thought they would hurt me if I did not cooperate, even though I cannot say if they would have killed me. I did not believe this child had to die. I was just scared.[39]

It is difficult to evaluate the actual risk that women would have faced had they refused to cooperate. On the one hand, some women Hogg interviewed said they were able to continue protecting people in their homes by bribing the *Interahamwe* to turn a blind eye. Penal Reform International (PRI) has similarly found relatively few cases of people who were actually killed or seriously injured for resisting the genocidal ideology but have noted the "formidable effectiveness of fear" in such circumstances.[40] On the other hand, a detailed report by the survivors' organization Ibuka found that in addition to a few well-known cases of Hutus who were killed with the Tutsis they were protecting, among 372 people who were reported to have helped save Tutsis during the genocide, almost 10 percent had been beaten by the killers, 16 percent had been "attacked," and 9 percent had their houses or goods destroyed.[41] In addition, in light of a culture of physical and sexual violence against women, the question arises as to whether "ordinary" women such as those in the above examples had an additional reason to fear the *Interahamwe*, even though women were probably under less pressure overall than men to participate.

Raising such questions is not an attempt to minimize the complicity of women in the genocide, as it seems that many women were active agents in it. Moreover, as the violence amplified, even people who had initially tried to help Tutsis often ended up handing them over to the killers. Josée Mukandamage, former vice president of the Rwandan Supreme Court, described the situation as follows:

Women were not usually part of the death squads, but they only went so far for others. Women had been conditioned by then to think it was normal for Tutsis to die. So, even if they tried to help someone, they would not resist if someone came searching for that person, and they would not risk their lives for others.[42]

This statement is probably largely true, though there are cases of women who did risk their lives for others, to which we will shortly return.

(c) Women and Property Crimes

Property crimes have been included under Rwanda's *Gacaca Law*,[43] as the looting and destruction of Tutsi property were part of the genocidal plan and were encouraged by the administrative and military authorities.[44] According to a report by PRI, "The large-scaled looting which took place during the

1994 tragedy and which, to a large extent, was organized from the top down, constitute a complex set of events [in which] many people were involved in one way or another."[45] Women's involvement in these crimes can be largely attributed to jealousy, greed, and opportunism, which in turn were fueled by the anti-Tutsi propaganda. According to one female genocide suspect, "Hutu women were jealous of Tutsis' wealth. Women wanted their goods."[46] The following stories by women who had confessed to property crimes speak for themselves:

> I did not even need the blankets. It was like the devil had got into us. We saw that those people were not there and that others were looking for them to kill, so we women went to take their property to sell and buy beer. I took ten blankets.[47]

> I was at home making beer when my neighbors were killed in their home. That night I went with two other women and a man to take their property. Their bodies were still there. . . . I took a blouse and a skirt; the other woman took a wrap and shoes. The man found a pig in another house and slaughtered it and we shared the meat. I looted because others were doing it and because those people did not need their belongings anymore since they were dead. But it was bad. I sinned, and that is why I had to ask for forgiveness from all Rwandans.[48]

Another woman went the extra step and looted clothing off the bodies of dead Tutsis following a massacre in the local parish. As she said,

> People started looting the belongings of Tutsis who had been killed in the Parish. . . . I do not know what made me go there because I already had everything I needed. I took three wraps from the bodies. . . . There were other women there, also taking things. . . . I have confessed to looting, but that is the only thing I did.[49]

Property offenses committed during the genocide are not punishable by prison sentences. Instead, perpetrators and victims (or their families) have been expected to try to reach an amicable solution for reparations. When this was not possible, the lower-level *gacaca* courts could hear the case and order perpetrators to pay compensation in monetary terms or in kind, such as through agricultural work.[50] It has, however, proven to be very difficult to enforce both the amicable agreements and *gacaca* court decisions, and a large percentage of orders have not been honored, partly due to a widespread incapacity to pay.[51] Many survivors consider the lack of reparations for property damage as an obstacle to reconciliation.[52] Others say that material compensation for property crimes, even if provided, will never be sufficient.[53]

(d) Resisting the Genocide: Family Relations and Women among Rwanda's "Righteous"

As emphasized above, the majority of "ordinary" Hutu women did not "actively" participate in the genocide (nor did the majority of men).[54] Yet they did not actively resist it either. When questioned about their capacity to act against the genocide, female genocide suspects consistently responded that it was impossible, especially when their husbands were involved. They often referred to their husbands as "beasts," and several said they feared their husbands would have hurt or killed them if they had tried to intervene. One woman recounted that after her husband had killed their Tutsi neighbors, "when I told him he had done a bad thing, he looked at me with eyes like an animal and told me it was not proper to speak to him like that."[55] According to another woman,

> I was hiding a Tutsi woman in our house. He [my husband] was always arguing with me, telling me not to feed her. . . . Because I was hiding her, I couldn't argue with him about what he was doing during the day.[56]

Another commented that "women couldn't stop their husbands from going to kill because women didn't have any power. Women could only sometimes convince their husbands to let someone hide in their house; they couldn't stop a whole group."[57]

Some observers are unsympathetic to the argument that women were powerless in the face of the genocide. Rakiya Omaar of African Rights, for example, maintained that "women were not helpless."[58] A female detainee agreed. She said:

> Women assisted the killers by preparing the meals, fetching drinks and encouraging their men. Women brought provisions to the roadblocks and fed their men at home. No women criticised their men for being killers. This was not because they feared their husbands but because they believed in the need to kill Tutsis.[59]

Kanzayire expressed a more nuanced view, suggesting,

> Before the genocide, women . . . followed the orders of their husbands and their families. But . . . women could have advised their husbands and sons or refused to prepare meals for them. Even if women did not have much power in Rwandan society they should have at least tried to do something.[60]

In fact, a number of women and men did try to do something, to the extent that "the majority of the survivors of the genocide benefited in one way or another from the aid of a Hutu."[61] Over recent years, often as part of reconciliation efforts, increasing attention has been paid to Hutus who tried to save Tutsis from the slaughter. For the most part, these people were "ordinary" Rwandans and not authority figures. Given the title of the "Righteous," they are seen as "living proof that a choice was possible" not to participate in the genocide.[62] Among the criteria for securing a place among the "Righteous" is that the person acted without any expectation of personal benefit. Those who assisted only family members, or who rescued some people but also participated in the genocide, have also been denied the title.

In the most extensive survey to date, conducted by the National University of Rwanda under sponsorship of the survivors' organization Ibuka, 372 individuals were initially identified as "Righteous," although this number was eventually reduced to 265 after applying the above criteria. The study showed that the motives for assisting Tutsis varied, but that friendship accounted for almost 31 percent, sympathy for the victim represented 25 percent, family ties motivated 17.5 percent (with these people being immediately disqualified from the list), while "categorical refusal of the genocidal ideology" accounted for only 3.5 percent of cases.[63]

Just over 20 percent of the 372 identified cases were women. However, the report emphasizes that "these figures must be nuanced, as we have noticed that in the majority of cases, the whole family participated in the act of rescue. . . . In this case, in accordance with Rwandan matrimonial law, which places the husband as the head of the family, it was him who was retained [by the survey team] to represent the household."[64] The 20 percent thus represents only women who acted against the will of her husband or children in the face of "enormous difficulties," women who were not married, or women who acted alone. It is therefore impossible to say if women were less, or more, inclined than men to have come to people's aid.

Female heroes have nevertheless emerged. The most well known is Sula Karuhimbi, a Hutu peasant and traditional healer who was almost seventy years old at the time of the genocide. She saved up to 100 Tutsis by hiding them on her own property or elsewhere. She challenged the *Interahamwe* when they came to search her house, braving gunfire and threats. She has remained a staunch opponent of the genocide, testifying against the perpetrators before the *gacaca* courts. Her source of inspiration, she says, were her parents, who also protected Tutsis from attacks when she was a child.[65] According to one of the survivors that Sula rescued,

> She made everyone welcome, even strangers. Karuhimbi found different hiding places for us all. . . . All the people she hid are alive today. I find her an amazing old lady. Her courage during the genocide was unequalled. Very few people could have done what she did.[66]

A Kigali midwife named Thérèse Nyirabayovu has also earned a place among Rwanda's "Righteous." Aged sixty-seven at the time of the genocide, she hid eighteen people in her house and took food to others staying at a nearby church, out of a belief that she had "a duty to save fellow human beings in danger."[67] She was questioned repeatedly, her home was searched, and a grenade was thrown at it. She was also under constant threat from the *Interahamwe* in the refugee camps in the DRC after the genocide. In the words of one of the survivors she helped,

> Thérèse has always been well known for her courage, her generosity and her skill as a midwife. She has always been poor, especially since she was widowed and had so many children to look after. But . . . Thérèse and her children hid us for nearly two months, knowing very well they were risking their lives.[68]

A third example of a "Righteous" woman is Félicitée Niyitegeka, a church assistant in the province of Gisenyi, who protected a group of girls staying in the diocese when the genocide erupted in April 1994. She searched for medicine to treat wounded Tutsis and began evacuating the most vulnerable across the border into the DRC when her plans were discovered. Refusing an opportunity to evacuate, she was murdered along with her protégés. One among the few survivors of this massacre said she should be proclaimed a saint.[69]

A number of men among the "Righteous" have also acknowledged the active contribution of women to their efforts to save Tutsis during the genocide. According to one man named Célestin, "If my wife had not been there they would all be dead. She helped me. Those children . . . who took people over by canoe, they nearly gave up once. It was that old woman who begged them to continue their work. . . . She said 'We have always been friends with their families. It is not now that you will let them die.'"[70]

In sum, "ordinary" women's desire to actively oppose the genocide was severely curtailed by their belief in the genocidal ideology, jealousy, greed, and fear. Their ability to take a stronger stance against the violence, including within the family, was also undoubtedly limited by gender dynamics. Yet, among the positive examples that have come to light are a number of "ordinary" Hutu peasant women who demonstrated that resistance was possible but required character and courage.

Moving from the participation of "ordinary women" in the genocide to that of women in leadership roles and positions of authority, the following section focuses on the imagery surrounding the trials of "powerful women" and the gendered tropes that emerged in this context.

Women as Authority Figures

(a) Three Ministers: A Martyr and Two Convicts

Three women were in Cabinet at the outbreak of the genocide, but one did not survive to see it unfold. Prime Minister Agathe Uwilingiyimana had previously served as Minister of Education and pushed merit-based approaches to school admission as opposed to ethnic quotas (which in colonial times had favored the Tutsi but following independence favored the Hutu).[71] A political moderate, and perceived as a foil to the genocidal movement, Uwilingiyimana was tracked down, sexually assaulted, and murdered by Rwandan army personnel (including members of the Presidential Guard) on April 7, 1994—the very start of the genocide. Her brutal execution allowed the most extreme group of *génocidaires* to cement their grip on the highest levers of power and permitted genocide to metastasize.

Pauline Nyiramasuhuko served as Rwanda's Minister of Family and Women's Development immediately prior to and during the genocide. She remains the highest-profile woman implicated in the genocidal violence. On June 24, 2011, Trial Chamber II of the ICTR convicted her of conspiracy to commit genocide and genocide; the crimes against humanity of extermination, rape, and persecution; and the war crimes of violence to life and outrages upon personal dignity.[72] She was sentenced to the harshest punishment possible, namely, life imprisonment.[73] At the time of her conviction, she was sixty-five years old.

The proceedings against Nyiramasuhuko were among the most complex ever undertaken by the ICTR. She was prosecuted, as the lead defendant, jointly with five other defendants, including her son, Arsène Shalom Ntahobali (who was also given a life sentence). All the defendants were from Butare, a prefecture in southern Rwanda. These defendants became colloquially known as the "Butare Group" or the "Butare Six." The other four defendants received sentences of twenty-five years, thirty years, thirty-five years, and life imprisonment. The Butare Six case remains in the appeals process at the ICTR, but Chief Prosecutor Hassan Jallow anticipates that the appeals judgment will be released only in September 2015.[74]

Nyiramasuhuko is the ICTR's only female accused. She is, moreover, the only woman tried and convicted by an international criminal tribunal for the specific crime of genocide and the only woman tried and convicted by an international criminal tribunal for rape as a crime against humanity.[75]

Overall, the trial judgment diligently pursued a neutral approach to Nyiramasuhuko's gender. Her gender, in fact, was never discussed. On the one hand, this deliberate silence avoids sensationalizing Nyiramasuhuko or scandalously accentuating her guilt just because she was a woman. And, arguably, this silence reflected what a criminal court is supposed to do—that is, microscopically assess the guilt or innocence of the person in the dock on the basis of what that person is alleged to have done. The degendering of the lead perpetrator might additionally have permitted a clearer assessment of the criminal responsibility of the five other accused, all men. This silence also brought into sharper relief the judgment's vivid exposition of the gender-based nature of many of the crimes, in particular the mass rape of Tutsi women. On this note, trial testimony, authenticated by the text of the judgment, demonstrated how Nyiramasuhuko ordered the rape of those "arrogant" Tutsi women who, alternately, tempted and stole Hutu men (an image aimed at galvanizing female support for the rapes) or spurned and humiliated them (an image aimed at encouraging men to commit acts of rape).[76]

On the other hand, this conscious textual gender neutrality also presents shortcomings and lost opportunities. It skipped over the reality that, when disaggregating the multiple motivations that prompt a person to commit atrocity, it is somewhat stilted (perhaps even scripted) not to consider the role of gender in that process. Moreover, degendering runs the risk of glossing over the acute etiological need to better understand the role of femininities and masculinities in how mass atrocity emerges and, by logical extension, the cultivation of more effective reintegration and preventative efforts in its aftermath.

Public representations of the Nyiramasuhuko trial, in any event, were rife with problematic essentialisms of femininity and motherhood. She has been cast as a "mother hen" type of character; media reports obsessed over her clothing and appearance; she was depicted as controlling her son; and articles and media reports about her were festooned with titles such as "A Woman Scorned," "Mother of Atrocities," and "A Woman's Work."[77] These caricatures informed the way in which the media expressively telegraphed the trial to the public. Essentialisms also suffused the strategic discourse of those invested in Nyiramasuhuko's conviction and, conversely, of those invested in her acquittal (including Nyiramasuhuko herself). Although the trial lawyers refrained from such discursive strategies in the courtroom, focusing instead on Nyiramasuhuko's presence (or not) at various crime scenes, they did pursue these strategies in the media. Within this public arena, those who condemned Nyiramasuhuko's conduct, including victims, turned to her status as woman and mother to underscore her personal culpability and individual deviance (viz., she was a worse perpetrator because she was a woman, mother, and grandmother). Those who defended her conduct, including Nyiramasuhuko herself, invoked tropes of womanhood and motherhood to emphasize the impossibility of her culpability (viz., she could not be a perpetrator, in particular of rape, because she was a woman, mother, and grandmother) and the utter implausibility that a mother could exhort her own son to rape.[78] Either way, however, sensationalizing her conduct led to troublesome outcomes—gender became a proxy for her helplessness or a proxy for her aberrant deviant evil.[79]

The relationship between "mother and son *génocidaires*"[80] has attracted greater media fascination than the relationship between another parent-child duo convicted inter alia for genocide at the ICTR, namely, Rev Elizaphan Ntakirutimana (father, a Seventh-Day Adventist pastor) and Gérard Ntakirutimana (his son, a physician), who were sentenced to ten and twenty-five years' imprisonment, respectively, in 2003 and whose sentences were affirmed on appeal in 2004.[81] Whereas the Ntahobali and Nyiramasuhuko proceedings tended to become diffused to the public as "mother and son," the proceedings concerning the Ntakirutimanas tended to become diffused as "pastor and son."[82] When it came to the elder parent figure, Ntakirutimana was reduced to his profession, not his fatherhood. Nyiramasuhuko, on the other hand, was reduced to her motherhood, not her profession. Her case was not presented as "minister and son *génocidaires*," nor was his case presented as "father and son *génocidaires*."

Nyiramasuhuko, however, was not the only female minister in the genocidal government. Agnès Ntamabyaliro served as Minister of Justice. Earlier in her career, she had "directed an NGO that raised micro-finance loans for poor Rwandan women."[83] She was one of the first women in Africa to serve in Parliament, but according to Jacqueline Novogratz, who had known her personally, "Agnes stood as a reminder that power corrupts on an equal-opportunity basis. Agnes loved the trappings of power, and when all was said and done, she'd traded integrity and whatever good she'd built for glitter and gold."[84] Ntamabyaliro was captured in Zambia and tried in Kigali—the only minister from the genocidal government tried before the Rwandan courts. In 2009, she received a life sentence in isolation for planning and inciting genocide, complicity to murder, and conspiracy.[85] Her sentence is currently on appeal.[86]

Ntamabyaliro's case has barely received any mention in the international media, even though, exactly like Nyiramasuhuko, she was a high-profile minister and another woman in the Rwandan Cabinet. Undoubtedly, the fact that she was prosecuted in Rwanda, as opposed to at the ICTR, contributes to this disparate reaction, but the disproportionate attention given to Nyiramasuhuko obfuscates the fact that many other Rwandan women, including authority figures, have been prosecuted, convicted, or acquitted or are serving sentences for genocide-related crimes.

(b) Other Influential Women Perpetrators

Looking beyond the kernel of national political power, other women of prominent social status participated in the genocide. Upon apprehension or investigation, some (but certainly not all) of these women turned to gender to explain away their behavior. In some cases, similarly although not as acutely as was the case with Nyiramasuhuko, media reports about these women were burdened with gender-based essentialisms.

These female perpetrators came from all walks of life, which underscored how *génocidaires* were unhindered by occupation or socioeconomic status. Euphrasie Kamatamu, a local political official in Kigali, was convicted in 1998; she was handed the death penalty, but ultimately died in prison three years later of natural causes.[87] Anne-Marie Nyirahakizimana, a major in the armed forces and a physician, was convicted in 1999 by a military court and sentenced to death.[88] She was retried a decade later—after the death penalty had been abolished in Rwanda—by a *gacaca* court and sentenced to life imprisonment in isolation.[89] Dr. Jeanne-Marie Nduwamariya, a physician in

Butare, "held meetings at her home to draw up lists and identify Tutsi to be killed"; she was tried *in absentia* by a *gacaca* court and sentenced on appeal in 2009 to life imprisonment.[90] Other prominent women *génocidaires* include Rose Karushara (a local official in Kigali), Odette Nyirabagenzi (known as "the terror of Rugenge," a *secteur* of Kigali), and Athanasie Mukabatana (a nursing school teacher).[91]

Valérie Bemeriki was a high-profile star journalist who worked for the notorious RTLM radio station, known for its dissemination of hate propaganda. During the genocide she reported on the progress of the genocide, read off lists of Tutsi to be hunted and killed, and congratulated the killers for their efforts. She was seen dressed in *Interahamwe* attire. Late in December 2009, a *gacaca* court in Rwanda sentenced her to life imprisonment for planning and inciting genocide and complicity to murder.[92] She had been arrested in 1999 in the DRC. Donna Maier, citing RTLM transcripts archived at the ICTR, reports that Bemeriki exhorted listeners to cut the cockroaches (the infamous code word for Tutsi) to pieces with a machete and that she had been told by the Virgin Mary that the Hutu will have the victory.[93] A week prior to her conviction, she publicly requested forgiveness for her actions and blamed her anti-Tutsi childhood socialization for her conduct.[94]

A few Rwandan women have also faced, and continue to face, legal process at the national level outside of Rwanda. Sister Gertrude (Consolata Mukangango) and Sister Maria Kizito (Julienne Mukabutera) were initially convicted in Belgium in 2001 for their role in the murders of thousands of Tutsi refugees in a monastery in Sovu, Butare, in 1994. Both nuns had sought asylum in Belgium. They were sentenced to fifteen and twelve years' imprisonment, respectively. Their unsuccessful defense was that they were terrified bystanders who lacked control over the circumstances at Sovu.

Arsène Shalom Ntahobali's wife, Béatrice Munyenyezi, moved to the United States in 1998, where she claimed asylum and became a citizen in 2003. In 2010, US prosecutors indicted her for allegedly falsifying her refugee and citizenship application by covering up her role in the 1994 genocide. Prosecutors "produced witnesses from Rwanda who testified that Munyenyezi was a Hutu extremist who helped orchestrate the rapes and killings . . . at a roadblock near her home."[95] The jury, however, deadlocked; a mistrial was declared. A new trial was set. The defense presented a number of unpersuasive arguments, including a belligerent reference to the superiority of US courts in which they implored that the jurors acquit insofar as "this is not a Rwandan kangaroo court."[96] Ultimately, on February 21, 2013, jurors convicted Munyenyezi of lying to obtain US citizenship by denying her role in the Rwandan genocide (she was not tried for genocide or war crimes).[97] She was sentenced on July 15, 2013 to the maximum term of ten years' imprisonment. She is appealing her conviction and sentence.

Munyenyezi's sister, Prudence Kantengwa, was also convicted in Boston—on charges of visa fraud, fraud in immigration documents, perjury, and obstruction—for lying about her role in the Rwandan genocide to gain US citizenship.[98] In October 2012, Kantengwa was sentenced to twenty-one months' imprisonment.[99] In another case, Marie Claire Mukeshimana, who had been convicted by a *gacaca* court in Rwanda to serve a nineteen-year prison sentence, was deported by US authorities to Rwanda in December 2011 after attempting to enter the United States on a travel visa.[100]

Agathe Habyarimana (Kanziga), whose influence greatly catalyzed Nyiramasuhuko's own political ascent, continues to elude criminal prosecution, despite her apparent place at the very heart of the extremists who incubated the genocidal campaign. She was the wife of Rwandan president Juvénal Habyarimana, whose assassination was the trigger event of the genocide. Kanziga, who was airlifted out of Rwanda only days after her husband's death and brought to France, was allegedly the pivot of an extremist clique of northern Rwandan Hutus known as the Akazu, believed to have hatched the plans for genocide. She was investigated by the ICTR prosecutors, but no indictment was ever issued.

Now in her seventies, Kanziga still lives in France, although her residency there remains contested. She brought an asylum claim in France in early 2007, which was rejected on the basis of a serious belief that she had been involved in the commission of an international crime in Rwanda and hence excludable under the Refugees Convention.[101] In December 2009, Rwandan prosecutors requested her extradition back to Kigali to face seven counts of genocide.[102] In 2010, however, the extradition request was dismissed by an appeals court in Paris on the basis that Rwandan courts did not satisfy international due process standards. In June 2013, her residence permit request in France was rejected anew.[103] She remains in a legal limbo, though she may end up facing criminal process in France, if France fails to extradite her to Rwanda in light of the outstanding international arrest warrant. She also faces civil proceedings in France that have been brought by a victims' organization and has been summoned as a witness in this regard.[104]

In her pleadings before the French Refugee Commission, Kanziga invoked gender essentialisms: she "stressed her role as mother of eight children," she "claim[ed] to have passed her time preparing meals for her family and taking care of the garden and livestock," and she "argued . . . she never listened to the radio or read newspapers, and never discussed politics with her husband."[105] The image thus presented was of a simple woman—a motherly figure—who was ignorant of political affairs. In many ways, this posture is similar to that advanced by Nyiramasuhuko at her criminal trial.

Gender discourses similarly informed the case brought against Yvonne Basebya (Ntacybatabara), aged sixty-six, who was convicted by the Hague District Court in March 2013 of inciting genocide. Basebya—a Rwandan-born Dutch citizen—was sentenced to six years and eight months' imprisonment, which was the maximum term available at the time.[106] Basebya was found to have "led meetings in the Rwandan capital, Kigali, of a radical Hutu party" and to have sung "a song that called for the murder of all Tutsis."[107] She was, however, acquitted of the charge of conspiracy to commit genocide and the charge of genocide. She plans on appealing the conviction. Somewhat similar to the press coverage of the Nyiramasuhuko trial, news reports mention—rather gratuitously—her fashion preferences, often in stereotypical language.[108] Both prosecutorial and defense strategies, moreover, also evoke gendered tropes. While "[t]he prosecutors say she was a 'General Mother' ... and 'genocide cheerleader,'" in response, "her defense paints a picture of a dedicated mother: married to a respectable MP."[109]

Conclusions and Areas for Further Research

This paper has demonstrated that "ordinary" women participated in the Rwandan genocide, though their involvement was characterized, most often, by acts of complicity rather than the wielding of weapons. Some acted impulsively or out of fear, others after closely assessing their options, while many were simply persuaded by the genocidal ideology that had swept the country. Simple greed and opportunism were other factors at play. A complex and uncomfortable reality is that sometimes the same individuals were both complicit in the violence and helped others to survive.

Women in leadership positions apparently participated as enthusiastically in the genocide as their male counterparts. (The one exception, Agathe Uwilingiyimana, paid for her moderate views with her life.) Nonetheless, the unashamed sensationalism and stigmatization by the media of Nyrimasahuko during her trial before the ICTR, as well as the gendered arguments used to defend many women accused of genocide-related crimes, demonstrate that gender stereotypes are rife around cases involving female perpetrators even while the law adheres to gender "neutrality." As Uwilingiyimana's case demonstrates, moreover, unremitting portrayals of women as victims nourish prejudicial stereotypes of helplessness and, thereby, gloss over the reality that some women are victimized precisely *because* they exercise resistance and, thereby, threaten the normalization of massacre.

Ultimately, a need arises to examine women perpetrators without the "tabooification" that currently pervades media accounts, the essentialisms that emerge in trial strategies, and also the forced invisibility of gender that emerges from, for example, the ICTR's judgment in the Nyiramasuhuko conviction. As Maier notes, "Many women, both humble and powerful, deliberately chose to embrace the genocidal ideology of hate and violence, and even chose to participate with enthusiasm and dedication."[110] Justice for their victims, many of whom also are women, requires a temperate, yet rigorous, approach shorn of stereotypes.

To develop a better understanding of women perpetrators and their treatment before the law, now that the *gacaca* trials as well as the vast majority of trials in the national courts in Rwanda have ended, comprehensive research could be conducted into the types of crimes for which women have been prosecuted, the arguments used in their defense, and their acquittal rates relative to men. Research could also explore if women's complicity in the genocide was adequately captured by the various criminal justice systems created in its aftermath, although this will always probably remain a matter of perception. This exercise is particularly relevant as the efforts of activists have succeeded in bringing the horrors of sexual violence, rape, forced marriage, and sexual slavery—crimes that affect both men and women, although women disproportionately—into the judicial frame. If both international criminal law and Rwandan law have managed to better cover crimes against women over recent years, have those systems done as well at capturing the crimes committed by women, especially without demonizing them or ignoring gender-specific circumstances?

The penal and rehabilitation needs of women convicted in Rwanda for genocide-related offenses also warrant consideration. Not only do women face particular problems in prison; Mark Drumbl notes that female ex-detainees face steep reintegration challenges and are among the most isolated demographic segments in contemporary Rwanda.[111] The families of imprisoned men also face ongoing stigma and are often in a precarious economic situation.[112] To be sure, emphasizing the obstacles confronting female perpetrators and the families of male perpetrators should not come at the expense of redressing the challenges that victims of the genocide continue to face.

Genocide destroys but, in the Rwandan case, it also ironically generated new socioeconomic possibilities, including for women. In postgenocidal Rwanda, women play more prominent roles in public life than they ever have historically. Customary land laws and practices that discriminated against women have been scaled back. Yet, many challenges remain, and one of those, as Rwanda looks to its future, is ensuring due recognition for the "Righteous" whose position in society often remains ambiguous and contested, including by survivors.[113] In terms of preventing future mass atrocities, it is crucial to better understand what distinguished these people from the masses and enabled them to defy the genocide. Twenty years after the genocide, there is not indefinite time for exploring all of these issues. Accordingly, efforts should now be expanded to gain a more profound understanding of both women's involvement in mass atrocities and their capacities for good.

Notes

1 Parts of section II are drawn from N. Hogg, "Women's Participation in the Rwandan Genocide: Mothers or Monsters?" *International Review of the Red Cross* 92:877 (2010), pp. 81–2; parts of section III are drawn from M. A. Drumbl, "'She Makes Me Ashamed to be a Woman': the Genocide Conviction of Pauline Nyiramasuhuko, 2011," *Michigan Journal of International Law*

34:3 (2013), pp. 586–93. Appreciations to Cody Phillips and Laura Durin for research assistance. The views expressed in this chapter reflect the authors' opinions and not necessarily those of the International Committee of the Red Cross (ICRC).

2   See the categorization of genocide-related crimes in Organic Law no 13/2008 of 19/05/2008, art. 9.

3   The *gacaca* trials commenced in June 2002 and finished in June 2012. "Genocide: le Rwanda clot officiellement ses jurisdictions populaires 'Gacaca,'" *Le Monde*, June 18, 2012; Ligue Rwandaise Pour la Promotion et la Defense des Droits de l'Homme (LIPRODHOR), *Situation des droits de la personne au Rwanda* (Kigali, Rwanda: 2013), pp. 16–17.

4   Female (Tutsi) genocide suspect Butare Prison (respondent #50), personal interview, July 24, 2001.

5   Women represented on average 7 percent of suspects (102 of 1,435) in *gacaca* trials at Sector and Appeal level observed by Avocats Sans Frontières (ASF) Belgium from October 2005 to March 2010. See ASF, *Rwanda: Rapport analytique des juridictions gacaca* (2006), p. 54; Ibid., (2007), p. 66; Ibid., (2009), p. 54; Ibid., (2006), p. 84. The ASF data is just slightly higher than the proportion of women among persons detained in Rwanda for genocide-related crimes as at February 2008 (almost 6 percent, or 2,133 from a total of 37,213). Among these, 1,738 women had been convicted of genocide-related offenses and 395 still awaited trial. LIPRODHOR, *Rapport de monitoring des prisons au Rwanda. Periode: 1er timestre 2008* (Kigali, 2008), p. 17.

6   According to ASF: "The participation of women is very marginal compared to that of men and often concerns acts of complicity or non-intervention." ASF, *Rwanda: Rapport analytique des juridictions gacaca* (2006), p. 32.

7   Penal Reform International (PRI), "The Righteous: Between Oblivion and Reconciliation? Example of the Province of Kibuye," *Report on Monitoring and Research on the Gacaca* (2004), p. 7.

8   D. J. Maier, "Women Leaders in the Rwandan Genocide: When Women Choose to Kill," *Universitas* 8 (2013), p. 2.

9   Female genocide suspect, Nsinda Prison (respondent #65), personal interview, August 6, 2001.

10   "Gacaca: 27 femmes condamnées à de lourdes peines à Cyangugu," *Porte Voix*, August 21, 2009. Available online: http://porte-voix.e-monsite.com/blog/publications/gacaca-27-femmes-condamnees-a-de-lourdes-peines-a-cyangugu-21-08-09.html (accessed August 18, 2014).

11   National Service of Gacaca Courts, *Gacaca Courts in Rwanda* (Republic of Rwanda, 2012), p. 218.

12   The *Interahamwe*, meaning "those who stand together" in Kinyarwanda, was a militia formed in the period leading up to the genocide and which led many of the killings during it.

13   Female genocide suspect, Gitarama Prison (respondent #37), personal interview, July 18, 2001.

14   Since colonial times, "customary rules existed in Rwanda governing the determination of ethnic group, which followed patrilineal lines of heredity."

Prosecutor *v.* Jean-Paul Akayesu, International Criminal Tribunal for Rwanda (ICTR), Case No. ICTR-96-4-T, Judgment (September 2, 1998), p. 171.

15 Female genocide suspect, Kigali Central Prison (respondent #23), personal interview, July 6, 2001.

16 Stereotypes about Tutsi women were also used to incite rapes. For example, see Prosecutor *v.* Nyiramasuhuko, Case No. ICTR-98-42-T, Judgment and Sentence, June 24, 2011, pp. 2268, 2764, 4985.

17 Woman convicted of genocide Gitarama Prison (respondent #10), personal interview, July 17, 2001.

18 Female genocide suspect, Gitarama Prison (respondent #46), personal interview, July 19, 2001.

19 Female genocide suspect, Kigali Central Prison (respondent #21), personal interview, July 6, 2001.

20 Ibid.

21 C. Cohn, "Woman and Wars: Toward a Conceptual Framework," *Woman and Wars: Contested Histories, Uncertain Futures*, ed. Carol Cohn (Cambridge, UK: Polity Press, 2012), p. 2.

22 A study on the weapons used to conduct the genocide in Kibuye province found that out of 59,050 victims of the genocide, 53 percent were killed by machete. See P. Verwimp, "Machetes and Firearms: The Organization of Massacres in Rwanda," *Journal of Peace Research* 43:1 (2006), p. 13.

23 Ibid., p. 7 (citing a National Agricultural Household Survey [1984]).

24 Ibid.

25 This was confirmed by at least one woman convicted of genocide. Female genocide suspect, Gitarama Prison (respondent #43), personal interview, July 19, 2001.

26 Female genocide suspect, Kigali Central Prison (respondent #13), personal interview, July 3, 2001.

27 Woman convicted of genocide, Gitarama Prison (respondent #10), personal interview, July 2, 2001.

28 Bernadette Kanzayire (lawyer, Kigali), personal interview, June 12, 2001.

29 Rwandan Penal Code, 2012, part 570.

30 National Service of *Gacaca* Courts, *Gacaca Courts in Rwanda* (Republic of Rwanda, 2012), pp. 201–2.

31 "*Gacaca* Law," 2004, p. 53.

32 Nyirabapfizina, cited in ASF, *Rwanda: rapport analytique des juridictions gacaca* (2005), p. 20.

33 Virtually none of the hundreds of detainees Drumbl interviewed in Kigali prison in 1998 (men and women, though the vast majority were men) revealed that they believed they had done anything "wrong" or that anything really "wrong" had happened in the summer of 1994. Those who recognized they had engaged in violent conduct never called it genocide or saw their involvement as willing but considered it as politically necessary self-defense in light of the war that was taking place at the time. M. A. Drumbl, "Rule of Law

Amid Lawlessness: Counselling the Accused in Rwanda's Domestic Genocide Trials," *Columbia Human Rights Law Review* 29 (1998), pp. 604–9.

34 Woman convicted of genocide, Gitarama Prison (respondent #10), personal interview, July 2, 2001.

35 Female genocide suspect, Gitarama Prison (respondent #43), personal interview, July 19, 2001.

36 Rakiya Omaar (codirector, African Rights, Kigali), personal interview, June 13, 2001. According to feminist criminologist Francis Heidensohn, "Women reject a criminal identity with especial rigour," in line with "appropriate" gender-role behavior. F. M. Heidensohn and M. Silvestri, *Women and Crime*, 2nd edn (New York, NY: New York University Press, 1995), p. 19.

37 Hogg, "Women's Participation in the Rwandan Genocide," pp. 81–2.

38 Female genocide suspect, Kigali Central Prison (respondent #19), personal interview, July 5, 2001.

39 Female genocide suspect, Gitarama Prison (respondent #30), personal interview, July 16, 2001.

40 PRI, "The Righteous," p. 8.

41 J. M. Kayishema and F. Masabo, *Les justes Rwandais "Indakemwa"* (Kigali, Rwanda: Ibuka, 2011), p. 20.

42 Josée Mukandamage (former vice president of the Rwandan Supreme Court), personal interview, July 23, 2001.

43 "*Gacaca* Law," 2004, art. 51.

44 Center for Conflict Management, *Research on Gacaca* (Ministry of Justice, Republic of Rwanda, 2013), p. 138.

45 PRI, "Trials of Offences against Property Committed during the Genocide: A Conflict between the Theory of Reparation and the Social and Economic Reality in Rwanda," *Report on Monitoring and Research on the Gacaca* (2007). Summary; as of October 2008, there were 612,151 people accused of property offenses, of whom 609,144 had been tried by that date. PRI, "The Settlement of Property Offense Cases Committed during the Genocide: Update on the Execution of Agreements and Restoration of Condemnations," *Report on Monitoring and Research on the Gacaca* (2009), p. 35.

46 Female genocide suspect, Kigali Central Prison (respondent #13), personal interview, July 3, 2001.

47 Female genocide suspect, Butare Prison, personal interview, July 24, 2001.

48 Female genocide suspect, Nsinda Prison, personal interview, August 6, 2001.

49 Female genocide suspect, Gitarama Prison, personal interview, July 19, 2001.

50 Ministry of Justice, Republic of Rwanda, *CCM Research on Gacaca* (2013), p. 140.

51 Ibid., p. 139.

52 "Trials of Offences against Property Committed during the Genocide," p. 16.

53 J. Schurr, "Rwandan Genocide Survivors Still Waiting for Reparation," *Pambazuka News* 547 (2011).

54 Based on the National Service of *Gacaca* Courts's data, PRI has estimated that at the national level, 13.5 percent of the adult population in 1994, or approximately one-quarter of the adult male population, were "real" genocide killers. PRI, "The Righteous," p. 8.

55 Female genocide suspect, Nsinda Prison (respondent #70), personal interview, August 7, 2001.

56 Female genocide suspect, Gitarama Prison (respondent #34), personal interview, July 16, 2001.

57 Female genocide suspect, Nsinda Prison (respondent #65), personal interview, August 6, 2001.

58 Rakiya Omaar (co director, African Rights, Kigali), personal interview, June 13, 2001.

59 Female genocide suspect, Kigali Central Prison (respondent #13), personal interview, July 3, 2001.

60 Bernadette Kanzayire (lawyer, Kigali), personal interview, June 12, 2001.

61 Hildebrand and Omar, in Kayishema and Masabo, *Les justes Rwandais "Indakemwa,"* p. 7.

62 PRI, "The Righteous: Between Oblivion and Reconciliation."

63 Kayishema and Masabo, *Les justes Rwandais "Indakemwa,"* p. 16. This "pilot" survey was conducted in all districts of Rwanda but only in two sectors (eight cells) per district.

64 Ibid., p. 13.

65 Genocide Archive Rwanda, *Oral Testimony of Sula Karuhimbi.*

66 African Rights, "16 Stories from 'Tribute to Courage,'" in *Reconciliation in Rwanda—Stories of Rescue* (London, UK: African Rights, 2002).

67 Ibid. See also, "Profile of Zura Karuhimbi, Candidate for the Nobel Peace Prize," *BeneRwanda* (2010).

68 African Rights, "16 Stories."

69 Ibid.

70 PRI, "The Righteous: Between Oblivion and Reconciliation," pp. 17–18.

71 P. R. Bartrop, *A Biographical Encyclopedia of Contemporary Genocide: Portraits of Evil and Good* (Santa Barbara, CA: ABC-CLIO, 2012), p. 320.

72 Prosecutor *v.* Nyiramasuhuko, Case No. ICTR-98-42-T, Judgment and Sentence, June 24, 2011.

73 When it came to sentencing, Trial Chamber II emphasized the vast number of victims and Nyiramasuhuko's abuse of her superior position.

74 H. Jallow, Lecture notes distributed at *Seventh Annual Humanitarian Law Dialogs* at Chautauqua, NY, on August 26, 2013.

75 The only other woman convicted by an international criminal tribunal (in this case, the International Criminal Tribunal for the former Yugoslavia) is Biljana Plavšić, a leading Bosnian Serb politician. Plavšić pleaded guilty in 2002 to one count of persecutions on political, racial, and religious grounds as crimes against humanity. She was sentenced in 2003 to eleven years' imprisonment,

which she served in Sweden. Plavšić was released in 2009, pursuant to early release guidelines, after completing two-thirds of her term.

76 Prosecutor v. Nyiramasuhuko, 2011, paragraphs 2268, 2764, 4985.

77 Gaël Lombart, "Pauline Nyiramasuhuko, une criminelle aux airs de 'mere-pule,'" *Le Monde International*, June 24, 2011. For a lucid overview and incisive commentary regarding academic and media representations of Nyiramasuhuko up until 2007, see L. Sjoberg and C. E. Gentry, *Mothers, Monsters, Whores: Women's Violence in Global Politics* (London, UK: Zed Books, 2007), pp. 158–71. For further and detailed discussion of these media depictions, including following 2007, see Drumbl, "'She Makes Me Ashamed to be a Woman,'" pp. 586–93.

78 Hogg, "Women's Participation in the Rwandan Genocide," pp. 82, 100; C. Sperling, "Mother of Atrocities: Pauline Nyiramasuhuko's Role in the Rwanda Genocide," *Fordham Urban Law Journal* 33 (2006), pp. 652–3.

79 Cf. Maier, "Women Leaders in the Rwandan Genocide," pp. 12–13.

80 E. Barad, "Mother and Son *Genocidaires*," *Arusha Times* 683 (2011).

81 Prosecutor v. Elizaphan & Gerard Ntakirutimana, (2003), pp. 919, 22.

82 See, for example, M. Simons, "Rwandan Pastor and his Son are Convicted of Genocide," *New York Times*, February 20, 2003, p. A3; "Hutu Pastor on Trial for Genocide," *CNN World*, September 17, 2001, p. 1; "Pastor Aided Rwanda Genocide," *BBC News*, February 19, 2003.

83 Maier, "Women Leaders in the Rwandan Genocide," p. 9.

84 J. Novogratz, *The Blue Sweater: Bridging the Gap between Rich and Poor in an Interconnected World* (Emmaus, PA: Rodale Books, 2009), p. 163.

85 LIPRODHOR, *Situation de droits de l'homme au Rwanda rapport 2007-2008* (2010), paragraph 2.2.1; "Former Rwandan Justice Minister Sentenced to Life Imprisonment," *Hirondelle News Agency*, January 20, 2009.

86 "Rwanda: Convicted Former Justice Minister Ntambyariro Appeals for Sentence Reduction," *News of Rwanda*, February 21, 2014.

87 During her trial, Kamatamu specifically argued she had no power to prevent the genocide. *Kamatamu Euphrasie* et al., Decision July 17, 1998.

88 Hogg, "Women's Participation in the Rwandan Genocide," p. 96.

89 Ibid., p. 156.

90 Maier, "Women Leaders in the Rwandan Genocide," p. 12 (also discussing other women convicts who had played notorious roles in the genocide).

91 African Rights, *Rwanda, Not So Innocent: When Women Become Killers* (London, UK: African Rights, 1995), pp. 27, 60, 67.

92 J. P. Chretien, "Prison a vie pour une journaliste: Valerie Bemeriki etait une journaliste vedette de RTLM et y a encourage le genocide," *Ibuka*, December 15, 2009. Available online: http://www.ibuka.ch/content/index. php?option=com_content&view=article&id=333:prison-a-vie-pour-une-journaliste-valerie-bemeriki-etait-une-journaliste-vedette-de-rtlm-et-y-a-encourage-le-genocide-&catid=44:memoire-a-justice&Itemid=38 (accessed August 19, 2014).

93 Maier, "Women Leaders in the Rwandan Genocide," p. 10.

94 Ibid.

95 T. Susman, "Jury Deadlocks in Case of Rwandan Immigrant Accused of Genocide," *Los Angeles Times*, March 16, 2012.

96 T. Haines, "Did this New Hampshire Woman Take Part in the Rwandan Genocide?" *The Atlantic*, February 20, 2013. (This article noted also that Munyenyezi "dressed sharply and wore black-framed glasses. On some days her hair was pulled back tight.")

97 L. Tuohy, "Jury: NH Woman Lied About Role in Rwanda Genocide," *Associated Press*, February 21, 2013; Haines, "Did this New Hampshire Woman Take Part in the Rwandan Genocide?" ("Witnesses flown from Rwanda testified that Munyenyezi shot a nun in the head, fed men hungry from hours of raping women, and more.")

98 K. Marchocki, "Boston Jury Convicts Sister of NH Woman Accused of Rwanda Genocide Role," *New Hampshire Union Leader*, May 7, 2012.

99 T. Andersen, "Woman Gets 21 Months for Lying About Ties to Rwandan Genocide," *Boston Globe*, October 12, 2012.

100 US Immigration and Customs Enforcement, "ICE Deports Convicted Rwandan to Serve Sentence for Role in 1994 Genocide," December 21, 2011.

101 Arrêt no. 311793 du Conseil d'État—October 16, 2009.

102 "France Will not Extradite Agathe Habyarimana," *Hirondelle News Agency*, September 28, 2011.

103 Arrêt no. 366219 du Conseil d'État—June 5, 2013.

104 *Plainte Avec Constitution de Parti Civile*, Collectif des Parties Civiles Pour Le Rwanda *v.* Habyarimana, 2007.

105 Hogg, "Women's Participation in the Rwandan Genocide," p. 91.

106 Associated Press, "Rwandan-Born Dutch Woman Jailed for Inciting Genocide," *Guardian*, March 1, 2013.

107 Ibid.

108 See for example, ibid (noting that Basebya was "wearing a pink top and earrings of small crosses at the end of long chains"); "Pastor aided Rwanda genocide," *BBC News*, February 19, 2013 (noting that "Basebya wore a pink jacket, black trousers"); B. Czerwinski, "Dutch Citizen in the Dock for Rwandan Genocide," *Daily Star*, October 22, 2012 (noting at the start of her trial that Basebya was "[d]ressed in a cream jacket and black trousers").

109 T. Bouwknegt, "Hague Court to Decide on Rwanda Genocide Case," *Radio Netherlands Worldwide*, September 27, 2012.

110 Maier, "Women Leaders in the Rwandan Genocide," p. 14.

111 Mark Drumbl, "The ICTR and Justice for Rwandan Women," *New England Journal of International and Comparative Law* 12 (2005), p. 115.

112 PRI, "The Righteous: Between Oblivion and Reconciliation," p. 28.

113 Ibid., p. 23.

Post-Genocidal Trauma and Memory

PART FOUR

Post-Genocidal Trauma and Memory

9

The Biopolitics of "Rescue": Women and the Politics of Inclusion after the Armenian Genocide[1]

Lerna Ekmekcioglu

Introduction

The once-glorious seat of the Ottoman Empire resembled a sprawling refugee camp in the immediate aftermath of the First World War. Several tragedies pulled groups of Greeks, Turks, Russians, Armenians, and others to Constantinople/Istanbul from various locations including Thrace, Anatolia, Levant, Mesopotamia, and southern Russia. Among the camps that sheltered the survivors of the 1915 Armenian genocide, the one in Galata served as the makeshift home of a teenaged girl who had spent the war years among Muslims. Like many of her counterparts, she had been kidnapped and raped. After the Ottoman defeat was sealed by the Mudros Armistice in October 1918, an unknown set of developments had led her to the capital. She may have been rescued by the Armenian relief organizations, or freed by her abductor, or perhaps she had escaped. Be that as it may, she was heavy with child, conceived by the man who had first forced her former fiancé, an Armenian, to witness her violation and had then killed him.

In Allied-occupied Istanbul and under the institutional care of fellow Armenians, she tried every means possible to terminate the pregnancy. Sometime in her first trimester she reached the house of a fellow Armenian woman, Zaruhi Kalemkiarian, who would later tell of her in her memoirs.[2]

I will refer to this "girl" as X, since Kalemkiarian did not provide her name. X pleaded with Kalemkiarian to help her get an abortion (*vizhoum*), but despite her deep sympathy for the girl, Kalemkiarian refused to help, even after X began visiting her house every day, banging her head on the wooden floor in an attempt to injure herself since "her soul was fired up with the need to curse and take revenge."[3]

X sought out Kalemkiarian's help because she was one of the founders of the Armenian Red Cross, which operated a hospital where X could possibly get an abortion. Instead, alarmed that X might commit infanticide, Kalemkiarian and other *khnamagal diginner* (female relief workers) ordered her incarcerated in the maternity ward of the Armenian Red Cross Şişli branch hospital. This ward only housed "forlorn young mothers" (*anderunch yeridasart mayrer*)—refugees expecting babies of Muslim fatherhood.[4] In that "special" ward, within hours of giving birth to a healthy boy, X committed suicide. Despite the customary practice of the shared nursing of infants, other mothers cursed the newborn by collectively refusing to nurse him. Kalemkiarian does not record the baby's fate.

Why did the Armenian authorities deny X an abortion?[5] Why did the expectant mother's perception of the fetus as "the continuation of the *vojrakordz* (criminal)" conflict so profoundly with what Kalemkiarian and other relief workers saw in such babies, whose "chirping cries elevated [their] souls"?[6] At first glance, Kalemkiarian's view may seem puzzling because both Muslims and Christians had long believed, and the law endorsed, that a baby belonged to its father and his group. Yet the Armenian National Relief Committee, the umbrella organization in charge of providing relief to refugees in Istanbul, referred to babies of Muslim fatherhood as "*our orphans*" (*mer vorpere*). What conditioned the decision to render fatherhood irrelevant in determining Armenianness?

I answer this question in the context of immediate postwar-era Istanbul (1918–22). My research is grounded in institutional reports, Ottoman state and Armenian Patriarchate archives, writings in the Armenian and Turkish press, unpublished private papers of intellectuals, and memoirs. During these immediate postwar years, the Ottoman capital was under Allied occupation. When the Great Powers convened in Paris to redraw the world map, one section on that map was claimed by Armenians and Turks alike. International diplomacy, revolving around the Wilsonian principle of self-determination, inextricably linked territorial claims to demographics, and this led Armenians and Turks to take all possible measures to increase their ranks. The intersection of this political context with the shared symbolic and functional importance of women and children for each group engendered not only a postwar Armenian effort to rescue the abducted but also fierce fights about who belonged where. The rescue effort was sometimes aggressive, and rape victims and babies of Muslim fatherhood were officially welcomed into the new coordinates of Armenian collectivity. I will demonstrate that these actions, in addition to exemplifying a common postgenocidal victim response, were intended to reverse the results of extermination campaigns and also represented a conscious choice on the part of Armenian leaders striving to revive their nation *and* their state.[7]

This analysis of a metamorphosis of rules of ethnoreligious belonging provides a striking example of how, under certain circumstances, patriarchy may relax one of its central tenets—the primacy of paternity over maternity. But this did not translate into women's agency in determining group belonging. On the contrary, Armenian rescue efforts left the target population with few options for controlling their own lives and bodies, and far from subverting patriarchal norms they reproduced patriarchal hierarchies and left intact long-established assumptions about women's nature, culture, and potential.

The Armenian Rescue Effort (*Vorpahavak*) in Istanbul

During the First World War, the ruling Young Turk party, the Committee of Union and Progress, openly tolerated and even encouraged the transfer of Armenian children and women of childbearing age into Muslim households, orphanages, and shelters, thus creating what I previously called "a climate of abduction."[8] Integration of Armenian females and minors into Muslim contexts was part of the genocidal policy of eliminating Armenians as a people, thus eliminating the threat of the establishment of an independent Armenian state by seizing "Ottoman" territory.

The signing of the Mudros Armistice on October 1918 sealed the Ottoman defeat and initiated a new political climate in which Armenians could rescue or be rescued. It stipulated the release of Ottoman prisoners of war, a clause that everyone interpreted to include Islamized women and children. Deported Armenians were given the right to return to their original hometowns. Soon after, the Allies occupied Istanbul and parts of Anatolia. The exiled Patriarch Zaven Der Yeghiayan returned to the capital in February 1919 and resumed his duties as the head of the Armenian *millet* (ethnoreligious community). The Armenian National Assembly, a semi-autonomous parliament composed of elected clerics and laymen that had overseen Armenian affairs since the 1860s, reopened. One of the first responsibilities that the patriarch took upon himself was the liberation (*azadakrum*) of Islamized Armenians.

Armenians' campaigns to find, liberate, and reintegrate children and women sequestered in Muslim households and orphanages were collectively called "*vorpahavak*"—"the gathering of orphans" in Armenian. Here the term "orphan" (*vorp*) referred to not only children without one or both parents but also women who lacked a surviving male family member. Rather than age or sex, orphanhood connoted the absence of a dependable male relative and was thus translated to and from Turkish as *bi-kes, kimsesiz,* or *sahipsiz* (unprotected, unclaimed, or forlorn), in addition to *yetim* (fatherless orphan) and *öksüz* (motherless orphan).

In Istanbul, the Patriarchate created and financially supported an Orphan Gathering Agency (*Vorphavak Marmin*) composed of a supervisor—Arakel Chakerian, a Paris-educated professor of chemistry at the University of Istanbul—and four young men personally known to and trusted by the patriarch.[9] Some young girls and women were also employed to facilitate easier and more respectful access to Muslim places.[10] The British Embassy gave each *vorpahavak* agent a letter of introduction addressed to the Allied police force asking them to provide assistance if needed. According to the memoirs of the patriarch, until the end of 1922 *vorpahavak* agents in Istanbul retrieved about three thousand of the five thousand kidnapped Armenians.[11]

The Sèvres Treaty, the first postwar peace treaty the Ottomans signed with the Allies (later superseded by the 1923 Lausanne Treaty), further boosted *vorpahavak* efforts. It not only annulled all conversions to Islam between 1914 and 1918 but also required the Ottoman Turkish government to assist in all efforts to find those concerned and deliver them back to their original communities. The newly formed League of Nations, too, became involved in uniting Near-Eastern families torn apart by the war.[12] Beginning in 1922, the League's Commission of Inquiry for the Protection of Women and Children in the Near East carried out rescue operations in Istanbul and Aleppo and opened shelters; from 1922 to 1926, it rescued four thousand adults and four thousand children, the majority of them Armenians.[13]

Especially in the months immediately following the Mudros Armistice and the de jure occupation of Istanbul, the Ottoman government remained supportive of the *vorpahavak*.[14] During the first months after the Armistice, some Turkish/Muslim families voluntarily gave their Armenians to the Patriarchate.[15] However, as 1919 unfolded, the government's support of *vorpahavak* diminished, and at times it turned openly hostile to it. Many Armenians now had to be extracted forcibly. The Turkish nationalist movement in Anatolia, which had been growing since the Armistice, was now organized around the leadership of Mustafa Kemal (later Atatürk) and was growing increasingly anti-Armenian and anti-Greek.

A problem that deeply troubled both Greek and Armenian rescue efforts was those persons who refused to be rescued. Many "captives" wanted to remain where they were. Research conducted in different parts of the world suggests that abducted people often resist being forcibly returned to their natal communities. This is most common when they have assimilated relatively well into the abductors' group and suffer no severe discrimination there, when they have spent several years away, and when they foresee being stigmatized if they return. Many abducted women in both India and Pakistan resisted efforts to "liberate" them from households into which they were forcibly integrated during the 1947 partition. Similarly, many white women and children held captive by Native Americans were reluctant to return to white society. These situations contrast sharply with those conflicts, such as in Central and West Africa, in which kidnapped girls have been isolated and confined in huts to serve as sex slaves and have usually welcomed rescue efforts.[16]

We can begin to understand why some women and children resisted re-Armenianization through eyewitness testimonies, memoirs, and oral history interviews, and also a report prepared in March 1919 for the Armenian National Delegation in Paris.[17] Their abduction, loss of chastity, abuse at enemy hands, or bearing of a child by an enemy man constituted such deep disgrace that many married women did not want to leave their relatively bearable situations for lives of certain stigmatization back in their native communities.[18] Those who had converted to Islam, even at gunpoint, and even men, were seen to have blackened their group's name.[19] Some assumed that Armenians would refuse to accept their "Muslim" children and did not want to leave them behind. Most knew they had no family to return to. Many had been purchased or saved from the *gendarmes* by "peaceful Muslims who ensured them a relatively tolerable life," for which the women remained grateful.[20] Some loved and were loved by their husbands.[21] Some women in unhappy marriages before the war may have found life with their new families an improvement and abduction to have bettered their lots as wives.[22]

Children were even less willing to return, and many younger returnees escaped back. By the time of their rescue they had spent an average of four to five years in their new households or institutions, and many knew no other life. Especially in cases where a child was happily integrated into a household, *vorpahavak* felt more like abduction than redemption. There were also cases where children were simply too afraid to admit their Armenianness.[23]

The Patriarchate's and the Ottoman government's policies of handling the reluctant abductee differed. In general, Armenians of all strands agreed that all Armenian children, regardless of their wishes or whether or not they claimed to be faithful Muslims, had to be returned to the nation's bosom. Ottoman regulations supported this policy by ordering that all former Armenians below age twenty, irrespective of their inclinations, be presumed to have converted to Islam by force—thus their conversions were annulled automatically.[24]

Where the two centers of authority diverged was on the question of how to deal with people older than twenty. The Ottoman government decreed that such individuals had the right to choose what was best for themselves. The main problem here was married women—the November 28, 1918 order to the provinces maintained "the constitution commands freedom of conscience" and that married women over twenty be free to re-Armenianize, in which case both their conversion to Islam and their Muslim marriages would be annulled. If they wished to return to their original religion but not divorce their Muslim husbands, they had to apply to the courts.[25] Married women under twenty, even though their conversions to Islam were considered invalid, would not be forced to re-Armenianize and divorce; their cases, the government said, would be resolved in court, in the presence of members of their natal family (if they had any), church authorities, Christian missionaries (or other Westerners), and Ottoman officials.[26]

The Patriarchate took a different stance, and insisted that irrespective of their age, choice, marital status, or self-identification, every former Armenian had to be reclaimed, and if they insisted on escaping, they would be imprisoned.[27] It is important to note that not every Armenian who took part in the *vorpahavak* initiatives agreed with this position. Some—including Avedis Aharonian, a member of the Armenian Republic's Parliament and the cochair of the Armenian delegation to the Paris Peace Conference—thought those women who lived with "relatively bearable Muslims," had children, and were accustomed to their way of life should be left where they were. Aharonian did not believe that women who were fine in the Muslim homes would be able to successfully reintegrate among Armenians. He emphasized that Armenians should spare no effort to rescue each and every Armenian girl and woman who was suffering at the hands of "savage races" (*vayrak tsegh*), then cautioned that if a woman chose the new Muslim family, to aggressively seize her against her husband's wishes would agitate such "savage races," who were Armenia's future neighbors with whom the survivors had to live.

For others, like Zaruhi Bahri, considerations of individual happiness occasionally demanded a respect for personal wishes. She was a colleague of Zaruhi Kalemkiarian, the recorder of X's story in this chapter's opening vignette. Like Kalemkiarian, she was a native Constantinopolitan from an elite intellectual background. During the Armistice era she remained very active by directing an orphanage/shelter, penning articles in periodicals, and working for the Armenian Red Cross, which she had helped found in Istanbul. The patriarch personally asked her for assistance in directing a Neutral House orphanage/shelter across from her house in Şişli, where women and children of contested identities were sheltered until their true identities were determined.

In her memoirs, Bahri took a cautiously critical tone when detailing how the patriarch himself never sympathized with liberated women who wanted to go back to the homes they had been abducted to. Bahri herself was clearly a tough inspector, who more than once brought out the Armenianness of children and women who veraciously and for days denied their origins, but in at least two cases she begged the patriarch to let captives go. In the first case, the patriarch suspected that Bahri might help the escape of a certain Aghavni Kazazian (who had already tried to run away twice) and so ordered Aghavni declared mentally ill and institutionalized in the Armenian National Hospital. This, even though Aghavni showed no signs of an illness except for longing for her husband and her son, whom Bahri defined as "a Turk, yes, but of her own blood and ultimately her very own child."[28] In the second case, a young Armenian woman was happily married to an Iranian who had saved her during the deportations. Though National Assembly officials forbade this woman returning to her husband, as Bahri bitterly noted, at about the same time her husband's equally Iranian brother was in the process of marrying an Armenian girl in Istanbul, freely and with the full consent of both parties.[29] The patriarch's memoir includes detailed passages on the Neutral House but is silent on the topic of orphans and women who preferred to stay among Muslims.

Turkish officials and the broader public were disturbed by news of such cases as well as by the many complaints that *vorpahavak*s were retrieving true Muslims, both mistakenly and intentionally. As women and children were transferred from one group to another, they found themselves caught up in fierce debates over who had kidnapped whom.[30] Turks accused Armenians of being baby snatchers "who hoped to replenish their wartime losses from the Muslim pool."[31] Government-led Turkish newspapers claimed that Armenians were beating and threatening Muslim children to make them "admit" their Armenian origin.[32] Armenian editors responded by accusing the Turkish press of maintaining the genocidal mentality by blaming victims for the perpetrators' crimes. One Armenian editor ended his piece about the issue with: "It would be naïve to talk about colors with a blind person, about sounds with a deaf person, and of conscience with a perpetrator [of massacres]."[33]

In the Ottoman lands, political competition over the redefinition of children's true belonging has a history reaching back to the late nineteenth century. Notwithstanding that children are allocated powerful symbolic roles by collectivities that imagine themselves as nations, the late-Ottoman battle over "nobody's children" expressed also the demographic concerns of a crumbling empire. These concerns, combined with the changing urban fabric of a fast-modernizing Istanbul, led to a competition over foundlings and abandoned children waged between the state, non-Muslim civil and religious leaders, and missionaries.[34] While the central state and the municipality wanted to assume all foundlings' Muslimness, non-Muslim leaders argued that at least those who were left in front of churches and synagogues should be taken in by the respective communities. Greek and Armenian patriarchates were alarmed at Catholic missionaries' active roles in foundling care, because the missionaries, who were forbidden to convert Muslims, continued to take in Christian children and convert them to Catholicism.

In immediate postwar Istanbul, the fights between opposing parties escalated to the degree that when the British occupying forces intervened, "Neutral Houses" were opened to determine which children or women belonged to which group. In Istanbul, the Neutral House (*Chezok Dun* in Armenian, *Bitarafhane* in Turkish) was established in Şişli, close to the Armenian Red Cross's special maternity ward that I described earlier in this chapter. It was managed by a joint committee composed of one Turk, one Armenian, and one American female director. There, children and young women who claimed Muslim identity but were suspected of hiding their Armenian identity out of fear of Muslim retaliation or simply due to brainwashing, were isolated from their Muslim families. After a few weeks' stay at the house, surrounded by Armenians, most admitted they were Armenian.[35] During this process, the Turkish director resigned in protest, claiming that Turkish Muslim children were being Armenianized.

Available evidence indicates that the *vorpahavak* initiative did not employ a conscious, widespread Armenianization policy, and some mistakes were corrected by returning children or women to their families.[36] They were corrected not only to straighten out the record, but also because Armenian authorities were wary of what they believed were Turkish plans to present Armenians to the occupation forces and the League of Nations as kidnappers of Turkish children. In a March 1922 internal report, Arakel Chakerian cautioned the patriarch that if Turks found even one Turkish child in an Armenian orphanage they would make a serious issue of it. He strongly advised letting go from Armenian orphanages the few children who still insisted that they were Turks. We do not know if this was done.[37]

Even though Armenianization was not the general policy, *vorpahavak* agents' criteria for considering someone Armenian were very broad: if a suspect did not protest otherwise, and if no other party claimed him or her, persons were considered Armenian whether or not they remembered their previous language, family, or location. Zaruhi Bahri narrated how a certain Zekiye, a Turkish woman who had introduced herself as an Armenian, was easily sheltered in Armenian orphanages despite the fact that she neither knew Armenian nor "looked like an Armenian."[38] Aghavni Kazazian's Muslim husband had hired Zekiye to enter the shelter and convince his wife to return to him.

In addition to always erring on the side of the potential Armenianness of any orphan, authorities at times forced confessions (true or possibly false), and they did occasionally Armenianize Muslim children or ignore when others did.[39] Aram Haygaz, a teenager at the Yesayan orphanage at the time, in his memoirs told of a ten-year-old boy who, unlike many others in a similar situation, would not admit his Armenianness and, even after some time at the orphanage and suffering threats and pressure, continued to insist that he was Turkish. Ultimately, Haygaz and his friends believed him, but they decided that "even if he was a pure-bred (*zdariun*) Turk, we would keep him to Armenianize him gradually (*asdijanapar hayatsnenk*)."[40]

Haygaz's explanation of why they kept this boy, who they knew had a Turkish mother and father outside the orphanage walls, leads us to ask why this rescue effort was at times so aggressive, passionate, and determined. One of the orphans who worked on this "case" with Haygaz maintained, "They Turkified thousands from among us. Now it is our turn to at least Armenianize one among them."[41] Haygaz, the sole survivor in his family, who had spent the war years in Ottoman Kurdistan where he was converted and adopted by Muslim families, noted that the issue here was one of reprisal (*pokhvrej*). Revenge was definitely part of the story, but it was only one part. To understand the whole we must understand the contemporary international political framework and the fight over territory that was ongoing.

Reclaiming People, Reclaiming Land

The fight at this time over women and children epitomized the larger, ongoing conflict between Armenians and Turks. It centered on a piece of land, today within eastern Turkey, that Ottomans referred to as their "Eastern Provinces" and Armenians as "Western Armenia." As with the minors and women, each side claimed and reclaimed the land as its own and fought for it militarily, or diplomatically, or both.

Around the same time that the story of X was unfolding in Istanbul, the great powers gathered at Versailles to redraw the world map. Armenians sent a well-equipped delegation to the Paris Peace Conference to lobby for their entitlement to a share of the soon-to-be-dismembered Ottoman Empire. The goal was to expand the tiny Republic of Armenia in Transcaucasia (established in May 1918) to include the western parts of the Armenian historical homeland that had been under Ottoman rule since the sixteenth century. The establishment of Greater Armenia or United Armenia would not only realize Armenians' "age-old dream" but would also gain revenge against "the Turk" who had recently attempted to exterminate the whole Armenian nation.[42]

Yet, having just survived this annihilation campaign, Armenians lacked the numbers needed to people the land—a particularly harsh challenge in the immediate postwar era. The Paris Peace Settlement negotiations, with their emphasis on Wilsonian "self-determination," came to an agreement that the nationality of a region was to devolve to that community that made up the majority of the population.[43] Armenians had to come up with numbers—and quickly.

Patriarch Zaven learned about the intricacies of international diplomacy firsthand during his European tour in support of the Armenian Delegation. In London, the commission charged with Armenia's future borders told him, "The more people you have the more land you will get."[44] British Foreign Secretary Lord Curzon's assistant also advised the patriarch to "hearten the dispersed Armenians to immediately return and populate Armenia."[45]

Both the Armenians and the leaders of the Kemalist movement anticipated the unleashing of a "war of statistics."[46] One of the most important tasks of the emerging defense committees was to prove, by "scientific means," that Muslims had always constituted the majority in the regions that Armenians claimed to be their historical homelands; places that the Armenian delegation in Paris attempted to prove, also statistically, had to belong to Armenians.

Armenian populations away from Paris were clearly aware of the link between numbers and territory. In December 1919, the editor of *Hay Gin* (*Armenian Women*), the prominent Armenian women's journal of the time, edited by Hayganush Mark (a colleague of Zaruhi Kalemkiarian and Zaruhi Bahri), wrote with alarm that Islamized Armenians had to return to their natal religion so that "we get our Armenia."[47] In order to accumulate statistical numbers and create the necessary demographic profile, Armenians launched a worldwide pronatalist campaign, which was part of a broader campaign called "National Revival/Rebirth" (*Azkayin Veradznunt*).[48] Their goal was to raise the Armenian population, Armenian landholdings, and Armenian life generally back to, or beyond, their prewar levels.

Predictably, this campaign placed women at the heart of the Armenian state-building project, both as real actors and as objects of discourse. To lower infant and juvenile mortality, columns in Armenian periodicals urged mothers to employ scientific childrearing practices. The pages of the press poured out detailed information on topics such as babies' breastfeeding, getting enough fresh air, and wearing proper clothing. Women's journals organized "pretty baby" contests to encourage mothers, while journalists and professionals urged young women and men to marry early and produce many children.[49] Abortion became tantamount to treason. The medical journal *Hay Puzhag* (*Armenian Healer*), which published regular reports on how many marriage certificates the Patriarchate had issued, characterized abortion-seeking women as "egoist and undutiful." Equating abortion with infanticide, it addressed the Armenian woman: "Keep away all thoughts and principles of degeneration and devote yourself to your procreation, which is your *sole duty*. It is the complete fulfillment of this duty that will realize our ideal."[50]

The push to realize this "ideal" justified policies that would have been nearly unthinkable before the war. Most significantly, Armenian authorities—political and religious leaders as well as intellectuals and professionals—were willing to change the coordinates of legitimate belonging. Both the administrative practices toward and discourses about rescued pregnant women and their offspring reveal that, facing a perceived existential crisis, Armenian authorities changed the criteria for inclusion in the national collectivity by making room for one group that would otherwise have been excluded—babies of Muslim fatherhood.[51]

In the summer of 1920, Dr. Yaghoubian, in charge of the Armenian Red Cross hospital where X was incarcerated, delivered a lecture at the center of the Armenian Women's Association. The doctor argued that depopulation was the "worst enemy of a nation's development" and therefore had to be fought with every medical, social, and material effort. After emphasizing mothers' unique role in realizing this national goal, he encouraged nonrefugee women and girls to become nurses and midwives so that they could prevent abortion and infanticide among refugees, especially rescued women and girls. He stated:

> We respect the offspring of lawful marriages and curse free love. The Armenian baby has to be parented by those who have been lawfully married in the Armenian Church. But we cannot dismiss some unfortunate realities of life; many of our deported sisters and wives became mothers by force, with the fear of the knife or death; many in half-dead state have become victims of savage races' pleasures. . . . A smart midwife knows how to support and console such poor women and will try to conceal [dzadzgel] their shame; more importantly, she will hinder them from aborting their unlawful baby. Big governments build special shelter houses for such unlucky people and they protect the children born out of wedlock [aboren] with special laws. We, however, as the tiniest of small nations, how can we exterminate our fetuses, even though they may be out of wedlock?[52]

That Yaghoubian considered products of rape to be "our fetuses" is telling, especially since it follows his statement that the fathers of these babies belonged to a "barbarian race." Given that Muslim and Christian traditions as well as law asserted that progeny was made up primarily of a fathers' substance and thus belonged to him, Yaghoubian's statement, like many vorpahavak practices, stood in stark contrast to established practice. Women were now seen to have a creative and not just a receptive role in procreation; they were assumed to have engendered, not simply contributed to, their progeny.

This response to rape babies of mixed heritage has by no means been the universal one in similar cases. For instance, in Bangladesh during the 1971 War of Independence, Pakistani army personnel raped about two hundred thousand women. In the war's aftermath, the Bangladeshi state elevated the rape victims to the status of "war heroines" but excluded their children by categorizing them as Pakistani. It was decided that the presence of these babies would adversely affect the country's social structures and perpetuate painful memories of the war, and abortion and foreign adoption, once criminal and unaccepted, were made legal.[53] In contrast to the Armenian case, where women were not allowed to abort their rape babies, Bangladeshi women were "de-kinned" from their offspring by coerced abortions or forced surrender of their babies for adoption.

What is perhaps most unique about the Armenian case is the lack of discussion of, let alone opposition to, the changed paternity rules. A contrasting case is that of the enfants du barbare, children of French women raped by Germans during the First World War. There were fierce debates in France over how to handle their situation: what to do with the babies, where they belonged, and to whom, and so forth. Some people, including even Catholic priests, advocated abortion in the name of racial purity. Others remained antiabortionists and argued that women's contribution to procreation was greater than men's; that, in any case, French "civilization" in a child would triumph over its German barbarism; and that France needed nationals.[54]

The lack of Armenian opposition to the Patriarchate's policies might be explained by the felt immanency of the realization of the "national ideal."[55] Perhaps the establishment of *Mayr Hayasdan* (Mother Armenia) justified these extraordinary measures. Moreover, the genocidal nature of the conflict might have influenced both the policy and the absence of discussions. We know, for another comparative instance, that after the Rwandan genocide the state forbade the international adoption of rape babies. Rwanda needed citizens, yes, but it did not go so far as to ban abortions. In fact, the former ban on abortions was temporarily relaxed so rape victims could obtain them. The Armenian administration's attitude regarding abortion, then, stands in contrast to comparable cases.

Marriageability and Re-masculinization

The alarmist tone of the above quotation from Dr. Yaghoubian reveals that not all refugees shared "the national agenda." Many of those on whom motherhood was forced simply did not want to have the babies, which, again, is a common response among genocidal rape survivors. Among the Bosnian Muslim and Rwandan Tutsi women, scholars documented soaring rates of self-induced abortion, infanticide, neglect, and child abandonment.[56] For Armenians, the rare anecdotal evidence comes from the writings of Constantinopolitan women, both Armenian and American, who worked with the rescued. They recount how some rescued pregnant women, like X, were relieved when their newborns died (and may had neglected them intentionally)[57] and that some explicitly asked orphanages to take their Muslim children from them so that they would not kill them as a rapist's offspring.[58] One, after being told that she was at an early stage of pregnancy, responded to her American doctor simply, "Very well, I will send it to its father."[59]

Under *vorpahavak* policy, authorities would not allow the baby to be sent to the father; it would be sheltered in an orphanage and baptized by the church.[60] Clearly, the "half-caste" progeny represented radically different things for their mothers, for their surviving maternal relatives, and for Armenian leaders. The Turkish state and public seem to have overlooked the issue, focused as they were on the threat of losing fully Muslim orphans, and integrated women, to the enemy.

Available evidence indicates a general pattern of surviving Armenian relatives being eager to get back their kidnapped women and children, whether or not they had been raped, or wanted to return, or had given birth to "wrong children." Indeed, they insisted on their return. But relatives sometimes did not want to bring "the enemy's children" into their midst.

One survivor in an interview recalled a woman who had been abducted at age twelve, was married to a Turk, and had two children by him. After the genocide, her father found out where she was and wrote to her to say that he wanted her to rejoin him but did not want her children, "who belonged to a Turk." "She kept crying and crying, not knowing what to do. Finally she decided to leave and went to Beirut; once in Beirut, she could not take it without her children but was too afraid to return. . . . She was miserable."[61]

Some mothers chose, and managed, to escape with their children. One of these women lived in the same refugee camp as Kerop Bedoukian, who was then a young boy. In his memoirs Bedoukian recalled that this 22-year-old's one-year-old son not only made impossible her marriage to an Armenian but "also branded her as a whore." This did not prevent the woman's skillful mother from marrying her to a handsome Armenian man from America, who had arrived in Istanbul to find a wife. The American was first engaged to his future wife's sister, a pretty eighteen-year-old who the mother apparently used as bait. Bedoukian told the story of the family sleeping in the next blanket in the refugee camp: "Their mother arranged it that he should go to America with the older girl and the child, to help them get settled or possibly find her a husband, before he sent for his own bride. Three months later, the bride-to-be flew into a great rage on receiving the news that her fiancé had married her sister. The mother tried to explain that it was easy to find her a husband, but for her sister it was another matter. If she loved her sister, she should be glad. Well! She did not love her sister and she did not mind telling the world about it!"[62]

For many rescued women and refugees, a proper marriage represented the most viable way to exchange the transient life for some sense of stability and security.[63] Here the goals of the rescued and their rescuers converged. For the *vorpahavak* agenda, marrying younger women and girls to Armenian men and placing their children with Armenian families as foster children or adoptees represented an ideal solution: they retrieved what the Turks had stolen and employed what they reclaimed to reproduce Armenianness.

Given the pregenocide ideas about purity and propriety, Armenian leaders had their work cut out for them in packaging rescued women as proper marriage candidates and future mothers. As early as 1916, *Hairenik* (*Fatherland*), a daily of Boston, announced, "An Armenian man should not reject a woman who has been abducted since she is an innocent victim who cannot be held morally responsible for her condition."[64] A contributor to *Hay Gin* warned that victims should not be blamed for the actions of "bestial packs of wolves that deflowered and mutilated Armenian virgins."[65]

As norms regarding paternal lineage were suspended, so too did ideas about proper marriageability change, at least temporarily. But unlike the new lineage norms, changing conceptions of marriageability seem to have been shared by the mass of the people—and for good reason. Men in the diaspora, at least, were eager to marry rescued women. In 1919, out of the seventy women sheltered in the Scutari Women's Shelter for the Rescued, twenty-one married within their first year there.[66] Most went to America, many as picture brides. Many of the grooms had settled in North America before the war, and had lost their families in the Ottoman lands during the war. A survivor observed that men "returned from America for the sole purpose of marrying orphans and widows to help heal and make them forget their tragic past, to give them a new home, and to create new hope—this was the least they thought they could do for those who had survived."[67] Even the tattoos that many of the rescued bore on their faces and hands (an Arab and Kurdish tradition) did not necessarily leave them unmarriageable.[68] Understandably, many of these women hated their tattoos, and some disfigured themselves trying to burn them away with acid.[69]

There were various reasons that men living abroad, many of them disempowered laborers, might want to marry rescued orphans, including a desire to partner with someone in their daily struggles and for someone to help them overcome the loss of their families. At the same time it was a way to re-masculinize. This was true for those men who rescued women, ordered their rescue, fathered them, married them, or married them off. Armenian men who were made to witness violations of their families, or were away when they were violated, now had a chance to do what they felt they should have been doing before: protecting their women and minors. While saving them, either literally or by marrying them despite their defiled state, they also saved themselves from feelings of guilt and emasculation. In addition to the chance to regain people and land, *vorpahavak* offered a chance to reclaim manhood.

The relevant discourse employed not an explicit language of masculinity but rather a vocabulary of protection (*der ganknil* in Armenian, *sahip çıkmak* in Turkish), benevolence, honor, and revenge.[70] For instance, when in 1921 the Armenian Church in Baghdad received hundreds of recently reclaimed children, among them many girls tattooed according to Bedouin traditions, the priest collectively baptized them "*Vrezh*" (Vengeance).[71] The patriarch himself, suiting his function as *parens patriae*, took the guardianship of his unprotected flock quite seriously.[72] All the rescued, even the prostitutes that he had saved in Mosul where he had been exiled, were the nation's "unfortunate sisters" (*darapakhd kuyrer*) and, crucially, they still represented the honor of the nation—the precious Armenian national honor that men had to protect by marrying them.[73]

The first such wedding in Istanbul was narrated by Anayis (Yeprime Avedisian), another prominent native Armenian woman of Constantinople, an activist and writer, and a colleague of Kalemkiarian, Bahri, and Hayganush Mark. The wedding celebration took place nowhere other than in the Neutral House, and the patriarch presided over the church ceremony, which Anayis described:

> Only rarely has a wedding ceremony been this serious and impressive. When the priest, amidst the smell of incense, was blessing the young

groom and the bride in white, we felt as if we recognized the smells of martyrs' souls, who (forgetting their tortures, the suffering of exile, the blood-filled lakes that they had seen, and the whip of the merciless Turkish sergeant) came, with the company of little angels, to witness the wedding of a sweet budding flower who was going to sprout on top of embellished mountains and give beautiful flowers so that the nation/race [*tsegh*] continues invincibly.[74]

The passage is striking from a number of perspectives. The bride wore the color of purity despite having been rescued from a Muslim household where she probably served as a wife or concubine. Her dressing in white negated her previous experiences, thus denying, both literally and figuratively, the rapist or perpetrator the right to violate an Armenian girl's virginity and, by extension, to dishonor what she represented: the honor of her male relatives and her nation. This was also a retaliation ceremony that the martyred dead would have watched with satisfaction: the wedding of two Armenians, including one who could have been lost to Turks forever, meant that Armenianness would continue despite the Turks. That this sweet budding flower was going to sprout atop "embellished mountains" takes us directly to the issue of land. Given that the ultimate territorial symbol of the Armenian historical homeland had long been Mount Ararat, the reference to mountains connected the reclamation of land to the reclamation of people: the two sides of the overall Armenian project.

Conclusion

Subsequent historical developments soon revealed that this Armenian project had failed: no Greater United Armenia was ever established, and the independent republic in the Caucasus lasted only twenty months until its Sovietization in December 1920. The 1923 Lausanne Treaty not only did not grant Armenians any territory, but also declared a general amnesty for war crimes, effectively pardoning the perpetrators of the Armenian genocide. Turkey, including the territories that Armenians claimed was part of their own homeland, was declared a republic that October, ending the rule of the 600-year-old Ottoman Empire.

The *vorpahavak* ended in the autumn of 1922, when the first Turkish officers victoriously entered Istanbul, and the Allied evacuation began. Many people associated with the *vorpahavak*, including the patriarch, Zaruhi Bahri, Anayis, Arakel Chakerian, and others who had worked in collaboration with the occupation forces, fled the country in panic or were expelled.[75] The League of Nations' rescue effort ended in Istanbul in 1926 and in Aleppo in 1927. Thousands of Armenian women and children who continued to live in Muslim households or orphanages, by their choice or against it, lived and died as Turkish citizens of Muslim religion. Some found ways to resume relationships with their former Armenian relatives by exchanging letters, money, or even visits.[76] Their stories remained mostly silent and silenced in Turkey until recently, when their memories began to resurface via their grandchildren.[77] For Armenians, orphans and orphanhood have remained central both to a defining national discourse and as a focus of humanitarian and charitable giving. By contrast, the attention given to the rescued girls and women slowly receded.

This chapter has remembered them as policy objects of a postgenocide nation that badly needed to people a promised land. Females were incredibly valuable assets both during the war—for the perpetrator group and afterward for survivors—because of not only what women possessed but also what they lacked. Wombs reproduced the group physically while their holders reproduced it socially. However, what rendered women golden for opposing nationalists with similar goals was the perceived female deficiency for naming: while performing these vital functions for each group's present and future, women could define neither the group nor their progeny. The same nationalist ideology that portrayed women as the national core, the nation's essence and critical difference, remained patriarchal at all times, denying women any creative potential. Perceived genetic ineffectiveness, then, needs to be added to the list of reasons why women may matter to national, ethnic, and state projects.

Herein lies the central *problematique* of this chapter: why a patriarchal structure like that of the Armenian community in Istanbul, led literally by a patriarch, reversed these assumptions in order to make space for those who would have otherwise been left out. Like many other states or state-like structures facing real or imagined existential crises, Armenians passed emergency laws and crafted new technologies with gendered implications. The temporary change in Armenian descent rules led to many children of Muslim fatherhood growing up Armenian. While some "hidden Armenian" grandparents in contemporary Turkey have become publicly visible, we have yet to learn the story of X's baby boy who, if he survived without breast milk, would have continued life as an Armenian.[78]

Notes

1   This is a shortened version of my earlier article: Lerna Ekmekcioglu, "A Climate for Abduction, A Climate for Redemption: The Politics of Inclusion during and after the Armenian Genocide," *Comparative Studies in Society and History* 55:1 (2013), pp. 522–53.

2   Kalemkiarian's piece, "Badmutiun me Tornigis Hamar, Yerp vor Medznas," written in New York in 1927, is included in her *Giankis Jampen* (Antilias: Dbaran Gatoghigosutian Giligio, 1952), pp. 293–8.

3   Ibid., p. 296.

4   *Yergamia Deghegakir H. G. Khachi Getr. Varchutian, 1918 Noy. 18-1920 Teg. 31* (Biennial report of the Armenian Red Cross in Constantinople covering the years from November 18, 1918 to December 31, 1920) (Constantinople, Ottoman Empire: M. Hovagimian, 1921), p. 30.

5   We lack studies of Armenian abortion laws, practices, and rates in the Ottoman Empire that would allow us to fully assess how unprecedented the relief workers' attitude was.

6   Kalemkiarian, "Badmutiun," p. 297.

7   This paper refutes Vahe Tachjian's claim that responsible Armenian leadership displayed "opposing forms of prejudice towards two integral components of . . . nation: positive towards orphans one the one hand, and negative towards some abandoned women and girls on the other hand." Vahe Tachjian, "Gender, Nationalism, Exclusion: The Reintegration Process of Female Survivors of the Armenian Genocide," *Nations and Nationalism* 15:1 (2009), pp. 60–80, here 65.

8   See Ekmekcioglu, "A Climate for Abduction, A Climate for Redemption," pp. 525–34.

9   Zaven Der Yeghiayan, *My Patriarchal Memoirs* (Barrington, RI: Mayreni Publishing, 2002), pp. 181–2.

10 One such girl, then nineteen, remembered how, with two male guards, she would go to Muslim households, and even when the lady of the house claimed that there were no "infidels" (non-Muslims) in the house she would forcibly enter the household and find children hidden in basements. Eliz Sanasarian, "Gender Distinction in the Genocidal Process: A Preliminary Study of the Armenian Case," *Holocaust and Genocide Studies* 4:4 (1989), pp. 449–61, here 455. Oral history interviews conducted with survivors in their old age, mostly in the United States, have not been explored with regard to *vorpahavak* efforts.

11 Der Yeghiayan, *My Patriarchal Memoirs*, p. 185. According to an April 1921 report prepared by the Patriarchate in Istanbul, the total number of kidnapped Armenians reached 63,000, out of which 6,000 were in Istanbul and its environs. Hikmet Özdemir, *Ermeniler: Sürgün ve Göç* (Ankara, Turkey: Türk Tarih Kurumu, 2004), p. 123. A similar table was reproduced in *Amenoun Daretsuytse* 15 (1922), pp. 261–5.

12 Keith David Watenpaugh, "The League of Nations' Rescue of Armenian Genocide Survivors and the Making of Modern Humanitarianism, 1920-1927," *American Historical Review* 115:5 (2010), pp. 1315–39, here 1315.

13 Vahram Shemmassian, "The League of Nations and the Reclamation of Armenian Genocide Survivors," in *Looking Backward, Moving Forward: Confronting the Armenian Genocide*, ed. Richard Hovannisian (New Brunswick, NJ: Transaction Publishers, 2003), p. 94.

14 Atnur, *Türkiye'de Ermeni Kadınları*, pp. 135–8.

15 The patriarch mentions this but provides no numbers. Der Yeghiayan, *My Patriarchal Memoirs*, p. 181.

16 For a comparative discussion, see Andrea Parrot and Nina Cummings, *Sexual Enslavement of Girls and Women Worldwide* (Westport, CT: Praeger, 2008).

17 The March 1919 report, "La liberation des Femmes et Enfants Nonmusulmans en Turquie," was prepared by Zabel Yeseyan, the most distinguished Armenian female writer and activist of the time, for the Armenian National Delegation in Paris; Nubarian Library, National Delegation archives, 1–15, correspondence February–March 1919, report titled 1919, p. 9.

18 One interviewed survivor said that a few Armenian men who had been in the United States during the war returned to Adana (in southern Turkey) to search for their wives. They found their wives, but they all had married Muslim men. The interviewee described the meeting of these women with their former and new husbands: "[The former wives] all came dressed like Turks with veils on their heads. [Their Muslim husbands] told [their Armenian husbands] that anything can happen during wartime. . . . [The Armenian women] would not leave—one of them said that if they returned, people would say that they have been Turks' wives and would mock them. [The Armenian husbands] all gave up. . . . They remarried. And all of them returned to the U.S." Derderian, "Common Fate," p. 13.

19 Aram Haygaz, *Bantog* (Beirut: Mshag, 1967).

20 Yesayan, "La liberation."

21 See my points regarding Zaruhi Bahri's cases in this article.

22 The Turkish press of the time and subsequent Turkish nationalist historiography interpreted Armenian women's reluctance as proof of their initial consent or eventual happiness, thus implying that women were happier among Muslims than among Armenians. Armenian historiography, on the other hand, has simply ignored reluctant women and children, reflecting the biases of male memoirists.

23 Zaruhi Bahri, "Inch er Chezok Doune?" *Aysor*, May 3, 1953.

24 From February 8, 1919, Başbakanlık Osmanlı Arşivleri, DH-ŞFR, 96/100, quoted in Atnur, *Türkiye'de Ermeni Kadınları*, p. 174.

25 Ibid., p. 180.

26 Ibid., p. 181.

27 Based on research on refugee women's memoirs, and Karen Jeppe's reports of incoming women refugees to her Reception House in Aleppo, Victoria Rowe reached a similar conclusion to mine, that the "Armenian and international community made it a policy to offer women the chance to return to the Armenian community." Victoria Rowe, "Armenian Women Refugees at the End of Empire: Strategies of Survival," in *Refugees and the End of Empire: Imperial Collapse and Forced Migration in the Twentieth Century*, ed. Panikos Panayi and Pipa Virdee (New York, NY: Palgrave Macmillan, 2011), p. 164.

28 Zaruhi Bahri, *Giankis Vebe* (Beirut, Lebanon: n.p., 1995), p. 189.

29 Ibid., p. 191.

30 Halide Edib Adıvar accused Armenians of brainwashing Muslim children; *The Turkish Ordeal: Being the Further Memoirs of Halidé Edib* (London, UK: Century Co., 1928), p. 17. Armenians, though, accused her of Islamizing Armenian children. For an example, see Aghavnie Yeghenian, "The Turkish Jeanne D'Arc: An Armenian Picture of Remarkable Halide Edib Hanoum,"

New York Times, September 17, 1922. Edib herself fostered a Kurdish (or possibly Armenian) war-orphan girl at home. İpek Çalışlar, *Halide Edib: Biyografisine Sığmayan Kadın* (Istanbul, Turkey: Everest, 2010), p. 158.

31 Even though written from a markedly Turkish nationalist perspective (Armenians are the only kidnappers of the story), the following work remains informative: Funda Selçuk, "Türk Basınında Ermeni Sorunu (Mayıs 1919-Aralık 1920)," MA thesis, Ankara Üniversitesi, Turkey, 2003.

32 Raymond Kévorkian, *The Armenian Genocide: A Complete History* (New York, NY: I. B. Tauris, 2011), pp. 760–2.

33 Dikran Zaven, "Miamedutiun E Khosil Kuynerou Vra Guyri Me, Khghji Vra Chartarari Me," *Zhoghovurti Tsayne*, June 26, 1919.

34 Nazan Maksudyan, "The Fight over Nobody's Children: Religion, Nationality and Citizenship of Foundlings in the Late Ottoman Empire," *New Perspectives on Turkey* 41 (Fall 2009), pp. 151–80.

35 Anahid Tavitian, *Yergo Dziranner (Arvesde yev Engerayin Dzarayutiune)* (Beirut, Lebanon: [published by her family], 2006), p. 168.

36 Chakerian personally returned the daughter of a certain Tevfik Efendi, whose daughter was mistakenly retrieved by *vorpahavak*s and kept for four days. Though Chakerian apologized to Tevfik Bey, another *vorphavak* agent named Garabed subsequently took the daughter away again, and again Chakerian returned the daughter to her father. Atnur, *Türkiye'de Ermeni Kadınları*, p. 165.

37 Archives of the Patriarchate of Constantinople, Armenian Patriarchate of Jerusalem, PCI Bureau, 3d report, March 6, 1922.

38 Bahri, *Giankis Vebe*, p. 187.

39 Even discussions within the National Assembly confirm this point, but only additional study will give us a deeper understanding of the policy. Armenian critics, including the assembly's chairman, Tavit Der Movsesian, accused the Neutral House of acting like an "inquisition court," selling the orphans or taking bribes from their Muslim families. A Patriarchal commission found these accusations unfounded, but this did not prevent T. Der Movsesian from repeating them in his memoirs: T. Der Movsesian, *Kaghutahayutian Hamar Yelits Miag Aghake* (Paris, France: Jarian, 1935), pp. 196–207.

40 Haygaz, *Bantog*, p. 138. Responsible authorities' memoirs either refute the accusations or remain silent on the topic. The head of the Armenian National Relief Committee in his memoir italicized the following: "*I affirm that we had no wish to Armenianize any Turk's child.*" Madteos Eblighatian, *Giank Me Azkis Giankin Mech: Aganadesi Yev Masnagtsoghi Vgayutiunner 1903–1923* (Beirut, Lebanon: Antilias, 1987), p. 185.

41 Haygaz, *Bantog*, p. 138.

42 See Haroutioun Khachadourian, "Hayun Vrezhe," *Amenun Daretsuytse* 15 (1921), pp. 134–5, here 135.

43 Eric Weitz, "From the Vienna to the Paris System: International Politics and the Entangled Histories of Human Rights, Forced Deportations, and Civilizing Missions," *American Historical Review* 113:5 (2008), pp. 1313–43.

44 Der Yeghiayan, *My Patriarchal Memoirs*, p. 205.

45 The patriarch assured him that the survivors living in foreign lands intended to return to the fatherland at first opportunity and did not even try to improve the condition of their (temporary) homes (ibid., p. 207).

46 Fatma Ülgen, "Reading Mustafa Kemal Atatürk on the Armenian Genocide of 1915," *Patterns of Prejudice* 44:4 (2010), pp. 369–91, here 376.

47 Hayganush Mark, "Khmpakragan: Hay Ellank," *Hay Gin* 1:3 (December 1919).

48 My discussion here excludes psychological dimensions of achieving or trying to achieve recuperation by physically reproducing; that is, substituting the dead with the living. We lack numbers to assess whether a "baby boom" occurred among Armenians following the genocide.

49 A contributor to *Hay Gin* proposed that the Armenian Patriarchate should collect extra taxes from singles and decrease taxes on families with multiple children. Armenag Salmaslian, "Pnagchutiun Yev Amurineru Vra Durk," *Hay Gin* 1:21 (September 1, 1920).

50 Original emphasis. Dokt. Derorti, "Ur Gertas Hay Gin," *Hay Puzhag* 3:9 (July 1922), p. 150.

51 If need be, Armenian spokespersons could even make room for Muslims in new definitions of Armenianness. See Sam Kaplan, "Territorializing Armenians: Geo-Texts and Political Imaginaries in French-Occupied Cilicia, 1919–1922," *History and Anthropology* 15:4 (2004), pp. 399–423.

52 Dr. Yaghoubyan, "Hay Gnoch Aroghchabahagan tere Hayasdani Mech III," *Hay Gin* 1:19 (August 1, 1920).

53 Nayanika Mookherjee, "Available Motherhood: Legal Technologies, 'State of Exception' and the Dekinning of 'War-Babies' in Bangladesh," *Childhood: A Global Journal of Child Research* 14:3 (2007), pp. 339–54.

54 Ruth Harris, "The 'Child of the Barbarian:' Rape, Race and Nationalism in France during the First World War," *Past and Present* 141 (1993), pp. 170–206.

55 The rare intellectual who refused to consider Armenian motherhood sufficient for eligibility for national belonging received little attention and no corresponding policy. For instance, "Yeghernayin Harsanik," in "*Yerevan*"*i Daretsuytse* (Constantinople, Ottoman Empire: n.p., 1920), p. 32.

56 Patricia Weitsman, "The Politics of Identity and Sexual Violence: A Review of Bosnia and Rwanda," *Human Rights Quarterly* 30 (2008), pp. 561–78.

57 Kohar Mazlmian, "Prni Mayrutian Bardatrvadz Teradi Mayreru Hokegan Vijage Yev Anonts Yerakhanerun Zrganknere," *Hay Gin* 1:11 (April 1, 1920). For interviews with survivors who had to neglect or abandon their rape babies, see Donald E. Miller and Lorna Touryan Miller, *Survivors: An Oral History of the Armenian Genocide* (Berkeley, CA: University of California Press, 1999), pp. 101–2.

58 Zaruhi Kalemkiarian, "Zavage," in her *Giankis Jampen* (Antilias: Dbaran Gatoghigosutian Giligio, 1952), p. 272.

59 Mabel Elliott, *Beginning Again at Ararat* (New York, NY: Fleming H. Revell Company, 1924), p. 25.

60 For example, see Varteres Garougian, *Destiny of the Dzidzernag: Autobiography of Varteres Mikael Garougian* (Princeton, NJ: Gomidas Institute, 2005), p. 96.

61 Quoted in Derderian, "Common Fate," p. 14.

62 Kerop Bedoukian, *Some of Us Survived: The Story of an Armenian Boy* (New York, NY: Farrar Straus Giroux, 1979), p. 201.

63 See Isabel Kaprielian-Churchill, "Armenian Refugee Women: The Picture Brides 1920–1930," *Journal of American Ethnic History* 12:3 (1993), pp. 3–29, here 3.

64 Ibid., p. 22, fn. 54, 29.

65 Nargiz Kipritjian, "Goch Me Hay Mayrerun," *Hay Gin* 1:10 (March 16, 1920).

66 *Yergamia Deghegakir H. G. Khachi Getr. Varchutian.*

67 John Minassian, *Many Hills Yet to Climb: Memoirs of an Armenian Deportee* (Santa Barbara, CA: J. Cook, 1986), p. 236.

68 This does not mean that everyone accepted them wholeheartedly. Yet various survivors and Western social workers mention how tattoos did not pose a fundamental obstacle to integration. See Mae M. Derderian and Virginia Meghrouni, *Vergeen: A Survivor of the Armenian Genocide* (Los Angeles, CA: ATMUS Press, 1997), p. 249. For a narrative construction of a tattooed woman's attempted return to her original family after thirty-seven years, see Hourig Attarian, "Lifelines: Matrilineal Narratives, Memory and Identity," PhD dissertation, McGill University, 2009.

69 A recent documentary, despite its ungrounded overgeneralizations, provides a glimpse into the life of a tattooed woman who continued her life as an Armenian. Suzanne Khardalian, *Grandma's Tattoos* (New York, NY: Cinema Guild, 2011).

70 The best-remembered precedent for such an attitude was Kegham Der Garabedian's marriage to Gulizar, a young girl who had recently rescued herself from the household of the Kurdish Musa Bey, into which she had been absorbed in 1893. For a sample of how Armenians remembered the case in postwar Istanbul, see "Musa Bey yev Gulizar," *Amenoun Daretsuytse* 10–14 (1916–20), pp. 151–2.

71 Sahag Mesrob, "Yegherni Hushartsan, Anonts Anune," *Aravodi Darekirk* 1 (1921), pp. 83–6 (this is an almanac).

72 The patriarch would not easily give away orphaned girls; even to their Armenian relatives, even when they provided extensive proof of their relationship. Haygaz, *Bantog*, p. 133.

73 Hayganush Mark, "Khmpakragan: Angial Gineru Hamar," *Hay Gin* 3:4 (December 16, 1921).

74 Anavis (Yeprime Avedisian), *Hushers* (Paris, France: [published by her family], 1949), p. 264.

75 Fifty thousand Greeks and Armenians left the city between October and December of 1922. Alexis Alexandris, *The Greek Minority of Istanbul and Greek-Turkish Relations, 1918–1974* (Athens, Greece: Center for Asia Minor Studies, 1983).

76 For a collection of interviews with their grandchildren, see Ayse Gül Altinay and Fethiye Çetin, *Torunlar* (Istanbul, Turkey: Metis, 2009).

77 It should be noted that among Turkish Muslim citizens in Turkey, having Armenian ancestry is still widely considered shameful and the person potentially disloyal. "*Ermeni dölü*" ("Armenian sperm") is still used as an insult.

78 The only known past case that acquired public attention, to a certain extent, was in 1962. A certain Ms. Pilibosian, born as Muslim but raised in Armenian orphanages in Istanbul and France, visited Turkey from France and found her Turkish siblings. The case was the lead story in a popular Turkish daily: Esin Talu, "Akşam Köşesi/Madam Pilibüsyan'ın Macerası," *Akşam*, December 17, 1962, cover page and p. 5.

10

Wartime Rape and Its Shunned Victims

Olivera Simić[1]

Sexual violence in conflict knows no geographical borders. From Colombia to Bosnia, from Cambodia to Democratic Republic of Congo; it knows no gender or age limits. Men and boys have also been victims, and I have met survivors as young as six months and women as old as 70 years.[2]

There are certain things you just don't believe can happen to a man, you get me? But I know now that sexual violence against men is a huge problem. Everybody has heard the women's stories. But nobody has heard the men's.[3]

That night they came again. They separated fathers from their sons. They took us on the podium and told us to strip off our clothes. I cannot tell you what they forced us to do to each other . . . they were particularly excited to see father and son doing it.[4]

Sexual Abuse of Men: Mapping the Problem

Over the past two decades, sexual violence in war against women has become a focus of feminist scholarship, policymaking, legal proceedings, and global media coverage. The first international reports on rampant sexual abuse of women and girls in armed conflicts emerged in the 1990s. Soon after, rape and sexual violence in war were recognized in gender-neutral terms for the first time in history as crimes against humanity and war crimes.[5] That is, the International Criminal Tribunal for Rwanda (ICTR) acknowledged that such violence was not merely a by-product of war but that it could constitute genocide and that it could be carried out against women *and* men.[6] Such recognition was unprecedented and represented a legal victory partially won due to the world attention to rape on a mass scale during the war in Bosnia-Herzegovina (BiH). Ever since this legal recognition, feminists scholars and activists have been preoccupied with reminding governments around the world that they need to prosecute those accountable for sexual violence. The recent Global Summit to End Sexual Violence in War[7] repeated (yet again) that the plethora of United Nations (UN) resolutions promulgated in the past decade with an aim to combat sexual violence in war still need to be acted upon.[8] While these efforts are welcomed and long overdue, they have focused almost exclusively on female sexual abuse in warfare, while male experiences of sexual assault have, for the most part, been ignored and silenced.[9] This form of violence against males, as some scholars argue, is still surrounded by "a wall of silence."[10]

So far, this issue has not attracted much academic, policymaking, or media attention. Sporadic and scant literature has not succeeded in generating wider interest into this topic. Sexual violence in which males are victims, rather than perpetrators, has not attracted many feminist researchers either.[11] Dubravka Zarkov was among the first feminist scholars to analyze male-on-male rapes in the context of the Bosnian War. In her groundbreaking paper, published in 1997, Zarkov notes that the number of scholarly papers that analyze males as victims of sexual violence "could be counted on the fingers of one hand":

> People who have lived through armed conflicts around the globe know that sexual violence against men, even if random and with fewer victims than violence against women, has been a fact of war for hundreds of years. In the contemporary wars, however, it is a rather well-hidden fact. Experts in the field of conflict studies, or aid workers, may know about it. But a war rape of a man was never a major story in the press, nor castration in a war camp on the evening television news. I had hardly heard of it myself.[12]

Male rape in a wartime context is still a taboo subject that is little understood and largely underreported, undertheorized,[13] and underinvestigated.[14] As Adam Jones argues, this issue "has barely begun"[15] to receive sustained attention, although the practice "is old as history itself"[16] and occurs regularly in armed conflicts.[17] While recent international attention to male sexual violence in war[18] may attract more scholarly interest in this topic, the popular belief that only women can be raped seems to be widespread.[19] Sexual violence against women has been "normalized," but sexual violence against men is not. This normalization of violence against women has had consequences, because, as David H. J. Morgan argues, such a process may be so effective that violence against women "disappears" and is ignored since it is taken for granted.[20]

On the other hand, the protection of strong traditional gendered norms and the reluctance to disrupt them have fostered a culture of silence surrounding sexual abuse of men. Elizabeth Stanko argues that popular images of violence thus rest upon unquestioned (normalized) understandings and constructions of gender, and of masculinity in particular, that perpetuate a myth of the inevitability of men's violence and, conversely, the abnormality or pathology of violence by women.[21]

This chapter is concerned with the male victims of sexual abuse and torture in the Bosnian War, which became notorious for the rape of women. The international and local media, researchers, and scholars widely reported on sexual violence against women by all warring parties, in particular by Serb soldiers. Although the Bassiouni report, the first comprehensive report on sexual violence in war in BiH, acknowledges widespread sexual abuse and torture of Bosnian men too, this topic has not attracted considerable interest.[22] The "rape victim identity" is exclusively reserved for women; the gender stereotypes that portray women as *rapable* and powerless, and men as *un-rapable* and powerful, were (as in other armed conflicts) firmly embedded in the tale of the Bosnian War.[23] This chapter aims to unpack the silence surrounding men who were sexually abused in Bosnian detention during the war (1992–5). It raises questions of silence and denial when it comes to male rapes as well as the consequences and effects that disinterest in this form of sexual violence produce in the long term in the lives of survivors.

This chapter will first provide a brief overview of masculinity studies and theorize connections between hegemonic masculinities, power, and domination, in which hegemonic and *victorious* masculinities (in the context of the Bosnian War) utilized sexual torture to subordinate *camp detainees'* masculinities.[24] This chapter will then turn to an analysis of the local Bosnian grassroots initiatives to assist male survivors. Although there is acknowledgment that men and boys have been subjected to sexual violence during the war, a strong patriarchal culture in BiH and societal unwillingness to recognize male survivors as "victims" of sexual torture mean there are no ongoing and long-term programs or assistance for this category of victims. This chapter will draw on an interview with Midheta Oruli, a general secretary of the Association of Camp Inmates in BiH (Savez logoraša u Bosni i Hercegovini), undertaken in Sarajevo in July 2014. The chapter will argue that sexually tortured men have not been recognized as "victims" and, as a consequence, have not received either material or symbolic reparation.

Hegemonic Masculinities and
Male-on-Male Sexual Abuse

Although the international human rights community developed set concepts and norms that defined sexual violence as an instrument of armed conflict, ethnic cleansing, and even genocide,[25] the current recognition and construction of sexual war crimes in humanitarian, legal, and scholarly circles is typically gendered.[26] Constructions of wartime sex crimes have been highly gendered, with analysis of wartime rape focusing solely on the victimization of women while leaving men visible only as agents of violence. This essentializing of gender roles that fails to recognize males as victims of sexual violence in armed conflicts[27] has been analyzed and problematized in scholarly literature.[28]

Dubravka Zarkov argues that portraying men only, and always, as offenders and never as victims of rape (and other forms of sexual violence) is a very specific gendered narrative of war, which eventually labels who "can or cannot be named a victim of sexual violence."[29] Any attempt to dismantle this gender power dynamic (in which women are victims and men are perpetrators) may threaten to dispel firmly established gender stereotypes. So, even when sexual violence in war against men and boys has been briefly mentioned, males are often juxtaposed to female victims and brushed over with the usual conclusion that "women much more than men"[30] suffer gender-based violence.[31] Due to the sheer number of women who experience sexual violence, coupled with the little material that exists on male-on-male violence, the issue tends to be "relegated to a footnote."[32] According to Nancy Dowd, while feminist theory "has been increasingly critical to differentiate among women"[33] and to examine the intersectionality of gender with race, class, age, and/or sexual orientation, male victims are presented in much legal theory largely as a group that is universal, almost undifferentiated.[34] As such, the men who are sexually abused are not only virtually ignored as victims, they are also homogenized. According to Adam Jones and Augusta Del Zotto, the elite discourses and practices that exclude men's experiences overall are reproduced by the nongovernmental sector too. According to their study, in 2001, there were 4,076 nongovernmental groups that addressed war rape and other forms of political sexual violence.[35] Out of this number, only 3 percent mentioned the experiences of males at all in their programs and informational literature.[36]

Such disinterest in the topic stands in sharp opposition to recent data on this form of abuse. Sexual violence against men and boys, including rape, sexual humiliation, sexual torture, mutilation of the genitals, sexual enslavement, and forced incest, has been reported in at least twenty-five recent armed conflicts across the world.[37] Male rape, according to Lara Stemple, "flourishes" in peacetime (prisons) and in armed conflicts (detentions).[38] For example, in the Democratic Republic of the Congo, 23.6

percent of men in the eastern region of the country have been the victims of sexual violence.[39] The prevalence of the rape of men is underreported partly due to the extreme stigma and humiliation attached to the sexual abuse of males.[40] It is also concealed by victims' shame in speaking out and by a society that is not willing or prepared to listen.[41]

Men who have been raped are seen as weak and less than men. They risk not only ostracism by their community but also criminal prosecution because they may be seen as homosexual, which is a crime in thirty-eight African countries.[42] Male victims are less likely to appear in court, and those who do are cast out in their villages and called "bush wives."[43] Mukuli, a male victim from Congo, reported, "I'm laughed at. The people in my village say: 'You're no longer a man. Those men in the bush made you their wife.'"[44] Despite growing empirical evidence that sexual violence against men and boys is used for strategic purposes during armed conflict, such offenses have not yet become visible in transitional justice processes.[45]

Hilmi Zawati argues that male rape in wartime is not about satisfying the perpetrator's sexual desire but is primarily an assertion of power, dominance, and aggression.[46] This is because masculinity is not only about men's relationships to women but also about men's relationships to other men. The key thread in theories of masculinity is that masculinity is not unitary but diverse; hence, it is necessary to use the plural *masculinities*. Michael Kimmel argues that "all masculinities are not created equal"[47] and that a dominant, "hegemonic" heterosexual masculinity is at the top of a hierarchy. More dominant masculinities must have a subordinate in order to thrive. Raewyn Connell, the leading scholar in masculinities studies, argues that masculinity is practised in a way that embodies dominance and inequality.[48] Being a man is defined in opposition to others; it is produced and reproduced in relation to the "Other," women in particular.[49] The so-called "feminized" male "Other" is likewise vital to the construction of modern masculinities, especially hegemonic ones.[50] Scholars have observed that the construction of gender identity is never fully achieved; thus masculinity needs to be constantly proved and reasserted through male affirming practices.[51]

Criminologists, such as James W. Messerschmidt, have argued that crime is an extension of "normal" masculinity. Messerschmidt sees the overrepresentation of men among perpetrators of crimes as explained by crime being another way of "doing gender." He also notes how gender intersects with class and race.[52] In his view, "Crime by men is not simply an extension of the 'male sex role.' Rather, crime by men is a form of social practice invoked as a resource, when other resources are unavailable, for accomplishing masculinity."[53] In other words, the men who perform their masculinity by engaging in crime are often (but not always) unable to realize their masculinity in more traditional ways.

In the military context, male rape is about the final act of an enemy's defeat and control.[54] Historically, when a dominant, victorious soldier sexually penetrated his enemy, it was believed that the victim would lose his manhood and could not be a ruler or a warrior anymore.[55] In times of war and/or conquest, women have been raped to humiliate the men they are related to, who are often forced to watch the assault.[56] Men are also raped in order to humiliate and emasculate not only the victims but their ethnic group as well.[57] Through this emasculation, the male victim is deconstructed as male and constructed as a woman. As Skjelsbæk argues, an important aspect of conquest involves turning male enemies into feminized subjects.[58]

Male rapes in armed conflict usually include rape in detention camps or prison-like conditions.[59] In these camps, inmates are often forced to penetrate each other or, less commonly, inmates are raped by opposite warring party soldiers. The gendered positioning of rapists and victims is something that Jones finds worthy of analysis; it allows a rapist to be confirmed in his active, hegemonic, and heterosexual masculinity, while victims who are in "passive" (receptive) role are feminized.[60] Traditionally, in a military, male environment, male-on-male rape has long been accepted and even celebrated.[61]

Surviving the Silence

According to the Association of Camp Inmates (ACI) in BiH, approximately 1,352 detention camps and other detention facilities existed during the war: 656 for Bosniaks, 523 for Serbs, and 173 for Croats.[62] Thousands of male inmates passed through these camps, and, according to some reports, several hundred men were subjected to sexual violence, including sexual assaults and castrations.[63] Due to such infamous evidence of abuse, the BiH war resulted in a groundbreaking and thorough accounting of sexual violence against males during conflict.[64] While case law has been scattered when it comes to male rape, there have been several cases that detail sexual abuse, torture, and mutilation that occurred in Serb camps for Bosniak camp inmates and, in two cases before the International Criminal Tribunal for the former Yugoslavia (ICTY), in Bosniak camps for Serb inmates.[65]

Zarkov argues that sexual assaults against men in war in the Balkans "were committed mainly in detention, and by all warring sides."[66] The Bosnian War was also the first armed conflict for which an international body, the Commission of Experts created by the UN Security Council, was formed in order to investigate sexual violence.[67] The Experts' Final Report, commonly known as the Bassiouni report, published in 1994, is perhaps the most extensive source of information on male sexual victimization during the Balkan Wars:

> Sexual assaults were also practised against men: one witness saw prisoners forced to bite another prisoner's genitals. In addition, 10 of those interviewed had witnessed deaths by torture and seven of the group

had survived or witnessed mass executions (there or in other camps). . . .
Another ex-detainee told of suffering electric shocks to the scrotum and
of seeing a father and son who shared his cell forced by guards to perform
sex acts with each other.[68]

In 1993, Amnesty International confirmed the evidence collected in the
Bassiouni report:

> It should . . . be mentioned that Amnesty International has received
> allegations of instances of male prisoners in detention under the control
> of both Serbian and Bosnian Government forces being made to perform
> sexual acts with each other. However, these reports are few in comparison
> with the numerous reports and allegations of rape or sexual abuse of
> women.[69]

The ICTY also instituted a Sexual Assault Investigation Team, which
included investigations into the rape of men during armed conflict.[70] The
team reported that men were castrated and otherwise sexually mutilated,
forced to rape other men, and forced to perform fellatio and other sex
acts on guards and one another.[71] Accounts of sexual abuse were often
graphic and included severe torture, genital mutilation, and forced incest.[72]
These acts were performed not only to inflict enormous pain but also as a
concerted attempt to humiliate the victims[73] and destroy their reproductive
role, heterosexual activity, and identification.[74] Undermining or rather
destroying male victims' identification with hegemonic forms of masculinity
further disempowered and feminized them.

Alongside these reports, the first international war crimes trial involving
charges of sexual violence included sexual violence against male prisoners in
the Omarska concentration camps in 1995.[75] Acts of rape and sexual violence
were recognized as forms of torture in the Tadic[76] and Celebici[77] judgments
by the ICTY. In terms of domestic prosecutions involving sexual violence
against males, the BiH court has finalized only four cases so far.[78] In all four
cases, the accused either ordered or forced the camp inmates themselves to
perform sexual acts on each other. For example, Zijad Kurtović, a member
of the Bosniak army, was convicted and sentenced to eleven years in prison
for, among other things, forcing two brothers and members of the Croatian
Defense to strip naked and have oral sex.[79]

Still, as of today, there have been no reports or research that have identified
the approximate number of male victims or the needs and challenges this
group of survivors has encountered in postwar BiH. While it is known that
the abuse was "significant and widespread,"[80] it is not known how many
men survived sexual abuse in Bosnian war camps. Like women, men who
survive sexual torture may experience shame and humiliation and, due to
their gender, are largely discouraged from talking about their emotions. Since
they may find it even more difficult than women to acknowledge what has

happened to them, it is suspected that the reported cases of sexual violence against males are a fraction of the true number of cases.[81]

Men in BiH do not talk about these experiences publicly, and only a small number of them of them have registered as victims of sexual abuse with the ACI in BiH. The ACI has around 55,000 members, but this number is not final since former camp inmates still come to the office to register. A few men have been willing to come forward about sexual abuse and torture they survived, and some of these testimonies have been collected in the book *Torture in Bosnia and Herzegovina During the War 1992–1995*.[82] Oruli noted that since 2006, when she first met a Bosniak man who survived sexual rape and torture in a Serb camp, around 100 men have come to register with the association and to ask for assistance in receiving a status of "civil victim of war." According to Oruli, male sexual torture is:

> still a taboo topic in BiH . . . and in the first few years after the war I never met such survivors. . . . As a victim of war, I heard stories and rumours about it but never met anyone in person . . . and then I met a man whom I befriended as a fellow camp inmate. I was curious why he did not marry, why he does not have a girlfriend and after two years he confessed to me. He was one of around 86 [Bosniak] men according to our data who survived sexual abuse in Dom Kulture in Zvornik . . . he never shared this info with anyone . . . he told me that he was haunted by his memories of that event; that he had no one to talk to about it and that he could not form any sexual relationship with women. . . . According to our experiences men survivors of sexual abuse who were married could not engage in sexual intercourse for at least 4, 5 years after that event.[83]

Such physical and psychological damage to men is inflicted intentionally so they can no longer play their role in group reproduction.[84] Male survivors encounter profound psychological difficulty in expressing their masculine sexuality,[85] and some describe impotence and difficulty in establishing relationships and trusting others.[86] Often they do not ask for psychological or psychiatric assistance for a long time or do not seek help at all.[87] But when they do open up, health workers may be the first to hear their stories, rather than lawyers. However, many trained health workers, such as psychiatrists and psychologists, have not been trained to recognize male sexual abuse or are not aware of it.[88] This complexity is often compounded by the fact that sexual torture may not leave visible scars, which may further divert the attention of medical workers from this type of brutalization.[89] As Zihnija, Bosniak ex-combatant and survivor of sexual abuse, recently reported: "When you lose your arm or leg that is something you can see. But, no one can see when your soul hurts. Maybe I look strong as a rock, but I am only a wreck. Just a wreck."[90]

While some authors, such as Zawatti, argue that the civilian community ought to encourage male survivors of rape to break their silence and address their specific needs,[91] Bosnian civil society activists are cautious and aware that by speaking up male survivors will not necessarily achieve anything other than stigma and ostracism. Edin Ramulić, from the Association of Women in Prijedor, "Izvor," stated:

> The victims of such crimes do not expect anything positive to happen to them if they speak up. First, perpetrators probably won't be punished, or won't be punished enough. For example, Dragan Kolumdžija, a guard in the notorious camp in Omarska who was present when the majority of camp inmates were sexually abused and then later killed, got only 3 years imprisonment in ICTY and he returned to live in his home in Prijedor. Second, there is no one to help these people and at the same time they will be exposed to bullying and psychological abuse from all those who did not survive it, who do not understand it, from their own community—we will all look at them with suspiciousness and pity. Simply, the community is not ready to listen to them and that is the reason why they are silent—because we are not ready to listen and do anything for them.[92]

Why would men tell the truth about sexual abuse if they are stigmatized for doing so? Trauma healing goes beyond alleviation of personal traumas and includes not only the mending of social relationships and divisions between communities, but also validation of experience and reparation.[93] As Naomi Aratza argues, truth telling without reparation or prosecution seems "meaningless for victims."[94] Male survivors cannot be expected to reveal their intimate suffering and pain without any mechanisms in place to deal with the effects of such violations and without proper reparation and rehabilitation measures.[95] This is so because the aim of reparation programs is not only to validate experiences and confirm that offenses have occurred but also to assist victims in coping with their impact by providing concrete programs and measures.[96]

Lack of community concern, along with male victims' hesitancy to report the crimes, makes reporting and making any assumptions about the numbers of males assaulted almost impossible. Due to the stigma attached to sexual violence, it is highly unlikely that males would be willing to identify themselves or to organize or mobilize themselves publicly to claim reparations.[97] According to Murat Tahirović, former president of the ACI,

> It is difficult to talk about this topic. You know how the society we live in operates. It is shaming and embarrassing to talk about it. It is difficult for women and let alone for men to talk about it. In patriarchal society as in ours, people are bullied. So, it is hard to know how widespread it was and that is the problem. In longer and more amicable conversation, they [men] will admit that [sexual abuse]. But very rarely anyone talks about it.[98]

One of the former camp inmates who witnessed the sexual violence and castration of his fellow inmate reported how difficult it is to talk about this issue:

> All of us, 200 men who heard this horrific human wail cried . . . when I think of that day I cannot sleep . . . it is extremely difficult to talk to those who survived a torture especially when we know that no one cares about us . . . what we survived was worse than hell . . . feelings of humiliation are forever with you and are killing you slowly.[99]

Sexual torture of males during the war in BiH is not understood and lacks an effective healing response and communal intervention. Male victims are not encouraged to talk; on the contrary, due to a lack of any state or NGO attention, they may be encouraged to infer that their experiences are "unworthy of redress."[100] In BiH there are no programs developed for male survivors of rape, and there is currently no law to assist victims of torture.[101] The associations of camp inmates have given their inputs in draft law on torture which, among other things, requests free legal aid, free health assistance, and the establishment of state funds for reparation for each day spent in camp.[102] Apart from material reparation, the associations request symbolic reparation, such as marking and remembering dates and places where crimes took place.

According to Jasmin Mešković, the president of the ACI in BiH, the request to mark and remember dates and places where crimes were committed "does not cost the government anything . . . that is important to all former camp inmates—that they can go and visit places of crimes and pay their respects without any troubles."[103] Material and symbolic reparation, restitution, and rehabilitation are all-important and, as Ruth Rubio-Marín argues, assume that harm has been done and that loss has unreasonably happened.[104] Reparations are possibly "the most victim-centered justice mechanism available and the most significant means of making difference in the lives of victims."[105]

So far, the government of BiH has been reluctant and unwilling to meet the ACI demands for material and symbolic reparation. A handful of NGOs, such as the Center for Victims of Torture and the Association, have offered ad hoc material, legal, or health assistance to former camp inmates. As the World Health Organization has reported, while legal and social networks often do exist in local communities for women and girls who have been victims of sexual torture, there is hardly anything comparable for male victims.[106] In BiH, some local women's organizations, such as "Medica Zenica" and "Žena žrtva rata" (although specialized to support women), offer legal and psychosocial support to male victims of sexual torture too.[107] A number of male rape survivors have received a status of civilian victim of war under its category of "sexual violence victim" with the help of local women's NGOs.[108]

Some countries, such as Peru and Guatemala, have had debates about whether reparations for victims of sexual violence should be reserved for women only. While Peru eventually decided to include both genders equally, in Guatemala, it was decided that only female victims of sexual abuse would qualify.[109] Such a decision not only is discriminatory but reinforces the popular notion that only females can be subjected to such offenses, underscoring gender stereotypes in which women are victims and men can be nothing but perpetrators.[110] A victim-centered and harm-centered reparation agenda cannot ignore the fact that men and boys are often victims of sexual violence and that their victimization deserves unequivocal acknowledgment.[111]

In BiH there was no debate as to whether both genders could qualify for laws that enable civilian victims of war to apply for reparation (thus making them gender-neutral).[112] By December 2013, 770 victims of sexual violence had been registered in the Federation of BiH.[113] Although it is not cited in NGO reports, among those registered civilian victims of sexual violence, 114 are males.[114] The fact that this is not an insignificant number and has not been publicly reported confirms the reluctance of local community organizations as well as government institutions to recognize sexual violence against men as a legitimate issue in their reports and activities.

As Susanne Buckley-Ziestel argues, the status of "ideal victim" has been preserved for women, who have the opportunity to use the victim position to speak up but also to claim a number of benefits, rights, and entitlements.[115] They can qualify for reparation—material and symbolic.[116] Women can acquire the identity of victim, which is an important step in gaining control over one's life and making sense of crime.[117] They are seen as vulnerable, passive, helpless, inferior, and in need of protection, which is in line with traditional models of passive femininity and active masculinity. Indeed, acknowledging males as "victims" would go contrary to such models and dispel popular gender stereotypes. The BiH society is not ready to disrupt this view and fails to acknowledge male victims of torture; more importantly, it fails to accept their vulnerability and need for reparation for the harm they suffered.

The ACI is one of three local NGOs in the Federation of BiH[118] that the BiH government has authorized to grant individuals the status of "camp inmate" and "sexually abused and tortured person" during the war in 1992–5. Upon receiving such status, individuals can apply for monthly compensation. During my visit to the ACI office, Oruli showed me a few thick folders, each containing the personal files of men who came to seek assistance in obtaining the status of victim of sexual torture. Each file has full medical documentation, a personal testimony, and other relevant documents. All these files have been archived according to date and year, starting from 2006 when the ACI encountered its first case of sexual abuse and torture. Oruli explained the difficulties that male victims faced in seeking assistance:

> When they come to our office, we ask them to tell us their stories. I type up each of them and file them in. Sometimes, our clients would cry and could not tell the story and then I would tell them to go home and write it on a piece of paper and then bring that paper to me. . . . I recently had a man who was sobbing uncontrollably and we had to stop the interview. I told him and others who cannot tell their story to ease their soul and write up everything that happened to them at their own home . . . it is very hard to tell these stories. But, people find strength to tell them so such evil never happens to anyone again.[119]

The people who work for the ACI invest significant emotional labor in registering and uncovering cases of male wartime sexual abuse. The private and confidential interviews are held in one of the three ACI rooms. Each new member has to fill in a form with personal details and details of the torture they survived. In order to avoid burying issues such as sexual assault and rape under the general rubric of "abuse" or "torture," the ACI asks members to tick the box if they experienced sexual abuse.[120] Under the rubric "the Type and Form of Torture in Camp," men can choose to circle "sexually abused" among other options such as "physically tortured," "beaten," "psychologically tortured," "deprived of food," "robbed," and "used as a living shield."[121]

The new male members of the ACI are composed of both locals and nonresidents. Currently, the ACI is processing more nonresident cases than local cases. According to Oruli, these men may have a greater interest in receiving the status of civilian victim of war, and they often seek assistance with full medical documentation. Oruli reported that if these men receive this status, "it increases men's benefits for early retirement by twenty percent in their countries of residency, so there is an incentive to come and open up about it." The recognition of male victims therefore has important psychological aspects as well as material ones. The recognition of this status also affords male victims health and housing support, which are crucial for men's recovery and rehabilitation.

Although the ACI does such vital and unique work, it struggles with funds, as do many other NGOs in BiH. When finances permit, the ACI provides legal aid and assistance with finding employment, housing, or food. The association has recently applied for government funds to open the "Psycho-Legal Center." However, the association has received no response to their application. The needs of male victims are great, since many of these people are not fit for work, are disabled, are elderly, have no health insurance, are often returnees, and have psychological disorders. The grassroots initiatives in BiH are vital for the male survivors as they are often the only service providers men can turn to for help. The BiH government is long overdue in supporting local associations that provide assistance to male survivors. Still, even if the state does support the ACI, it has a larger obligation to provide legal material and other assistance to its most vulnerable population—whether female or male.

Conclusion

This chapter has argued that male rape is a marginalized topic at best, and utterly neglected at worst. Victims of male rape are shunned, and the offenses against them are not fully recognized as violations and crimes against humanity that need to be prosecuted and punished. There seems to be a lack of willingness to accept the fact that male-on-male rape, as Janine Natalya Clark argues, "is no less a crime than the rape of wom[e]n."[122] This chapter has offered some reasons why such a crime may be viewed as *less of* a crime. Recognizing male survivors of sexual torture as victims may disrupt gender power dynamics in which women are seen as victims and men as perpetrators. Societal unwillingness to abandon gender norms and stereotypes and to accept males as victims of sexual torture needs to be systematically addressed. Only such willingness can bring visibility to the victims and their rehabilitation. Sexual torture leaves males, as is the case with female victims, with lifelong trauma. However, it triggers some specific gender traumas that are unique to men, such as feeling emasculated, feminized, and stripped of their sense of manhood. It is very important to understand how the performance of masculinities in a wartime context contributes to male-on-male violence but also to its denial and cover-up.

Victorious masculinities and *subordinated* masculinities are the main protagonists of violence and victimhood. Male rape is about power and control, and each group that is in a position to exercise it will use that opportunity to exert its dominance. Seen as protectors and warriors, males who survive some form of sexual torture will rarely publicly confess what happened to them. Not allowing men to express their vulnerability brings stigma and shame and results in silence and denial. Governments, policymakers, communities, and scholars have the responsibility not only to encourage men to talk about their difficult experiences in a space free of stigma and shame but also to guarantee recovery and reparation for the victims of this heinous crime.

Notes

1   I would like to thank the editor, Associate Professor Amy Randall, for her thoughtful and valuable comments on previous drafts of this paper. My thanks also are due to Ms. Zoe Rahtus, Dr. Karen Crawley, and Dr. Kylie Burns for their insights and comments.

2   Zainab Bangura, "History's Greatest Silence," in *Preventing Sexual Violence in Conflict* (London, UK: Foreign and Commonwealth Office, November 2013). Available online: http://preventsexualviolenceinconflict.tumblr.com/post/68968721475/historys-greatest-silence-un-special (accessed June 13, 2014).

3   Will Storr, "The Rape of Men: The Darkest Secret of War," *Guardian*, July 17, 2011. Available online: http://www.theguardian.com/society/2011/jul/17/the-rape-of-men (accessed July 6, 2014).

4   *Nidžara Ahmetašević*, "Zločin o kojem se ne govori," *H-Alter*, April 20, 2006. Available online: http://h-alter.org/vijesti/ljudska-prava/zlocin-o-kojem-se-ne-govori (accessed June 2, 2014).

5   Prosecutor *v.* Kunarac, Kovac and Vukovic, Case No. IT—96-23T, Judgement, February 22, 2001. This was the first indictment in history of international war crimes prosecutions with charges based solely on crimes of sexual violence against women.

6   The Akayesu case was the first conviction ever for genocide, and it was the first time that an international tribunal ruled that rape and other forms of sexual violence could constitute genocide. It was also the first conviction of an individual for rape as a crime against humanity. Prosecutor *v.* Jean-Paul Akayesu, International Criminal Tribunal for Rwanda, Trial Chamber I, Case No. ICTR-96-4-T, Judgement, September 2, 1998, paragraph 731.

7   The summit was held in London in June 2014. Available online: https://www.gov.uk/government/topical-events/sexual-violence-in-conflict.

8   Such as, United Nations Security Council Resolution 1325, S/Res/1325 (2000); United Nations Security Council Resolution 1820, S/Res/1820 (2008); United Nations Security Council Resolution 1888, S/RES/1888 (2009).

9   N. King, *Speaking Our Truths: Voices of Courage and Healing for Male Survivors of Childhood Sexual Abuse* (New York, NY: Harper Collins, 1995).

10   Augusta DelZotto and Adam Jones, "Male-on-Male Sexual Violence in Wartime: Human Rights Last Taboo?" paper presented to the Annual Convention of the International Studies Association (New Orleans, LA: ISA, March 23–27, 2002). Available online: http://adamjones.freeservers.com/malerape.htm (accessed May 5, 2014).

11   On the contrary, some argue that acknowledgment of male rape victims, with respect to lobbying for more inclusive polices and laws, "is part of the backlash against feminism." See Phillip Rumney and Martin Morgan-Taylor, "The Construction of Sexual Consent in Male Rape and Sexual Assault," in *Making Sense of Sexual Consent*, ed. Mark Cowling and Paul Reynolds (Aldershot, UK: Ashgate, 2004).

12   Dubravka Zarkov, "The Body of the Other Man: Sexual Violence and the Construction of Masculinity, Sexuality and Ethnicity in Croatian Media," in *Victims, Perpetrators or Actors? Gender, Armed Conflict and Political Violence*, ed. Caroline O. N. Moser and Fiona C. Clark (London, UK: Zed Books, 2001), p. 72.

13   Adam Jones, "Straight as a Rule: Heteronormativity and Gendercide, and the Noncombatant Male," *Men and Masculinities* 8 (2006), p. 462.

14 Eric Stener Carlson, "Sexual Assault on Men in War," *Lancet* 349 (1997), p. 129.

15 Jones, "Straight as a Rule," p. 458.

16 DelZotto and Jones, "Male-on-Male Sexual Violence in Wartime."

17 Pauline Oosterhoff, Prisca Zwanniken, and Evert Ketting, "Sexual Torture of Men in Croatia and Other Conflict Situations: An Open Secret," *Reproductive Health Matters* 12 (2004), p. 75.

18 See, for example, the Global Summit to End Sexual Violence in War (held in London, UK in June 2014) that had a separate panel on men and boys in war.

19 Carlson, "Sexual Assault on Men in War," p. 129.

20 David Hopcraft John Morgan, "Masculinity and Violence," in *Women, Violence and Social Control*, ed. Jalna Hanmer and Mary Maynard (London, UK: McMillan, 1987), pp. 180–3.

21 Elizabeth A. Stanko, Louise Marian, and Debbie Crisp, *Taking Stock: What Do We Know About Interpersonal Violence?* (Surrey, UK: ESRC Violence Research Programme, Royal Holloway University of London, 2002), p. 33.

22 United Nations Security Council, *Final Report of the Commission of Experts Established Pursuant to Security Council Resolution 780 (1992), S/1994/674* (May 27, 1994).

23 Dubravka Zarkov, "War Rapes in Bosnia: On Masculinity, Femininity and Power of the Rape Victim Identity," *Tijdschrift voor Criminologie* 39:2 (1997), 140–51.

24 Jones, "Straight as a Rule," p. 454.

25 B. Allen, *Rape Warfare* (Minneapolis, MN: University of Minnesota Press, 1996).

26 DelZotto and Jones, "Male-on-Male Sexual Violence in Wartime."

27 Lara Stemple, "Male Rape and Human Rights," *Hastings Law Journal* 60 (2008–09), p. 612.

28 Caroline O. N. Moser and Fiona C. Clark, "Introduction," in *Victims, Perpetrators or Actors?*, ed. Moser and Clark, p. 3.

29 Zarkov, "The Body of the Other Man," p. 69.

30 E. Rehn and E. J. Sirleaf, *Women, War and Peace: The Independent Experts' Assessment on the Impact of Armed Conflict on Women and Women's Role in Peacebuilding* (New York, NY: UNIFEM, 2002), p. 10.

31 The intention of the author here is not to deny this well-established fact but to emphasize some possible reasons why this issue has not attracted much scholarly (or other) attention.

32 Sandesh Sivakumaran, "Sexual Violence against Men in Armed Conflict," *The European Journal of International Law* 18 (2007), p. 253.

33 Nancy E. Dowd, "Masculinities and Femininities Legal Theory," *Wisconsin Journal of Law, Gender and Society* 23 (2008), p. 203.

34 Ibid., p. 204.

35 DelZotto and Jones, "Male-on-Male Sexual Violence in Wartime."

36 Ibid.

37 Wynne Russell, "Sexual Violence against Men and Boys," *Forced Migration Review* 27 (2007), p. 22.

38 Stemple, "Male Rape and Human Rights," p. 605.

39 L. Melhado, "Rates of Sexual Violence Are High in Democratic Republic of the Congo," *International Perspectives on Sexual and Reproductive Health* 36 (2010): 210.

40 IRIN, "Analysis: Rethinking Sexual Violence in Democratic Republic of the Congo," *Integrated Regional Information Networks*, August 6, 2010. Available online: http://www.unhcr.org/refworld/docid/4c64f1071e.html (accessed February 18, 2013). See also Refugee Law Project, "Gender against Men" (Refugee Law Project, Video Advocacy Unit, May 2012). Available online: https://www.youtube.com/watch?v=mJSl99HQYXc (accessed May 30, 2014).

41 G. G. Mezey, and M. B. King, eds., *Male Victims of Sexual Assault* (Oxford, UK: University of Oxford Press, 2000).

42 Amnesty International, "Making Love a Crime: Criminalization of Same-Sex Conduct in Sub-Saharan Africa," *Amnesty International USA*, June 24, 2013. Available online: http://www.amnestyusa.org/research/reports/making-love-a-crime-criminalization-of-same-sex-conduct-in-sub-saharan-africa (accessed June 2, 2014).

43 Dunia Prince Zongwe, "The New Sexual Violence Legislation in the Congo: Dressing Indelible Scars on Human Dignity," *African Studies Review* 55 (2012), p. 44.

44 Jeffrey Gettleman, "Symbol of Unhealed Congo: Male Rape Victims," *New York Times*, August 4, 2009. Available online: http://www.nytimes.com/2009/08/05/world/africa/05congo.html?_r=0 (accessed August 14, 2014). "Bush wives" has a particular meaning and weight in African countries and is used to refer primarily to women who were abducted and forced to be "spouses of soldiers." In the landmark verdict against members of the Sierra Leone Revolutionary United Front, the court found all three men guilty of "forced marriage." Prosecutor *v.* Brima, Kamara, and Kanu, Appeal Judgement (February 22, 2008). Special Court for Sierra Leone, paragraph 184 (finding that forced marriage is "not predominantly a sexual crime" and overruling the Trial Chamber's conclusion that forced marriage may constitute the crime against humanity of sexual slavery). Also, Ms. Zainab Hawa Bangura stated that "wives were constantly sexually abused, physically battered during and after pregnancies, and psychologically terrorised by their 'husbands' who thereby demonstrated their control over their wives." Prosecutor *v.* Brima Ors, Special Court for Sierra Leone Trial Chamber Judgement. Partly Dissenting Opinion of Judge Doherty, paragraph 15. This marks the first time that anyone has been convicted of "forced marriage" as a crime against humanity in an international criminal tribunal.

45 Susanne Buckley-Ziestel, "Redressing Sexual Violence in Transitional Justice and the Labelling of Women as 'Victims,'" in *Victims of International Crime: An Interdisciplinary Discourse*, ed. T. Bonacker and C. Safferling (The Hague, Netherlands: Asser Press, 2013), p. 98.

46 Hilmi Zawait, "Impunity or Immunity: Wartime Male Rape and Sexual Torture as a Crime Against Humanity," *Torture* 7 (2007), p. 33. See also Sivakumaran, "Sexual Violence Against Men in Armed Conflict," p. 270.

47 Michael Kimmel, "Masculinity as Homophobia: Fear, Shame, and Silence
    in the Construction of a Gender Identity," in *The Masculinities Reader*, ed.
    Stephen M. Whitehead and Frank Barrett (Cambridge, UK: Polity Press, 2001),
    pp. 271–2.

48 Raewyn W. Connell, *Gender* (Cambridge, UK: Polity, 2009).

49 Kimmel, "Masculinity as Homophobia."

50 Jones, "Straight as a Rule," p. 453.

51 Susan Faludi, *Stiffed: The Betrayal of the American Man* (New York, NY:
    William Morrow & Company, 1999).

52 James W. Messerschmidt, *Masculinities and Crime: Critique and
    Reconceptualization of Theory* (Lanham, MD: Rowman & Littlefield,
    1993), p. 185.

53 Ibid., p. 85.

54 Ibid.

55 Ibid., p. 34.

56 Ibid.

57 Zarkov, "The Body of the Other Man," p. 78.

58 Inger Skjelsbæk, "Sexual Violence in Times of War: A New Challenge for Peace
    Operations?" *International Peacekeeping* 8:2 (2001), pp. 69–84; L. H. M. Ling,
    *Postcolonial International Relations: Conquest and Desire between Asia and
    the West* (London, UK: Palgrave 2001).

59 Stemple, "Male Rape and Human Rights," p. 611.

60 Jones, "Straight as a Rule," p. 459.

61 Ibid.

62 Center for Democracy and Transitional Justice, "Mapping Detention Camps in
    BiH: 1992-1995," press release, February 2014. Available online: http://cdtp.
    org/en/dokumentovanje-logora-drugih-zatocenickih-objekata-u-bih/(accessed
    March 14, 2014).

63 Nela Porobic Isakovic, "UN Action Against Sexual Violence: MPTF Office
    Generic Final Programme 1 Narrative Report Reporting Period: From 11.2010
    to 06.2013" *Multi-Partner Trust Fund Office*. Available online: http://mptf.
    undp.org/document/download/11738 (accessed March 18, 2014).

64 M. Cherif Bassiouni and Marcia McCormick, "Sexual Violence: An Invisible
    Weapon of War," Occasional Paper No. 1 (Chicago, IL: International Human
    Rights Law Institute, DePaul University College of Law, 1996), p. 2.

65 Prosecutor *v.* Delalic et al., Judgement, Case No IT-96-21, November 16, 1988.
    In the Celebic prison camp, on one occasion guards put a burning stick in
    the genitalia of Vukasin Mrkojevic and Dusko Bendzo. On another occasion,
    inmates were forced to perform fellatio on each other. Vaso Dordjic described
    an event when Esad Landzo forced him and his brother to fellate each other
    in camp before the other inmates. In the Naser Oric case, on one occasion, a
    guard, after torture, urinated in Serb inmate Nedeljko Radic's mouth, forcing
    him to swallow urine (Prosecutor *v.* Naser Oric, Judgement, Case No IT-03-
    68-T, June 30, 2006, pp. 154–5). There are other documentary testimonies

and personal narratives in which Serb inmates testify about sexual violence and torture performed by Bosniak and Croat soldiers; see, for example, Obrad Bubić, *Ljetovanje na Golgoti* (Prosvjeta, 2004) and Strahinja Živak, *Logor Čelebići: 1992-1995* (Edicija Srpske,1997).

66 Zarkov, "The Body of the Other Man," p. 71.

67 Ibid.

68 United Nations Security Council, *Final Report of the Commission of Experts.* See IV, Sec F: "Rape and Other Forms of Sexual Assault."

69 Amnesty International, "Bosnia-Herzegovina: Rape and Sexual Abuse by Armed Forces," Report No. EUR 63/001/1993 (January 21, 1993), p. 3.

70 Carlson, "Sexual Assault on Men in War," p. 129.

71 Ibid.

72 Prosecutor *v.* Dusko Tadic, International Criminal Tribunal for the former Yugoslavia, Trial Chamber Judgement, Trial Chamber II, Case No. IT-94-1-T, May 7, 1997, paragraphs 198, 206, 238. A prisoner in a Bosnian Serb prison camp was forced, in front of other detainees, to bite off another prisoner's testicle. See also, M. Olujic, "Embodiments of Terror: Gender Violence Peacetime and Wartime in Croatia and Bosnia and Herzegovina," *Medical Anthropology Quarterly* 12 (1998), pp. 31–50.

73 Bassiouni and McCormick, "Sexual Violence: An Invisible Weapon of War," p. 18.

74 Jones, "Straight as a Rule," p. 455.

75 In the Omarska camp, held by Serb forces, one of the detainees was forced by uniformed men, including Duško Tadić, to bite off another detainee's testicles. See Prosecutor *v.* Dusko Tadic (Trial Chamber Judgement) (International Criminal Tribunal for the former Yugoslavia, Trial Chamber II, Case No. IT-94-1-T, May 7, 1997).

76 Prosecutor *v.* Dusko Tadic (Trial Chamber Judgement) (International Criminal Tribunal for the former Yugoslavia, Case No. IT-94-11, February 10, 1995).

77 Prosecutor *v.* Delalic, Mucic, Delic, and Landzo (Trial Judgement) (International Tribunal for the former Yugoslavia, Trial Chamber, Case No. IT-96-21-T, November 16, 1998), paragraph 770.

78 Organization for Security and Cooperation in Europe, *Combating Impunity for Conflict-Related Sexual Violence in Bosnia and Herzegovina: Progress and Challenges: An Analysis of Criminal Proceedings Before the Court of Bosnia and Herzegovina Between 2005 and 2013* (Sarajevo, BiH: OSCE, 2014), p. 42.

79 Prosecutor *v.* Zijad Kurtović, Case No. X-KR-06/229, Second Instant Verdict, March 25, 2009 (Kurtović Appeal Judgement).

80 According to Senadin Ljubović, a psychiatrist from Sarajevo who treated a number of male survivors; see Žana Kovaćević, "Silovani muškarci rijetko progovore o svojoj trauma," *Radio Slobodna Evropa.* Available online: http://www.slobodnaevropa.org/content/plp_silovani_muskarci_rijetko_govore_o_svojoj_traumi/2239393.html (accessed July 22, 2014).

81 World Health Organization, "Reproductive Health During Conflict and Displacement," Report no. WHO/RHR/00.13, ch. 17. Available online:

http://www.who.int/reproductive-health/publications/RHR_00_13_RH_
conflict_and_displacement/RH_conflict_chapter17.en.htm (accessed
March 20, 2002).

82 The book is published only in its local language. The original title is *Torture u
    Bosni i Hercegovini za vrijeme rata 1992-1995* (Sarajevo, BiH: Savez logoraša
    BiH, 2003).

83 Author interview, Sarajevo, July 9, 2014. Midheta's story is also one of
    victimization, as her own mother and brother were killed in front of her and
    their home in Goražde in 1992.

84 Jones, "Straight as a Rule," p. 461.

85 Ibid.

86 For more on consequences, see Oosterhoff, Zwanniken, and Ketting, "Sexual
    Torture of Men in Croatia and Other Conflict Situations," p. 71.

87 Kovaćević, "Silovani muškarci rijetko progovore o svojoj traumi."

88 Carlson, "Sexual Assault on Men in War," p. 129.

89 A. Burnett and M. Peel, "The Health of Survivors of Torture and Organised
    Violence," *British Medical Journal* 322 (2001), p. 608; M. Peel, "Men as
    Perpetrators and Victims," in *Rape as a Method of Torture*, ed. M. Peel
    (London, UK: Medical Foundation for the Care of Victims of Torture, 2004),
    pp. 55, 65.

90 Bojan Arežina, "Pretukli su me, razderali mi hlaće i zabili lopatu u mene,"
    Vecernji List April 1, 2014. Available online: http://www.vecernji.hr/balkan/
    pretukli-su-me-razderali-mi-hlace-i-zabili-lopatu-u-mene-930412 (accessed
    April 13, 2014).

91 Zawatti, "Impunity or Immunity: Wartime Male Rape and Sexual Torture
    as a Crime Against Humanity," p. 40.

92 Kovaćević, "Silovani muškarci rijetko progovore o svojoj traumi."

93 Mark Forshaw, ed., "Global Trauma and Scripture Engagement," Report
    (Wayne, PA: Global Scripture Impact, May 2012), p. 27.

94 Naomi Aratza, "The New Landscape of Transitional justice," in *Transitional
    Justice in the Twenty-First Century—Beyond Truth versus Justice*, ed. Naomi
    Roht-Arriaza and Javier Mariezcurrena (New York, NY: Cambridge University
    Press, 2006), p. 8.

95 See also, *The Final Report of the Truth and Reconciliation Commission in
    Sierra Leone* (Accra, Ghana: Graphic Packaging, 2004): "Truth telling without
    reparations could be perceived by the victims as an incomplete process in
    which they revealed their pain and suffering without any mechanism in place
    to deal with the consequences of that pain or to substantially alter the material
    circumstances of their lives . . . without adequate reparation and rehabilitation
    measures, there can be no healing or reparation."

96 Ruth Rubio-Marín, "The Gender of Reparations in Transitional Societies," in
    *The Gender of Reparations: Unsettling Sexual Hierarchies while Redressing
    Human Rights Violations*, ed. Ruth Rubio-Marín (New York, NY: Cambridge
    University Press, 2009), p. 89.

97 Ruth Rubio-Marín, "Reparations for Conflict-Related Sexual and Reproductive Violence: A Decalogue," *William & Mary Journal of Women and the Law* 19:1 (2012), p. 81.

98 *Ahmetašević*, "Zločin o kojem se ne govori." Blog, Sefik Kilic comment, December 17, 2006. Available online: http://kozarac.ba/modules.php?name=News&file=article&sid=1632.

99 Ibid.

100 Stemple, "Male Rape and Human Rights," p. 637.

101 It was rejected by Parliament in February 2014.

102 Zoran Matkić, "BiH još uvijek bez zakona o žrtvama torture," *Slobodna Evropa*, March 31, 2013. Available online: http://www.slobodnaevropa.org/content/plp-bih-jos-uvijek-bez-zakona-o-pravima-zrtava-torture/24943306.html (accessed June 2, 2014); also see note 108.

103 Ibid.

104 Rubio-Marín, "The Gender of Reparations in Transitional Societies," p. 89.

105 UN Secretary-General, "The Rule of Law and Transitional Justice in Conflict and Post-Conflict Societies," Report, UN Doc.S/2011/634 (October 12, 2011), p. 26. The report calls upon the Security Council to "encourage further attention to the rights of victims to a remedy and reparations, in particular the victims of conflict-related sexual and gender-based violence."

106 World Health Organization, "Reproductive Health During Conflict and Displacement," p. 111.

107 This is true for neighboring Croatia, where male victims of wartime sexual abuse use programs and assistance for female rape survivors organized and offered by NGOs for women. See Snježana Vućković, "Poniženi i osramoćeni: Muškarci silovani po srpskim logorima- žrtve su o kojima se ne rado govori," *Dnevno*, March 17, 2014. Available online: http://www.dnevno.hr/vijesti/hrvatska/117779-ponizeni-i-osramoceni-muskarci-silovani-po-srpskim-logorima-zrtve-su-o-kojima-se-nerado-govori.html (accessed July 27, 2014).

108 However, this has been possible for men who live in the Federation of Bosnia-Herzegovina, which is one of two BiH entities. The other entity, Republika Srpska (RS), does not recognize victims of sexual violence during the war as a special category of victims.

109 Claudia Paz y Paz Bailey, "Guatemala: Gender and Reparations for Human Rights Violations," in *What Happened to Women? Gender and Reparations for Human Rights Violations*, ed. Ruth Rubio-Marín and International Center for Transitional Justice (New York, NY: Social Science Research Council, 2006), pp. 106–7.

110 Colleen Duggan and Ruth Jacobson, "Reparation of Sexual and Reproductive Violence: Moving from Codification to Implementation," in *The Gender of Reparations*, ed. Ruth Rubio-Marín, p. 138.

111 See UN High Commissioner for Refugees, "Working with Men and Boys Survivors of Sexual and Gender-based Violence in Forced Displacement," Guidelines (July 2012), p. 10; Rubio-Marín, "Reparations for Conflict-Related Sexual and Reproductive Violence: A Decalogue," p. 87.

112 "Persons who have suffered sexual assault and rape are defined as a special category of civilian victims of war": International Commission on Missing Persons et al., "Guide for civilian victims of war," *International Commission on Missing Persons* (Sarajevo, BiH: 2007), p. 5.

113 Data is from December 2013. On file with the author.

114 Document is on file with the author.

115 Buckley-Ziestel, "Redressing Sexual Violence," p. 95.

116 Ibid.

117 C. G. Davis, S. Nolen-Hoeksema, and J. Larson, "Making Sense of Loss and Benefiting from the Experience: Two Construals of Meaning," *Journal of Personality and Social Psychology* 75 (1998), pp. 561–7.

118 The local women's association "Žena žrtva rata" [Women Victim of War] and camp inmates' association "Hrvatska udruga logorasa domovinskog rata u BiH" [The Croatian Association of Former Detention Camp Prisoners of the Homeland War in BiH] are the other two NGOs which can issue certificates. The Law on principles of social protection, protection of all civilian victims of war and protection of families with children (Official Gazette of the FBiH, 36/99). The RS has a similar law, but determination of status of civilian victims of war is preserved for the government institutions only.

119 A written statement by male victims of sexual abuse is used in the courtrooms too. The protected witness RM-081 in the Ratko Mladić trial has provided a written statement about the sexual abuse and torture that he and his family survived in Rogatica Serb camp. He witnessed the sexual abuse of his then thirteen-year-old son and seven-year-old daughter. He said he could never "summon up the courage" to ask his wife whether she was raped too since they were held in the same camp. FENA, "Svjedok: Nisam imao snage da pitam suprugu da li je silovana," *Oslobođenje*, October 5, 2012. Available online: http://www.oslobodjenje.ba/vijesti/bih/svjedok-nisam-imao-snage-sa-pitam-suprugu-da-li-je-silovana (accessed June 18, 2014).

120 Carlson, "Sexual Assault on Men in War," p. 129.

121 The blank sample of the form that each new member needs to fill in is called "Komplet dosije" and is on file with the author.

122 Janine Natalya Clark, "A Crime of Identity: Rape and Its Neglected Victims," *Journal of Human Rights* 13:2 (2014), p. 153.

11

Distortions in Survivors' Narratives from Srebrenica: The Impossibility of Conveying Their Truth

Selma Leydesdorff

Life stories do not just describe the historical trajectory of the self. They also express someone's being. Narratives of the self demonstrate how we are interwoven with our families, communities, and traditions. They show how we interpret the past and our experiences, and they reveal our background and expectations of our future. In short, these narratives disclose who we want to be and who we think we are. In order to affirm and assert the self, our narratives need to be believed and recognized. Others need to acknowledge that our life story is important, and they need to listen to our voices. Survivors of genocidal trauma have a right to be heard. Indeed, one could argue that it is a precondition for reestablishing a sense of self and a sense of connection with others. After all, genocidal trauma destroys social bonds and human relations and demolishes one's self-image.

This chapter discusses how women survivors of the genocide of Srebrenica, the largest genocide since the Second World War, lost their relationship with the world and with others and, in the process, lost their sense of self. It focuses on the stories these women tell about their pasts and what they tell us about life before and during the Bosnian War of 1992–95. It examines women survivors' search for words to express their fear, anxiety, trauma, and other feelings. And it explores the consequences of the international community's failure to really hear these women, listen to their complex stories, and recognize them. Ultimately, the chapter argues, this failure has contributed to the distortion of women's narratives about the past.

From 2002 to 2008, I traveled to Bosnia to interview female survivors of Srebrenica. I worked closely with the three major organizations of survivors: The "Mothers of Srebrenica and Zepa Enclaves," "Women of Srebrenica," and "Women of Podrinje." At that time, they had offices in Sarajevo, Ilidža, and Tuzla (a provincial capital in eastern Bosnia). My other major contact for setting up interviews was an NGO, *Snaga Zene*, in Tuzla. I was particularly supported by a doctor from *Snaga Zene* who worked in several remote refugee camps—sad places of exclusion that few people from the outside world visited. Many of the life stories that came out of my work are discussed in my book, *Surviving Genocide: The Women of Srebrenica Speak*, and several other publications, and they form the basis for this chapter.[1]

From the outset, my intent in conducting the interviews was to produce a historical account that included the voices of the Srebrenica survivors. I was distressed by the various inquiries into the fall of Srebrenica.[2] Although the United Nations (UN) and various governments commissioned official reports to investigate what went wrong, none of these reports included the voices, histories, and experiences of the survivors, even though historians agree that such voices cannot be left out of any historical account of genocide.[3] The validity of women survivors' stories was not recognized. Perhaps people thought such an undertaking was impossible.

I must admit that being confronted with the immense grief of survivors is frightening. Moreover, as is typical in narratives of traumatized people, the stories I heard were not self-evident. I was also confronted with the inability of the interviewees to put their experiences into words. There seemed to be no framework or genre for their stories. There was nothing to hold onto. Psychoanalysts Francois Davoine and Jean Max Gaudillière have called this inability to express "history beyond trauma,"[4] describing the limbo of the seriously wounded and their difficulty in reestablishing contact with others. For these survivors, the traumatic event has been isolated from their life story; it seems unconnected in the brain.

My interviews provided a fresh historical image of the genocide and its survivors: an image different from the image frequently recorded elsewhere—such as in many television programs—in which the women survivors had been stigmatized as hysterical victims with whom it is impossible to communicate. For example, when women survivors who had traveled to the Netherlands walked out of the meeting at which the Dutch NIOD report (Netherlands Institute for War Document) was officially presented, some saw this as evidence of their "hysteria." It has taken many discussions between me and the writers of the official report and the general Dutch audience to convince people that these women were and are as angry and disobedient as, for instance, the mothers of the Plaza de Mayo. And anger is not the same thing as hysteria.

The women survivors I talked to were hospitable and open, and often very sweet. They were able to communicate the complexity of their trauma, although not directly. The interviews revealed how the massive historical trauma the survivors had experienced had impregnated their personalities, resulting in what is known in psychological terms as *dissociation*. For these women, every subsequent event had become visible only through the prism of massive slaughter, betrayal, and feelings of loneliness. Moreover, this trauma had destroyed their connections with others and their sense of self. However, during the interviews, I noticed that telling a story can be healing and can help in the long process of putting fragments of memory together. To bear witness seemed to create a place where the past could be told—a place in which the women could make connections once again. This helped the women to reconstruct their life stories, and they often felt excited and "free" after telling their story to me, the outsider.

Fragmented and Chaotic Stories

In their interviews, women survivors were often too traumatized to describe exactly what happened during the genocide, and, as with all severely traumatized people, chronology was a major problem, lapses in memory occurred, and confusion reigned. The women's accounts were not always immediately understandable. But this is not surprising. Narratives of trauma are not straightforward. Rather, they are what Cathy Caruth has called expressions of "a crisis of witnessing." As a result, Caruth explains, trauma becomes layered in language and literature, and eyewitness accounts are rooted in dislocations of history.[5] Normal bounds do not exist any longer; there is confusion over where they belong since trauma is as much about surviving with the experience of trauma as the traumatic event itself.

Talking about trauma often means reliving it in all of its pain, difficulty, fear, confusion, and shame. Accordingly, the American psychiatrist Dori Laub proposes that "there is a need for tremendous libidinal investment in those interview situations: There is so much destruction recounted, so much death, so much loss, so much hopelessness, that there has to be an abundance of holding and of emotional investment in the encounter."[6] For the interviewer, then, absolute freedom of speech is required, and patience is obligatory. Answers are never given, but the desire to answer always leads to the beginning of a new story. One memory brings forth new memories. The narrator is often unaware of how much he or she has to tell. There is an emotional dynamic between the interviewer and interviewee, who are both committed to the story. In this difficult process of remembering, using existing narration genres is a way to escape personal memories. Collective memories are redundant. This complicates any understanding of what is told. The interviewer has to continually question whether the story is indeed personal, or if the language of others is being used.

Women's fragmented and chaotic stories reflected the confusion and panic consciously promoted by the Serbs to dominate thousands of people during the genocide in Srebrenica/Potočari. The Serbian chaos was unlike other stories of mass killings, such as the Holocaust, where those who survived talked about organization as part of the domination. After the enclave of Srebrenica fell, the Serbs utilized disorder—as well as fear and incredible violence—to assert their control. As Bosniak refugees hurriedly fled toward the Potočari compound that was supposed to be protected by the Dutch battalion of UN soldiers, mayhem reigned; many refugees were pushed, run over, and separated from others. During three days of Serbian aggression, more than 30,000 Bosniaks faced killings, beatings, rape, and other atrocities. Women and girls were raped on the spot. Men were taken away to be murdered. Bosniaks experienced psychological torture from the total insecurity of their situation. The women did not know if they were going to be killed, and they did not know where their men were; they were scared. Parents feared for their children. We know now that 731 children went missing and that more than 5 percent of the victims were under the age of 15. While thousands of babies, children, sick, and elderly were herded into the Potočari compound, without sanitation and food, the Dutch soldiers sealed off part of the compound, and thousands of others were forced to remain outside the enclosure. There was a horrible stench.

In the midst of this deliberate and violent chaos, the refugees were terrified and confused. Ajsa, one of the survivors, recalled her terror and powerlessness:

> They got drunk and walked around us with rifles. We were just sitting. We did not know what would happen. They were drunk and had blood-shot eyes. We were sitting, helpless, waiting for what would happen. We sat with our hands in our laps, and they did what they wanted to do. I sat on a concrete floor. They separated my father and my husband. They told them where they should go and later they would come back.[7]

Then, after enumerating how many she lost, Ajsa softly told how people were taken to the so-called white house: "They were taken there. Now they say they disappeared. They did not disappear. They were alive when they were taken from us."

The women I interviewed were reluctant to talk about the atrocities and the pain they experienced. The chaos of Srebrenica/Potočari became chaos in their heads. It was a memory that was best muted. Silence was everywhere, and it had many meanings. How can victims/survivors find words for the horror that unfolded before their eyes? Is it not better to be silent, as the task of remembering and speaking is so horrendous?

Even though remembering the terrible events that unfolded in Srebrenica/Potočari seemed impossible, women survivors did recall them, mostly in broken stories. Moreover, some women found that talking about the past was *both* impossible and unavoidable. Bida, for example, could not initially talk when I interviewed her in her house near the collective graveyard. Her voice was blocked by a sore throat, and apparently her throat always hurts when she talks about "certain events." But she tried:

> I do not know, I tell you I cannot; it is so hard for me. When I start talking about it, I cannot go on, believe me, I lose my voice. We left the house. That moment was difficult for me, I just cannot talk about it. Believe me. Everything up to then and departure from home, that was so hard for me, and children and worry, it makes my hair stand on end. I lose my voice, and that is that. I wish that all that was over and never talked about.
>
> You do not know how difficult it is for me. After this, I do not know how, but I know that I will get a headache, I will get ill, believe me. Whenever we sit somewhere, we talk about the war, about our survival, about fear. Somebody says, "Why do you talk about it?" I do not know, I wish we could avoid it. As soon as I start talking, I lose my voice. I wish we could avoid all this, but we cannot, it stays inside us, it persists.
>
> But regardless of everything, we sit together and talk and cry; we cannot do it differently. But the worst thing with me is that I lose voice, something happens. Most of us are like that, it cannot be different, so accept it.[8]

Women such as Bida could not stand to talk about the past, and yet they found themselves frequently talking about it with other survivors. They developed a coded language to deal with what had happened, a language that suppressed emotions since it avoided naming what had taken place.

Although Bida and many other women managed to talk to me, despite the difficulties, their stories contained important omissions, particularly when it came to sexual violence. Bida, for example, never told me that her daughter was raped, since rape is a wall of silence I was seldom able to break, even though her husband had committed suicide when he had found out. Her husband could not tell her, and he did not see any other solution than to kill himself. Instead of talking about these issues, Bida talked about her brother who was killed. She grieved and missed him; she had loved him. His death was a memory template for what could not be told.

Women's comments underscored how they had lost their sense of place in the world. Grief and loss permeated their whole personality and their sense of self. For some women, this made them feel as though nothing was left and that they had no meaningful identity. For example, after describing how she had lost her father, husband, and son, Nezira no longer cared for life. She explained, "I cannot help crying, I think that this is the end of my life. First my father's remains were found and then my son's. My husband died."[9] Other women found that their ability to connect with others had been shattered. All that remained for them was their story of great sorrow and suffering, which they knew others preferred not to hear, and thus they could no longer relate well to people. In Zumra's words,

> Not one day passes that I haven't said something about it. That means it is on my mind all the time. I can't understand. Sometimes I visit a happy family, where all the members are there together, and they have problems buying a fridge, or they need to change the curtains or something else in their house. I'm not interested in that. I don't have the power inside me to listen to that. I don't worry anymore about which dress I have on, what kind of shoes, which bag. All I worry about now is that I'm neat, that I'm not filthy, and I pray to dear Allah to keep me sane, to keep me aware and reasonable, so that I can communicate normally with people.[10]

The major trauma that the women endured, including the loss of loved ones, made social interactions and carrying on in life extremely difficult.

Significantly, the events in Srebrenica/Potočari were not integrated into women's personal life stories. Instead, these traumatic events stood apart and constituted a part of a more general, confused memory about what had happened. Women's inability to incorporate these events into their life stories was related to their inability to make sense of these events, to understand how they had happened. For many women, their memories almost seemed like someone else's, and/or their memories seemed like a dream. As Nermina said,

> It is a dream, I mean a nightmare. But one moment stands out: My husband began to kiss our children. He took the eldest one and cried and he wailed: "Armin, my son, maybe your father will never see you again." He cried. Then he took little Omer. "Omer, my son, your father will never see you again." The whole war, everything we went through, was not so terrible as this farewell, this saying good-bye. He came to the youngest one and only then stepped back. He went to the gate and stood there, crying.[11]

Nermina added that this memory did not seem to be her own and that instead it seemed like a film that replayed in her head. Many other women recounted a similar story of parting—and the dreamlike nature of it. There was always that last moment engraved in the memory: A husband, a son, a father, a member of the family. A man and a woman embraced for the last time, their eyes full of tears. A father embraced his daughter, and both knew it was the last time. A child cried and begged: "Daddy, please come back." A mother begged: "Don't take my son away; he is so small." She tried in vain to free him from the Serb soldiers. Her life seemed over.

Women who watched their loved ones being taken away frequently expressed shame about not doing more. As Zumra explained,

> I couldn't say anything at the time. I had the feeling that I was paralyzed and I cried rivers of tears. I didn't shriek or scream. I didn't say that they

must not take him. I didn't ask, "Why him?" Nothing, nothing. I'm not saying now that, if I had said something, it might have saved him. But I couldn't help. They just told us to go along. I couldn't do anything, not a thing. And he was so gentle, worrying all the time. It was very hot that day, to faint. I felt a bit sick. He held my hand all the time, kept telling me everything is going to be all right. His arm on my shoulder was so heavy. I felt it so deep in my body. Heavy, shaky, with fear of what will happen to us. Although he knew everything, was aware of everything, he kept saying everything would be all right. Five minutes before they separated us, I turned around to see his eyes. Now I can say, he was looking at death. He was speechless. His eyes were focused at one point. He wasn't saying anything. He held his jacket in his hands.[12]

Women's failure to act, to do anything to try to prevent the murder of their husbands and other male relatives, contributed not only to their sense of remorse, but also to their sense of guilt. This survivor's guilt was similar to what Judith Zur has described in regard to Guatemalan women.[13] Guatemalan women, who were forced to see their husbands slaughtered, were ashamed they did not intervene. This shame, which the officials manipulated, contributed to the public silence about what had happened.

Over the years, victims' voices became an accepted and essential source for Holocaust historiography, but only after fierce historical debate. This is not yet the case with Srebrenica. And yet the stories I was told, though fragmented and chaotic, shed light on important aspects of the events that unfolded in Srebrenica/Potočari—aspects that are not presented in the official reports from the various states that were involved. Moreover, the interviews demonstrated how it was only possible within the framework of women's life stories to understand the depth of their trauma and grief.

In spite of their traumatic memories, the interviewees brought back to life a world that had been lost. Of course, the women preferred to forget about this world, which no longer made sense. As a result, women frequently started their interviews with the story of their childhood, focusing on good times. Significantly, women's stories provided a glimpse of how much their lives had been turned upside down. Speaking specifically of life before the war and before the genocidal events was a source of great confusion: "Many bad guys had been good guys at another time."

Confusion and Betrayal

It took a long time for me to realize that Srebrenica survivors' life stories were fragmented not only by the trauma of 1995, but also by the impossibility of telling the longer story. Women's confusion was aggravated because any narrative of the past is interwoven with a vision of the future. The women remembered the multicultural society they originally came from, and they still thought it was important to live together. They were raised with a brand of Communism that suppressed any expression of cultural difference, and they had internalized positive feelings toward other ethnic groups. The Yugoslav identity, although imposed, was about unity, and this unitarian ideology became a part of everyday perceptions of the world.

On a psychological level, the collapse of the former Yugoslavia and the fast rise of nationalist policies were very disorienting, undermining survivors' sense of self. Despite the current nationalist myth that the region has always been rife with war and hostility, even the most illiterate women were able to describe the alliance between nationalism and state politics that was the origin of all the destruction and bloodshed that followed. For the women survivors, the war in Bosnia had resulted not only in terrible genocidal events, but also in the loss of interethnic friendships and the loss of trust in the world and loved ones. These losses left survivors with unsettling grief and conflicting emotions, with no sense of normality to provide counterbalance.

The women survivors were bewildered by those who became enemies and murderers: their neighbors whom they knew so well and had been so close to. The women had trusted and shared many experiences with them. The trust was sometimes so great that the women asked for help even while their neighbors were "on the other side" as uniformed rapists and murderers. When the women were among those be to killed or evacuated, they appealed to old friends and acquaintances for assistance, such as when the women recognized some of them as military staff in the compound where they had been taken. One interviewee told how, before the genocide began but during the war, she had exchanged sex with a former neighbor for the safety and protection of her children. She said that the man who raped her every night had always been in love with her and wanted her. Before the war she had liked him, as a neighbor. She knew him quite well, and even during those miserable weeks of sexual violence, she had trusted his promises of protection.

Survivors were confused about the disintegration of Yugoslavia and the way various groups became enemies after many years of "unity." The people of the town had gone to school together and lived on the same streets. The auxiliaries or perpetrators were not only neighbors, but also people they had often known for a very long time, some of whom had been friends. Although some (but not all) survivors had felt slow but increasing estrangement and greater social distance from Bosnian Serbs in the two decades prior to the genocide, the degree of exclusion, aggression, and violence that they subsequently experienced during the war did not belong to the society in which they had lived. In the former Yugoslavia, there had been a safety net, and violence among ethnicities was punished.

Good memories of coexistence with "the other" were problematic. It was easier not to talk about them and to deny past feelings and replace them with stronger emotions of hatred and disappointment. Memories of previous lives were eclipsed by feelings of loss. This is why the women I interviewed could hardly imagine positive feelings when they thought about the past. Everything that was normal was disrupted. The moment of disruption was clearly grafted onto their memory, but it is precisely that moment that also concealed all positive feelings about the time before.

When emptiness replaces memory, connectedness, context, and a place in society, and there is no positive memory or future, it can be better to forget. Remembering the past requires the survivor to explore positive feelings that resurface, and these feelings disrupt the negative paradigm that the survivor has embraced to make sense of the incomprehensible. Remembering might prompt questions about the need to think about past friendships and love. One woman who lost twenty-two members of her family, including her husband and three sons, managed to talk about the positive feelings she had toward her Serb former friend. Yet while she spoke, the pain was clearly visible on her face.

> I dreamed about her, and I was amazed to hear that her sons had served in the army, a special unit. When I returned to my village and went to her mother's house she wanted to embrace me and kiss me. But I told her, "We are not what we were before." She started to cry and told me that her sons had not killed my son. But I told her, "They didn't do anything to save him either." Deep inside, I still love her, though I would never admit it. I don't want to forgive her.[14]

Forgiving her former friend would only further complicate her feelings, which were already confused by the love she still felt.

The Right to be Recognized

In 2007, lawyers for a group of 6,000 women survivors of Srebrenica sent a writ of summons to the Dutch government and to the UN, asking for a judicial declaration that the UN and the Netherlands were guilty of failing to fulfill their obligations to the UN Genocide Convention, which obliges countries to assist people under extreme threat, and suing them for damages, that is, for financial compensation for lost livelihoods, education, material, and health.[15] The plaintiffs leveled accusations against the UN, which had declared that the enclave of Srebenica would be safe, and the Dutch, who had represented the UN in the enclave. The Dutch soldiers had promised protection, even though they were no match for the heavily armed Serbian forces; nor was the Dutch army familiar with real war. The Dutch soldiers also did not have an order to fight. Their mandate was to separate the warring parties, even though there were no instructions on how to do that. Instead of providing protection, the Dutch forces had looked on while men and women were separated, and women with small children were evacuated to safe territory. Dutch soldiers even witnessed the murder of some Bosniak men by Serbian forces, although most Bosniak men were massacred at killing sites.

Incredibly, however, the women's demands were turned down. The District Court of The Hague ruled that the UN enjoys immunity from prosecution. The Dutch government was able to escape blame because its army was under UN command. Perhaps, decades from now, the women of Srebrenica's rights will be acknowledged, and so will their stories. As far as the women are concerned, the court's ruling demonstrated the international community's inability to acknowledge its failure in response to the Balkan Wars of the 1990s and its unwillingness to take survivors seriously. The court's ruling signaled that the door of international law was closed, and it made the women feel unrecognized, unheard, and rejected.

After the carnage in Bosnia, many women survivors offered testimonies in a variety of legal venues: lawsuits, the aforementioned writ of summons, the International Criminal Tribunal for the former Yugoslavia (ICTY), regional tribunals, and local courts. Initially, the possibility of giving such testimony brought hope to many women. Moreover, women survivors were pleased with the establishment of the ICTY and its determination that the massacre in Srebrenica/Potočari constituted genocide. Going to court was emotionally challenging, however, and many survivors ended up crying and becoming hysterical. The women assumed that court proceedings would help them find answers to the many questions that haunted them (often framed by the words "search for justice and truth about what happened to their beloved"). The answers they wanted and the truth they sought, however, were not always the same answers and truth that the court pursued. As a result, the women sometimes clashed with judges.

An example is the testimony of Kada Hotić in the Orić case at the ICTY. She wanted to talk about the stream of refugees from Bratunac to Srebrenica. Bratunac was conquered in 1992. It was a massacre. Neighbors suddenly turned against each other, and there was unprecedented violence. Refugees felt betrayed by friends. Hotić wanted to explain to the court what had happened. However, the judge was only interested in how the people of Srebrenica had raided the area surrounding the town in 1993–94. The accused, Orić, was supposedly the leader of those raids, in which many were killed. The court wanted details from 1993 to 1994, but Hotić's mind was focused on 1992. The resulting testimony was chaos. It lacked chronology. Events from the past flashed before her eyes. She wanted to tell all at once, and she wanted to accuse someone because she was angry. From her perspective, all Serbs were criminals, and her anger could not be focused.

Going to court was not the solution for survivors. Some important spokeswomen I interviewed loudly declared that they did not trust the legal system. Others protested that such a procedure would not bring back the missing people and that attention should be focused on building a collective cemetery and commemoration site. They were also worried that while they focused on legal procedures, the women would forget to rebuild their lives or improve the horrible living conditions in their dilapidated neighborhoods and camps. Most of all, they dreaded the psychological effects of women's rage being presented in a lawsuit. It became clear that going to The Hague to testify was also problematic, because the women who testified were threatened when they returned to Bosnia.

Women's difficulty in speaking and the lack of recognition afforded to their complex and chaotic stories resulted in the distortion of their narratives. The victims began to recount a new version of past events. Survivors tried to create testimony that could be used as evidence to convince the world of Serbian aggression. They provided "facts" the way the prosecution told them to in staged testimonies. These new testimonies looked like an edited version of what had been initially testified in court. At the courts and in the writ of summons, women's stories of sadness and pain were transformed by juridical language into stories of denunciation and self-defense. This new language of accusation became the master narrative, preventing freedom of expression. As I have already suggested, there was so much more in the long and open interviews I conducted. Survivors' voices also became distorted, quite literally, in another way: when the women bore witness, the ICTY had their voices altered so that they would be unrecognizable, and this version of their voices is available on the Internet. One can hear them, since excerpts of the witness testimonies are posted on the web.[16]

Legal and historical discourses try to understand the history of an epoch and its causality, but their outcomes are different. As a historian, I researched the daily life of Srebrenica during the siege (1992–95). Early on, most information came from official reports and the ICTY. This information presented an image of the town under siege, filtered through the lens of knowing that the people would be slaughtered. The reports' and the ICTY's common task was to discover who was accountable and to assign responsibility. However, the people living in Srebrenica were not aware they were going to be killed. When the town came under siege, most Bosniaks believed the UN would protect them as it had promised. The women recounted the arrival of the Serb soldiers and the disruption of previously good relations between ethnic groups. They also described how they tried to give meaning to what happened to them and resume their lives. They tried to educate their children by creating schools and a library. They cleaned the town and stimulated social cohesion. They organized daily life and sought to plan for the future.

If legal language and the demands of law become the dominant narrative for framing eyewitness accounts of genocide, we risk erasing a representation of how deeply survivors' lives were disrupted.[17] We erase the fragmentations, silences, and dislocations. By not allowing the full truth of the stories in all their layered and unfinished forms, and dismissing them as emotional outbursts, we deny their mediated authenticity and how they might reconfigure (or even remake) the world for those who have lost their place in it. In turn, we dislocate the meaning and place assigned to an event.

In this clash between the legal truth and the victim's need to speak out, material compensation became one of many ways to reclaim a place in the world. The women demanded compensation in the lawsuits. They wanted material recognition of their losses. However, money never restores lost social and cultural capital. It does not validate the right to exist as a human being, which is crucial in order to go on living.[18] Nor does any juridical act or decision do that. Material compensation also does not bring back the dead. As one survivor, Nermina, observed, "When I heard that we were going to get compensation for war damages, I was happy. Believe me. But there is no money that can make up for losing my husband. It hurts every time one of my children says 'Papa.' My soul hurts, and my heart is heavy."[19]

We tend to forget that victims' core desire is to be recognized, which goes far beyond compensation. What does it mean to be recognized? The political philosopher, Nancy Fraser, describes the Hegelian idea of recognition:

> A reciprocal relation between subjects, in which each sees the other both as its equal and also as separate from it. This relation is constitutive for subjectivity: one becomes an individual subject only by virtue of recognizing, and being recognized by, another subject. Recognition from others is thus essential to the development of a sense of self. To be denied recognition is to suffer both a distortion of one's relation to the self and an injury to identity.[20]

Failing to recognize victims—or "misrecognizing" them — harms them further, because survivors need to reconnect to a society and world that seem to have been lost.

The language of the law and juridical thinking hijacked the possibility of reintegrating feelings of deep traumatization. The people who testified at the ICTY or in local courts were often so hurt that they were unable to give a place to what happened. Also, the judges did not want to hear their story. I wonder if speaking up and telling the whole story would ever have been possible. The loss of loved ones, of course, also made reintegration difficult, as did the misery of poverty. Many of the women I interviewed suffered from terrible living conditions after the war. They often lived in deserted schools and lodgings that were actually refugee camps. Although many of the women had come from wealthy families in Yugoslavia before the war, after the war they were unable to give their children a decent education and standard of living. For women survivors, years of poverty were not just an additional psychological and physical strain that made dealing with the past challenging; this unimaginable destitution without any help was another form of nonrecognition even from the local government. In looking at the survivors' wishes or reading the many psychological reports, it emerges that the survivors' main desire was to return to a normal daily life, to escape their poverty, and to escape the legal and administrative webs. Money was the materialization of women's grief.

Moving Forward?

Narrowing the survivors' desires down to material compensation and juridical procedures reduced their life stories to the demands and format of legal language. In preparation for court proceedings and testimonies, exact information was required. However, the women victims struggled with something incomprehensible, beyond any traditional concept of history. The significance of remembered life stories lies not in absolute truth, but in how one remembers, gives meaning, and represents events. Stories do not exist until they are told, and an adequate history cannot be written without including victims' suffering and memories. Therefore, we should not dismiss them as constructions that lack factual authority but rather regard them as being ontologically authentic. This view of survivor subjectivity is not in line with how witness accounts are perceived in the public arena, which requires the "true" story of what "really" happened and the exact timeline.

Although women's voices have been distorted by a juridical framework, I concluded from my interviews that the main problem is not how memories are constructed as compared to reality. The main problem is that what cannot be remembered cannot be put into words. The women I interviewed were reluctant to talk about the atrocities and pain they went through. At a deeper level, the survivors either did not wish to remember or, more frequently, found certain episodes too difficult to recall in the light of their present lives. I am not referring to traumatic episodes but rather to their past peaceful coexistence with those who eventually betrayed them. This past could hardly be understood now. The betrayal they witnessed— the participation of friends, neighbors, and loved ones in murder and genocide—also prevented them from developing any vision of the future. Such a vision can only be based on feelings about what they perceived as "good" in the past.

In the interviews I conducted, memories often manifested in bitterness about this betrayal and feelings that such cruelty cannot remain unpunished. Interviewees wanted people to be held accountable for their terrible actions. The desire for revenge and punishment is in opposition to rebuilding a town and a countryside where people can live together again.[21] Although the 1995 Dayton agreement stopped the bloodshed, it instituted territorial separation on the basis of ethnicity. Since the town of Srebrenica is part of the Republika Srpska, survivors returned to hostile environments where they felt threatened and dealt with the administration of a hostile entity. They had to live on the same street with men who committed crimes against Bosniaks. Sometimes, the next plot of land over was owned by a Serb. Other survivors were too traumatized to return.

In order for women survivors to move forward and to reconstitute a sense of self, they need to be able to tell their traumatic stories in all their complexity. Moreover, to tell and to speak are as important as other measures—such as depolarizing education systems, promoting tolerance, strengthening independent media, challenging dominant national narratives, hearing other voices (such as women's groups), instituting truth and reconciliation commissions, finding a place for mourning, and, finally, prosecuting the criminals—in helping Bosnian society move forward. International institutions have privileged the prosecution of criminals. Talking about one's past, however, is an important way for women to negotiate their trauma, construct a meaningful identity, and restore their sense of connection to others.

Trauma is a constitutive element in a problematic interplay between not being able to remember and not wanting to remember. The significance of remembered life stories lies not in absolute truth but in how one remembers; how one gives meaning and representation to events. Stories do not exist until they are told, and an adequate history cannot be written without including the victims' suffering and the survivors' memories. Therefore, we should not dismiss women's stories as constructions that lack factual authority but rather regard them as being ontologically authentic. We historians should work, and not only in this case, to create a public sphere that recognizes the need to include those other and more historical voices. Without the victim's voice, a history of genocide is no History.

Notes

1   Selma Leydesdorff, *Surviving the Bosnian Genocide: The Women of Srebrenica Speak* (Bloomington, IN: Indiana University Press, 2011).

2   Research is done in the international network created by Charles Ingrao called the Scholars Initiative. Available online: http://www.cla.purdue.edu/academic/history/facstaff/Ingrao/si/scholars.htm. Also see NIOD, *Srebrenica, een'veilig gebied:. Reconstructie, achtergronden, gevolgen en analyses van de val van een Safe Area* (Amsterdam, Netherlands: Boom, 2002); Rapport d'information de MM. René André et Francois Lamy, no.3413, deposé le novembre 22, 2001, en application de l'article 145 du réglement (Paris, France: l'Assemblée Nationale, 2002); Rpublika Serpska, *The Events in and around Srebrenica between 10th and 19th July 1995* (The Commission for Investigation of the Events in and around Srebrenica between 10th and 19th July 1995) (Banja Luka, Bosnia-Herzegovina: June 2004 with appendix October 2004); Jan W. Honing and, Norbert Both, *Srebrenica: Record of a War Crime* (London, UK: Penguin, 1996). Major research and major historical descriptions have mainly been made by journalists. I mention some of the excellent works: David Rhode, *Endgame, The Betrayal and Fall of Srebrenica. Europe's Worst Massacre since World War II* (Boulder, CO: Westview Press, 1997); Roy Gutman, *A Witness to Genocide* (New York,

NY: Palgrave Macmillan, 1993); Sylvie Matton, *Srebrenica, un génocide annoncé* (Paris, France: Flammarion, 2005).

3   There is a vast array of sources for describing the suffering of genocide. See, for instance: Dominique LaCapra, *Writing History, Writing Trauma* (Baltimore, MD and London, UK: 2001); Donald E. Miller and Lorna T. Miller, *Survivors: An Oral History of the Armenian Genocide* (Berkeley, CA: 1993); Gadi BenEzer, "Trauma Signals in Life Stories," in *Trauma and Life Stories: International Perspectives (Routledge Studies in Memory and Narrative)*, ed. Kim Lacy Rogers, Selma Leydesdorff, and Graham Dawson (London, UK and New York, NY: Routledge, 1999), pp. 29–45; Samuel Totten, William S. Parsons, and Israel W. Charny, eds., *A Century of Genocide: Eyewitness Accounts and Critical Views* (New York, NY: 1997); Cathy Caruth, *Unclaimed Experience: Trauma, Narrative, and History* (Baltimore, MD; Johns Hopkins University Press, 1996).

4   Francois Devoine and, Jean Max Gaudilliere, *History beyond Trauma* (New York, NY: Other Press, 2004).

5   Caruth, *Unclaimed Experience: Trauma, Narrative, and History*.

6   Shoshana Feldman and Dori Laub, *Testimony: Crises of Witnessing in Literature, Psychoanalysis and History* (New York, NY and London, UK: Routledge, 1992), p. 71; Erika Apfelbaum, "And Now What, After Such Tribulations? Memory and Dislocation in the Era of Uprooting," *American Psychologist* 55 (2000), pp. 1008–13; Dori Laub, "Truth and Testimony, The Process and the Struggle," in *Trauma: Explorations in Memory*, ed. Cathy Caruth (Baltimore, MD: Johns Hopkins University Press, 1995), pp. 61–76; Paul Gready, *Writing as Resistance: Life Stories of Imprisonment, Exile, and Homecoming from Apartheid South Africa* (Lanham, MD: Lexington Books, 2003).

7   Interview, Ajša Betić, 2006.

8   Bida Smajlovic, interview by Selma Leydesdorff, 2006.

9   Nezira Sulejmanović, interview by Selma Leydesdorff, September 2005.

10 Zumra Šehomerović, interview by Velma Sarić, 2007.

11 Interview, Nermina Smaljović, 2004.

12 Šehomerović, interview.

13 Judith Zur, "Remembering and Forgetting: Guatemalan War Widows' Forbidden Memories," in *Trauma and Life Stories*, ed. Rogers, Leydesdorff, and Dawson, pp. 45–59.

14 Anonymous interviewee, 2005.

15 Writ of summons (June 4, 2007) against the State of the Netherlands and the United Nations, District Court, The Hague. Van Diepen and Kroes.

16 Lynn Abrams, *Oral History Theory* (London, UK: Routledge, 2010). Also see Nanci Adler and Selma Leydesdorff, *Tapestry of Memory, Evidence and Testimony in Life-Story Narratives* (New Brunswick, NJ and London, UK: Transaction Publishers, 2013).

17 Shoshana Felman and Dori Laub, *Testimony: Crises of Witnessing in Literature, Psychoanalysis and History* (New York, NY and London, UK:

Routledge, 1992); Michael G. Levine, *The Belated Witness: Literature, Testimony and the Question of Holocaust Survival* (Palo Alto, CA: Stanford University Press, 2006).

18 Shoshana Felman, *The Juridical Unconsciousness: Trials and Traumas in the Twentieth Century* (Cambridge, MA and London, UK: Harvard University Press, 2002).

19 Interview, Nemira Smaljović, 2004.

20 Nancy Fraser, "Rethinking Recognition," *New Left Review* 3 (May–June 2000), pp. 107–20; Nancy Fraser and Axel Honneth, *Redistribution or Recognition? A Political-Philosophical Exchange* (London, UK: Verso, 2003).

21 Laurel E. Fletcher and Harvey M. Weinstein, "Violence and Social Repair: Rethinking the Contribution of Justice to Reconciliation," *Human Rights Quarterly* 24 (2002), pp. 601–3.

PART FIVE

Genocide Prevention and International Law

12

Making Sense of Genocide, Making Sense of Law: International Criminal Prosecutions of Large-Scale Sexual Violence

Doris Buss

As the essays in this volume make clear, there is a growing recognition that gender plays a role in shaping the conditions, mechanisms, and representations of large-scale violence. As a crime committed against a group, genocide invariably engages issues of gender. Gender ideologies, symbols, and norms often feature in the ways group membership is marked and regulated. The gendered roles of women and men are targeted for genocidal violence precisely because those roles are seen as crucial to the group's ability to constitute itself, whether culturally or biologically. Gendered social structures, meanwhile, can shape the conditions that lead to vulnerability or survivability, while gendered access to postconflict power can impact the accounts of genocide that emerge as authoritative.[1]

While gender seems so obviously core to the modalities and representations of genocidal violence, the particularly gendered harms experienced by women and men during times of large-scale violence are surprisingly difficult to unravel. Prior to the 1990s, scholarship excavating the role of gender in shaping the trajectories of genocidal violence was minimal, and the legal and policy architecture pertaining to international crimes was largely gender blind (hence gendered male). This situation has changed substantially since the 1990s, when the wars and atrocities committed in Rwanda and the former Yugoslavia sparked international outrage and mobilized legal and scholarly responses. The field of genocide studies has grown significantly since then, though gender remains underexamined, and new institutions, particularly international criminal courts, have been built to respond to and, hopefully, to prevent genocide.[2] But even these institutions have been slow to explore the range of gender harms experienced during large-scale violence.

Feminist transitional justice scholars have argued persuasively that naming and officially recognizing gendered forms of harm is essential to the postconflict transitional constitution of social and political order.[3] International criminal courts have become a key site where this process of recognition unfolds. While other transitional justice mechanisms, such as the *gacaca* courts in Rwanda, also provide some accountability for gendered forms of genocidal violence, international criminal courts have emerged as the most authoritative site for the production of official knowledge about what happened to women and men during large-scale violence, like genocide, and hence what harms need to be addressed as part of the transition from atrocity to "peace."[4]

In this chapter, I consider the role of international criminal prosecutions in feminist efforts to secure legal recognition of the gendered harms that accompany genocide. My focus is on the prosecution of sexual violence crimes by the Rwanda and Yugoslav war crimes tribunals. While sexual violence is only one dimension of gendered harm, it has become the most common form recognized as an international crime and the crime of genocide in particular. For good reasons, feminist scholars have raised concerns about the overattention to sexual violence and the presumption that this form of harm is most definitive of women's experience of genocide and other large-scale atrocities.[5] I analyze the prosecution of sexual violence harm as genocide precisely because it has become emblematic of gendered harm more generally. Gendered dimensions of violence accompanying genocide are both revealed and obscured by the prosecution of sexual violence as a genocide crime.

The Yugoslav and Rwanda tribunals, both established in the 1990s, have generated the most significant legal precedents on sexual violence as genocide. As I write this chapter in 2014, both tribunals are in the process of winding up their work, but they have established important precedents in exploring the gendered contours of contemporary genocide and large-scale atrocity. These two tribunals were the focus of feminist activism around the legal recognition of gendered forms of harm in the last two decades, and their judgments remain among the most comprehensive and groundbreaking.

My interest in this chapter is in the role of law in advancing understandings of, and international responses to, large-scale violence. The limits of law in the field of genocide are well known. The legal definition of genocide has been much analyzed and critiqued for its narrow focus on state-planned genocides, aimed at the biological rather than cultural existence of a community and with a high threshold for determining genocidal intent.[6] The international criminal trial, meanwhile, with its formal processes, constraining rules of evidence, and vulnerability to political interference, is seen as ill-suited to a thick accounting of the causes and circumstances of genocide. But, these accounts of the limits of law have not been entirely borne out by the operation of international criminal courts, some of which have provided detailed, contextual accounts of genocide and its social and political contexts. While the legal definition of genocide can constrain an accounting of genocide as a crime, in this chapter I suggest that some of the limits encountered in the criminal prosecution of genocide may reflect contemporary dynamics around dominant conceptions of the causes and solutions to large-scale violence. International criminal prosecutions are sites where various narratives about conflict, atrocity, and justice are shaped and given expression. This expressive capacity of international criminal law is equally as important in understanding the limits, and the possibilities, of law in securing an accounting of the complexity of genocide.

In both the Rwanda and Yugoslav tribunals, conceptions of the violence have been shaped by a particular "interpretive narrative" in which the atrocities in each of Rwanda and Yugoslavia are understood solely as the product of elite-orchestrated, ethnically inflected violence.[7] Sexual violence, in this account, is similarly reduced to a single causation—rape as an instrument of the genocide. These "meta-narratives," I argue, produce a number of troubling omissions that make a full accounting of gendered forms of harm difficult, even within the legal limits of the crime of genocide.

The final section of the chapter examines the ways in which international genocide prosecutions remain, despite these limitations, an important arena for the recognition of gendered forms of harm. International criminal law serves to express symbolic condemnation and "forg[e] an emerging consensus regarding international norms."[8] Law thus occupies a contradictory place: most scholars bemoan its limitations yet see it as offering a political opening for transformation unavailable elsewhere. In this chapter, I explore in more detail how international criminal law, and the prosecution of genocide crimes in particular, can be both these things—limited and open.

The first part of my analysis begins with a discussion of political and legal campaigns by feminists to secure legal recognition of rape as genocide. Here, I provide some introduction to the historical context in which a feminist "politics of presence" emerged, and I then highlight some of the important legal decisions by the Rwanda and Yugoslav tribunals on rape, genocide, and crimes against humanity that resulted.[9] The second section investigates the "meta-narrative" of the violence in Rwanda and Yugoslavia that structured the work of the tribunals, particularly in the early stages of their operation. The third section addresses how this meta-narrative is found also in the dominant political and legal conceptions of rape "as a weapon of war."

Seeing Rape as Genocide

When war broke out in Yugoslavia in the early 1990s, reports of violence revealed that civilian populations were being specifically targeted for acts of brutality. The widespread use of rape against women, in particular, received significant press coverage. These rapes were described by international and local observers as a targeted policy to force or coerce civilians from one group to leave a geographical area claimed by another.[10] Women from particular ethnic or national communities were often publicly raped as a means to terrorize local populations. Later reports would document the rapes of women held in prison camps in different locations in Bosnia.[11]

These and other atrocities appeared to be unfolding along "identity" lines. That is, the women from one "nationality" or ethnic community were being targeted for sexual and other violence by the men from another. The work of feminist sociologists, such as Floya Anthias and Nira Yuval-Davis, has mapped the ways in which "nation" is often understood in highly gendered terms: nation as mother; language as mother tongue; women as guardians of custom and national memory; and finally, women as keepers of the "home-fires" in times of war.[12] Mass rape of women in Yugoslavia was a phenomenon where gender, sexual violence, and nationalism were woven together.[13] The atrocities, like the conflicts themselves, seemed to confirm that the world was witnessing a war that was identity-based, where nationalism as an expression of identity had reached a tragic extreme.[14]

Leading feminist analyses published in the 1990s, such as Alexandra Stiglmayer's edited collection, *Mass Rape: The War Against Women in Bosnia*,[15] came to focus on rape as a weapon of war.[16] Other terms found in this literature include rape as an "instrument" of genocide,[17] an "engine of war,"[18] a "war tactic,"[19] and so on. Like "rape as a weapon of war," these expressions reflect a conception of rape as having a function[20] or use[21] in, for example, furthering militaristic, masculinist, and/or nationalist goals, such as the destruction of a community.[22]

The ethnic contours of the conflicts in Yugoslavia were central to this conception of rape as a "weapon" used by one side against the other. In the logic of ethnic difference, so went the argument, the attack of a woman was an attack on the community. Rape was widespread precisely because it was being used to achieve a goal in the conflict: the humiliation, forced removal, or even destruction of the "other" group.

This understanding of rape served, in turn, to highlight the utter inadequacy of international law and policy in addressing this violence. To the extent that rape was recognized as violating international law, it was characterized as a lesser offense and one linked to a woman's honor.[23] In this context, feminist scholars, activists, lawyers, and politicians lobbied to ensure that women's experiences of conflict violence would be recognized as an international crime, worthy of prosecution and condemnation. The focus of that effort was on including rape in the list of crimes that could be prosecuted by the international criminal tribunals for the former Yugoslavia and Rwanda. The overall results were mixed, and the statutes establishing the legal reach of the tribunals do not make much reference to rape or sexual violence. But subsequent judgments, and extensive feminist lobbying, began to deepen and extend the legal recognition of sexual violence and rape as international crimes, including the crime of genocide.

The question of whether rape could be a component of genocide surfaced as an issue among feminists in the early 1990s, and Catherine MacKinnon's 1993 article in *Ms. Magazine*[24] was an early intervention arguing strongly that rape in Bosnia should be seen as genocide.[25] While feminists themselves were divided about the tactical wisdom of arguing for rape as genocide (would this serve simply to make invisible rapes that did not fit the definition of genocide?), the legal case for recognizing rape as genocide was also not straightforward.

Genocide—like its close, legal neighbor "crimes against humanity"—has two main parts: first, the underlying, intentional criminal act ("killing," for example) that is committed; second, the intent to "destroy in whole or in part" a group. The Rwanda tribunal statute, as one example, defines genocide as the commissioning of certain listed acts with the intent of destroying a "national, ethnical, racial or religious" group. The list of acts that can form the underlying basis for genocide is not open-ended and includes only "killing members of the group; causing serious bodily or mental harm to members of the group; deliberately inflicting on the group conditions of life calculated to bring about its physical destruction in whole or in part; imposing measures intended to prevent births within the group; and forcibly transferring" children of the group to another group.[26] The problem facing those who argued that rape constituted genocide was that rape and sexual violence are not specifically included in this list. Compounding the omission, the drafts of the 1945 Genocide Convention, on which both the Rwanda and Yugoslav tribunal definitions are based, also did not include any mention of rape or sexual violence.[27] In order for rape to legally constitute the crime of genocide, then, judges would need to make an innovative ruling that sexual violence could be read into one of the five underlying acts listed above.

The first Rwanda tribunal decision in Prosecutor *v.* Akayesu made exactly this ruling, but only after prompting by feminist activists.[28] The Akayesu trial got underway in 1997 with the defendant, a mayor of Taba commune, charged with genocide but not with rape or sexual violence crimes. Two witnesses who were testifying during the trial "spontaneously" spoke of rapes they had experienced or observed. The judges questioned the witnesses further about the rapes, and more evidence came to light. In the vacuum created by a prosecutor's office seemingly disinterested in pursuing rape charges, an NGO—the Coalition for Women's Human Rights in Conflict Situations—stepped in and submitted an *amicus curiae* (friends of the court) brief calling on the Trial Chamber judges to amend the indictment to include rape charges and, further, to investigate why rape charges were not being properly brought in the first place.[29] The Office of the Prosecutor apparently relented and brought its own motion requesting permission to amend the indictment to include charges of rape or sexual violence, including rape as genocide. The chamber agreed, the indictment was amended, evidence and argument were presented about rapes that took place in Taba commune, and Jean-Paul Akayesu was eventually found guilty of genocide, including rape as genocide. The Trial Chamber ruled that the rapes committed in Taba commune were part of the genocidal violence and constituted serious bodily or mental harm to the Tutsi group, and thus fit the crime of genocide.

In making this determination, the Trial Chamber highlighted a number of factual elements about the rapes: they were widespread[30]; they were often public, including acts intended to humiliate the women[31]; they were frequently accompanied by mutilation of sexual organs, with women often killed after the rapes[32]; and, crucially, they were systematically targeted at Tutsi women "and solely against them."[33] The Trial Chamber concluded that rape and sexual violence could:

> constitute genocide in the same way as any other act as long as they were committed with the specific intent to destroy, in whole or in part, a particular group, targeted as such. Indeed, rape and sexual violence certainly constitute infliction of serious bodily and mental harm and are even ... one of the worst ways of inflict (sic) harm on the victim as he or she suffers both bodily and mental harm.[34]

The trial judgment was upheld on appeal, and the Akayesu ruling that rape and sexual violence could constitute genocide stands as one of the oft-cited achievements of the Rwanda tribunal. Akayesu was followed by several other judgments that also established legal precedent in recognizing that harm in conflict can take on gendered qualities that are instrumental to the commission of international crimes. The decision by the Yugoslav tribunal in Prosecutor v. Kunarac, Kovac, and Vukovic[35] was the first case where the charges related solely to sexual violence crimes, though genocide charges were not pursued.[36] The Trial Chamber found the three defendants guilty of rape and torture, both as constituting a crime against humanity and a war crime, and two of the defendants guilty of enslavement (for exercising de facto ownership and power over women in their custody) as a crime against humanity.

In Prosecutor v. Krstic, the Yugoslav tribunal also made an innovative ruling, not on sexual violence this time, but on the gendered social relations that influenced how genocidal violence was planned and then impacted the surviving community.[37] The Trial Chamber ruled that the Bosnian Muslim community in eastern Bosnia was patriarchal in nature, which meant the community was effectively destroyed, in whole or in part, as a result of the Srebrenica massacre that killed 7,000–8,000 Bosnian Muslim men and boys. The chamber further ruled that Serb forces were aware of the patriarchal nature of the community and the devastation that the deaths of the men would have on the surviving women, children, and elderly.[38] The chamber determined that the Srebrenica massacre constituted the crime of genocide.[39]

These and other decisions have begun to offer a more detailed accounting of how gendered norms, beliefs, and practices are implicated in large-scale violence, in understanding both the types of violence used and its effect on victims. The commitment to prosecuting sexual violence crimes dropped off substantially after these cases, and the overall record of rape and sexual violence cases in international courts is dismal.[40] While these landmark cases, and a few others, have established important precedents for the legal recognition of the gendered harms caused by international crimes, there is another reason to be cautious. Daniel Bloxham and Dirk Moses have argued that genocide studies need to move beyond simply considering the outcomes deemed to constitute "upper case *Genocide*" and broaden the analysis to consider the "context in which genocide occurs."[41] The same is true of legal decisions adjudicating genocide charges.

While written judgments, including precedent-setting decisions like Akayesu and Krstic, are important to consider, it is equally imperative to place those decisions in their particular historical and institutional context. In the following discussion, I argue that these notable decisions unfolded in a context where violence and its causes were understood almost exclusively in terms of identity-based conflict, whereas violence was understood as resulting from elite orchestration of latent ethnic grievance. This framework, I argue below, has exerted a powerful conceptual pull on the work of the Yugoslav and Rwanda tribunals and has implications for how, and in what terms, gendered harms are recognized as aspects of genocide and other international crimes.

Making Sense of Violence

In the mid- to late 1990s, when both the Yugoslav and Rwanda tribunals were beginning their work, there was a growing consensus in some international policy and scholarly circles that the conflicts in these two regions were problematically portrayed as resulting from tribal, atavistic hatreds. Scholars and policy practitioners began emphasizing the conflicts as constructed, elite-driven, modern, and intentional.[42] Robert Hayden, a US-based scholar of the Balkan region and two-time expert witness at the Yugoslav tribunal, describes Western state and institutional responses to the war in Yugoslavia as "informed by a particular teleology—in which the demise of Yugoslavia was an aberration, a disaster caused by evil politicians, whose culpability needs to be shown so that normalcy can be obtained."[43] Scott Straus, writing on the Rwanda genocide, refers to a "new consensus" about Rwanda that emerged in scholarly and activist work in the 1990s. "Rather than seeing the violence as chaotic frenzy, as state failure, or an explosion of atavistic animosities, scholars and human rights activists alike stress the violence was modern, systematic and intentional."[44]

The "new consensus," as Straus calls it, emerged partly in response to simplistic characterizations by Western media, and some political leaders, of the conflicts as "ethnic" or "tribal" violence. Warren Christopher, then secretary of State in the United States, described the violence in the Yugoslav regions in 1993 as a "problem from hell": "The hatred between all three groups . . . is almost unbelievable. It's almost terrifying, and it's centuries old."[45] Christopher's phrase—"a problem from hell"—became the title of Samantha Power's Pulitzer prize-winning book, which was a strongly argued *tour de force* about US government failure to officially recognize and respond to genocide and mass violence in various non-US locations, including Yugoslavia and Rwanda. For Power, Christopher's comment reflected a US government strategy to absolve itself of responsibility by characterizing the violence in Yugoslavia as an amoral mess; centuries-old grievances that were beyond US intervention.[46]

Against the powerful trope of "tribal violence," the new consensus was, in some respects, an attempt to insert complexity and responsibility (of local leaders but also Western decision-makers) into the discussions about mass atrocity. Within this framing, identity markers such as ethnicity and race remain important, but not as leading inevitably to violence. Rather they are understood as devices, or cultural codes, that could be manipulated by criminal elites to foster fear and violence.

For example, in the Rwanda tribunal case Prosecutor *v.* Nahimana, Barayagwiza, and Ngeze the three defendants, all charged with multiple counts of genocide and crimes against humanity, were depicted by the prosecution as ideologues of the Hutu power movement and as instigators of a propaganda campaign waged on radio, in print, and through the extremist political party, the *Coalition pour la defense de la république* (CDR), to incite ethnic fear, hatred, and then violence against Rwandan Tutsi.[47] In its judgment, the Trial Chamber found that the radio station, RTLM, and the newspaper, *Kangura*, did engage in incitement to ethnic hatred and violence. It ruled that RTLM broadcasts "exploited the history of Tutsi privilege and Hutu disadvantage, and the fear of armed insurrection, to mobilize the population, whipping them into a frenzy of hatred and violence that was directed largely against the Tutsi ethnic group."[48] The three defendants, including in their roles as leaders and managers of RTLM, *Kangura*, and CDR, were found guilty of multiple genocide charges, including direct and public incitement to genocide.[49]

The Trial Chamber's determinations in this and other cases are not, in my view, necessarily *in*accurate. My point here is that the careful depiction of the violence as resulting from elite manipulation of ethnic identities (rather than inexplicable atavistic hatred) is itself an epistemological claim that serves, among other things, to make it possible to conceive of international criminal prosecutions as a justifiable international response to large-scale violence. If the conflicts are understood as resulting from the actions of rational, calculating individuals, then it is possible that the events in Rwanda and

Yugoslavia were "not tribalism run amok" but, instead, were international crimes, like genocide.[50]

The understanding of large-scale violence as resulting from cynically contrived, local, elite-orchestrated ethic conflict, I suggest, exerted a powerful conceptual pull at least in the early days of the tribunals. The lawyers, judges, and clerks hired to work at the tribunals were drawn from various regions across the globe, and almost none of them had any working knowledge of the conflict regions or even the local languages. Faced with the enormity of prosecuting the most serious of international crimes—genocide and crimes against humanity—the judges and lawyers sought a framework within which they could explain what had happened. According to Robert Donia, a fourteen-time expert witness at the Yugoslav tribunal, "What they [ICTY judges] pretty much all feel is a need for a vehicle to frame the alien world they are being asked to render judgments on."[51] Navanethem Pillay, former judge of the Rwanda tribunal, described the approach of judges in the first Rwanda tribunal case of Akayesu in similar terms: "We judges agreed that you can't avoid this question of history of Rwanda, otherwise it's just one ethnic group killing another ethnic group with no reason why. History is necessary for an understanding of why the conflict occurred. Our first judgment—Akayesu—did this."[52]

The prosecutors Robert Donia encountered at the Yugoslav tribunal were not looking for just any kind of historical narrative, he found, but "one that could be inserted in indictments, could impute motivations of actors as rational rather than crazed and wild; in general, that could make some sense."[53] Making "sense," for both Donia and Judge Pillay, is rooted in a dichotomous way of conceiving the violence: as tribal or atavistic hatred on the one hand, or as intentional elite orchestration on the other. Within the logic of this dichotomy, the tribunals' focus on elite responsibility is not seen as a "version" of what happened but simply as common sense; a laudable rejection of the "ancient ethnic hatreds" characterization.

Once again, and to be clear, there are many aspects of this account of the violence that I find persuasive, particularly as it pertains to the Rwanda conflict and genocide. But the "new consensus," as a type of "master narrative," also offers an additional "level of information" about the conditions in which certain (gendered) accounts of the causes and consequences of violence are possible at a given time.[54] Attending to master or meta-narratives also helps reveal the true effects that result when a particular framing of events exerts such comprehensive explanatory power. The difficulty, I suggest, is that forms of violence, and categories of perpetrators and victims that do not fit within the common sense understanding of the violence, are simply disregarded or otherwise dismissed. In the following section, I focus on the judgments of the Rwanda tribunal in particular, to argue that the legal recognition of gendered harms, including sexual violence, has been constrained by the gravitational pull of an understanding of the violence in terms of elite manipulation of ethnic identities.

Making Sense of Rape

An understanding of rape and sexual violence as a means to target a community of people for violence and destruction fits well within the "new consensus" that emerged to explain the violence in Bosnia and Rwanda. In many of the feminist accounts discussed above, the significance of women's cultural location as the symbols of the nation was emphasized. In the political and scholarly context of the 1990s, these arguments were important to make. Women were largely excluded from discussions about war and its effects, except when they were seen as the wives and mothers of brave soldiers.[55] Emphasizing the sexual victimization of women disrupted some of the dominant narrative scripts about war and its location, participants, and effects. Placing women's (violated) bodies into policy and legal discussions about war highlighted that women were a part of war, that the violence against them was not incidental and minor, and that women were targets for violence because of, for example, the gendered norms of motherhood and marriage.[56]

Fionnuala Ní Aoláin refers to feminist activism of this period as engaging in a "politics of presence" that sought to move "women into view as relevant actors."[57] This was a "hard-headed" feminist activism, she argues, that emphasized women as victims and strategically highlighted women's roles as mothers and wives in structuring their violence and suffering.[58] In many ways, this was also a successful feminist intervention. The recognition of rape as a "weapon of war" or an "instrument of the genocide" took hold in legal, policy, and public consciousness. It has become the dominant frame within which the gendered nature of conflict violence is understood. The United Nations Security Council has passed six landmark resolutions recognizing the impact of armed conflict on women and the need for women's participation in peacebuilding activities. A significant theme throughout these "women, peace and security" resolutions, as they are known, is the recognition of women's experience of sexual violence in armed conflict.[59] Similarly, in the legal prosecution of war crimes, including genocide, rape as a weapon of war or as an instrument of the genocide has also become the dominant explanatory framework within which discussions of sexual harm are placed.[60]

While these political and legal developments are important in making visible and taking seriously conflict sexual violence, they also portray violence and its effects in narrow ways that produce some troubling omissions. Rape as a "weapon of war" or "instrument of the genocide" has resulted in a disproportionate focus on both sexual violence and sexual violence in connection with orchestrated atrocities that fit the model of the "new consensus." That is, conflict rape is predominantly, almost exclusively, now understood as an instrument wielded by militias and armies against the women of a different community in order to harm or destroy that community.

But this narrative, while an important explanation of some sexualized violence, is not accurate for all rapes and all conflicts. Some research has begun to challenge the too-easy assumptions about the perpetrators, victims, and contexts of conflict sexual violence woven into assertions about rape as a weapon of war.[61] Elisabeth Wood, for example, broke important ground by specifically challenging assumptions about the inevitability of rape in war.[62] She studied examples of armed conflicts where rape was "rare," revealing a "neglected fact" that rape is not always a substantial feature of conflict, and, by closely examining when and in what contexts conflict rape is widespread, we can help identify conditions that impact its prevalence.[63]

Other researchers have revealed the different kinds of rape and different categories of perpetrators and victims omitted from accounts premised on the singular explanation of rape "as a weapon of war."[64] "Everyday" rape, rape in "peace" time, rape by civilians, and rape against certain kinds of victims may be overlooked or minimized when "rape as a weapon of war" is the dominant lens.[65]

Genocide prosecutions, particularly of rape as genocide, tend to exacerbate these omissions. In an understanding of conflict and violence as emanating from elite manipulation of ethnic identity designed to destroy a group within the polity, legal attention is focused on the elite and their (criminal) responsibility. Evidence that will demonstrate this responsibility, such as chains of command but also continuity in the types and mechanism of violence, are prioritized. The resulting "top-down" focus on violence perpetuates the omission of the range of harms suffered by women and men and the complexities of the labels "perpetrator" and "victim."

In the Rwanda tribunal, for example, the focus of many of the sexual violence determinations by Trial Chambers was on the patterns of rape. In Akayesu, the Trial Chamber's assessment of the genocidal nature of the rapes was underpinned by the conclusion that in "most cases" Tutsi women were raped and then killed.[66] In other cases, the Trial Chambers emphasized that the rapes were highly public, often occurring at roadblocks.[67] And throughout, there was particular attention to the deemed ethnic identities of the victims and perpetrators.

In this emphasis on patterns and commonalities, acts of violence that do not fit within larger patterns can be too easily discounted as idiosyncratic, or as not sufficiently systematic to warrant prosecution. For example, "forced marriage"—or "forced enslavement" as it is sometimes called[68]— has not been prosecuted by the Rwandan tribunal, even while there is some evidence that women were "married" or held in sexual servitude during the genocide.[69] Given the disappointing record of the International Criminal Tribunal for Rwanda (ICTR) on sexual violence prosecutions generally, this particular omission on its own is not too surprising.[70] But "forced marriage" or "sexual enslavement" also does not fit well within the depiction of rape as genocide outlined by the Trial Chamber in Akayesu and other cases, where the patterns of the rapes are identified as a prelude to killing and as taking place in very public surroundings.

Certain categories of perpetrators and victims who do not fit the dominant account of rape as genocide can also be difficult to see. In Akayesu, the Trial Chamber concluded that rape was "perpetrated against all Tutsi women and solely against them."[71] This same determination can be found in the dissenting judgment in Kajelijeli, in which Judge Ramaroson concluded that "rape and sexual violence were exclusively perpetrated against Tutsi women (of which only some cases were reported to us) and were committed on grounds of their ethnicity."[72]

Yet, Hutu women were also raped and killed, particularly in the early days of the genocide, because of their presumed political opposition to the Habyarimana government and/or extremist Hutu elements.[73] Hutu women married to Tutsi men were likewise targeted for rape, as were Hutu women accused of helping Tutsi to escape. But the violence surrounding the genocide made all women, irrespective of their deemed ethnic identity or political affiliation, vulnerable to rape.[74] Just as Hutu women were hard to see as victims of the genocide, so too were the men subjected to rape and sexual violence. The ICTR did not prosecute any sexual violence cases where men were the victims, though there is evidence that sexual violence, including rape and forms of sexual slavery against men, was a feature of the genocide.[75]

Finally, rape as genocide may also have an impact on how other gender harms are not seen as part of genocidal violence. Ní Aoláin has argued that international criminal law has, for the most part, ignored the:

experiences that women might describe as most damaging . . . [such as] harms to their children, destruction and insecurity to their private spaces, humiliation and discrimination based on sex, economic deprivations, and the range of sex-based acts that constitute violent experiences to the female person but are not formally acknowledged as such by international or domestic law.[76]

Further, she notes that the dominant focus on the violence experienced by specific individuals overlooks the ways in which families and communities who are "emotionally tied to the victim or in a relationship of co-dependency with them" are also affected.[77] These "connected harms" are largely invisible within a legal framework preoccupied with the civil and political harms experienced by individual men and women.

The Krstic decision on the Srebrenica genocide stands out as a notable exception in this regard. The Trial Chamber in this case gave substantial consideration to evidence about the ways in which the surviving members of the community of Bosnian Muslims were impacted by the killings of large numbers of men and boys. The chamber, for example, recognized the existence of "Srebrenica syndrome," a "new pathology category" that refers to the unique difficulties arising from the (then) large number of unconfirmed deaths of the Muslim men from Srebrenica. The 7,000–8,000 men killed in Srebrenica had been buried and then moved out of mass grave sites, making identification of their bodies difficult. At the time of the trial, many of the men were still classified as "missing." The suffering caused by this uncertainty posed a particular problem for this community, the chamber ruled, because "for Bosnian Muslim women it is essential to have a clear marital status."[78] For this and other reasons connected to the patriarchal nature of the affected community, the Trial Chamber concluded that "by killing all the military aged men, the Bosnian Serb forces effectively destroyed the community of the Bosnian Muslims in Srebrenica as such and eliminated all likelihood that it could ever reestablish itself on that territory."[79] These acts constituted the crime of genocide.[80]

But the decision in Krstic has been criticized by legal scholars for overreaching in its analysis of genocide and for a "patronizing" speculation about the effects of the Srebrenica massacre on the surviving community.[81] While I share some of these critiques, the legal judgment in Krstic, despite its limitations, remains a rare exception to the rule that gendered harms of genocide are most likely to be seen as rape and related forms of sexual violence and that these acts are understood as a highly efficient "instrument" by which the genocide was enacted.[82]

The account of rape as an "instrument of the genocide" has epistemological effects, I argue, much like the "new consensus" outlined above. In addition to producing a range of omissions in the types of harms and victims that can be recognized, this instrumentalized account of rape also limits the questions that are asked about sexual violence and about the range of harms and violence that accompany genocide. "Rape as an instrument of the genocide" leads away from questions about *why* rape (or other modalities of violence) happened. Violence is understood exclusively as the product of a two-sided, identity-based conflict, minimizing, in turn, the social, political, and economic structures within which genocide and other large-scale atrocities unfold.

Making Sense of Law

The limitations that result from criminal prosecutions of rape as an instrument of genocide reflect what Ní Aoláin refers to as the "capture problem"; the difficulty that transitional justice institutions, such as international criminal courts, have in accounting for the range of conflict harms that women experience.[83] The "capture problem" is found in multiple areas of law, not just genocide prosecutions, and feminist lawyers and academics have long been wary about criminal prosecution of sexual violence crimes even in national legal contexts. British sociologist Carol Smart, for one, writing in the 1980s, warned about the limits for feminists in seeking to better use law for women's benefit. She argued that law gives itself the sole authority to determine "the truth of things," disqualifying, in turn, feminist knowledges that fall outside law's truth. The rape trial exemplifies this power, she said, and demonstrates the enduring authority of phallocentric sexuality. Women's accounts of sexuality and violence are "strained" through the legal form of the trial, with the result that law "consistently fails to 'understand' accounts of rape which do not fit with the narrowly constructed legal definition (or Truth) of rape."[84]

While Smart's account of the limits of the rape trial is somewhat overdrawn, her analysis of law's power holds some lessons for contemporary feminist engagement with international criminal law. International criminal prosecutions, and the focus on prosecuting genocide crimes in particular, may be a limiting forum within which to seek a full accounting of women's experiences of large-scale violence. Other transitional justice mechanisms such as reparations and lustration should be explored as additional, important sites to bring about a more gender-sensitive account of conflict and harm.[85] Yet, as Smart herself noted, law may have its limits, but it is also a powerful arena. For all its limitations, international criminal law is not a forum that feminists can easily dismiss. Smart urged feminists to revisit their strategic goals in light of law's power. As a tool to promote women's interests, law can be limiting and produce effects antithetical to feminist goals. But precisely because law has the power to "redefine the truth of events," it "cannot go unchallenged."[86]

The postgenocide transitional period, as is now widely recognized, is a time of great flux, where political, social, and economic institutions are being rebuilt and often transformed. Transitional justice processes, in this period of change, are important sites at which the terms of postconflict public life and citizenship are constituted. The criminal trial, for all its deficiencies, has become the most important of the transitional institutions—truth commissions, memorialization, and the like—that are deployed in transitioning countries.[87] For reasons too complex to develop here, international criminal trials offer an authoritative arena in which internationally agreed norms and values are given expression.[88]

In the important performative space of the international criminal trial, a feminist "politics of presence," even with all the reservations noted above, is still required. The legal recognition of gendered forms of harm and particular categories of victims and perpetrators provide an important basis for claims to full inclusion in both the accounting of large-scale atrocity and the social rebuilding that follows.[89] The dismissal or exclusion of women's experiences of large-scale crimes can be seen as a form of "misrecognition" and social subordination.[90] In this context, the demand for recognition of the full range of gendered harms experienced by women and men, for example, is a means to "overcome status subordination by changing the values that regulate interaction."[91]

International criminal prosecution as a form of recognition is arguably even more crucial in the area of genocide crimes. Genocide is generally considered the "crime of crimes" and as occupying a higher status in the list of crimes prosecuted by international courts.[92] Both the Rwanda and Yugoslav tribunals have prioritized genocide convictions over the prosecution of other crimes, for example, and the label "genocide" is often sought after in other contexts to secure heightened attention to situations of mass atrocity.[93] As Payam Akhavan notes, the label "genocide" offers the prospect of "meta-legal recognition."[94] In this context, the legal recognition of the gendered dimensions of genocide is particularly important, even while the legal arena offers a mixed, and at times limiting, space for this to happen.

Conclusion

Contemporary understandings of genocides in the twentieth and twenty-first centuries have highlighted the significance of the "body politic" to the rationality and mechanisms of orchestrated violence.[95] Gendered norms, relations, and beliefs are important devices by which the very idea of the body politic coheres. Women's bodies, in particular, often figure in representations of the borders of the political unity of a given population. It is perhaps not surprising that violence against women, and sexual violence against women and men, can sometimes feature as mechanisms by which communities are targeted for harm and possible destruction. What is more surprising is how difficult it is to "capture" the ways in which gender, and gendered forms of harm, are woven into genocidal violence.

In this chapter, I have explored international criminal prosecutions as one setting in which the role of gender in some contemporary examples of genocide has been examined. I have argued that international law offers a paradoxical site for this exploration. It is a limited arena, and the legal definition of genocide further constrains the types of harms that can be visible as linked to genocide. But even within these restrictions, I have argued, more attention is needed on the dominance of meta-narratives about contemporary forms of identity-based conflicts and the role of instrumentalized sexual violence—rape as a weapon of war—within that framing.

Yet, I conclude by noting that law offers the possibilities for pushing the range of voices and knowledges that can be placed before it, even with its tendency to dismiss or colonize dissonant accounts. It remains an important arena, for all its limitations, within which to contest and, hopefully, expand official accounts of the gender dimensions of contemporary forms of genocide and other large-scale violence.

Notes

1   A. Hájková, "Sexual Barter in Times of Genocide: Negotiating the Sexual Economy of the Theresienstadt Ghetto," *Signs* 38:3 (Spring 2013), pp. 503–33.

2   A. Curthoys and J. Docker, "Defining Genocide," in *The Historiography of Genocide*, ed. D. Stone (Cambridge, UK: Cambridge University Press, 2008).

3   F. Ní Aoláin, "Emerging Paradigms of Rationality: Exploring a Feminist Theory of Harm in the Context of Conflicted and Post-Conflicted Societies," *Queen's Law Journal* 35:1 (Fall 2009), pp. 219–44; F. Ní Aoláin, "Advancing Feminist Positioning in the Field of Transitional Justice," *International Journal of Transitional Justice* 6:2 (2012), pp. 205–28; D. Buss, "Performing Legal Order: Some Feminist Thoughts On International Criminal Law," *International Criminal Law Review: Special Issue on Women & International Criminal Law* 11 (2011), pp. 409–23.

4   D. Buss, "Knowing Women: Translating Patriarchy in International Criminal Law," *Social & Legal Studies* 23:1 (2014), pp. 73–92; P. Dixon and C. Tenove, "International Criminal Justice as a Transnational Field: Rules, Authority and Victims," *International Journal of Transitional Justice* 7:3 (2013), pp. 393–412.

5   For a more detailed discussion, see N. Henry, "The Fixation on Wartime Rape: Feminist Critique and International Criminal Law," *Social & Legal Studies* 23:1 (2014), pp. 93–111.

6   W. Schabasl, *Genocide in International Law: The Crime of Crimes*, 2nd edn (Cambridge, UK: Cambridge University Press, 2009); for an overview see Curthoys and Docker, *Defining Genocide*.

7   P. Akhavan, *Reducing Genocide to Law: Definition, Meaning and the Ultimate Crime* (Cambridge, UK: Cambridge University Press, 2012), p. 108.

8   D. Bloxham and D. O. Pendas, "Punishment as Prevention? The Politics of Prosecuting Génocidaires," in *The Oxford Handbook of Genocide Studies*, ed. D. Bloxham and A. Moses (Oxford, UK: Oxford University Press, 2010), pp. 617–35.

9   Ní Aoláin, "Advancing Feminist Positioning."

10 See, for example, R. Gutman, *A Witness to Genocide: The 1993 Pulitzer Prize-Winning Dispatches on the "Ethnic Cleansing" of Bosnia* (New York, NY: Macmillan, 1993); Helsinki Watch, *War Crimes in Bosnia-Hercegovina*, vol. I (New York, NY: Human Rights Watch, 1992).

11 Prosecutor *v.* Kunarac, Kovac, and Vukovic, Case nos ICTY-IT-96-23-T and ICTY-IT-96-23-1-T, Judgment (February 22, 2001).

12 F. Anthias and N. Yuval-Davis, *Racialized Boundaries: Race, Nation, Gender, Colour and Class and the Anti-Racist Struggle* (London, UK: Routledge, 1992).

13 D. Buss, "Women at the Borders: Rape and Nationalism in International Law," *Feminist Legal Studies* 6:2 (1998), p. 171; S. A. Sofos, "Inter-Ethnic Violence and Gendered Constructions of Ethnicity in Former Yugoslavia," *Social Identities* 2:1 (1996): p. 73; J. Mertus, "'Women' in the Service of National Identity," *Hastings Women's Law Journal* 5 (Winter 1994), p. 5.

14 M. Kaldor, *New and Old Wars: Organized Violence in a Global Era* (Stanford, CA: Stanford University Press, 1999); M. Ignatieff, *Blood and Belonging: Journey into the New Nationalism* (Toronto, Canada: Penguin Canada, 1994).

15 A. Stiglmayer, *Mass Rape: The War Against Women in Bosnia-Herzegovina* (Lincoln, NE: University of Nebraska Press, 1994).

16 See, for example, B. Allen, *Rape Warfare: The Hidden Genocide in Bosnia-Herzegovina and Croatia* (Minneapolis, MN: University of Minnesota Press, 1996); R. Seifert, "War and Rape: A Preliminary Analysis;" C. MacKinnon, "Rape, Genocide, and Women's Human Rights;" and R. Copelon, "Surfacing Gender: Reconceptualizing Crimes Against Women in Time of War," in *Mass Rape: The War Against Women in Bosnia-Herzegovina*, ed. A. Stiglmayer (Lincoln, NE: University of Nebraska Press, 1994), pp. 54–72, 183–95, 197–218, respectively; E. Kohn, "Rape as a Weapon of War: Women's Human Rights During the Dissolution of Yugoslavia," *Golden Gate University Law Review* 24 (1994), pp. 199–223; Hastings Law Symposium, "Rape as a Weapon of War in the Former Yugoslavia," *Hastings Women's Law Journal* 5:1 (1994), pp. 69–88.

17 K. D. Askin, "Prosecuting Wartime Rapes and Other Gender-Related Crimes under International Law: Extraordinary Advances, Enduring Obstacles," *Berkeley Journal of International Law* 21:2 (2003), pp. 288–349.

18 Copelon, *Surfacing Gender*, p. 205.

19 T. L. Tompkins, "Prosecuting Rape as a War Crime: Speaking the Unspeakable," *Notre Dame Law Review* 70 (1995), p. 859.

20 Seifert, *War and Rape*, p. 55.

21 C. MacKinnon, "Turning Rape into Pornography: Postmodern Genocide," *Ms. Magazine* 5:1 (July/August, 1993), pp. 24–30.

22 Copelon, *Surfacing Gender*, p. 206; MacKinnon, "Rape, Genocide, and Women's Human Rights," p. 75; Seifert, *War and Rape*, p. 62; Kohn, "Rape as a Weapon of War," p. 203.

23 Ní Aoláin, "Advancing Feminist Positioning," pp. 205–28.

24 MacKinnon, "Turning Rape into Pornography," pp. 24–30.

25 For a discussion, see Elisa von Joeden-Forgey, "Gender and Genocide," in *The Oxford Handbook of Genocide Studies*, pp. 69–71; D. Buss, "Sexual Violence, Ethnicity, and the Limits of Intersectionality in International Criminal Law," in *Intersectionality and Beyond: Law, Power and the Politics of Location*, ed. E. Grabham, D. Cooper, J. Krishnadas, and D. Herman (London, UK: Routledge, 2008), pp. 105–23.

26 International Criminal Tribunal for Rwanda, Article 2: 2, ICTR Statute.

27 For a discussion, see A. L. M. de Brouwer, *Supranational Criminal Prosecution of Sexual Violence: The ICC and the Practice of the ICTY and the ICTR* (Antwerp, Belgium: Oxford Intersentia, 2005), p. 43.

28 Prosecutor *v.* Akayesu, Case no. ICTR-96-4-T, Judgment (September 2, 1998).

29 For a discussion, see B. Van Schaack, "Engendering Genocide: The Akayesu Case Before the International Criminal Tribunal for Rwanda," in *Human*

Rights Advocacy Stories (Law Stories), ed. D. R. Hurwitz, M. L. Satterthwaite, and D. B. Ford (New York, NY: Foundation Press, 2008).

30 Prosecutor *v.* Akayesu, paragraph 706.

31 Ibid., paragraph 731.

32 Ibid., paragraph 733.

33 Ibid., paragraph 732.

34 Ibid., paragraph 731.

35 Prosecutor *v.* Kunarac, Kovac, and Vukovic, Case nos. IT-96-23-T and IT-96-23-1-T (February 22, 2001).

36 Genocide charges were rarely pursued by the ICTY for reasons too complex to discuss here.

37 Prosecutor *v.* Krstic, Case no. ICTR-IT-98-33-T, Judgment (August 2, 2001).

38 Ibid., paragraph 595.

39 For further discussion see Buss, "Knowing Women."

40 D. Buss, "Rethinking Rape as a Weapon of War," *Feminist Legal Studies* 17:2 (2009), pp. 145–63; K. Campbell, "The Gender of Transitional Justice: Law, Sexual Violence and the International Criminal Tribunal for the Former Yugoslavia," *International Journal of Transitional Justice* 1:3 (2007), pp. 411–32; Henry, *The Fixation on Wartime Rape.*

41 Bloxham and Pendas, *Punishment as Prevention*, p. 8.

42 See, for example, African Rights, *Rwanda: Death, Despair and Defiance*, rev. edn (London, UK: African Rights, 1995); A. Des Forges, *Leave None to Tell the Story: Genocide in Rwanda* (New York, NY: Human Rights Watch, 1999); N. Malcolm, *Kosovo: A Short History* (London, UK: Papermac, 1998). The discussion in this section is narrowly focused on what I see as a meta-narrative about these conflicts as elite-orchestrated. A close reading of the vast scholarly literature that provides detailed analyses of the contexts of the violence in these two regions is beyond the scope of this chapter.

43 R. M. Hayden, *Blueprints for a House Divided: The Constitutional Logic of the Yugoslav Conflicts* (Ann Arbor, MI: University of Michigan Press, 1999), pp. 155–6.

44 S. Straus, *The Order of Genocide: Race, Power, and War in Rwanda* (Ithaca, NY: Cornell University Press, 2006), p. 33.

45 Interview with Warren Christopher, *Face the Nation*, CBS, March 28, 1993, cited in S. Power, *"A Problem from Hell:" America and the Age of Genocide* (New York, NY: Basic Books, 2002), p. 306.

46 Ibid., p. 306.

47 Prosecutor *v.* Nahimana, Barayagwiza and Ngeze, Case no. ICTR-99-52-A, Sentence and Judgment (November 28, 2007) ("media" case).

48 Ibid., paragraph 488.

49 Several of the convictions were, however, reversed on appeal, a full discussion of which is beyond the scope of this chapter.

50 Straus, *The Order of Genocide*, p. 33.

51 Interview with author via Skype, December 8, 2010.

52 R. Wilson, *Writing History in International Criminal Trials* (Cambridge, UK: Cambridge University Press, 2011), p. 72.

53 Interview with author via Skype, December 8, 2010.

54 See also Hájková, *Sexual Barter in Times of Genocide*, p. 504.

55 J. B. Elshtain, *Women and War* (New York, NY: Basic Books, 1987).

56 For further discussion, see D. Buss, "Seeing Sexual Violence in Conflict and Post-Conflict Societies: The Limits of Visibility," in *Sexual Violence in Conflict and Post-Conflict Societies: International Agendas and African Contexts*, ed. D. Buss, J. Lebert, B. Rutherford, and D. Sharkey (London, UK: Routledge Press, 2014).

57 Ní Aoláin, "Advancing Feminist Positioning," p. 220.

58 Ibid., p. 219.

59 L. J. Shepherd, "Sex, Security and Superhero(in)es: From 1325 to 1820 and Beyond," *International Feminist Journal of Politics* 13:4 (2011), p. 507.

60 Buss, "Rethinking Rape"; Buss, "Seeing Sexual Violence."

61 See, for example, C. Dolan, "*War is Not Yet Over*": *Community Perceptions of Sexual Violence and its Underpinnings in Eastern DRC* (London, UK: International Alert, 2010); Harvard Humanitarian Initiative and Oxfam International, "*Now the World is Without Me*": *An Investigation of Sexual Violence in Eastern Democratic Republic of the Congo* (April 2010); J. Kelly, "Rape in War: Motives of Militia in DRC," *Special Report: United States Institute of Peace* (2010), p. 243.

62 E. Wood, "Variations in Sexual Violence During War," *Politics & Society* 34:3 (2006), pp. 307–41; E. Wood, "Armed Groups and Sexual Violence: When is Wartime Rape Rare?" *Politics & Society* 37:1 (March 2009), pp. 131–62.

63 Ibid., p. 132.

64 M. E. Baaz and M. Stern, "The Complexity of Violence: A Critical Analysis of Sexual Violence in the Democratic Republic of Congo (DRC)," *Working Paper on Gender Based Violence* (Uppsala, Sweden: Swedish International Development Agency, 2010), pp. 1–70; J. Boesten, "Analyzing Rape Regimes at the Interface of War and Peace in Peru," *The International Journal of Transitional Justice* 4:1 (2010), pp. 110–29; Kelly, *Rape in War*; K. Theidon, "Gender in Transition: Common Sense, Women, and War," *Journal of Human Rights* 6 (2007), pp. 453–78; J. True, *The Political Economy of Violence Against Women* (New York, NY: Oxford University Press, 2012).

65 M. E. Baaz and M. Stern, "Why Do Soldiers Rape? Masculinity, Violence, and Sexuality in the Armed Forces in the Congo (DRC)," *International Studies Quarterly* 53:4 (2009), pp. 495–518; Baaz and Stern, *The Complexity of Violence*; Boesten, *Analyzing Rape Regimes*; Dolan, "*War is Not Yet Over*"; Harvard Humanitarian Initiative, *Now the World is Without Me*; Buss, "Rethinking Rape."

66 Prosecutor *v.* Akayesu, paragraph 733.

67 See, for example, Prosecutor *v.* Bagasora, Case no. ICTR-96-7-T (December 18, 2008), paragraph 1728.

68 A. Bunting, "'Forced Marriage' in Conflict Situations: Researching and Prosecuting Old Harms and New Crimes," *Canadian Journal of Human Rights* 1:1 (2012), pp. 165–85.

69 Human Rights Watch, *Shattered Lives: Sexual Violence during the Rwandan Genocide and its Aftermath* (New York, NY: Human Rights Watch, 1996).

70 Buss, "Rethinking Rape."

71 Prosecutor *v.* Akayesu, p. 732.

72 Prosecutor *v.* Kajelijeli, Case no. ICTR-98-44A-T, Dissenting Opinion of Judge Arlette Ramaroson (December 1, 2003), p. 97.

73 Human Rights Watch, *Shattered Lives*, pp. 40–1.

74 Ibid., p. 40.

75 Interview with Florida Kabasinga, Assistant Appeals Counsel, International Criminal Tribunal for Rwanda, May 6, 2008.

76 Ní Aoláin, "Emerging Paradigms of Rationality," p. 23.

77 Ibid., p. 25.

78 Prosecutor *v.* Krstic, paragraph 93.

79 Ibid., paragraph 597.

80 For a more detailed discussion, see Buss, "Knowing Women."

81 See for example, Schabas, *Genocide in International Law*, p. 881.

82 Buss, "Knowing Women."

83 Ní Aoláin, "Advancing Feminist Positioning," p. 224.

84 C. Smart, *Feminism and the Power of Law: Sociology of Law and Crime* (New York, NY: Routledge, 1989), p. 26.

85 Ní Aoláin, "Advancing Feminist Positioning."

86 Smart, *Feminism and the Power of Law*, p. 164.

87 Dixon and Tenove, "International Criminal Justice," pp. 393–412.

88 J. B. Elander, "The Victim's Address: Expressivism and the Victim at the Extraordinary Chambers in the Courts of Cambodia," *International Journal of Transitional Justice* 7:1 (2013), pp. 95–115; D. M. Amann, "Group Mentality, Expressivism, and Genocide," *International Criminal Law Review* 21:2 (2002), pp. 92–143; M. A. Drumbl, *Atrocity, Punishment and International Law* (Cambridge, UK: Cambridge University Press, 2007).

89 Ní Aoláin, "Advancing Feminist Positioning."

90 N. Fraser, "Rethinking Recognition," *New Left Review* 3 (May/June 2000), p. 113; Henry, *The Fixation on Wartime Rape*, p. 106.

91 Ibid., pp. 114–15.

92 For a discussion, see Akhavan, *Reducing Genocide to Law*.

93 M. Mamdani, "The Politics of Naming: Genocide, Civil War, Insurgency," *London Review of Books* 29:5 (March 2007), pp. 5–8. Available online:

http://www.lrb.co.uk/v29/n05/mahmood-mamdani/the-politics-of-naming-genocide-civil-war-insurgency.

94 Akhavan, *Reducing Genocide to Law*, p. 147.

95 M. Fleming, "Genocide and the Body Politic in the Time of Modernity," in *The Specter of Genocide: Mass Murder in Historical Perspective*, ed. R. Gellately and B. Kiernan (Cambridge, UK: Cambridge University Press, 2003), pp. 97–113.

13

Gender and the Future of Genocide Studies and Prevention

Elisa von Joeden-Forgey[1]

Gender-based violence, particularly mass rape, has become a core element of scholarly, legal, and activist approaches to genocide in the past ten years. There are many reasons for this: the ubiquity of sexual violence during the Bosnian, Rwandan, and Darfur genocides; the activist efforts of international feminists; the existence of women judges on international courts; and key legal findings, particularly the decision of the International Criminal Tribunal for Rwanda (ICTR) in the Prosecutor *v.* Akayesu trial, which established the myriad ways in which sexual violence can be a tool of genocide. This chapter will explore some of the less-developed implications of gender-sensitive research for our study of the subject in the future. I will focus principally on how gender research can productively engage our understanding of genocide as a historical process, how it can contribute to our conceptualization of the groups being targeted, how it can shape ideas of perpetrator intent, and, finally, how it can impact the way we define the crime. The upshot of the discussion presented here is that a gendered understanding of atrocity offers important tools for an early warning system—tools that should be incorporated into the research methodology and reporting strategies of the United Nations (UN), the International Criminal Court (ICC), human rights organizations, and other NGOs, as well as government agencies and intelligence services.

The study of gender and genocide began with the study of women, whose particular stories had been largely excluded from scholarship on the Holocaust and genocide up to the 1980s. It has not been an easy road. Bringing women back into the narrative required that scholars argue that these specific experiences mattered.[2] For doing this, they were sometimes accused of fomenting unnecessary discord between the sexes, as if the horror of genocide made gendered inquiry somehow irrelevant and even unseemly.[3] As gender research became more accepted by mainstream scholarship, feminist inquiry was then occasionally accused of ignoring the suffering of men and boys as well as the participation of women as perpetrators of genocide. Unfortunately, the critiques of feminist approaches to conflict tended to place gender analysis within a "competitive framework," where the fates of men and women too often become weighed in accordance with their perceived severity.[4] Just as feminists once argued (rather indisputably) that women's lives were being ignored by male scholars, their critics began to argue that men's fates were now being ignored by feminists.

It has been crucial, of course, to unearth men as gendered subjects in order to understand the complex ways in which gender informs the genocidal process. Of particular importance has been Adam Jones's work on the ways in which men, especially civilian men of "battle age," are victimized in times of genocide.[5] In "root-and-branch" genocides, they are often the first group to be separated out and massacred; in more common articulations of genocide, they can be the group slated for outright massacre while women and children suffer a range of fates involving rape, sexual exploitation, torture, forced maternity, murder, and expulsion.[6] Equally important has been the attempt to bring to light the ways in which women are perpetrators of genocide.[7] This latter subject in particular requires greater empirical and theoretical development. However, despite raising the very important subjects of men as victims and women as perpetrators of genocide, critiques of feminist inquiry have had a tendency to reject or ignore the gendered relations of domination that permeate all levels of patriarchal societies and inform, therefore, the context in which male victimization and female perpetration occur. The subtle argument sometimes seems to be that (civilian) men suffer the worst fate because they are so often targeted for direct killing. This casts men and women as opposing sides within a victim group and misses a key characteristic of genocidal violence: its targeting, through various means, of relations of affinity within victim groups in order to render these groups vulnerable to eventual elimination as historical agents.

Focusing on men, then, can and often does have the effect of marginalizing women's experiences once again or denying their centrality and importance, leading to definitions of genocide that prioritize the "strictly murderous dimension," usually understood as outright massacre, above all else.[8] This seriously underestimates the severity of rape and other forms of sexual torture during genocide, its lifelong effects, and the number of women and girls who die over time as a consequence of sexual violence. One side effect, then, of a "competitive framework" can be the failure to apprehend genocidal processes in the early stages, before we have mass murder; it can also unproductively muddy the waters in cases where women and children were "allowed" to continue living after suffering severe trauma that was intended by the perpetrators as part of an overarching plan to destroy a group.

Thankfully, the study of gender has now become an established and respected subfield within the genocide studies community, and competitive frameworks are gradually giving way to more sophisticated analyses that appreciate that the power of gender analysis lies not in prioritizing one victim group over another but in helping us to better understand the crime and therefore to better devise protocols for preventing and responding to it. It is therefore a propitious time to begin to draw out the implications of gender studies for our broader understanding of genocide as a process— its roots, its immediate causes, its shape, its aftermath, and ultimately its definition.

Although it is often assumed that gender research is limited to the stories of women, or to sexual violence, the "gender question" in genocide goes well beyond the experiences of women and girls, the perpetration of gender-based crimes (against both men and women), or even the comparative study of the experiences of men and women. It involves examining the network of gendered relationships that go into creating groups, whether in the objective world or in perpetrator subjectivity, and how ideas about creative power inform annihilatory violence. Gender follows the crime from its long-term origins, to short-term facilitators, to immediate indicators, to intervention, to justice and reconstruction after the fact. The gendered study of genocide therefore involves considering the simultaneous operation of gender within several different layers that contribute to the perpetration of the crime: the gendered concepts through which perpetrators understand power; the gendered ways in which they define their own group and the group(s) they are targeting; the gender dynamics that organize the economic, political, social, and familial spheres within perpetrator and victim societies; the gendered strategies pursued in the course of group destruction; the influence of gender on conceptions of self and on experiences of conflict among perpetrators, victims, bystanders, and witnesses; the gendered nature of international representations of and responses to a conflict; the use of gender in propaganda and in denial strategies; the gendered inflection of justice systems; and so forth. With the exception of extensive studies on the Holocaust, most of these topics have yet to be researched in great detail.

The growing number of gender-sensitive studies of genocide has added tremendously to our understanding of the crime and has challenged some of our thinking about its definition.[9] Gender, in fact, goes to the very heart of the crime of genocide. Because gender studies raises questions about the biological and cultural reproduction of groups, the construction of group identities, and the formation of perpetrator ideologies and perpetrator intent, any study of genocide in one way or another addresses gender, whether explicitly or implicitly. Because gender considerations open up for reflection the horrifying details of the crime scene, they also force us to reconstruct and catalog with excruciating specificity the crimes that were committed against each single member of a community and demand that we think anew about the nature of the crime. When considering all these things, genocide begins to emerge as a highly gendered crime.

Bringing the Women (and the Men) Back In

The study of women and genocide most recently has tended to focus on the phenomenon of mass rape. The genocides in Bosnia, Rwanda, and Darfur have forced changes in the way that the international community viewed mass rape, because in each case mass rape was clearly used systematically as a tool of genocide. The ad hoc tribunals, after much lobbying by feminists and women's NGOs, such as the authors of the CUNY *Clinic Memorandum* and the participants in the Women in the Law Project of the International Human Rights Law Group, began to prosecute rape as a war crime, a crime against humanity, and a crime of genocide, establishing important legal precedents that were incorporated into the statute of the ICC. The full and dramatic story of the "surfacing" of rape as a serious international crime in the past two decades has still to be written, but several shorter studies have sketched its general outline.[10]

The near ubiquity of mass rape during genocide raises important questions about its historical origins, its perpetrator intent, and, ultimately, what constitutes the crime of genocide. As Cynthia Enloe pointed out almost two decades ago, "We cannot completely understand any war—its causes, its paths, its consequences—unless male soldiers' sexual abuse of women on all sides is taken seriously, described accurately, explained fully, and traced forward and backward in time."[11] The same could be said of genocide. Focusing on rape in genocide puts gender-based violence front and center in our analysis, pointing in new directions forward and backward in time. It highlights a common experience of women victims, drawing their reality into our representations. The implications of this for genocide studies have only begun to be explored.

Although we commonly refer to "rape" in the singular, there are many crimes of rape that happen during genocidal processes. There are those rapes that are not part of an overarching plan and are the consequence of opportunity and impunity (often referred to as wartime rape); there is systematic mass rape, forced maternity, rape as a means of murder, sexual torture, gang rape, coerced rapes between family members, sexual mutilation, forced prostitution, sexual slavery, rape in rape camps, women forced to "marry" *génocidaires*, and so forth. We need to be specific in the way that we speak of sexual violence during genocide, examining each case and each type for its particular relationship to genocidal intent. The purpose would not be to rank types of rape in terms of degrees of severity but rather to better understand the words and actions of different groups of perpetrators so that we can begin to interpret rape's multiple functions during genocidal processes. Complicating our view of sexual violence, and understanding the implications of this for research on the origins and the function of mass rape during genocide, has the potential to yield important insights into perpetrators.

For example, to the extent that it has been addressed, it is generally assumed in cases of genocide that the rape of women and girls in the targeted victim group is a secondary phenomenon to the ideological hatred of the group. Genocidal ideology came first, followed by the use of rape as one tool among many. In many cases, such as Bosnia and Rwanda, mass rape was indeed systematic and intentional—implemented from the top down for the purposes of destroying, respectively, the Bosniak and Tutsi communities as such. In other cases, such as the Armenian genocide, new research has suggested that much of the sexual violence that attended the genocide was not centrally directed or part of the genocidal plan; instead there is evidence that certain perpetrators may in fact have joined the killing voluntarily, primarily because it gave them license to commit rape rather than out of a general hostility to Armenians. According to Henry Theriault, in certain cases "rape was not a tool of genocide; genocide was a tool of rape."[12] This would mean that a violently masculinized atmosphere of impunity is a potentially strong recruitment strategy available to *génocidaires*.

If some (and the Armenian case would suggest many) men can be recruited to commit genocide because it gives them a chance to commit rape and other sexual tortures against women and girls for an extended period of time, then the history of genocide will also have to be written within the framework of violent masculinity and patterns of violence against women more generally. Gender-based violence will not simply be an aspect of the story of the genocide itself, but also a key component in how we understand the emergence of genocidal ideologies and societal vulnerabilities to them over the *longue-durée*. A central question of this research would be whether there is a specific kind of violent masculinity—symbolic or actualized in the physical world—that makes societies more receptive to genocidal ideas.

Even in cases where much of the rape is committed outside the bounds of a direct order from superiors, there are in almost all genocides specific sorts of rape that involve the intentional brutalization—and often subsequently the murder en masse—of entire families and communities. These ritualized forms of rape as "total destruction" raise two important questions. The first is how historical investigations of specific types of masculinity might help explain the coincidence of genocidal ideology among the architects and genocidal rape rituals among the foot soldiers in instances when there is no specific training or indoctrination ordering rape. Do some perpetrators interpret genocidal language and policies in terms that encourage the performance of genocidal rape rituals? The second question raised by genocidal rape rituals is what, exactly, perpetrators are targeting. Rape, when used as a tool of genocide, targets women both as individual women and as members of a specific group.[13] Two threads from peacetime thus weave their way into the tactic of mass rape: group hatred and misogyny. The history of genocide should, therefore, explore the contribution made by each to genocidal ideology and implementation.[14] But there is another apparent target to genocidal rape: life-giving. The elaborate rape rituals and ritual rape spaces that perpetrators create are potent symbolic spaces in which to enact the annihilation of a people. Usually going beyond the rape and gang rape of individual women, genocidal rapists prey on the social context in which they find women and exploit the symbols and the relationships available to them in order to exert maximum damage to the woman or girl, to the community, to the group's regenerative capacity, and perhaps even to that metaphysical dimension that they believe accounts for the group's existence. Thus in genocidal contexts we frequently see public rapes, particularly rapes in front of family members, and rapes coerced between family members, and rapes involving sexual mutilation and torture, and rapes attended by the murder of a woman's or girl's family members. The intention seems to go well beyond compromising the physical and psychological ability of women and girls to carry children. It seems to be to puncture, to wound, that invisible space that may just be inside a woman's body that is the source of the group in the first place. Is that the message being told to us through the perpetrators' use of sharpened sticks to rape and kill Tutsi women during the Rwandan genocide in 1994?

As some perpetrators seem to know when they allow women victims to live, the consequences of sexual violation extend well beyond the genocide. The long-term physical, psychological, and sociopolitical effects of wartime rape are well known, though still in need of further study, particularly in terms of remediation.[15] Specific protocols need to be created to address the specific circumstances of "genocidal rape" and related atrocities. In most cases, women rape victims are often rejected by their families and communities, unable to find work, and left to raise children born of war alone and in abject poverty. We also know that in postconflict societies women face increased vulnerability to rape, sexual exploitation, and domestic violence from their old tormenters, from other perpetrators who are still walking free, from international peacekeepers, from liberating armies, and from men in their own communities and families. There is even some evidence that the sexual abuse of children increases after genocide.[16] Explanations for this trend range from wartime brutalization and humiliation of men, to the persistence of patriarchal dehumanization of women, to the culture of impunity that comes with the breakdown of traditional social institutions, and more. All of these explanations suggest a different shape and chronology to genocide than what we assume when we do not take women's stories into consideration.

This is especially true of where we decide to place the "end" of the crime in our narratives. Women die long after genocide from suicide, "honor killings," and HIV and other illnesses that are the direct result of genocidal atrocities including rape. They are often ostracized, or completely alone in the world, or raising children born of war, or caring for children orphaned in the conflict. Women are often very poor, lacking in access to jobs, resources, land, and basic services. Although in places like Rwanda postgenocide conditions can offer new opportunities for women's political engagement, by and large women survivors of genocide are marginalized from their own communities and from public life. For those women whose children were killed in front of them (often because they were trying to protect their mothers), the genocide simply never ends. Choman Hardi has written, regarding women survivors of the Anfal genocide of Iraqi Kurds, "For the women in this research, the aftermath of this catastrophe is as much a part of the Anfal story as the facts and figures that make up the grand narrative."[17]

Bringing women back into scholarly representations of genocide favors those definitions of the crime that do not limit the genocidal element to physical killing. Women and girls often die as a consequence of gang rape and sexual mutilation, but they are less frequently slated for direct massacre en masse.[18] Given the apparent ubiquity of mass rape during genocide, even during the Holocaust, it is hard to see how we would carve off this aspect of the crime as inessential to our genocide determinations.[19] And yet, this is what often happens, as is the case with Bosnia. Definitions that focus too much on massacre—mass bodies, mass graves, distinct moments of mass murder—erase almost completely the women victims and stand, therefore, in the way of deeper and more penetrating understandings of the crime.

To include women's experiences in our definition of genocide is to recognize something that the perpetrators have known for centuries: that one can destroy a group by destroying that group's ability to reproduce. What that means in each instance will differ according to cultural beliefs about reproduction and the perpetrators' understanding of their target group, but it is not unthinkable that future genocides could be committed solely through the use of sexual violence and related atrocities. Some of the fighting forces in the Democratic Republic of the Congo seem to be using strategies that come close to genocide-by-rape.[20]

The "social" aspect of the crime thus takes on an added importance when we consider the way that so many women victims have experienced it. Definitions that include concepts like "social death" (Daniel Feierstein), the destruction of "social power" (Martin Shaw), and "the interdiction of the biological and social reproduction of group members" (Helen Fein) incorporate (in my opinion) the ground-level realities of this crime for men and women, boys and girls, individuals, families, and collectivities much better than ones that get caught up in the numbers and the identities of those killed.[21] They come closer to capturing what this crime essentially is and arguably remain, as Martin Shaw has argued, more true to the spirit of the Genocide Convention and the work of Raphael Lemkin.[22]

The research on the mass rape of women during conflict, and the attention now being paid to this by policymakers and NGOs, has gradually also brought out evidence of the frequency of rape, sexual exploitation, and sexual torture of men. Treating women as gendered subjects of history has amplified attention to men as gendered subjects as well. This has made it possible to "see" male civilians as victims in entirely new ways, outside of the image of impregnability favored by militarized masculinist and nationalist narratives.[23] The scant research that exists on male victims of wartime (and genocidal) rape and sexual torture suggests that the postgenocide experiences of these men are very similar to those of women victims.[24] Clearly, we need to factor men and women survivors of rape into our understanding of the crime and into the protocols we devise to address its long-term effects.

All of this points to a key feature of sexual violence during genocide: that it is intended to desecrate the ways that members of collectivities, male and female, are bound together and thereby destroy permanently their capacity to rebuild themselves as stable and active collective agents in human history.

Reading Genocide from the "Bottom Up"

One thing that becomes apparent when we centralize gender-based violence during genocide is just how multifarious (and creative) are the means by which perpetrators go about destroying a group. Culture-specific studies of all of the tiny but essential details of the crime scene need to be undertaken in order to round out our understanding of genocide. As the discussion thus far has indicated, the rape of women during genocide is attended by multiple other crimes committed against the women themselves and their family members, many of whom are men. Taken together these make up what I have called "life force atrocities," that is, ritualized atrocities that target the life force of a group by destroying the physical integrity and the emotional and spiritual bonds of family members and of other strong symbols of group cohesion, such as religious and intellectual leaders.[25]

If we understand genocide as the intent to destroy a group specifically by destroying its source of life, the shared pattern of cruelties that we see across genocides would begin to make more sense. Gendered studies of genocide must therefore go beyond gender-based violence—including rape and sex-selective massacre—to truly grasp the extent to which ideas about gender are implicated in the crime. When communities are assaulted by forces with genocidal intent, individual members are usually targeted based on their (perceived) symbolic status within the forces of social and biological group reproduction. These perceived statuses are unequivocally gendered: men are assaulted as protectors, fathers, husbands, heads of families, political leaders, religious icons, leading intellectuals; past, present, and future patriarchs. Women are assaulted as mothers, wives, daughters, bearers of future life, protectors of children, providers of food, and so forth. The stereotypical gender roles that determine the exact nature of life force atrocity will vary with respect to the cultures committing the genocide, and perpetrators will draw on their own emotional and social experiences when devising ritual tortures, but by and large we can identify patterns across various different instances of the crime.

By giving us the means to begin to identify some of these "gender relational" atrocities during genocide, research on gender has also given us powerful tools to read genocide from the "bottom up."[26] This may be one of the greatest contributions it has made to genocide prevention efforts. Because gender operates in ways that are often unspoken, gender research requires that we interpret the nature of the forces and processes we study through myriad means that go well beyond the language of the actors involved. In a genocidal context, such a method involves searching for patterns that may not be immediately evident and certainly are not clearly articulated by perpetrators.

Such a contextualized approach was taken by the US Atrocities Documentation Team (ADT) that was sent in 2004 to refugee camps in Chad to document the experiences of survivors of the violence in neighboring Darfur, Sudan. The genocide determination that resulted from this research, while not explicitly based upon gender criteria, was sophisticated in its understanding of the multiple ways in which gendered strategies, specifically widespread and systematic sexual violence, can be exploited and deployed by perpetrators in committing the crime.[27] Interviewers in the field even updated the code list of crimes printed on the ADT questionnaire to account for things like mosque burning and the disembowelment of pregnant women.[28] The ADT methodology seems to have signified a return to "contextualized" understandings of the crime that consider the experience of victims and the ground-level behavior of perpetrators alongside statements of the purported architects and the general political and historical context of the conflict. The latter two elements—statements by leaders and macropolitical contexts— have dominated debates about genocide in the past decades, largely because they are assumed to more clearly indicate the presence or absence of what counts as "genocidal intent." The price of an exclusive focus on large-scale, elite, largely male, and highly reified phenomena is that the substantive experience of the victims—who occupy the space in which genocide occurs and are the bodies on whom the crime is committed—becomes lost in a sea of abstractions. As a consequence of this form of debate, the term "genocide" often is treated as little more than a political or legal "label" rather than something substantive in and of itself.[29]

Rituals targeting people specifically in terms of their gender and family roles are defining characteristics of violence in Bangladesh (1971), Bosnia (1992–95), Rwanda (1994), Sudan (the past decade), and the Democratic Republic of the Congo (the past decade-and-a-half). In every genocide, we can find these scenarios in the testimony of survivors. Perpetrators seem to have uncannily similar ideas about what most deeply and terribly destroys a person, a family, a community, and a group. So we need to better understand what is behind these rituals. And we need to find ways to use these rituals to ask new questions about the crime we are studying. The stories, told often by solitary survivors, are, in all their horror, also gifts. In them, perpetrators overplay their hands; they risk letting us in on their secrets, on the deep-seated and perhaps only vaguely recognized reasons for their terrible actions.

Unfortunately, human rights reports frequently fail to contextualize crimes and instead tend to disaggregate related crimes according to the gender and sometimes the age of the victim. We will be told that X number of men were killed, and X number of women raped, with special mention of the murder and rape of small children and the elderly. It is essential that we find ways to bring the narrative link between atrocities back into our statistical reporting strategies, since the narrative is what can help us identify the meaning perpetrators are making from their violence—and this meaning helps us identify and better understand genocidal intent.

Gender and Genocide Determinations

The logic of localized life force atrocities, which seek to destroy a deep cohesion within family units that, during genocidal processes, stand in for the cohesion of a more extensive group, can help us begin to go about making genocide determinations by starting with the "facts on the ground," using the Genocide Convention as a guide in deciding how these facts should best be organized while not relying solely on our abstract interpretations of its wording to make the case. The job becomes one of figuring out what the perpetrators are telling us about what they think they are doing by their behavior. Daniel Feierstein made this point quite elegantly when he wrote, regarding the question of genocide against "political" groups, that "the crime is not defined by the identity of the victim . . . but by the characteristics of the material action which is carried out."[30]

A good deal of pertinent information about this "material action" can be unearthed through gender-sensitive research that creates maps of affinity and atrocity to help us understand what perpetrators might have thought they were doing. Even in cases where the objective target of genocide was a political, social, or economic group, we know that *génocidaires* tend to view their victims as organic collectivities and persecute families based on the alleged status of one of its members.[31] In Argentina (i.e., during "The Dirty War," which has just recently been deemed a genocide), for example, the interior minister from 1976 to 1995, General Diaz de Bessone, framed the target of state violence in the following way:

> Founding a new republic is no easy matter. . . . The armed forces must be sufficiently alert, determined and resourceful to act simultaneously as an efficient fighting force against guerrillas and terrorists; an efficient surgeon that will remove the evil from all social classes and walks of life; and last but not least, parents of the new republic, strong, united,

just, free, supportive of others, clean, exemplary. . . . But it is only fair to point out that since no national project was outlined beforehand, little has been achieved so far to accomplish the remaining objectives, which are to defeat not only the guerrillas but subversion "in totum," so laying strong foundations for the birth of the new republic.[32]

As Feierstein points out, the general is here framing the counterinsurgency as a war on the "forces of evil," as "a clearly defined 'surgical operation' on previously defined sections of the population whose disappearance is meant to have an 'irreversible' effect on Argentinean society."[33] There is a gendered link between the plan of achieving the partial destruction of the Argentinean national group by carving out its "evil" and "subversive" elements and the atrocities committed against "suspect" families and networks.[34] Judging from Diaz de Bessone's understanding of the conflict, these families were the cosmic and reproductive opponents of the new national family to which the armed forces—"parents of the new republic"—were supposed to give birth. The torture of family members was a way for junta members to perform in a site-specific, localized way the broader genocidal intent to excise the generative units of opposition from the nation. It is as if annihilating one family makes room for the birth of the new, national family. The coincidence of statements like the one above and a pattern of life force atrocities strongly suggests genocide, even when all the reports have yet to be written; all the individual human lives have yet to be murdered; all the bodies have yet to be buried and, if found, exhumed and identified and counted. It is one way to identify a genocidal pattern within what is thought to be a brutal counterinsurgency.

In other cases of genocide we can also identify a perpetrator preoccupation with family dramas, with the generative power of violence; an understanding of their own actions in familial terms, whereby the armed forces, or the party, or the executive branch of the state, or the individual torturer are the generative unit—the parents—giving birth to something new and better through the total destruction of other generative units, not simply in physical terms but affectively and spiritually as well.[35] The precise relationship of these life force atrocities to genocide needs to be investigated in more depth. We should be curious about why the parental theme crops up so much in the language of the architects of genocide. Is it merely a by-product of their embrace of the rhetoric of extreme nationalism? Or do they see or experience their killing as an act of creation akin to fathering children?

Whatever the case, since there is such a strong correlation between the existence of life force atrocities and the existence of a genocidal logic to violence and persecution, they can help us avoid the pitfalls created by the constraints imposed through the four protected categories in the Genocide Convention, namely, "national, ethnical, racial and religious" groups. Before trying to determine whether the victims conform to these criteria, it might be more useful to determine whether people are being subjected to the types of atrocities that are common during genocides, especially before there are high numbers of the dead.

A benefit of focusing on the presence of gendered atrocities and identifying those patterns in them that are correlated most directly with genocide is that it would give us another empirical means of identifying situations in which "genocidal" violence is threatened without having to make an airtight argument for the presence of genocide. We may even be able to identify potentially genocidal cadres within armed forces, or potentially genocidal supporters of specific political parties, by documenting who has engaged or is engaging in ritual atrocities that appear to target a group's life force. If, during occupations, riots, and communal violence—more limited patterns of warfare—a small group of people, as part of an armed force or not, commits life force atrocities, that tells us something important about how things might progress and offers up new and crucial research agendas involving chains of command. At the very least we will know better who to watch in order to prevent a generalization of those atrocities into genocide somewhere down the road.

Identifying potentially genocidal violence in its early stages is important for many reasons. Genocide, unlike conflicts with more limited and strategic goals, is a type of violence that has ever-expanding horizons once it has become the organizing principle of a conflict. History has shown that perpetrators tend to enlarge their list of targeted victim groups as their power and reach grow. Furthermore, societies and groups that have faced genocide in the past require particular sorts of interventions afterward, both to rebuild a social fabric whose core institutions were targeted for destruction and to prevent the reignition of genocidal violence, either by the old perpetrators or by descendants of the victims.

Gender and Genocide Denial:
Darfur and Bosnia

Apart from the clear benefit of gender analysis to genocide prevention mechanisms, rethinking genocide in gendered terms can help cut through some of the ideological layering that has made genocide determinations so particularly fraught since the 2003 US war in Iraq. The current political debate about the use of the term tends to cluster around a few controversial cases, notably Bosnia and Darfur. These cases are accepted as genocides by the vast majority of genocide scholars, but opposition to the use of the term has come from high places and has been quite visible and vocal. Much of this opposition is coming from the left of the political spectrum and is a direct response to what is considered to be a double standard used by the United States and its allies in their deployment of the term.[36] These works show little concern for the evidence and none for the experiences of the many victims. Genocide is merely a label here.

More seriously, the political scientist Mahmood Mamdani, in his work on Darfur, has argued against the applicability of the term genocide largely because he believes that the advocates for its applicability to the situation there are not using the term consistently; if they did, he argues, they would also use it with reference to Iraq and Afghanistan. There are many threads to his argument, and in making it he offers a serious and enlightening study of the historical dynamics of identity and conflict in Sudan. His book, *Saviors and Survivors: Darfur, Politics and the War on Terror,* seeks to show that the conflict in Darfur is more properly considered to be a counterinsurgency, not unlike the wars being waged by the United States in Iraq and Afghanistan. Mamdani's book is surprising in its failure to take seriously the atrocities suffered by the victims of Janjaweed attacks, even if he does not consider these crimes to amount to genocide. When we begin to look at the nature of the atrocities committed in Darfur, the differences between counterinsurgency as such and genocide become clear. What matters so much is not the objective or even the subjective definition of the groups of people involved but rather the excruciating detail with which perpetrators go about destroying everything sacred and meaningful among the victims, particularly family bonds. This takes Darfur beyond any reasonable characterization as counterinsurgency and generalized atrocity. In Darfur, as in Bosnia, the death toll may fall well short of the mass killings that attended the key twentieth-century genocides; nevertheless, the focused assault on generative symbols, relations of affection and loyalty, all those deep recesses of the human heart and soul—this is the evidence of genocide that I think is most difficult to refute and that ultimately makes the case for genocide in both these instances.

In reconstructing the narratives of the individual acts of atrocity, we see emerging a tapestry of relational violence that is a core element of the crime. The ADT discovered a systematic pattern of attack that was sustained across hundreds of villages in Darfur, involving encirclement by mounted Janjaweed militias, strafing and bombing from Antonov bombers and helicopters belonging to the army of the government of Sudan, murder and disappearances of men and boys, sexual exploitation of women and girls, and the wholesale destruction of property, food, and water supplies. Mamdani does not engage these findings analytically or explain why they do not point to genocide in the way that was argued by the US Department of State legal team. Indeed, he dismissed one of the key findings that—in concert with all the others—seems to point to genocide: evidence of systematic mass rape. To critique the inclusion of this charge in the ICC arrest warrant for president Omar al-Bashir, who is charged with conspiracy to commit genocide, among other things, Mamdani writes: "To claim that ongoing rape in the [internally displaced person] camps is the result of official government policy is to ignore the simple fact that rape occurred in all camps, those controlled by the government and by the rebels."[37]

Mamdani's statement about rape is misleading. In his efforts to normalize and depoliticize the conflict in Darfur, he has ended up undervaluing, indeed entirely neglecting, the stories of women and girl survivors, which are so valuable precisely because they give us access to the behavior of perpetrators during the moment of attack. Simply because rape occurs in many different contexts and is committed by many different types of men does not mean that mass rape by one particular group, such as Janjaweed militias or government soldiers, is not itself part of a genocidal strategy. But, even more important than such an obvious point is the narrative framework in which these atrocities take place. These were frequently not "rapes" in the generic sense that Mamdani seems to use the term. Survivors of the attacks in Darfur describe a multipronged strategy of attack on villages in which rape occurred alongside a host of ritualized atrocities all aimed at destroying the life foundations of a group—the family unit, the connection to land and community, and the future social and biological reproduction of the group. These atrocities included: eviscerating pregnant women, raping women and girls in public, mutilating victims of rape and sexual violence, raping women and girls with sharp objects, killing infants (especially infant boys), murdering men, humiliating and torturing village leaders, and inciting cruel performances involving family members, all while screaming racist epithets at the victims.[38]

These types of atrocities are common to all other genocides and place Darfur clearly within the ranks of genocidal violence. These atrocities share a "genealogical" link with the type of violence that has attended every other known case of genocide in past centuries. When such atrocities all begin to point toward the five elements of the crime enumerated in the 1948 Convention on the Prevention and Punishment of the Crime of Genocide, then a working genocide determination seems entirely reasonable.

The key to understanding how gendered violence and life force atrocities work together in a genocidal strategy is, of course, to examine how they contribute to the destruction of the group as such. A recent work in criminology, *Darfur and the Crime of Genocide*, makes fruitful use of the ADT interviews to reconstruct the crime scene in several settlements in Darfur, generating data for shifts in the family size of respondents as a consequence of the attacks and creating charts of the age and gender of people killed and missing. On this latter point, the authors discovered that the groups with the greatest number killed (and missing) were comprised of young men between the ages of fifteen and twenty-nine and girls between the ages of five and fourteen. They note "about a third of both the young adult males and the preadolescent girls are represented among the dead or missing."[39] This suggests that young men were not simply being killed as potential combatants, a common defense against genocide charges; the presence of such a high number of young girls alongside the high number of young men seems to point to an attempt to destroy the ability of the group to organize and reproduce itself in the future. When placed along other evidence of atrocity patterns and more macro-level indications of intent, such crime scene statistics are invaluable.

Gender data underscore the importance of empirical evidence in making genocide determinations. Overarching schemas and analytical abstractions cannot replace this evidence in our attempts to understand the genocidal process and make determinations about its existence. Legal, political, and rhetorical arguments can be made to support all sorts of positions in regard to the crime. The debate about its nature goes right back to the debates about the wording of the Genocide Convention. This is why the ADT's "atrocity statistics" are such an important innovation in the struggle against the crime. They allow us to navigate through the heavy storm of ideology and politics and enter the moment of victimization. By categorizing crimes that together are suggestive of genocide, they offer us an empirical means of determining whether what we see could in fact be or become the crime of crimes.

It is true, as Mamdani and others emphasize, that in Darfur a great number of women and children have been allowed to survive after experiencing or witnessing rape, murder, and the destruction of their families and communities. The absence of the annihilation of most members in some of the villages targeted (though many villages were completely annihilated) challenges one of the most common working definitions of genocide: genocide as mass killing. Defining genocide simply as mass killing becomes very difficult when one takes seriously the issue of gender and gender-specific acts of violence. Studies that have considered the experiences of women and girls alongside men and boys have shown that a common pattern in the early stages of genocide is the systematic execution of male members of a community alongside the terrorization, sexual exploitation, torture, and expulsion of women, children, and the very old. When we limit our definitions to killing, we can end up artificially separating processes that are part of the same phenomenon.

The consequence of this can be that massacres of men and boys are defined as genocide, while the attendant rape, torture, and expulsion of the women and girls who were their mothers, wives, children, girlfriends, colleagues, and so forth are either ignored entirely or described as something other than genocide, such as "ethnic cleansing," crimes against humanity, war crimes, or uncategorized "atrocities." This approach is clearly inadequate and inaccurate, for it is unlikely that perpetrator intent can be broken up in a similar fashion. Furthermore, the evidence contained within witness testimony shows time and again that perpetrators understand quite well the meaning and function of people's family and community relationships and that they appear to intend to use these relationships in gender-determined ways in order to destroy the group. Nevertheless, the survival of women and children, even when they have been forced out of a territory, is often pointed to as evidence that even a sex-selective massacre of men and boys cannot be construed as genocide, since the entire community was not slated for physical annihilation. This latter approach assumes that genocidal massacres must include victims of both sexes indiscriminately in order to prove intent. It also potentially underestimates the long-term destructive trauma caused by the systematic and intentional harm on the expelled women and children as well as the effect that the massacre of men and boys can have on a community's reproductive capacity.

The best example of a case that has raised the two issues above is the 1995 Srebrenica massacre of over 8,000 Bosniak (Bosnian Muslim) men and boys by Bosnian Serb forces under the command of Ratko Mladić. These massacres were determined by the International Criminal Tribunal for the former Yugoslavia (ICTY) to constitute genocide. Its finding was upheld by the International Court of Justice.[40] Like Darfur, most genocide scholars view the Serb war in Bosnia to have been a genocidal assault on Bosniaks. Even when the status of the war as a whole is in doubt, scholars tend to accept Srebrenica as an instance of genocide. However, because the ICTY has been conservative in its use of the term, and because the nebulous concept of "ethnic cleansing" has confused characterizations of the war in Bosnia as a whole, the Serbian attacks on Bosnian populations between 1992 and 1995 have not been determined in a court of law to fit the definition of genocide. This has opened up ample space for confusion, and one rarely sees reference to the "Bosnian genocide." The conflict in general is instead referred to as ethnic cleansing and civil war. With the exception of the massacres at Srebrenica after July 13, 1995, most of the atrocities committed by Serbs in the course of the war have been punished as crimes against humanity and war crimes, and public perceptions follow suit.

Paying attention to the experiences of women and to the gendered dynamics of the Serb onslaught on the UN safe haven can help us maneuver this difficult definitional terrain. When we examine, from a gendered perspective, what went on in Srebrenica from the fall of the enclave on July 11, 1995 to the forced relocation of women, girls, and very young boys two days later (an occurrence that directly preceded the start of the massacres), we can see that there are several threads that connect the massacres at Srebrenica in 1995 to a systematic Bosnian Serb policy that had been pursued since the outbreak of war in 1992. The case of Srebrenica in fact demonstrates how important it is that we consider the testimony of women survivors of violence in making our determinations about what is and what is not genocide and in thinking about which conflicts are likely to have genocidal outcomes. Their testimonies, because they are often the lone survivors of a given massacre, offer us evidence that is just as important as body counts in establishing genocide and genocidal intent. Specifically, their testimonies can establish a systematic pattern of atrocity aimed directly at the institutions, symbols, and relations of reproduction as well as the biological capacity to reproduce.

314 GENOCIDE AND GENDER IN THE TWENTIETH CENTURY

Ramiza Gurdić gave the following testimony to the Dutch law firm Van Diepen/Van der Kroef, which is representing the surviving victims of the Srebrenica massacres in a suit against the government of the Netherlands and the UN for failing to protect civilians in the UN "safe haven":

> At one time, I saw how a young boy of about ten was killed by Serbs in Dutch uniform. This happened in front of my own eyes. The mother sat on the ground and her young son sat beside her. The young boy was placed on his mother's lap. The young boy was killed. His head was cut off. The body remained on the lap of the mother. The Serbian soldier placed the head of the young boy on his knife and showed it to everyone. . . . The woman was hysterical and began to call out for help. . . . The Serbs forced the mother to drink the blood of her child. Chaos broke out among the refugees.[41]

Another survivor, Munira Šubašić, tells us,

> There was a girl, she must have been about nine years old. At a certain moment some Chetniks recommended to her brother that he rape the girl. He did not do it and I also think that he could not have done it for he was still just a child. Then they murdered that young boy.[42]

These are just two of the many stories of specific atrocities witnessed by survivors of Srebrenica. But rarely do such stories work themselves into narratives and analyses of the crime. Certainly they are not part of dominant images of the Srebrenica massacre. The fact is that during the two days preceding the "evacuation" of an estimated 23,000 women and children, many women and girls as young as nine were raped by Serb forces; frequently they were killed afterward; small girls and boys, including infants, were murdered, often by having their throats cut in front of their families; pregnant women were eviscerated; and boys and men were seemingly randomly picked out of crowds of families and dragged off, never to return. These atrocities, targeted as they were at family bonds, need to find their way into scholarly, legal, and public images of Srebrenica.

The reasons that we need to know the details surrounding the separation of women and men before the Srebrenica evacuations and deportations is that they demonstrate the extent to which people were being persecuted relationally, specifically as members of families. This, in turn, suggests that Bosnian Serb forces were seeking to compromise and destroy the most important unit of group cohesion, the family. Rather than being instances of random and excessive violence in a madhouse, the atrocities committed against family members, *in front of one another,* are some of the strongest indicators of genocidal intent. They suggest something much more malicious than attempts to rid Serbian forces of a military foe. Indeed, they conform to several elements of the crime as articulated in the Genocide Convention.

These atrocities only come to light in the testimony of those who survived, the majority of whom are women and girls. The stories, and their implications, are not considered by legal scholars who argue against the genocide finding in the Prosecutor *v.* Krstic case tried by the ICTY.[43]

Conclusion

These types of atrocities committed in Argentine prisons, the Srebrenica enclave, and within villages in Darfur could serve to further specify exactly those limited crimes that we would consider to be "atrocity crimes" with a high risk of turning into genocide.[44] The Srebrenica massacres, for example, came on the heels of over three years of violence and "ethnic cleansing" against Bosnian Muslims perpetrated by Bosnian Serb forces, including several "special forces" that seem to have operated with orders from Slobodan Milošević in Belgrade.[45] We can trace back from the atrocities committed in Srebrenica on July 11–12, 1995 to similar atrocities committed in eastern Bosnian towns from April 1992 through July 1995. The atrocities we see in Srebrenica also can be linked to atrocities in the various Serb-controlled concentration and rape camps that operated in Bosnia between 1992 and 1995. When we draw lines from one atrocity to another, across time and space, we begin to see the dense tapestry of genocide in Bosnia above and beyond the evidence of single cases of massacre, murder, rape, and ethnic cleansing. It therefore becomes difficult to cordon off the Srebrenica massacres as the only case of genocide within a wider war that was characterized by other things.[46]

Atrocity statistics that are sensitive to the contextual frame in which discrete crimes are committed point to the usefulness of an approach to genocide that understands the crime spatially, not only in terms of the geography of the attacks, but also in terms of the geography of atrocity. Data and maps (similar to Hagan and Rymond-Richmond's for Darfur) could be created for those specific types of atrocities that have a high correlation with the crime of genocide. If early on in a conflict we could see a map of specific types of atrocities reported by witnesses, such as public rape or the evisceration of pregnant women, this would contribute to determining if a conflict is threatening genocide and, if so, which group or cadre is of particular concern. If we could begin to correlate the specific types of atrocities that are highly suggestive of genocide with specific ways of envisioning reproduction, women's sexuality, men's power, and so forth, we may begin to tease out the very specific types of thinking—genealogies—of atrocity that can lead to genocide way down the road.

In our new century most of us will probably be drawn into the terrible position of witnesses to genocide, if only by virtue of the international media. The first, and the most fundamental, question is how we can know genocide before it announces itself with mass graves and how we can offer direction to others on identifying genocidal situations in crises and conflicts at an early stage. A great deal of work has been done on this already, but we are still at the beginning of an effort to develop effective early indicators, as is evidenced by the endless debates about definitions that followed the US recognition of genocide in Sudan in 2004. Considering the small, but momentous, gendered details of the space of genocide, like the premassacre killing spree in Srebrenica from July 11 through 13, and the similar atrocities committed by Serb forces in eastern Bosnia three years beforehand, can help us refine what it is we are looking for, with ramifications for the ways that we define genocide and work toward prevention. To borrow from Jacobo Timerman, the stakes are, as they always have been, nothing short of rescuing civilization as we know it from those who would bring about the disappearance of the universal, human family.[47]

Notes

1   I would like to thank the editors of *Genocide Studies and Prevention*, as well as Benjamin Forgey, for their vital comments and help in the editing of the article form of this chapter. This chapter version has been slightly modified.

2   For an overview of the development of gender research within Holocaust and Genocide studies, see especially Sonja Hedgepath and Rochelle Saidel, eds., *Sexual Violence Against Jewish Women During the Holocaust* (Waltham, MA: Brandeis University Press, 2010); Lisa Pine, "Gender and the Family," in *Historiography of the Holocaust*, ed. Dan Stone (New York, NY: Palgrave Macmillan, 2004), pp. 364–82; Atina Grossmann, "Women and the Holocaust: Four Recent Titles," *Holocaust and Genocide Studies* 16: 1 (Spring 2002), pp. 94–108; Elisa von Joeden-Forgey, "Gender and Genocide," in *The Oxford Handbook of Genocide Studies*, ed. Donald Bloxham and A. Dirk Moses (London, UK: Oxford, 2010), pp. 61–80; Adam Jones, "Gendering Genocide," in *Genocide: A Comprehensive Introduction*, 2nd edn (New York, NY: Routledge, 2011), pp. 464–98.

3   For a particularly bellicose example, see Gabriel Schoenfeld, "Auschwitz and the Professors," *Commentary* 105:6 (1998), pp. 42–7. More moderate critiques of gender analysis are discussed in Roger Smith, "Women and Genocide: Notes on an Unwritten History," *Holocaust and Genocide Studies* 8:3 (1994), pp. 215–334.

4   See, for example, Adam Jones, "Does Gender Make the World Go Round? Feminist Critiques of International Relations," *Review of International Studies* 22:4 (1996), pp. 405–29; Adam Jones, "Gender and Ethnic Conflict in Ex-Yugoslavia," *Ethnic and Racial Studies* 17:1 (1994), pp. 115–34. Although Jones is sensitive to and aware of the multifarious ways in which women are victimized in genocide, his definition of the crime, based on Steven Katz's, depends on the crime of murder and therefore does not incorporate mass rape as a central, determining element: "[Genocide is] the actualization of the intent, however successfully carried out, to *murder in whole or in part*, any national,

ethnic, racial, religious, political, social, gender or economic group, as these groups are defined by the perpetrator, by whatever means." (emphasis added). See: Adam Jones, *Genocide: A Comprehensive Introduction*, p. 18.

5 For a definition of "root-and-branch" genocide, visit Chapter 2, "Masculinities and Vulnerabilities in the Rwandan and Congolese Genocides," by Adam Jones in this volume. A comprehensive synopsis of this work can be found in Jones, "Gendering Genocide."

6 For a comprehensive discussion of gender patterns in genocides, see Helen Fein, "Genocide and Gender: The Uses of Women and Group Destiny," *Journal of Genocide Research* 1:1 (1999), pp. 43–64.

7 The study of women perpetrators is most developed for the Holocaust, where research has been carried out largely by women scholars. Wendy Lower, *Hitler's Furies: German Women in the Nazi Killing Fields* (Boston, MA: Houghton Mifflin Harcourt, 2013); Claudia Koontz, *Mothers in the Fatherland: Women, the Family and Nazi Politics* (New York, NY: St. Martin's Press, 1987); Smith, "Women and Genocide," pp. 215–334; Laura Sjoberg and Caron E. Gentry, "Gendered Perpetrators of Genocide," in *Mothers, Monsters, Whores: Women's Violence in Global Politics* (London, UK: Zed Books, 2007), pp. 141–73; Christina Herkommer, "Women under National Socialism: Women's Scope for Action and the Issue of Gender," in *Ordinary People as Mass Murderers*, ed. Olaf Jensen and Claus-Christian W. Szejnmann (New York, NY: Palgrave MacMillan, 2008), pp. 99–119; Irmtraud Heike, "Female Concentration Camp Guards as Perpetrators: Three Case Studies," in *Ordinary People*, ed. Jensen and Szejnmann, pp. 120–44; Wendy Adele-Marie Sarti, *Women and Nazis: Perpetrators of Genocide and Other Crimes During Hitler's Regime, 1933-1945* (Palo Alto, CA: Academica Press, 2010).

8 Jones, "Gendering Genocide," p. 467.

9 Gender-sensitive literature on the Holocaust is cited in the works listed in FN2. Important works that address various genocides include Alexandra Stiglmayer, *Mass Rape: The War Against Women in Bosnia-Herzegovina* (Lincoln, NE: University of Nebraska Press, 1994); Smith, "Women and Genocide"; Beverly Allen, *Rape Warfare: The Hidden Genocide in Bosnia-Herzegovina and Croatia* (Minneapolis, MN: University of Minnesota Press, 1996); Christopher Taylor, *Sacrifice as Terror* (Oxford and London, UK: Berg Publishers, 2001); Claudia Koontz, *The Nazi Conscience* (Cambridge, MA: Harvard University Press, 2003); R. Charli Carpenter, *"Innocent Women and Children:" Gender, Norms and the Protection of Civilians* (Aldershot, UK: Ashgate Press, 2006); R. Charli Carpenter, *Born of War: Protecting Children of Sexual Violence Survivors in Conflict Zones* (Bloomfield, CT: Kumarian Press, 2007); Adam Jones, *Gender Inclusive: Essays on Violence, Men, and Feminist International Relations* (New York, NY: Routledge, 2009); Samuel Totten, *Plight and Fate of Women During and Following Genocide* (New Brunswick, NJ: Transaction Publishers, 2009); Choman Hardi, *Gendered Experiences of Genocide: Anfal Survivors in Kurdistan-Iraq* (Burlington, VT: Ashgate Publishing Limited, 2011); Selma Leydesdorff, *Surviving the Bosnian Genocide: The Women of Srebrenica Speak* (Bloomington, IN: Indiana University Press, 2011); Carol Rittner and John Roth, *Rape: Weapon of War and Genocide* (St. Paul, MN: Paragon House, 2012).

10 Janet Halley, "Rape at Rome: Feminist Interventions in the Criminalization of Sex-Related Violence in Positive International Criminal Law," *Michigan Journal of International Law* 30 (2008–09), pp. 1–123; Mark Ellis, "Breaking the Silence: Rape as an International Crime," *Case Western Reserve Journal of International Law* 225 (2006), pp. 225–47; Karen Engle, "Feminism and Its (Dis)contents: Criminalizing Wartime Rape in Bosnia and Herzegovina," *The American Journal of International Law* 99:4 (2005), pp. 778–816; Kelly Dawn Askin, "Prosecuting Wartime Rape and Other Genocide-Related Crimes under International Law: Extraordinary Advances, Enduring Obstacles," *Berkeley Journal of International Law* 21 (2003), pp. 288–349.

11 Cynthia Enloe, *The Morning After: Sexual Politics at the End of the Cold War* (Berkeley, CA: University of California Press, 1993), p. 240.

12 Henry Theriault, "Gender and Genocide: New Perspectives for Armenian Genocide Research," paper presented at the Armenian Genocide Workshop, *Strassler Center for Holocaust and Genocide Studies*, Clark University, April 8–10, 2010.

13 For an excellent discussion of sexual exploitation during genocide, see Catherine MacKinnon, *Are Women Human?* (Cambridge, MA: Harvard University Press, 2006), pp. 209–36.

14 One of the few studies to do this to date is Taylor, *Sacrifice as Terror.*

15 On the social and economic impact of rape on women after genocide, see for example, Samuel Totten, ed., "The Darfur Genocide: The Mass Rape of Black African Girls and Women," in *Plight and Fate of Women*, pp. 137–68.

16 See, for example, Human Rights Watch, *Struggling to Survive: Barriers to Justice for Rape Victims in Rwanda* (New York, NY: Human Rights Watch, September 2004).

17 Hardi, *Gendered Experiences of Genocide: Anfal Survivors in Kurdistan-Iraq*, p. 7.

18 Fein, "Genocide and Gender."

19 For an overview of the evidence for this, see MacKinnon, "Genocide's Sexuality," *Are Women Human?*

20 Elisa von Joeden-Forgey, "Sexual Violence and Genocide in the DRC," *Institute for the Study of Genocide Newsletter* 45 (Winter 2010). Available online: http://www.instituteforthestudyofgenocide.org/newsletters/isg45/ISG45.pdf (accessed July 22, 2011).

21 Martin Shaw, ed., *What is Genocide?* (Cambridge, UK: Polity Press, 2007); Daniel Feierstein, "Political Violence in Argentina and Its Genocidal Characteristics," in *State Violence and Genocide in Latin America*, ed. Marcia Esperanza, Henry R. Huttenbach, and Daniel Feierstein (London, UK: Routledge, 2010), pp. 44–63; Helen Fein, "Genocide: A Sociological Perspective," *Current Sociology* 38:1 (1990): 1–126.

22 Martin Shaw, ed., "Neglected Foundations," in *What is Genocide?* (Cambridge, UK: Polity Press, 2007), pp. 17–36.

23 Along these lines, Dubravka Zarkov, in an essay on male victims of rape in the Yugoslav war, has shown how a masculinist construction of national identity can have the effect of erasing men's sexual exploitation precisely because

such exploitation feminizes the victim. Dubravka Zarkov, "The Body of the Other Man: Sexual Violence and the Construction of Masculinity, Sexuality and Ethnicity in Croatian Media," in *Victims, Perpetrators or Actors? Gender, Armed Conflict and Political Violence*, ed. Caroline O. N. Moser and Fiona C. Clark (London, UK and New York, NY: Zed Books, 2001), p. 75.

24 For an extensive newspaper treatment of this subject, see Will Storr, "The Rape of Men," *Observer*, July 17, 2011. Available online: http://www.guardian. co.uk/society/2011/jul/17/the-rape-of-men (accessed July 11, 2014). Thanks to Adam Jones for drawing my attention to this.

25 Elisa von Joeden-Forgey, "Devil in the Details: 'Life Force Atrocities' and the Assault on the Family in Times of Conflict," *Genocide Studies and Prevention* 5:1 (April 2010), pp. 1–19.

26 I am borrowing the "relational" designation from Adam Jones, "Gendering Genocide," p. 25.

27 Gregory Stanton, "Proving Genocide in Darfur: The Atrocities Documentation Project and Resistance to Its Findings," in *Genocide in Darfur: Investigating Atrocities in Sudan*, ed. Samuel Totten and Eric Markusen (New York, NY: Routledge, 2006), pp. 181–8. For an analysis of the gendered violence documented by the ADT, see Kelly Dawn Askin, "Prosecuting Gender Crimes Committed in Darfur: Holding Leaders Accountable for Sexual Violence," in *Genocide in Darfur*, ed. Totten and Markusen, pp. 141–62.

28 Jonathan P. Howard, "Survey Methodology and the Darfur Genocide," in *Genocide in Darfur*, ed. Totten and Markusen, p. 69.

29 As we know, Raphael Lemkin understood genocide in highly contextualized terms. Much of his thinking about the crime was clearly formed by the attention he paid to the (generally assumed) familial composition of the groups being targeted. See, for example, Raphael Lemkin, "Biological Techniques of Genocide," *Axis Rule in Occupied Europe: Analysis, Proposals for Redress* (Washington, DC: Carnegie Endowment for International Peace, 1944), pp. 86–7. For a discussion of Lemkin's contextual approach, see Shaw, "Neglected Foundations," pp. 17–36. Shaw rightly credits Helen Fein with continuing Lemkin's tradition of incorporating a wide range of destructive social and biological policies and actions into a definition of genocide.

30 Feierstein, "Political Violence," p. 154.

31 There is a great deal of work emerging on this topic. See, for example, Norman Naimark, *Stalin's Genocides* (Princeton, NJ: Princeton University Press, 2010).

32 Daniel Feierstein, "National Security Doctrine in Latin America: The Genocide Question," in *The Oxford Handbook of Genocide Studies*, pp. 504–5.

33 Ibid.

34 See, for example, atrocities witnessed by Jacobo Timerman and related in *Prisoner Without a Name, Cell Without a Number*, trans. Toby Talbot (New York, NY: Alfred A. Knopf), pp. 146–58.

35 For a rudimentary treatment of this theme, see my Elisa Von-Joeden Forgey, "Genocidal Masculinity," in *New Directions in Genocide Research*, ed. Adam Jones (New York, NY: Routledge, 2011), 76–95.

36 A recent example of this tendency is Edward Herman and Scott Peterson, *The Politics of Genocide* (New York, NY: Monthly Review Press, 2010) and Edward Herman and Phillip Corwin, *The Srebrenica Massacre* (Montreal, Canada: Centre for Research on Globalization, 2011). For cogent critiques of these works see Martin Shaw, "Left Wing Genocide Denial." Available online: http://martinshaw.org/ (accessed July 11, 2014); George Monbiot, "Left and Libertarian Right Cohabit in the Weird World of the Genocide Belittlers," *Guardian*, June 13, 2011. Available online: http://www.guardian. co.uk/commentisfree/2011/jun/13/left-and-libertarian-right?INTCMP=SRCH (accessed July 7, 2014); and Adam Jones, "On Genocide Deniers: Challenging Herman and Peterson," *Pambazuka News*, 490 (July 15, 2010). Available online: http://pambazuka.org/en/category/features/65977 (accessed July 7, 2014).

37 Mahmood Mamdani, *Saviors and Survivors: Darfur, Politics and the War on Terror* (New York, NY: Doubleday, 2009), pp. 271–2.

38 There are many reports on the specific atrocities committed by the Janjaweed and the government of Sudan in Darfur. See, for example, Human Rights Watch, "Darfur in Flames: Atrocities in Western Sudan," in *Sudan* 16:5 (New York, NY: Human Rights Watch, 2004).

39 John Hagen and Wenona Rymond-Richmond, *Darfur and the Crime of Genocide* (New York, NY: Cambridge University Press, 2009), p. 212.

40 ICTY, Prosecutor *v.* Krstić, April 19, 2004. Available online: www.un.org/icty/ krstic/Appeal/judgement/index.htm; ICJ, Press Release, February 26, 2007.

41 Van Diepen/Van der Kroef, Writ of Summons, The Hague, Netherlands, 2007. Full text, with witness testimonies. Available online: http://www/vandiepen. com/uploads/media/1376917704_issuu.pdf (accessed July 7, 2014).

42 Ibid.

43 See, for example, William Schabas, *Genocide in International Law: The Crime of Crimes*, 2nd edn (Cambridge, UK: Cambridge University Press, 2009), pp. 221–34; Katherine Southwick, "Srebrenica as Genocide? The Krstić Decision and the Language of the Unspeakable," *Yale Human Rights & Development Law Journal* 8 (2005), pp. 188–227.

44 David Scheffer, "Genocide and Atrocity Crimes," *Genocide Studies and Prevention* 1:3 (2006), pp. 229–50.

45 Norman Cigar, *The Bridge Betrayed: Religion and Genocide in Bosnia* (Berkeley and Los Angeles, CA: University of California Press, 1996), pp. 72–8.

46 Two recent works by Bosnian scholars argue that the Srebrenica massacre was a culmination of a genocidal policy toward eastern Bosnia pursued by Serb forces since the conflict began in 1992: Daniel Toljaga, "Prelude to the Srebrenica Genocide: Mass Murder and Ethnic Cleansing of Bosniaks in the Srebrenica Region During the First Three Months of the Bosnian War (April– June 1992)." Available online: http://www.bosnia.org.uk/news/news_body. cfm?newsid=2771 (accessed July 7, 2014); Edina Bećirević's *Na Drini genocide* (Sarajevo, Bosnia-Herzegovina: Buybook, 2009).

47 Timerman, *Prisoner*, p. 14.

SELECTED COMBINED BIBLIOGRAPHY

Abrams, Lynn. *Oral History Theory*. London, UK: Routledge, 2010.

Abrams, Lynn. *The Making of Modern Woman*. London, UK: Longman, 2002.

Adler, Nanci, and Selma Leydesdorff. *Tapestry of Memory: Evidence and Testimony in Life-Story Narratives*. New Brunswick, NJ and London, UK: Transaction Publishers, 2013.

African Rights. *Not So Innocent: When Women Become Killers*. London, UK: African Rights, 1995.

African Rights. *Rwanda: Death, Despair and Defiance*. Rev. edn. London, UK: African Rights, 1995.

African Rights. *Rwanda-Broken Bodies, Torn Spirits: Living with Genocide, Rape and HIV/AIDS*. Kigali, Rwanda: African Rights, 2004.

Akçam, Taner. *A Shameful Act: The Armenian Genocide and the Question of Turkish Responsibility*. New York, NY: Metropolitan Books, 2006.

Akhavan, Payam. *Reducing Genocide to Law: Definition, Meaning and the Ultimate Crime*. Cambridge, UK: Cambridge University Press, 2012.

Alexandris, Alexis. *The Greek Minority of Istanbul and Greek-Turkish Relations, 1918–1974*. Athens, Greece: Center for Asia Minor Studies, 1983.

Allen, Beverly. *Rape Warfare: The Hidden Genocide in Bosnia-Herzegovina and Croatia*. Minneapolis, MN: University of Minnesota Press, 1996.

Altinay, Ayse Gül, and Fethiye Çetin. *The Hidden Legacy of "Lost" Armenians in Turkey*, translated by Maureen Freely. New Brunswick, NJ: Transaction Publishers, 2014.

Altinay, Ayse Gül, and Fethiye Çetin. *Torunlar*. Istanbul, Turkey: Metis, 2009.

Amnesty International. "Bosnia-Herzegovina, Rape and Sexual Abuse by Armed Forces." 1993. Available online: http://www.amnesty.org/en/library/info/EUR63/001/1993.

Amnesty International. "Making Love a Crime: Criminalization of Same-Sex Conduct in Sub-Saharan Africa." Available online: http://www.amnestyusa.org/research/reports/making-love-a-crime-criminalization-of-same-sex-conduct-in-sub-saharan-africa.

Amnesty International. *Rwanda: "Marked for Death," Rape Survivors Living with HIV/AIDS in Rwanda*. London, UK: Amnesty International, 2004.

Andre, Catherine. "Terre rwandaise, accès, politique et reforme foncières." *L'Afrique des Grands Lacs Annuaire* (1998): 141–73.

Anthias, Floya, and Nira Yuval-Davis. *Racialized Boundaries: Race, Nation, Gender, Colour and Class and the Anti-Racist Struggle*. London, UK: Routledge, 1992.

Amann, Diane Marie. "Group Mentality, Expressivism, and Genocide." *International Criminal Law Review* 21, no. 2 (2002): 92–143.

Apfelbaum, Erika. "And Now What, After Such Tribulations? Memory and Dislocation in the Era of Uprooting." *American Psychologist* 55 (2000): 1008–13.

Appadurai, Arjun. "Dead Certainty: Ethnic Violence in the Era of Globalization." *Public Culture* 10, no. 2 (1998): 225–47.

Apsel, Joyce, and Ernesto Verdeja, eds. *Genocide Matters: Ongoing Issues and Emerging Perspectives.* Oxon, UK and New York, NY: Routledge, 2013.

Aratza, Naomi. "The New Landscape of Transitional Justice." In *Transitional Justice in the Twenty-First Century—Beyond Truth versus Justice*, edited by Naomi Roht-Arriaza and Javier Mariezcurrena, 1–16. New York, NY: Cambridge University Press, 2006.

Arendt, Hannah. *Eichmann in Jerusalem: A Report on the Banality of Evil.* New York, NY: The Viking Press, 1965.

Aretxaga, Begoña. *Shattering Silence: Women, Nationalism, and Political Subjectivity in Northern Ireland.* Princeton, NJ: Princeton University Press, 1997.

Askin, Kelly Dawn. "Omarska Camp, Bosnia: Broken Promises of 'Never Again.'" *Human Rights* 30, no. 1 (2003): 12–14, 23.

Askin, Kelly Dawn. "Prosecuting Gender Crimes Committed in Darfur: Holding Leaders Accountable for Sexual Violence." In *Genocide in Darfur: Investing the Atrocities in the Sudan*, edited by Samuel Totten and Eric Markusen, 141–62. London, UK: Routledge, 2006.

Askin, Kelly Dawn. "Prosecuting Wartime Rapes and Other Gender-Related Crimes under International Law: Extraordinary Advances, Enduring Obstacles." *Berkeley Journal of International Law* 21, no. 2 (2003): 288–349.

Attarian, Hourig. "Lifelines: Matrilineal Narratives, Memory and Identity." PhD diss., McGill University, 2009.

Avakian, Arlene Voski. "A Different Future? Armenian Identity Through the Prism of Trauma, Nationalism and Gender." *New Perspectives on Turkey* 42 (2014): 203–14.

Avakian, Arlene Voski. "Surviving the Survivors of the Armenian Genocide: Daughters and Granddaughters." In *Voices of Armenian Women: Papers Presented at the International Conference on Armenian Women, Paris, France*, edited by Barbara Mergeurian and Joy Renjilian-Burgy, 1–14. Belmont, MA: AIWA Press, 2000.

Baaz, Maria Eriksson, and Maria Stern. *The Complexity of Violence: A Critical Analysis of Sexual Violence in the Democratic Republic of Congo (DRC).* (Working Paper on Gender Based Violence, Swedish International Development Agency). Uppsala, Sweden: SIDA, 2010.

Baaz, Maria Eriksson, and Maria Stern. "Why Do Soldiers Rape? Masculinity, Violence, and Sexuality in the Armed Forces in the Congo (DRC)." *International Studies Quarterly* 53, no. 4 (2009): 495–518.

Baer, Elizabeth, and Myrna Goldenberg. *Experience and Expression: Women, the Nazis and the Holocaust.* Detroit, MI: Wayne State University Press, 2003.

Bailey, Claudia Paz y Paz. "Guatemala: Gender and Reparations for Human Rights Violations." In *What Happened to Women? Gender and Reparations for Human Rights Violations*, edited by Ruth Rubio-Marín and International

Center for Transitional Justice, 92–135. New York, NY: Social Science Research Council, 2006.

Baldwin, Annabelle. "Sexual Violence and the Holocaust: Reflections on Memory and Witness Testimony." *Holocaust Studies: A Journal of Culture and History* 16, no. 3 (2010): 112–34.

Banerjee, Sukanya, Angana Chatterji, Lubna Nazir Chaudry, Manali Desai, Saadia Toor, and Kamala Visweswaran. "Engendering Violence: Boundaries, Histories, and the Everyday." *Cultural Dynamics* 16 (2004): 125–39.

Barkan, Joanne. "As Old as War Itself: Rape in Foca." *Dissent* 49, no.1 (2002): 60–7.

Barsony, Janos and Agnes Daroczi. *Pharrajimos: The Fate of the Roma during the Holocaust.* Budapest, Hungary: Central European University Press, 2008.

Bassiouni, M. Cherif, and Marcia McCormick. "Sexual Violence: An Invisible Weapon of War." Occasional Paper no. 1. Chicago, IL: International Human Rights Law Institute, DePaul University College of Law, 1996.

Bauer, Yehuda. *Rethinking the Holocaust.* New Haven, CT: Yale University Press, 2001.

Bauman, Zygmunt. *Modernity and the Holocaust.* Cambridge, UK: Polity Press, 1989.

Baumann, Gerd. "Grammars of Identity/Alterity." In *Grammars of Identity/Alterity: A Structural Approach*, edited by Gerd Baumann and Andre Gingroch. Oxford, UK: Berghahn Books, 2004.

Baumel, Judith. *Double Jeopardy: Gender and the Holocaust.* London, UK: Vallentine Mitchell, 1998.

Bećirević, Edina. *Na Drini Genocide.* Sarajevo, Bosnia-Herzegovina: Buybook, 2009.

Benezer, Gadi. "Trauma Signals in Life Stories." In *Trauma and Life Stories: International Perspectives*, edited by Kim Lacy Rogers, Selma Leydesdorff, and Graham Dawson, 29–44. London, UK and New York, NY: Routledge, 1999.

Bergen, Doris. "Sexual Violence in the Holocaust: Unique and Typical?" In *Lessons and Legacies VII: The Holocaust in International Context*, edited by Dagmar Herzog, 179–200. Evanston, IL: Northwestern University Press, 2006.

Berger, Maurice, Brian Wallis, and Simon Watson, eds. *Constructing Masculinity.* New York, NY: Routledge, 1995.

Binaifer, Nowrojee. *Shattered Lives: Sexual Violence During the Rwandan Genocide and its Aftermath.* New York, NY: Human Rights Watch, 1996.

Bjørnlund, Matthias. "'A Fate Worse than Dying:' Sexual Violence during the Armenian Genocide." In *Brutality and Desire: War and Sexuality in Europe's Twentieth Century*, edited by Dagmag Herzog, 16–58. Evanston, IL: Northwestern University Press, 2006.

Beachler, Donald W. *The Genocide Debate: Politicians, Academics, and Victims.* Basingstoke, UK and New York, NY: Palgrave Macmillan, 2011.

Blok, Anton. "Zinloos en Zinvol Geweld." *Amsterdams Sociologisch Tijdschrift* 18, no. 3 (1991): 189–207.

Bloxham, Donald. *The Final Solution: A Genocide.* Oxford, UK: Oxford University Press, 2009.

Bloxham, Donald. *The Great Game of Genocide: Imperialism, Nationalism and the Destruction of the Ottoman Armenians.* Oxford, UK: Oxford University Press, 2005.

Bloxham, Donald, and Devin O. Pendas. "Punishment as Prevention? The Politics of Prosecuting Génocidaires." In *The Oxford Handbook of Genocide Studies*, edited by Donald Bloxham and A. Dirk Moses, 617–35. Oxford, UK: Oxford University Press, 2010.

Bloxham, Donald, and A. Dirk Moses, eds. *The Oxford Handbook of Genocide Studies*. Oxford, UK: Oxford University Press, 2010.

Bock, Gisela. "Racism and Sexism in Nazi Germany: Motherhood, Compulsory Sterilization, and the State." In *When Biology Became Destiny*, edited by Renate Bridenthal, Atina Grossman, and Marion Kaplan, 271–96. New York, NY: Monthly Review Press, 1984.

Boesten, Jelke. "Analyzing Rape Regimes at the Interface of War and Peace in Peru." *The International Journal of Transitional Justice* 4, no. 1 (2010): 110–29.

Bonnet, Catherine. *Le viol comme arme de guerre au Rwanda: du silence a la reconnaissance*. Paris, France: Médecins Sans Frontières, 1995.

Boose, Lydna, E. "Crossing the River Drina: Bosnian Rape Camps, Turkish Impalement, and Serb Cultural Memory." *Signs: Journal of Women and Culture in Society* 28, no. 1 (2002): 71–96.

Borchelt, Gretchen, and Andrea Barnes. "Sexual Violence Against Women in War and Armed Conflict." In *The Handbook of Women, Psychology, and the Law*, edited by Gretchen Borchelt and Andrea Barnes, 293–327. Hoboken, NJ: John Wiley & Sons Inc., 2005.

Bos, Pascale R. "Women and the Holocaust: Analysing Gender Difference." In *Experience and Expression: Women, the Nazis, and the Holocaust*, edited by Elizabeth Baer and Myrna Goldenberg, 23–52. Detroit, MI: Wayne State University Press, 2003.

Bossen, Laurel. "Toward a Theory of Marriage: The Economic Anthropology of Marriage Transactions." *Ethnology* 27, no. 2 (1988): 127–44.

Boyd, Stephen B., W. Merle Longwood, and Mark W. Muesse, eds. *Redeeming Men: Religion and Masculinities*. Louisville, KY: Westminster/John Knox, 1996.

Bringa, Tone. "Averted Gaze: Genocide in Bosnia-Herzegovina 1992-1995." In *Annihilating Difference: The Anthropology of Genocide*, edited by Alex L. Hinton, 194–228. Berkeley, CA: University of California Press, 2002.

Brod, Harry. "Introduction: Themes and Theses." In *The Making of Masculinities: The New Men's Studies*, edited by Harry Brod. Boston, MA: Unwin Hyman, 1987.

Brod, Harry. "The Case for Men's Studies." In *The Making of Masculinities: The New Men's Studies*, edited by Harry Brod, 39–62. Boston, MA: Allen and Unwin, 1987.

Browning, Christopher. *Ordinary Men: Reserve Police Battalion 101 and the Final Solution in Poland*. New York, NY: HarperCollins, 1992.

Brunet, Ariane, and Isabelle Solon Helal. "Monitoring the Prosecution of Gender-Related Crimes in Rwanda: A Brief Field Report." *Peace and Conflict: Journal of Peace Psychology* 4, no. 4 (1998): 393–7.

Buckley-Ziestel, Susanne. "Redressing Sexual Violence in Transitional Justice and the Labelling of Women as 'Victims.'" In *Victims of International Crime: An Interdisciplinary Discourse*, edited by Thorsten Bonacker and Christopher Safferling, 91–9. The Hague, Netherlands: Asser Press, 2013.

Burnett, Angela, and Michael Peel. "The Health of Survivors of Torture and Organised Violence." *British Medical Journal* 322 (2001): 606–9.

Burnet, Jennie E. "Gender Balance and the Meanings of Women in Governance in Post-Genocide Rwanda." *African Affairs* 107, no. 428 (2008): 361–86.

Burnet, Jennie E. *Genocide Lives in Us: Women, Memory, and Silence in Rwanda.* Madison, WI: University of Wisconsin Press, 2012.

Burnet, Jennie E. "(In)justice: Truth, Reconciliation, and Revenge in Rwanda's Gacaca." In *Transitional Justice: Global Mechanisms and Local Realities After Genocide and Mass Violence*, edited by Alex Laban Hinton, 95–118. New Brunswick, NJ: Rutgers University Press, 2010.

Burnet, Jennie E. "The Injustice of Local Justice: Truth, Reconciliation, and Revenge in Rwanda." *Genocide Studies and Prevention* 3, no. 2 (2008): 173–93.

Burnet, Jennie E. "Whose Genocide? Whose Truth? Representations of Victim and Perpetrator in Rwanda." In *Genocide: Truth, Memory and Representation*, edited by Alex Laban Hinton and Kevin Lewis O'Neill, 80–110. Durham, NC: Duke University Press, 2009.

Burnet, Jennie E., and Rwanda Initiative for Sustainable Development. "Culture, Practice, and Law: Women's Access to Land in Rwanda." In *Women and Land in Africa: Culture, Religion and Realizing Women's Rights*, edited by L. Muthoni Wanyeki, 176–206. New York, NY: Zed Books, 2003.

Bunting, Annie. "'Forced Marriage' in Conflict Situations: Researching and Prosecuting Old Harms and New Crimes." *Canadian Journal of Human Rights* 1, no. 1 (2012): 165–85.

Buss, Doris. "Knowing Women: Translating Patriarchy in International Criminal Law." *Social & Legal Studies* 23, no. 1 (2014): 73–92.

Buss, Doris. "Performing Legal Order: Some Feminist Thoughts On International Criminal Law." *International Criminal Law Review: Special Issue on Women & International Criminal Law* 11 (2011): 409–23.

Buss, Doris. "Rethinking Rape as a Weapon." *Feminist Legal Studies* 17, no. 2 (2009): 145–63.

Buss, Doris. "Seeing Sexual Violence in Conflict and Post-Conflict Societies: The Limits of Visibility." In *Sexual Violence in Conflict and Post-Conflict Societies: International Agendas and African Contexts*, edited by Doris Buss, Joanne Lebert, Blair Rutherford, and Donna Sharkey. London, UK: Routledge, 2014.

Buss, Doris. "Sexual Violence, Ethnicity, and the Limits of Intersectionality in International Criminal Law." In *Intersectionality and Beyond: Law, Power and the Politics of Location*, edited by Emily Grabham, Davina Cooper, Jane Krishnadas, and Didi Herman, 105–123. London, UK: Routledge, 2008.

Buss, Doris. "Women at the Borders: Rape and Nationalism in International Law." *Feminist Legal Studies* 6, no. 2 (1998): 171–203.

Çalışlar, İpek. *Halide Edib: Biyografisine Sığmayan Kadın.* Istanbul, Turkey: Everest, 2010.

Campbell, Kirsten. "The Gender of Transitional Justice: Law, Sexual Violence and the International Criminal Tribunal for the Former Yugoslavia." *International Journal of Transitional Justice* 1, no. 3 (2007): 411–32.

Caplan, Jane. "Gender and the Concentration Camps." In *Concentration Camps in Nazi Germany: The New Histories*, edited by Jane Caplan and Nikolaus Wachsmann, 82–107. London, UK and New York, NY: Routledge, 2010.

Card, Claudia. "Rape as a Weapon of War." *Hypatia* 11, no. 4 (1996): 5–18.

Carlson, Eric Stener. "Sexual Assault on Men in War." *The Lancet* 349 (1997): 129.

Carpenter, R. Charli, ed. *Born of War: Protecting Children of Sexual Violence Survivors in Conflict Zones*. Bloomfield, CT: Kumarian Press, 2007.

Carpenter, R. Charli. *Forgetting Children Born of War*. New York, NY: Columbia University Press, 2010.

Carpenter, R. Charli. *Innocent Women and Children: Gender, Norms and the Protection of Civilians*. Aldershot, UK: Ashgate Press, 2006.

Carpenter, R. Charli. "Recognizing Gender-Based Violence against Men and Boys." *Security Dialogue* 37 (2006): 83–103.

Carpenter, R. Charli. "Surfacing Children: Limitations of Genocidal Rape Discourse." *Human Rights Quarterly* 22, no. 2 (2000): 428–77.

Caruth, Cathy. *Unclaimed Experience: Trauma, Narrative, and History*. Baltimore, MD: Johns Hopkins University Press, 1996.

Chalk, Frank and Kurt Jonassohn. *The History and Sociology of Genocide: Analyses and Case Studies*. New Haven, CT: Yale University Press, 1990.

Charny, Israel. *How Can We Commit the Unthinkable? Genocide: The Human Cancer*. Boulder, CO: Westview Press, 1982.

Chesterman, Simon. *Civilians in War*. Boulder, CO: Lynne Rienner Publishers, Inc., 2001.

Chinkin, Christine. "Rape and Sexual Abuse of Women in International Law." *European Journal of International Law* 5, no. 1 (1994): 326–41.

Chitjian, Hampartzoum Mardiros. *A Hair's Breadth From Death: The Memoirs of Hampartzoum Mardiros Chitjian*. London, UK: Taderon Press, 2003.

Choko, Isabelle, Frances Irwin, Lotti Kahana-Aufleger, Margit Kalina, and Jane Lipski. *Stolen Youth: Five Women's Survival in the Holocaust*. New York, NY and Jerusalem: Yad Vashem, 2005.

Cigar, Norman. *The Bridge Betrayed: Religion and Genocide in Bosnia*. Berkeley and Los Angeles, CA: University of California Press, 1996.

Clark, Janine Natalya. "A Crime of Identity: Rape and Its Neglected Victims." *Journal of Human Rights* 13, no. 2 (2014): 146–69.

Clendinnen, Inga. *Reading the Holocaust*. Cambridge, UK: Cambridge University, 1999.

Cockburn, Cynthia. *The Space Between Us: Negotiating Gender and National Identity in Conflict*. London, UK: Zed Books, 1998.

Cohn, Carol. "Women and Wars: Toward a Conceptual Framework." In *Women and Wars: Contested Histories, Uncertain Futures*, edited by Carol Cohn, 1–35. Cambridge, UK: Polity Press, 2012.

Connell, Raewyn W. *Gender*. Cambridge, UK: Polity, 2009.

Connell, R. W. *Masculinities*. Berkeley, CA: University of California, 1995.

Copelon, Rhonda. "Surfacing Gender: Reconceptualizing Crimes against Women in Time of War." In *Mass Rape: The War Against Women in Bosnia-Herzegovina*, edited by Alexandra Stiglmayer, 197–218. Lincoln, NE: University of Nebraska Press, 1994.

Curthoys, Ann and John Docker. "Defining Genocide." In *The Historiography of Genocide*, edited by Dan Stone. Cambridge, UK: Cambridge University Press, 2008.

Damir, Arsenijević. "Gendering the Bone: The Politics of Memory in Bosnia Herzegovina." *Journal for Cultural Research* 15, no. 2 (2011): 193–205.

Danielyan, Edward G. *The Armenian Genocide of 1894-1922 and the Accountability of the Turkish State*. Yerevan, Armenia: Noyan Tapan, 2005.

Das, Veena. "Language and the Body: Transactions in the Construction of Pain." *Daedalus* 125, no. 1 (1996): 67–91.

Das, Veena. "National Honour and Practical Kinship: Of Unwanted Women and Children." In *Critical Events: An Anthropological Perspective on Contemporary India*, edited by Veena Das, 55–83. Oxford, UK: Oxford University Press, 1995.

Das, Veena. "Sexual Violence, Discursive Formations and the State." *Economic and Political Weekly* 31 (1996): 2411–23.

Das, Veena. "Violence, Gender and Subjectivity." *Annual Review Anthropology* 37 (2008): 283–99.

Davis, Christopher G., Susan Nolen-Hoeksema, and Judith Larson. "Making Sense of Loss and Benefiting from the Experience: Two Construals of Meaning." *Journal of Personality and Social Psychology* 75 (1998): 561–74.

Day, Sophie. "What Counts as Rape? Physical Assault and Broken Contracts: Contrasting Views of Rape Among London Sex Workers." In *Sex and Violence: Issues in Representation and Experience*, edited by Penelope Harvey and Peter Gow, 172–89. New York, NY: Routledge, 1994.

Debnath, Angela. "The Bangladesh Genocide: The Plight of Women." In *Plight and Fate of Women During and Following Genocide*, edited by Samual Totten, 47–66. London, UK and New Brunswick, NJ: Transaction Publishers, 2009.

de Brouwer, Anne-Marie. *Sexual Violence as an Act of Genocide: Supranational Criminal Prosecution of Sexual Violence: The ICC and the Practice of the ICTY and the ICTR*. Cambridge, UK: Intersentia, 2005.

de Brouwer, Anne-Marie. *Supranational Criminal Prosecution of Sexual Violence: The ICC and the Practice of the ICTY and the ICTR*. Antwerp, Belgium and Oxford, UK: Intersentia, 2005.

de Brouwer, Anne-Marie and Sandra Ka Hon Chu, eds. *The Men Who Killed Me: Rwandan Survivors of Sexual Violence*. Vancouver, Canada: Douglas & McIntyre, 2009.

Decker, John F., and Peter G. Baroni. "'No' Still Means 'Yes' the Failure of the 'Non-Consent' Reform Movement in American Rape and Sexual Assault Law." *Journal of Criminal Law & Criminology* 101, no. 4 (2011): 1081–169.

de Lame, Danielle. *A Hill Among a Thousand: Transformations and Ruptures in Rural Rwanda (English translation: Une colline entre mille, ou, Le calme avant la tempête)*. Madison, WI: University of Wisconsin Press, 2005 (1994).

Del Zotto, Augusta and Adam Jones. "Male-on-Male Sexual Violence in Wartime: Human Rights' Last Taboo?" Paper presented at the Annual Convention of the International Studies Association (ISA), New Orleans, LA, 2002.

Derderian, Katherine. "Common Fate, Different Experience: Gender-Specific Aspects of the Armenian Genocide, 1915-1917." *Holocaust and Genocide Studies* 19, no. 1 (2005): 1–25.

Der Yeghiayan, Zaven. *My Patriarchal Memoirs*. Waltham, MA: Mayreni Publishing Inc., 2002.

Des Forges, Alison L. *Leave None to Tell the Story: Genocide in Rwanda*. New York, NY: Human Rights Watch, 1999.

Des Forges, Alison L., and David S. Newbury, eds. *Defeat is the Only Bad News: Rwanda under Musinga, 1896-1931*. Madison, WI: The University of Wisconsin Press, 2011.

Devoine, Francois, and Jean Max Gaudilliere. *History Beyond Trauma*. New York, NY: Other Press, 2004.

Dixon, Peter, and Chris Tenove. "International Criminal Justice as a Transnational Field: Rules, Authority and Victims." *International Journal of Transitional Justice* 7, no. 3 (2013): 393–412.

Dolan, Chris. "*War is Not Yet Over:*" *Community Perceptions of Sexual Violence and its Underpinnings in Eastern DRC*. London, UK: International Alert, 2010.

Don-Yehiya, Eliezer. "Memory and Political Culture: Israeli Society and the Holocaust." *Studies in Contemporary Jewry* 9 (1993): 139–61.

Drumbl, Mark A. *Atrocity, Punishment and International Law*. Cambridge, UK: Cambridge University Press, 2007.

Drumbl, Mark A. "Rule of Law Amid Lawlessness: Counseling the Accused in Rwanda's Domestic Genocide Trials." *Columbia Human Rights Law Review* 29 (1998): 545–639.

Drumbl, Mark A. "'She Makes Me Ashamed to be a Woman': The Genocide Conviction of Pauline Nyiramasuhuko, 2011." *Michigan Journal of International Law* 34, no. 3 (2013): 559–603.

Drumbl, Mark A. "The ICTR and Justice for Rwandan Women." *New England Journal of International and Comparative Law* 12 (2005): 105–17.

Dowd, Nancy E. "Masculinities and Femininities Legal Theory." *Wisconsin Journal of Law, Gender and Society* 23 (2008): 201–48.

Drumond, Paula. "Invisible Males: A Critical Assessment of UN Gender Mainstreaming Policies in the Congolese Genocide." In *New Directions in Genocide Research*, edited by Adam Jones, 96–112. London, UK: Routledge, 2012.

Duggan, Colleen, and Ruth Jacobson. "Reparation of Sexual and Reproductive Violence: Moving from Codification to Implementation." In *The Gender of Reparations*, edited by Ruth Rubio-Marín, 121–61. New York, NY: Cambridge University Press, 2009.

Dwork, Deborah, and Robert Jan van Pelt. *Auschwitz: 1270 to the Present*. New York, NY: W. W. Norton, 1996.

Eblighatian, Madteos. *Giank Me Azkis Giankin Mech: Aganadesi Yev Masnagtsoghi Vgayutiunner 1903-1923*. Beirut, Lebanon: Antilias, 1987.

Ekmekcioglu, Lerna. "A Climate for Abduction, A Climate for Redemption: The Politics of Inclusion during and after the Armenian Genocide." *Comparative Studies in Society and History* 55, no. 3 (2013): 522–53.

Elander, Maria. "The Victim's Address: Expressivism and the Victim at the Extraordinary Chambers in the Courts of Cambodia." *International Journal of Transitional Justice* 7, no. 1 (2013): 95–115.

Ellis, Mark. "Breaking the Silence: Rape as an International Crime." *Case Western Reserve Journal of International Law* 225 (2006): 225–47.

Elshtain, Jean Bethke. *Women and War*. New York, NY: Basic Books, 1987.

Engle, Karen. "Feminism and Its (Dis)contents: Criminalizing Wartime Rape in Bosnia-Herzegovina." *The American Journal of International Law* 99, no. 4 (2005): 778–816.

Enloe, Cynthia. *The Morning After: Sexual Politics at the End of the Cold War*. Berkeley, CA: University of California Press, 1993.

Fabri, Mary, Jianhong Lu, Agnes Binagwaho, Kathryn Anastos, Mardge Cohen, Davis Kashaka, and Henriette Mukayonga. "Chronic PTSD and HIV in Rwanda." Paper presented at the Politics, Policy, & Public Health Conference, Washington, DC: APHA, 2007.

Farrell, Warren. *The Myth of Male Power: Why Men Are the Disposable Sex.* New York, NY: Simon & Schuster, 1993.

Faludi, Susan. *Stiffed: The Betrayal of the American Man.* New York, NY: William Morrow & Company, 1999.

Fearon, James D., and David D. Laitin. "Violence and the Social Construction of Ethnic Identity." *International Organization* 54, no. 4 (2000): 845–77.

Feierstein, Daniel. "National Security Doctrine in Latin America: The Genocide Question." In *Oxford Handbook of Genocide Studies*, edited by Donald Bloxham and A. Dirk Moses, 489–508. Oxford, UK: Oxford University Press, 2010.

Feierstein, Daniel. "Political Violence in Argentina and Its Genocidal Characteristics." In *State Violence and Genocide in Latin America*, edited by Marcia Esperanza, Henry R. Huttenbach, and Daniel Feierstein, 44–63. London, UK: Routledge, 2010.

Fein, Helen. "Genocide and Gender: The Uses of Women and Group Destiny." *Journal of Genocide Research* 1, no. 1 (1999): 43–63.

Fein, Helen. "Genocide: A Sociological Perspective." *Current Sociology* 38, no. 1 (1990): 1–126.

Felman, Shoshana. *The Juridical Unconsciousness: Trials and Traumas in the Twentieth Century.* Cambridge, MA and London, UK: Harvard University Press, 2002.

Felman, Shoshana, and Dori Laub. *Testimony: Crises of Witnessing in Literature, Psychoanalysis and History.* New York, NY and London, UK: Routledge, 1992.

Finkelstein, Norman G., and Ruth Bettina Birn. *A Nation on Trial: The Goldhagen Thesis and Historical Truth.* New York, NY: Holt, 1998.

Fisher, Siobhan K. "Occupation of the Womb: Forced Impregnation as Genocide." *Duke Law Journal* 46, no. 1 (1996): 91–133.

Fleming, Marie. "Genocide and the Body Politic in the Time of Modernity." In *The Specter of Genocide: Mass Murder in Historical Perspective*, edited by Robert Gellately and Ben Kiernan, 97–113. Cambridge, UK: Cambridge University Press, 2003.

Fletcher, Laurel E., and Harvey M. Weinstein. "Violence and Social Repair: Rethinking the Contribution of Justice to Reconciliation." *Human Rights Quarterly* 24 (2002): 573–639.

Foucault, Michel. *The Will of Knowledge: The History of Sexuality v. 1.* London, UK: Penguin Books, 1978.

Fraser, Nancy. "Rethinking Recognition." *New Left Review* 113 (2000): 107–20.

Fraser, Nancy, and Axel Honneth. *Redistribution or Recognition? A Political-Philosophical Exchange.* London, UK: Verso, 2003.

Fujii, Lee Ann. *Killing Neighbors: Webs of Violence in Rwanda.* Ithaca, NY: Cornell University Press, 2009.

Gagnon, V. P., Jr. *The Myth of Ethnic War: Serbia and Croatia in the 1990s.* Ithaca, NY: Cornell University Press, 2004.

Gaunt, David. *Massacres, Resistance, Protectors: Muslim-Christian Relations in Eastern Anatolia During World War I.* Piscataway, NJ: Gorgias Press, 2006.

Gellately, Robert, and Ben Kiernan, eds. *The Specter of Genocide: Mass Murder in Historical Perspective.* Cambridge, UK and New York, NY: Cambridge University Press, 2003.

Goldenberg, Myrna. "Different Horrors, Same Hell: Women Remembering the Holocaust." In *Thinking the Unthinkable: Meanings of the Holocaust*, edited by Roger Gottlieb, 150–66. New York, NY: Paulist Press, 1991.

Goldenberg, Myrna. "Memoirs of Auschwitz Survivors: The Burden of Gender." In *Women in the Holocaust*, edited by Dalia Ofer and Lenore Weitzman, 327–39. New Haven, CT: Yale University Press, 1998.

Goldenberg, Myrna. "Rape during the Holocaust." In *The Legacy of the Holocaust: Women and the Holocaust*, edited by Zygmunt Mazur, Jay T. Lees, Arnold Krammer, and Wladyslaw Witalisz, 159–69. Kraków, Poland: Jagiellonian University Press, 2005.

Goldhagen, Daniel Jonah. *Hitler's Willing Executioners: Ordinary Germans and the Holocaust*. New York, NY: Knopf, 1996.

Gottesfeld, Heller Fanya. *Love in a World of Sorrow: A Teenage Girl's Holocaust Memoirs*, New York, NY: Devora Publishing Company, 2005.

Grau, Gunter, ed. *Hidden Holocaust? Gay and Lesbian Persecution in Germany, 1933-1945*, translated by Patrick Camiller. Chicago, IL: Fitzroy Dearborn, 1995.

Grossmann, Atina. "Women and the Holocaust: Four Recent Titles." *Holocaust and Genocide Studies* 16, no. 1 (2002): 94–108.

Grossman, Atina. "Victims, Villains, and Survivors: Gendered Perceptions and Self-Perceptions of Jewish Displaced Persons in Postwar Germany." *Journal of the History of Sexuality* 11:1–2 (2002): 291–318.

Grossman, Atina. *Jews, Germans, and Allies: Close Encounters in Occupied Germany*. Princeton: Princeton University Press, 2007.

Gurewitsch, Brana. *Mothers, Sisters, Resisters: Oral Histories of Women Who Survived the Holocaust*. Tuscaloosa, AL: University of Alabama Press, 1998.

Gutman, Ray. *A Witness to Genocide: The 1993 Pulitzer Prize-Winning Dispatches on the "Ethnic Cleansing" of Bosnia*. New York, NY: Macmillan Publishing Company, 1993.

Hague, Euan. "Rape, Power and Masculinity: The Construction of Gender and National Identities in the War in Bosnia-Herzegovina." In *Gender and Catastrophe*, edited by Ronit Lentin, 50–63. London: Zed Books, 1997.

Hagen, John, and Wenona Rymond-Richmond. *Darfur and the Crime of Genocide*. New York, NY: Cambridge University Press, 2009.

Hájková, Anna. "Sexual Barter in Times of Genocide: Negotiating the Sexual Economy of the Theresienstadt Ghetto." *Signs* 38, no. 3 (2013): 503–33.

Halley, Janet. "Rape at Rome: Feminist Interventions in the Criminalization of Sex-Related Violence in Positive International Criminal Law." *Michigan Journal of International Law* 30 (2008–09): 1–123.

Halsell, Grace. "Women's Bodies a Battlefield in War for 'Greater Serbia.'" *Washington Report on Middle East Affairs* 11, no. 9 (1993): 8–9.

Hancock, Ian. "Romanies and the Holocaust: A Reevaluation and an Overview." In *The Historiography of the Holocaust*, edited by Dan Stone, 383–96. Basingstoke, UK and New York, NY: Palgrave Macmillan, 2004.

Hardi, Choman. *Gendered Experiences of Genocide: Anfal Survivors in Kurdistan-Iraq*. Burlington, VT: Ashgate Publishing Limited, 2011.

Hardmann, Anna. *Women and the Holocaust*. London, UK: Holocaust Educational Trust, 2000.

Harris, Ruth. "The 'Child of the Barbarian': Rape, Race and Nationalism in France during the First World War." *Past and Present* 141 (1993): 170–206.

Harvard Humanitarian Initiative and Oxfam International. "*Now the World is Without Me*": *An Investigation of Sexual Violence in Eastern Democratic Republic of the Congo*, 2010.

Harvey, Elizabeth. *Women and the Nazi East: Agents and Witnesses of Germanization*. New Haven, CT: Yale University Press, 2003.

Harvey, Penelope. "Domestic Violence in the Peruvian Andes." In *Sex and Violence: Issues in Representation and Experience*, edited by Penelope Harvey and Peter Gow, 66–89. New York, NY: Routledge, 1994.

Hastings Law Symposium. "Rape as a Weapon of War in the Former Yugoslavia." *Hastings Women's Law Journal* 5, no. 1 (1994): 69–88.

Hayden, Robert McBeth. *Blueprints for a House Divided: The Constitutional Logic of the Yugoslav Conflicts*. Ann Arbor, MI: University of Michigan Press, 1999.

Hayden, Robert McBeth. "Rape and Rape Avoidance in Ethno-National Conflicts: Sexual Violence in Liminalized States." *American Anthropologist* 102, no. 1 (2000): 27–41.

Hedgpeth, Sonja M., and Rochelle G. Saidel. *Sexual Violence Against Women During the Holocaust*. Waltham, MA: Brandeis University Press, 2010.

Heike, Irmtraud. "Female Concentration Camp Guards as Perpetrators: Three Case Studies." In *Ordinary People as Mass Murderers: Perpetrators in Comparative Perspective (Holocaust and Its Contexts)*, edited by Olaf Jensen and Claus-Christian W. Szejnmann, 120–44. London, UK: Palgrave Macmillan, 2008.

Heinemann, Marlene. *Gender and Destiny: Women Writers and the Holocaust*. Santa Barbara, CA: Praeger, 1986.

Helsinki, Watch. *War Crimes in Bosnia-Hercegovina Vol I*. New York, NY: Human Rights Watch, 1992.

Henry, Nicola. "The Fixation on Wartime Rape: Feminist Critique and International Criminal Law." *Social & Legal Studies* 23, no. 1 (2014): 93–111.

Herkommer, Christina. "Women Under National Socialism: Women's Scope for Action and the Issue of Gender." In *Ordinary People as Mass Murderers: Perpetrators in Comparative Perspective (Holocaust and Its Contexts)*, edited by Olaf Jensen and Claus-Christian W. Szejnmann, 99–119. New York, NY: Palgrave MacMillan, 2008.

Herman, Edward and Phillip Corwin. *The Srebrenica Massacre*. Montreal: Centre for Research on Globalization, 2011.

Herman, Edward, and Scott Peterson. *The Politics of Genocide*. New York, NY: Monthly Review Press, 2010.

Herzog, Dagmar, ed. *Brutality and Desire: War and Sexuality in Europe's Twentieth Century*. Basingstoke, UK: Palgrave Macmillan, 2009, 2011.

Herzog, Dagmar. *Sexuality and German Fascism*. New York, NY and Oxford, UK: Berghahn, 2005.

Herzog, Dagmar. "Sexual Violence Against Men." In *Rape: Weapon of War and Genocide*, edited by Carol Rittner and John K. Roth, 29–44. St. Paul, MN: Paragon House, 2012.

Heschel, Susannah. "Does Atrocity Have A Gender? Feminist Interpretations of Women in the SS." In *Lessons and Legacies: New Currents in Holocaust Research, Vol. IV.*, edited by Jeffry Diefendorf, 300–21. Evanston, IL: Northwestern University Press, 2004.

Hilberg, Raul. *The Destruction of the European Jews*. New York, NY: Holmes & Meier, 1961.

Hilberg, Raul. *Perpetrators, Victims, Bystanders: The Jewish Catastrophe, 1933 to 1945*. London, UK: HarperCollins, 1993.

Hinton, Alexander Laban. "The Dark Side of Modernity: Toward an Anthropology of Genocide." In *Annihilating Difference: The Anthropology of Genocide*, edited by Alexander Laban Hinton, 1–42. Los Angeles, CA: University of California Press, 2002.

Hirsch, Marianne, and Valerie Smith. "Feminism and Cultural Memory: An Introduction." *Signs: Journal of Women in Culture & Society* 28, no.1 (2002): 1–19.

Hochschild, Adam. *King Leopold's Ghost*. Boston, MA: Houghton Mifflin, 1998.

Hogg, Nicole. "Women's Participation in the Rwandan Genocide: Mothers or Monsters?" *International Review of the Red Cross* 92, no. 877 (2010): 69–102.

Hooper, Charlotte. *Manly States: Masculinity, International Relations, and Gender Politics*. New York, NY: Columbia University Press, 2001.

Honing, Jan W., and Norbert Both. *Srebrenica: Record of a War Crime*. London, UK: Penguin, 1996.

Horowitz, Sara. "Memory and Testimony of Women Survivors of Nazi Germany." In *Women of the Word: Jewish Women and Jewish Writing*, edited by Judith Baskin, 258–82. Detroit, MI: Wayne State University Press, 1994.

Howard, Jonathan P. "Survey Methodology and the Darfur Genocide." In *Genocide in Darfur: Investigating the Atrocities in Sudan*, edited by Samuel Totten and Eric Markusen, 59–74. London, UK: Routledge, 2006.

Hubbard, Jessica A. "Justice for Women? Rape as Genocide and the International Criminal Tribunal for Rwanda." In *Rape: Weapon of War and Genocide*, edited by Carol Rittner and John K. Roth, 101–16. St. Paul, MN: Paragon House, 2012.

Human Rights Watch. *Beyond the Rhetoric: Continuing Human Rights Abuses in Rwanda*. New York, NY: Human Rights Watch, 1993.

Human Rights Watch. "Darfur in Flames: Atrocities in Western Sudan." *Sudan* 16, no. 5. New York, NY: HRW, 2004.

Human Rights Watch. *Shattered Lives: Sexual Violence During the Rwandan Genocide and its Aftermath*. New York, NY: Human Rights Watch, 1996.

Human Rights Watch. *Struggling to Survive: Barriers to Justice for Rape Victims in Rwanda*. New York, NY: Human Rights Watch, 2004.

Human Rights Watch. "*You Will Be Punished:*" *Atrocities in Eastern Congo*. New York, NY: Human Rights Watch, 2009.

Hunter, Mark. "The Changing Political Economy of Sex in South Africa: The Significance of Unemployment and Inequalities to the Scale of the AIDS Pandemic." *Social Science & Medicine* 64, no. 3 (2007): 689–700.

Hunter, Mark. "The Materiality of Everyday Sex: Thinking Beyond 'Prostitution.'" *African Studies* 61, no. 1 (2002): 99–120.

Ignatieff, Michael. *Blood and Belonging: Journey into the New Nationalism*. Toronto, Canada: Penguin Canada, 1994.

Ingelaere, Bert. "'Does the Truth Pass Across the Fire Without Burning?' Locating the Short Circuit in Rwanda's Gacaca Courts." *Journal of Modern African Studies* 47, no. 4 (2009): 507–28.

Integrated Regional Information Networks. "Analysis: Rethinking Sexual Violence in Democratic Republic of the Congo." Available online: http://www.unhcr.org/refworld/docid/4c64f1071e.html.

Jacobs, Janet. *Memorializing the Holocaust: Gender, Genocide, and Collective Memory.* London, UK and New York, NY: I. B. Tauris, 2010.

Jansen, Stef, and Elissa Helsm. "The 'White Plague:' National-Demographic Rhetoric and Its Gendered Resonance after the Post-Yugoslav Wars." In *Gender Dynamics and Post-Conflict Reconstruction*, edited by Christine Eifler and Ruth Siefert, 219–43. Frankfurt, Germany: Peter Lang, 2009.

Jefremovas, Villia. *Brickyards to Graveyards: From Production to Genocide in Rwanda.* Albany, NY: State University of New York Press, 2002.

Jefremovas, Villia. "Loose Women, Virtuous Wives and Timid Virgins: Gender and Control of Resources in Rwanda." *Canadian Journal of African Studies* 25, no. 3 (1991): 378–95.

Jensen, Erik. "The Pink Triangle and Political Consciousness: Gays, Lesbians, and the Memory of Nazi Persecution." *Journal of the History of Sexuality* 11, no. 1 and 2 (2002): 319–49.

Jensen, Olaf, and Claus-Christian W. Szejnmann, eds. *Ordinary People as Mass Murderers: Perpetrators in Comparative Perspective.* Basingstoke, UK: Palgrave Macmillan, 2008.

Johnson, Kirsten, Jennifer Scott, Bigy Rughita, Michael Kisielewski, Jana Asher, Ricardo Ong, and Lynn Lawry. "Association of Sexual Violence and Human Rights Violations with Physical and Mental Health in Territories of the Eastern Democratic Republic of the Congo." *Journal of the American Medical Association* 304, no. 5 (2010): 553–62.

Jones, Adam. "Does Gender Make the World Go Round? Feminist Critiques of International Relations." *Review of International Studies* 22, no. 4 (1996): 405–29.

Jones, Adam. "Gender and Ethnic Conflict in Ex-Yugoslavia." *Ethnic and Racial Studies* 17, no.1 (1994): 115–34.

Jones, Adam. "Gendercidal Institutions against Women and Girls." In *Women in an Insecure World: Violence against Women: Facts, Figures and Analysis*, edited by Marie Vlachová and Lea Biason, 15–24. Geneva, Switzerland: Centre for the Democratic Control of Armed Forces, 2005.

Jones, Adam. "Gendercide and Genocide." *Journal of Genocide Research* 2, no. 2 (2000): 185–211.

Jones, Adam, ed. *Gendercide and Genocide.* Nashville, TN: Vanderbilt University Press, 2004.

Jones, Adam. "Gender and Genocide in Rwanda." *Journal of Genocide Research* 4, no. 1 (2002): 65–94.

Jones, Adam. *Gender Inclusive: Essays on Violence, Men, and Feminist International Relations.* New York, NY: Routledge, 2009.

Jones, Adam. *Genocide: A Comprehensive Introduction.* 2nd edn. London, UK and New York, NY: Routledge, 2010.

Jones, Adam. "Genocide and Humanitarian Intervention: Incorporating the Gender Variable." In *Gender Inclusive, Essays on Violence, Men, and Feminist International Relations*, edited by Adam Jones, 255–83. London, UK: Routledge, 2011.

Jones, Adam. "Of Rights and Men: Toward a Minoritarian Framing of Male Experience." *Journal of Human Rights* 1, no. 3 (2002): 387–403.

Jones, Adam. "On Genocide Deniers: Challenging Herman and Peterson." *Pambazuka News* 490 (July 15, 2010).

Jones, Adam. "Preface: A Pilgrim's Progress." In *Gender Inclusive, Essays on Violence, Men, and Feminist International Relations*, edited by Adam Jones, xi–xx. London, UK: Routledge, 2009.

Jones, Adam. "Straight as a Rule: Heteronormativity, Gendercide, and the Non-Combatant Male." In *Gender Inclusive: Essays on Violence, Men, and Feminist International Relations*, edited by Adam Jones, 292–308. London, UK: Routledge, 2009.

Kaldor, Mary. *New and Old Wars: Organized Violence in a Global Era.* Stanford, CA: Stanford University Press, 1999.

Kamatali, Jean-Marie, and Philippe Gafishi. *Situation des Enfants et des Femmes du Rwanda: Survie, Développement et Protection.* Kigali, Rwanda: Gouvernement de la République Rwandaise et UNICEF, 2000.

Kaplan, Marion. *Between Dignity and Despair: Jewish Life in Nazi Germany.* Oxford, UK: Oxford University Press, 1998.

Kaplan, Marion. "Jewish Women in Nazi Germany: Daily Life, Daily Struggles, 1933-1939." *Feminist Studies* 16, no. 3 (1990): 579–606.

Kaplan, Marion. "Keeping Calm and Weathering the Storm: Jewish Women's Responses to Daily Life in Nazi Germany." In *Women in the Holocaust*, edited by Dalia Ofer and Lenore Weitzman, 39–54. New Haven, CT: Yale University Press.

Kanchan, Chandra. "What Is Ethnic Identity and Does it Matter?" *Annual Review of Political Science* 9 (2006): 397–424.

Kaprielian-Churchill, Isabel. "Armenian Refugee Women: The Picture Brides 1920–1930." *Journal of American Ethnic History* 12, no. 3 (1993): 3–29.

Katz, Esther, and Joan Ringelheim, eds. *Proceedings of the Conference on Women Surviving the Holocaust.* New York, NY: Institute for Research in History, 1983.

Kaufman, Joyce P., and Kristen P. Williams. *Women, the State, and War: A Comparative Perspective on Citizenship and Nationalism.* Lanham, MD: Lexington Books, 2007.

Kayishema Jean-Marie V., and François Masabo. *Les Justes Rwandais "Indakemwa."* Kigali, Rwanda: Ibuka, 2011.

Kelly, Jocelyn. "Special Report: Rape in War: Motives of Militia in DRC." Washington, DC: United States Institute of Peace, 2010.

Kévorkian, Raymond. *The Armenian Genocide: A Complete History.* New York, NY: I. B. Tauris, 2011.

Kimmel, Michael. "Masculinity as Homophobia: Fear, Shame, and Silence in the Construction of a Gender Identity." In *The Masculinities Reader*, edited by Stephen M. Whitehead and Frank Barrett, 266–87. Cambridge, UK: Polity Press, 2001.

King, Neal. *Speaking Our Truths: Voices of Courage and Healing for Male Survivors of Childhood Sexual Abuse.* New York, NY: Harper Collins, 1995.

King, Richard, and Dan Stone, eds. *Hannah Arendt and the Uses of History: Imperialism, Nation, Race, and Empire.* New York, NY and London, UK: Berghahn Books, 2007.

Klee, Ernst, Willi Dressen, Volker Riess, and Hugh Trevor-Roper, eds. *The Good Old Days: The Holocaust as Seen Through the Eyes of Perpetrators and Bystanders*. New York, NY: Free Press, 1994.

Kohn, Elizabeth. "Rape as a Weapon of War: Women's Human Rights during the Dissolution of Yugoslavia." *Golden Gate University Law Review* 24 (1994): 199–223.

Kolinsky, Eva. *After the Holocaust: Jewish Survivors in Germany After 1945*. London, UK: Pimlico, 2004.

Koonz, Claudia. *Mothers in the Fatherland: Women, the Family and Nazi Politics*. New York, NY: St. Martin's, 1987.

Koonz, Claudia. *The Nazi Conscience*. Cambridge, MA: Harvard University Press, 2003.

Kuper, Leo. *Genocide: Its Political Use in the Twentieth Century*. Harmondsworth, UK: Penguin, 1981.

LaCapra, Dominique. *Writing History, Writing Trauma*. Baltimore, MD: John Hopkins University Press, 2001.

Lagerway, Mary. *Reading Auschwitz*. London, UK: Sage, 1998.

Landsberg, Alison. "America, the Holocaust, and the Mass Culture of Memory: Toward a Radical Politics of Empathy." *New German Critique* 71 (1997): 63–86.

Laub, Dori. "Truth and Testimony, The Process and the Struggle." In *Trauma: Explorations in Memory*, edited by Cathy Caruth, 61–76. Baltimore, MD: John Hopkins University Press, 1995.

Leatherman, Janie L. *Sexual Violence and Armed Conflict*. Cambridge, UK: Polity Press, 2011.

Ledgerwood, Judy. "Death, Shattered Families, and Living as Widows in Cambodia." In *Plight and Fate of Women During and Following Genocide*, edited by Samual Totten, 67–81. London, UK and New Brunswick, NJ: Transaction Publishers, 2009.

Lemkin, Raphael. *Axis Rule in Occupied Europe: Laws of Occupation, Analysis of Government, Proposals for Redress*. Washington, DC: Carnegie Endowment for International Peace, 1944.

Levene, Mark. *Genocide in the Age of the Nation State, Vol. 1 & 2*. London, UK: I. B. Tauris, 2005.

Levine, Michael G. *The Belated Witness: Literature, Testimony and the Question of Holocaust Survival*. Palo Alto, CA: Stanford University Press, 2006.

Leydesdorff, Selma. *Surviving the Bosnian Genocide: The Women of Srebrenica Speak*. Bloomington, IN: Indiana University Press, 2011.

Lifton, Robert J. *The Nazi Doctors: Medical Killing and the Psychology of Genocide*. London, UK: Macmillan, 1986.

Lonçar, Mladen. "Sexual Torture of Men in the War." In *War Violence, Trauma and the Coping Process: Armed Conflict in Europe and the Survivor Response*, edited by Libby Tata Arcel, 45–79. Copenhagen, Denmark: University of Copenhagen Press, 1998.

Lower, Wendy. "'Anticipatory Obedience' and the Nazi Implementation of the Holocaust in the Ukraine: A Case Study of Central and Peripheral Forces in the Generalbezirk Zhytomer, 1941-1944." *Holocaust and Genocide Studies* 16, no. 1 (2002): 1–22.

Lower, Wendy. *Hitler's Furies: German Women in the Nazi Killing Fields*. New York: Houghton Mifflin, 2013.

Lubkemann, Stephen C. *Culture in Chaos: An Anthropology of the Social Condition in War*. Chicago, IL: University of Chicago Press, 2008.

MacKinnon, Catherine A., ed. *Are Women Human? And Other International Dialogues*. Cambridge, MA: Harvard University Press, 2006.

MacKinnon, Catherine A., ed. "Genocide's Sexuality." In *Are Women Human? And Other International Dialogues*, edited by Catherine MacKinnon, 209–36. Cambridge, MA: Harvard University Press, 2006.

MacKinnon, Catherine A., ed. "Rape, Genocide, and Women's Human Rights." *Harvard Women's Law Journal* 17, no. 5 (1994): 5–16.

MacKinnon, Catherine A., ed. "Rape, Genocide, and Women's Human Rights." In *Mass Rape: The War Against Women in Bosnia-Herzegovina*, edited by Alexandra Stiglmayer, 183–95. Lincoln, NE: University of Nebraska Press, 1994.

MacKinnon, Catherine A., ed. "Trafficking, Prostitution, and Inequality." *Harvard Civil Rights—Civil Liberties Law Review* 46, no. 2 (2011): 271–309.

MacKinnon, Catherine A., "Turning Rape into Pornography: Postmodern Genocide." *Ms. Magazine* 5, no. 1 (1993): 24–30.

Maier, Donna J. "Women Leaders in the Rwandan Genocide: When Women Choose to Kill." *Universitas* 8 (2012–13).

Mahoney, Michael R. "The Zulu Kingdom as a Genocidal and Post-genocidal Society, c. 1810 to the Present." *Journal of Genocide Research* 5, no. 2 (2003): 251–68.

Maksudyan, Nazan. "The Fight over Nobody's Children: Religion, Nationality and Citizenship of Foundlings in the Late Ottoman Empire." *New Perspectives on Turkey* 41 (2009): 151–80.

Malkki, Liisa. *Purity and Exile: Violence, Memory, and National Cosmology Among Hutu Refugees in Tanzania*. Chicago, IL: University of Chicago Press, 1995.

Marcuse, Harold. "The Revival of Holocaust Awareness in West Germany, Israel, and the United States." In *1968: The World Transformed*, edited by Carole Fink, Philipp Gassert, and Detlev Junker, 421–38. Cambridge, UK: Cambridge University Press, 1998.

Marrus, Michael. *The Holocaust in History*. Hanover, NH and London, UK: University Press of New England, 1987.

Mason, Christine. "Women, Violence and Nonviolent Resistance in East Timor." *Journal of Peace Research* 42, no. 6 (2005): 737–49.

Matokot-Mianzenza, Sidonie. *Viol des femmes dans les conflits armés et thérapies familiales: cas du Congo Brazzaville*. Paris, France: L'Harmattan, 2003.

Matossian, Nouritza. *Black Angel: A Life of Arshile Gorky*. London, UK: Pimlico, 2001.

Matton, Sylvie. *Srebrenica: Un génocide annoncé*. Paris, France: Flammarion, 2005.

McKelvey, Tara, ed. *One of the Guys: Women as Aggressors and Torturers*. Emeryville, CA: Seal Press, 2007.

Medić, Adil, and Melike Malešević. *Torture u Bosni i Hercegovini za vrijeme rata 1992-1995*. Sarajevo: Savez logoraša Bosne i Hercegovine, 2003.

Melhado, L. "Rates of Sexual Violence Are High in Democratic Republic of the Congo." *International Perspectives on Sexual and Reproductive Health* 36 (2010): 210.

Melson, Robert F. *Revolution and Genocide: On the Origins of the Armenian Genocide and the Holocaust*. Chicago, IL: The University of Chicago Press, 1992.

Melson, Robert F. "The Armenian Genocide as Precursor and Prototype of Twentieth-Century Genocide." In *Is the Holocaust Unique?*, edited by Alan S. Rosenbaum, 205–30. Boulder, CO: Westview Press, 2001.

Mendelson, Sarah E. *Barracks and Brothels: Peacekeepers and Human Trafficking in the Balkans*. Washington, DC: Centre for Strategic and International Studies, 2005.

Mertus, Julie. "'Women' in the Service of National Identity." *Hastings Women's Law Journal* 5 (1994): 5–23.

Messerschmidt, James W. *Masculinities and Crime: Critique and Reconceptualization of Theory*. Lanham, MD: Rowman & Littlefield, 1993.

Mezey, Gillian C., and Michael B. King, eds. *Male Victims of Sexual Assault*. Oxford, UK: University of Oxford Press, 2000.

Micheler, Stefan. "Homophobic Propaganda and the Denunciation of Same-Sex Desiring Men under National Socialism." *Journal of the History of Sexuality* 11, no. 1 and 2 (2002): 105–30.

Miller, Donald E., and Lorna Touryan Miller. *Survivors: An Oral History of the Armenian Genocide*. Berkeley, CA: University of California Press, 1999.

Milton, Sybil. "Hidden Lives: Sinta and Roma Women." In *Experience and Expression: Women, the Nazis and the Holocaust*, edited by Elizabeth Maer and Myrna Goldenberg, 53–75. Detroit, MI: Wayne State University Press, 2003.

Milton, Sybil. "Women and the Holocaust: The Case of German and German-Jewish Women." In *When Biology Became Destiny: Women in Weimar and Nazy Germany*, edited by Renate Bridenthal, Atina Grossman, and Marion Kaplan, 297–333. New York, NY: Monthly Review Press, 1984.

Mintz, Alan. *Popular Culture and the Shaping of Holocaust Memory*. Seattle, WA: University of Washington Press, 2001.

Mitchell, Helen B., and Joseph R. Mitchell, eds. *The Holocaust: Readings and Interpretations*, New York, NY: McGraw-Hill, 2001.

Mitterauer, Micheal, and Reinhard Sieder. *The European Family*. Oxford, UK: Blackwell, 1981.

Mookherjee, Nayanika. "Available Motherhood: Legal Technologies, 'State of Exception' and the Dekinning of 'War-Babies' in Bangladesh." *Childhood: A Global Journal of Child Research* 14, no. 3 (2007): 339–54.

Mookherjee, Nayanika. *The Spectral Wound: Sexual Violence, Public Memories and the Bangladesh War of 1971*. Durham, NC: Duke University Press, 2012.

Morgan, David Hopcraft John. "Masculinity and Violence." In *Women, Violence and Social Control*, edited by Jalna Hanmer and Mary Maynard, 180–92. London, UK: Palgrave McMillan, 1987.

Moser, Caroline O. N., and Fiona C. Clark. "Introduction." In *Victims, Perpetrators or Actors?*, edited by Caroline O. N. Mosner and Fiona C. Clark, 3–12. London, UK: Zed Books Ltd, 2001.

Moses, Dirk, ed. *The Historiography of Genocide*. Basingstoke, UK: Palgrave Macmillan, 2008.

Mostov, Julie. "Sexing the Nation/Desexing the Body Politics of National Identity in the Former Yugoslavia." In *Gender Ironies of Nationalism: Sexing the Nation*, edited by Tamar Mayer, 89–112. London, UK: Routledge, 1999.

Mühläuser, Regina. *Eroberungen. Sexuelle Gewalttaten und intime Beziehungen Deutscher Soldaten in der Sowjetunion 1941-1945*. Hamburg, Germany: Hamburger Edition, 2010.

Mühläuser, Regina. "Between 'Racial Awareness' and Fantasies of Potency: Nazi Sexual Politics in the Occupied Territories of the Soviet Union, 1942, 1945." In *Brutality and Desire: War and Sexuality in Europe's Twentieth Century*, edited by Dagmar Herzog, 197–220. Basingstoke, UK: Palgrave Macmillan, 2009, 2011.

Mukamana, Donatilla, and Petra Brysiewicz. "The Lived Experience of Genocide Rape Survivors in Rwanda." *Journal of Nursing Scholarship* 40, no. 4 (2008): 379–84.

Mullins, Christopher. "'He Would Kill Me with His Penis': Genocidal Rape in Rwanda as a State Crime." *Critical Criminology* 17, no. 1 (2009): 15–33.

Musabyimana, Gaspard. *Pratiques et rites sexuels au Rwanda*. Paris, France: L'Harmattan, 2006.

Naimark, Norman. *Stalin's Genocides*. Princeton, NJ: Princeton University Press, 2010.

Nduwimana, Françoise. *The Right to Survive: Sexual Violence, Women and HIV/AIDS*. Montreal, Canada: International Center for Human Rights and Democratic Development, 2004.

Nelson, James B. *The Intimate Connection: Male Sexuality, Masculine Spirituality*. Philadelphia, PA: Westminster, 1998.

Ní Aoláin, Fionnuala. "Advancing Feminist Positioning in the Field of Transitional Justice." *International Journal of Transitional Justice* 6, no. 2 (2012): 205–28.

Ní Aoláin, Fionnuala. "Emerging Paradigms of Rationality: Exploring a Feminist Theory of Harm in the Context of Conflicted and Post-Conflicted Societies." *Queen's Law Journal* 35, no. 1 (2009): 219–44.

Novick, Peter. *The Holocaust in American Life*. New York, NY: Houghton Mifflin Company, 1999.

Ofer, Dalia, and Lenore J. Weitzman, eds. *Women in the Holocaust*. New Haven, CT: Yale University, 1998.

Olujic, M. B. "Embodiments of Terror: Gender Violence Peacetime and Wartime in Croatia and Bosnia and Herzegovina." *Medical Anthropology Quarterly* 12 (1998): 31–50.

Oomen, Barbara. "Donor-Driven Justice and its Discontents: The Case of Rwanda." *Development and Change* 36, no. 5 (2005): 887–910.

Oosterhoff, Pauline, Prisca Zwanikken, and Evert Ketting. "Sexual Torture of Men in Croatia and Other Conflict Situations: An Open Secret." *Reproductive Health Matters* 12 (2004): 68–77.

Otto, Diane. "The Sexual Tensions of UN Peace Support Operations: A Plea for 'Sexual Positivity.'" *Finnish Yearbook of International Law* 18 (2007): 33–57.

Özdemir, Hikmet, Kemal Çiçek, Ömer Turan, Ramazan Calık, and Yusuf Halacoğlu. *Ermeniler: Sürgün ve Göç*. Ankara, Turkey: Türk Tarih Kurumu, 2004.

Parrot, Andrea and Nina Cummings. *Sexual Enslavement of Girls and Women Worldwide*. Westport, CT: Praeger, 2008.

Peel, Michael. "Men as Perpetrators and Victims." In *Rape as a Method of Torture*, edited by Michael Peel. London, UK: Medical Foundation for the Care of Victims of Torture, 2004.

Peroomian, Rubina. "Historical Memory: Threading the Contemporary Literature of Armenia." In *The Armenian Genocide: Cultural and Ethical Legacies*, edited by Richard G. Hovannisian, 97–120. New Brunswick, NJ: Transaction Publishers, 2007.

Peroomian, Rubina. "Women and the Armenian Genocide: The Victim, the Living Martyr." In *Plight and Fate of Women During and Following Genocide*, edited by Samuel Totten, 7–24. New Brunswick, NJ: Transaction Publishers, 2009.

Pine, Lisa. "Gender and the Family." In *Historiography of the Holocaust*, edited by Dan Stone, 364–82. New York, NY: Palgrave Macmillan, 2004.

Pine, Lisa. *Nazi Family Policy, 1933-1945*. Oxford, UK: Berg, 1997.

Plümper, Thomas, and Eric Neumayer. "The Unequal Burden of War: The Effect of Armed Conflict on the Gender Gap in Life Expectancy." *International Organization* 60, no. 3 (2006): 723–54.

Podolsky, Anatoly. "The Tragic Fate of Ukrainian Jewish Women during the Holocaust." In *Sexual Violence Against Women During the Holocaust*, edited by Sonja M. Hedgpeth and Rochelle G. Saidel, 94–108. Waltham, MA: Brandeis University Press, 2010.

Power, Samantha. *"A Problem from Hell": America and the Age of Genocide*. New York, NY: Basic Books, 2002.

Price, Lisa S. "Finding the Man in the Soldier-Rapist: Some Reflections on Comprehension and Accountability." *Women's Studies International Forum* 24, no. 2 (2001): 211–27.

Proctor, Robert N. "The Destruction of Lives Not Worth Living." In *Deviant Bodies: Critical Perspectives on Difference in Science and Popular Culture*, edited by Jennifer Terry and Jacqueline Urla, 170–96. Bloomington and Indianapolis, IN: Indiana University Press, 1995.

Prunier, Gérard. *The Rwanda Crisis: History of a Genocide*. New York, NY: Columbia University Press, 1997.

Rehn, Elisabeth, and Ellen Johnson Sirleaf. *Women, War and Peace: The Independent Experts' Assessment on the Impact of Armed Conflict on Women and Women's Role in Peacebuilding*. New York, NY: UNIFEM, 2002.

Rettig, Max. "Gacaca: Truth, Justice, and Reconciliation in Postconflict Rwanda?" *African Studies Review* 51, no. 3 (2008): 25–50.

Reyntjens, Filip. *The Great African War: Congo and Regional Geopolitics, 1996-2006*. Cambridge, UK: Cambridge University Press, 2009.

Rhode, David. *Endgame, The Betrayal and Fall of Srebrenica. Europe's Worst Massacre since World War II*. Boulder, CO: Westview Press, 1997.

Richter-Lyonette, Elenor. "Women after the Genocide in Rwanda." In *In the Aftermath of Rape: Women's Rights, War Crimes and Genocide*, edited by Elenor Richter-Lyonette. Givrins, Switzerland: Coordination of Women's Advocacy, 1997.

Ringelheim, Joan. "Thoughts about Women and the Holocaust." In *Thinking the Unthinkable: Meanings of the Holocaust*, edited by Roger Gottlieb, 141–9. New York, NY: Paulist Press, 1990.

Ringelheim, Joan. "Women and the Holocaust: A Reconsideration of Research." In *Different Voices: Women and the Holocaust*, edited by Carol Rittner and John Roth, 373–405. New York, NY: Paragon House, 1993.

Ringelheim, Joan. "Women and the Holocaust: A Reconsideration of Research." *Signs: Journal of Women in Culture and Society* 10, no. 4 (1985): 741–61.

Rittner, Carol, and John Roth, eds. *Different Voices: Women and the Holocaust.* New York, NY: Paragon House, 1993.

Rosenbaum, Alan, ed. *Is the Holocaust Unique: Perspectives on Comparative Genocide.* Boulder, CO: Westview Press, 1996.

Ross, Andrew. *Mixed Emotions: Beyond Fear and Hatred in International Conflict.* Chicago, IL: University of Chicago Press, 2014.

Rowe, Victoria. "Armenian Women Refugees at the End of Empire: Strategies of Survival." In *Refugees and the End of Empire: Imperial Collapse and Forced Migration in the Twentieth Century*, edited by Panikos Panayi and Pipa Virdee, 152–74. New York, NY: Palgrave Macmillan, 2011.

Rubio-Marín, Ruth. "The Gender of Reparations in Transitional Societies." In *The Gender of Reparations: Unsettling Sexual Hierarchies while Redressing Human Rights Violations*, edited by Ruth Rubio-Marin, 63–120. New York, NY: Cambridge University Press, 2009.

Rubio-Marín, Ruth. "Reparations for Conflict-Related Sexual and Reproductive Violence: A Decalogue." *William & Mary Journal of Women and the Law* 19, no. 1 (2012): 69–104.

Rumney, Phillip, and Martin Morgan-Taylor. "The Construction of Sexual Consent in Male Rape and Sexual Assault." In *Making Sense of Sexual Consent*, edited by Mark Cowling and Paul Reynolds, 141–70. Aldershot, UK: Ashgate, 2004.

Russell, Wynne. "Sexual Violence Against Men and Boys." *Forced Migration Review* 27 (2007): 22–3.

Ruvinsky, Elysia. *"My Heart Bleeds, But Where To Take My Grief Is Not There": Wartime Sexual Violence Against Men in the Balkan and Great Lakes Regions.* Thesis, University of Amsterdam, 2012.

Saidel, Rochelle. *The Jewish Women of Ravensbruck Concentration Camp.* Madison, WI: University of Wisconsin Press, 2004.

Saikia, Yasmin. "Overcoming the Silent Archive in Bangladesh: Women Bearing Witness to Violence in the 1971 'Liberation' War." In *Women and the Contested State*, edited by Monique Skidmore and Patricia Lawrence, 64–82. Notre Dame, IN: University of Notre Dame Press, 2007.

Saikia, Yasmin. *Women, War, and the Making of Bangladesh: Remembering 1971.* Durham, NC: Duke University Press, 2011.

Salzman, Todd A. "Rape Camps as a Means to Ethnic Cleansing: Religious, Cultural, and Ethical Responses to Rape Victims in the Former Yugoslavia." *Human Rights Quarterly* 20, no. 2 (1998): 348–78.

Salzman, Todd A. "Rape Camps, Forced Impregnation, and Ethnic Cleansing." In *War's Dirty Secret: Rape, Prostitution, and Other Crimes Against Women*, edited by Anne Llewellyn Barstow, 63–92. Cleveland, OH: Ohio Press, 2000.

Sanasarian, Eliz. "Gender Distinction in the Genocidal Process: A Preliminary Study of the Armenian Case." *Holocaust and Genocide Studies* 4, no. 4 (1989): 449–61.

Sarafian, Ara. "The Absorption of Armenian Women and Children Into Muslim Households as a Structural Component of the Armenian Genocide." In *In God's Name: Genocide and Religion in the Twentieth Century*, edited by Omer Bartov and Phyllis Mack, 209–21. New York, NY and Oxford, UK: Berghahn Books, 2001.

Sarti, Wendy Adele-Marie. *Women and Nazis: Perpetrators of Genocide and Other Crimes During Hitler's Regime, 1933-1945*. Palo Alto, CA: Academica Press, 2010.

Schabas, William. *Genocide in International Law: The Crime of Crimes*, 2nd edn. Cambridge, UK: Cambridge University Press, 2009.

Scheffer, David. "Genocide and Atrocity Crimes." *Genocide Studies and Prevention* 1, no. 3 (2006): 229–50.

Schiessel, Christoph. "An Element of Genocide: Rape, Total War, and International Law in the Twentieth Century." *Journal of Genocide Research* 4, no. 2 (2010): 197–210.

Schilling, Donald G., ed. *Lessons and Legacies, Volume II: Teaching the Holocaust in a Changing World*. Evanston, IL: Northwestern University, 1998.

Schlegel, Alice, and Rohn Eloul. "Marriage Transactions: Labor, Property, Status." *American Anthropologist* 90, no. 2 (1988): 291–309.

Schoppmann, Claudia. "National Socialist Policies towards Female Homosexuality." In *Gender Relations in German History: Power, Agency and Experience from the Sixteenth to the Twentieth Century*, edited by Lynn Abrams and Elizabeth Harvey. Durham, NC: Duke University Press, 1996.

Segalman, Ralph. "The Psychology of Jewish Displaced Persons." *Jewish Social Service Quarterly* 23, no. 4 (1947): 363–5.

Seifert, Ruth. "War and Rape: A Preliminary Analysis." In *Mass Rape: The War Against Women in Bosnia-Herzegovina*, edited by Alexandra Stiglmayer, 54–72. Lincoln, NE: University of Nebraska Press, 1994.

Selçuk, Funda. "Türk Basınında Ermeni Sorunu (Mayıs 1919-Aralık 1920)." MA thesis, Ankara Üniversitesi, 2003.

Sémelin, Jacques. *Purify and Destroy: the Political Uses of Massacre and Genocide*. London, UK: Hurst and Co., 2007.

Sharlach, Lisa. "Gender and Genocide in Rwanda: Women as Agents and Objects of Genocide." *Journal of Genocide Research* 1, no. 3 (1999): 387–99.

Sharlach, Lisa. "Rape as Genocide: Bangladesh, the Former Yugoslavia, and Rwanda." *New Political Science* 22, no. 1 (2000): 89–102.

Sharratt, Sara and Ellyn Kaschak, eds. *Assault on the Soul: Women in the Former Yugoslavia*. New York, NY: The Haworth Press, 1999.

Shaw, Martin. *What is Genocide?* Cambridge, UK: Polity Press, 2007.

Shemmassian, Vahram. "The League of Nations and the Reclamation of Armenian Genocide Survivors." In *Looking Backward, Moving Forward: Confronting the Armenian Genocide*, edited by Richard Hovannisian, 81–112. New Brunswick, NJ: Transaction Publishers, 2003.

Shepherd, Laura J. "Sex, Security and Superhero(in)es: From 1325 to 1820 and Beyond." *International Feminist Journal of Politics* 13, no. 4 (2011): 504–21.

Shik, Na'ama. "Sexual Abuse of Jewish Women in Auschwitz-Birkenau." In *Brutality and Desire: War and Sexuality in Europe's Twentieth Century*, edited by Dagmar Herzog, 221–46. Basingstoke, UK: Palgrave Macmillan, 2009, 2011.

Simić, Olivera. "What Remains of Srebrenica? Motherhood, Transitional Justice & Yearning for the Truth." *Journal of International Women's Studies* 10, no. 4 (2009): 220–236.

Simić, Olivera. *Surviving Peace: A Political Memoir*, Spinifex, 2014.

Sinnreich, Helene. "'And It Was Something We Didn't Talk about:' Rape of Jewish Women during the Holocaust." *Holocaust Studies: A Journal of Culture and History* 14, no. 2 (2008): 1–22.

Sinnreich, Helene. "The Rape of Jewish Women during the Holocaust." In *Sexual Violence Against Jewish Women During the Holocaust*, edited by Sonja M. Hedgepeth and Rochelle G. Saidel, 108–23. Waltham, MA: Brandeis University Press, 2010.

Sinnreich, Helene. "Women and the Holocaust." In *Plight and Fate of Women During and Following Genocide*, edited by Samuel Totten, 25–46. London, UK and New Brunswick, NJ: Transaction Publishers, 2009.

Sivakumaran, Sandesh. "Sexual Violence Against Men in Armed Conflict." *European Journal of International Law* 18 (2007): 253–76.

Sivakumaran, Sandesh, and Paula Drumond. "Lost in Translation: UN Responses to Sexual Violence against Men and Boys in Situations of Armed Conflict." *International Review of the Red Cross* 92, no. 877 (2010): 259–77

Sjoberg, Laura, and Caron E. Gentry. *Mothers, Monsters, Whores: Women's Violence in Global Politics*. London, UK: Zed Books, 2007.

Skjelsbæk, Inger. "Sexual Violence in Times of War: A New Challenge for Peace Operations?" *International Peacekeeping* 8, no. 2 (2001): 69–84.

Smart, Carol. *Feminism and the Power of Law: Sociology of Law and Crime*. New York, NY: Routledge, 1989.

Smith, Karen E. *Genocide and the Europeans*. Cambridge, UK: Cambridge University Press, 2010.

Smith, Roger W. "Women and Genocide: Notes on an Unwritten History." *Holocaust and Genocide Studies* 8, no. 3 (1994): 315–34.

Snyder, Cindy S., Wesley J. Gabbard, J. Dean May, and Nihada Zulčić. "On the Battleground of Women's Bodies: Mass Rape in Bosnia-Herzegovina." *Afflia* 21 (2006): 184–95.

Sofos, Spyros A. "Inter-Ethnic Violence and Gendered Constructions of Ethnicity in Former Yugoslavia." *Social Identities* 2, no. 1 (1996): 73–91.

Soh, C. Sarah. *The Comfort Women: Sexual Violence and Postcolonial Memory in Korea and Japan*. Chicago, IL: University of Chicago Press, 2008.

Sommer, Robert. "Camp Brothels: Forced Sex Labour in Nazi Concentration Camps." In *Brutality and Desire: War and Sexuality in Europe's Twentieth Century*, edited by Dagmar Herzog, 168–96. Basingstoke, UK: Palgrave Macmillan, 2009, 2011.

Sommers, Marc. *Stuck: Rwandan Youth and the Struggle for Adulthood*. Athens, GA: University of Georgia Press, 2012.

Southwick, Katherine. "Srebrenica as Genocide? The Krstić Decision and the Language of the Unspeakable." *Yale Human Rights and Development Law Journal* 8, no. 188 (2005): 188–227.

Sperling, Carrie. "Mother of Atrocities: Pauline Nyiramasuhuko's Role in the Rwanda Genocide." *Fordham Urban Law Journal* 33 (2006): 637–64.

Stanko, Elizabeth A., Louise Marian, Debbie Crisp. Rachel Manning, Jonathan Smith, and Sharon Cowan. *Taking Stock: What Do We Know About Interpersonal Violence?* Surrey, UK: ESRC Violence Research Programme, Royal Holloway University of London, 2002.

Stanton, Gregory H. "Eight Stages of Genocide." In *The Genocide Studies Reader*, edited by Samuel Totten and Paul Robert Bartrop, 127–32. New York, NY: Routledge, 2009.

Stanton, Gregory H. "Proving Genocide in Darfur: The Atrocities Documentation Project and Resistance to Its Findings." In *Genocide in Darfur: Investigating*

Atrocities in Sudan, edited by Samuel Totten and Eric Markusen, 181–8. New York, NY: Routledge, 2006.

Staub, Ervin. "The Origins of Genocide and Mass Killing: Core Concepts." In *The Genocide Studies Reader*, edited by Samuel Totten and Paul Robert Bartrop, 97–107. New York, NY: Routledge, 2009.

Staub, Ervin. *The Roots of Evil: The Origins of Genocide and Other Group Violence*. Cambridge, UK: Cambridge University Press, 1989.

Steinmacher, Sybille. *Auschwitz: A History*. London, UK: Penguin Books, 2005.

Stemple, Lara. "Male Rape and Human Rights." *Hastings Law Review* 60 (2009): 605–46.

Stiglmayer, Alexandra, ed. "The Rapes in Bosnia-Herzegovina." In *Mass Rape: The War Against Women in Bosnia-Herzegovina*, edited by Alexandra Stiglmayer. Lincoln, NE: University of Nebraska Press, 1994.

Stone, Dan, ed. *The Historiography of the Holocaust*. Basingstoke, UK and New York, NY: Palgrave Macmillan, 2004.

Storr, Will. "The Rape of Men." *Observer*. Available online: http://www.guardian.co.uk/society/2011/jul/17/the-rape-of-men (accessed July 17, 2011).

Straus, Scott. *The Order of Genocide: Race, Power, and War in Rwanda*. Ithaca, NY: Cornell University Press, 2006.

Tachjian, Vahé. "Gender, Nationalism, Exclusion: The Reintegration Process of Female Survivors of the Armenian Genocide." *Nations and Nationalism* 15, no. 1 (2009): 60–80.

Tavitian, Anahid. *Yergo Dziranner (Arvesde yev Engerayin Dzarayutiune)*. Beirut, Lebanon: Published by her family, 2006.

Taylor, Christopher C. *Sacrifice as Terror: The Rwandan Genocide of 1994*. London, UK: Berg Publishers, 1999.

Taylor, Christopher C. "The Cultural Face of Terror in the Rwandan Genocide of 1994." In *Annihilating Difference: The Anthropology of Genocide*, edited by Alexander Laban Hinton, 137–78. Los Angeles, CA: University of California Press, 2002.

Tec, Nechama. *Resilience and Courage: Women, Men and the Holocaust*. New Haven, CT: Yale University Press, 2004.

Theidon, Kimberly. "Gender in Transition: Common Sense, Women, and War." *Journal of Human Rights* 6 (2007): 453–78.

Theriault, Henry. "Gender and Genocide: New Perspectives for Armenian Genocide Research." Paper presented at the Armenian Genocide Workshop, Strassler Center for Holocaust and Genocide Studies, Clark University, Worcester, MA, April 8–10, 2010.

"The United Nations Convention on the Prevention and Punishment of the Crime of Genocide." In *The Genocide Studies Reader*, edited by Samuel Totten and Paul Bartrop, 30–3. London, UK and New York, NY: Routledge, 2009.

Toal, Gerald, and Carl T. Dahlman. *Bosnia Remade: Ethnic Cleansing and its Reversal*. New York, NY: Oxford University Press, 2011.

Toljaga, Daniel. "Prelude to the Srebrenica Genocide: Mass Murder and Ethnic Cleansing of Bosniaks in the Srebrenica Region during the First Three Months of the Bosnian War (April-June 1992)." Accessed July 11, 2014. http://www.bosnia.org.uk/news/news_body.cfm?newsid=2771.

Tompkins, Tamara L. "Prosecuting Rape as a War Crime: Speaking the Unspeakable." *Notre Dame Law Review* 70 (1995): 845–90.

Totten, Samuel. *Impediments to the Prevention and Intervention of Genocide (Genocide: A Critical Bibliographic Review)*. New Brunswick, NJ and London, UK: Transaction Publishers, 2013.

Totten, Samuel, ed. *Plight and Fate of Women During and Following Genocide*. New Brunswick, NJ: Transaction Publishers, 2009.

Totten, Samuel, ed. *Teaching About Genocide: Issues, Approaches, and Resources*. Greenwich, CT: Information Age Publishing, 2004.

Totten, Samuel, ed. "The Darfur Genocide: The Mass Rape of Black African Girls and Women." In *Plight and Fate of Women During and Following Genocide*, edited by Samuel Totten, 137–68. New Brunswick, NJ: Transaction Publishers, 2009.

Totten, Samuel, and Steven Leonard Jacobs, eds. *Pioneers of Genocide Studies*. London and New Brunswick, NJ: Transaction Publishers, 2002.

Totten, Samuel, William S. Parsons, and Israel W. Charny, eds. *A Century of Genocide: Eyewitness Accounts and Critical Views*. New York, NY: Routledge, 1997.

Totten, Samuel, William S. Parsons, and Israel W. Charny, eds. *Genocide in the Twentieth Century: Critical Essays and Eyewitness Testimony*. New York, NY: Garland Publishing, Inc., 1995.

True, Jacqui. *The Political Economy of Violence Against Women*. New York, NY: Oxford University Press, 2012.

Turshen, Meredeth. "The Political Economy of Rape: An Analysis of Systematic Rape and Sexual Abuse of Women during Armed Conflict in Africa." In *Victims, Perpetrators or Actors?: Gender, Armed Conflict and Political Violence*, edited by Caroline O. N. Moser and Fiona C. Clark, 55–68. London, UK: Zed Books, 2001.

Turshen, Meredeth, and Clotilde Twagiramariya. "The Sexual Politics of Survival in Rwanda." In *What Women Do in Wartime: Gender and Conflict in Africa*, edited by Meredeth Turshen and Clotidle Twagiramariya, 101–21. New York, UK: Zed Books, 1998.

Tyrnauer, Gabrielle. "The Fate of the Gypsies During the Holocaust." In *The Gypsies of Eastern Europe*, edited by David Crowe and John Kolsti. Armonk, NY: M. E. Sharpe, 1991.

Ülgen, Fatma. "Reading Mustafa Kemal Atatürk on the Armenian Genocide of 1915." *Patterns of Prejudice* 44, no.4 (2010): 369–91.

United Nations. "Convention on the Prevention and Punishment of the Crime of Genocide." Available online: http://www.preventgenocide.org/law/convention/text.htm.

United Nations. *Final Report of the Group of Experts on the Democratic Republic of the Congo*. (S/2014/42), January 22, 2014.

Valentino, Benjamin. *Final Solutions: Mass Killing and Genocide in the 20th Century*. Ithaca, NY: Cornell University Press, 2005.

Van Schaack, Beth. "Engendering Genocide: The Akayesu Case Before the International Criminal Tribunal for Rwanda." In *Human Rights Advocacy Stories (Law Stories)*, edited by Deena R. Hurwitz, Margaret L. Satterthwaite, and Douglas B. Ford, 196–228. New York, NY: Foundation Press, 2008.

Verwimp, Philip. "Machetes and Firearms: The Organization of Massacres in Rwanda." *Journal of Peace Research* 43, no. 1 (2006): 5–22.

Villa, Susie H., and Mary K. Matossian. *Armenian Village Life Before 1914*. Detroit, MI: Wayne State University Press, 1982.

von Joeden-Forgey, Elisa. "Devil in the Details: 'Life Force Atrocities' and the Assault on the Family in Times of Conflict." *Genocide Studies and Prevention 5*, no. 1 (2010): 1–19.

von Joeden-Forgey, Elisa. "Gender and Genocide." In *The Oxford Handbook of Genocide Studies*, edited by Donald Bloxham and A. Dirk Moses, 69–80. Oxford, UK: Oxford University Press, 2010.

von Joeden-Forgey, Elisa. "Genocidal Masculinity." In *New Directions in Genocide Research*, edited by Adam Jones, 76–95. New York, NY: Routledge, 2011.

von Joeden-Forgey, Elisa. "Sexual Violence and Genocide in the DRC." *Institute for the Study of Genocide Newsletter* 45 (2010). Available online: http://www. instituteforthestudyofgenocide.org/newsletters/isg45/ISG45.pdf (accessed July 22, 2011).

Vranic, Seada. *Breaking the Wall of Silence: The Voices of Raped Bosnia*. Zagreb, Croatia: Anti Barbarus, 1996.

Vrdoljak, Ana Filipa. "Human Rights and Genocide: The Work of Lauterpacht and Lemkin in Modern International Law." *The European Journal of International Law* 20, no. 4 (2010): 1163–94.

Vušković, Linda, and Zorica Trifunović, eds. *Women's Side of War*. Belgrade, Serbia: Women in Black, 2008.

Waldorf, Lars. "Mass Justice for Mass Atrocity: Rethinking Local Justice as Transitional Justice." *Temple Law Review* 79, no. 1 (2006): 1–87.

Warren, Mary Ann. *Gendercide: The Implications of Sex Selection*. Totowa, NJ: Rowman & Allanheld, 1985.

Watenpaugh, Keith David. "'Are There Any Children for Sale?': Genocide and the Transfer of Armenian Children (1915-1922)." *Journal of Human Rights* 12, no. 3 (2013): 283–95.

Watenpaugh, Keith David. "The League of Nations' Rescue of Armenian Genocide Survivors and the Making of Modern Humanitarianism, 1920-1927." *American Historical Review* 115, no. 5 (2010): 1315–39.

Waxman, Zoë. "Rape and Sexual Abuse in Hiding." In *Sexual Violence Against Women During the Holocaust*, edited by Sonja M. Hedgpeth and Rochelle G. Saidel, 124–35. Waltham, MA: Brandeis University Press, 2010.

Waxman, Zoë. "Testimony and Silence: Sexual Violence and the Holocaust." In *Feminism, Literature and Rape Narratives*, edited by Sorcha Gunne and Zoe Brigley Thompson, 117–29. London, UK: Routledge, 2010.

Waxman, Zoë. "Towards an Integrated History of the Holocaust: Masculinity, Femininity, and Genocide." In *Years of Persecution, Years of Extermination: Saul Frielander and the Future of the Holocaust Studies*, edited by Christian Wiese and Paul Betts, 311–22. London, UK: Continuum, 2010.

Waxman, Zoë. "Unheard Stories: Reading Women's Holocaust Testimonies." *The Jewish Quarterly* 47, no. 177 (2000): 661–77.

Waxman, Zoë. *Writing the Holocaust: Identity, Testimony, Representation*. Oxford, UK: Oxford University Press, 2006.

Weitsman, Patricia A. "Children Born of War and the Politics of Identity." In *Born of War: Protecting Children of Sexual Violence Survivors in Conflict Zones*, edited by R. Charli Carpenter, 110–27. Bloomfield, IN: Kumarian Press, 2007.

Weitsman, Patricia A. "The Politics of Identity and Sexual Violence: A Review of Bosnia and Rwanda." *Human Rights Quarterly* 30, no. 3 (2008): 561–78.

Weitz, Eric D. *A Century of Genocide: Utopias of Race and Nation.* Oxford, UK: Princeton University Press, 2003.

Weitz, Eric D. "From the Vienna to the Paris System: International Politics and the Entangled Histories of Human Rights, Forced Deportations, and Civilizing Missions." *American Historical Review* 113, no. 5 (2008): 1313–43.

Wierzynska, Aneta. "Consolidating Democracy Through Transitional Justice: Rwanda's Gacaca Courts." *New York University Law Review* 79, no. 5 (2004): 1934–69.

Wilson, Richard A. *Writing History in International Criminal Trials.* Cambridge, UK: Cambridge University Press, 2011.

Wood, Elisabeth J. "Armed Groups and Sexual Violence: When is Wartime Rape Rare?" *Politics & Society* 37, no. 1 (2009): 131–62.

Wood, Elisabeth J. "Variation of Sexual Violence during War." *Politics and Society* 34, no. 3 (2006): 307–42.

World Health Organization. "Sexual Violence." In *World Report on Violence and Health*, 149–81. Geneva, Switzerland: World Health Organization, 2002.

Zarkov, Dubravka. "The Body of the Other Man: Sexual Violence and the Construction of Masculinity, Sexuality and Ethnicity in Croatian Media." In *Victims, Perpetrators or Actors? Gender, Armed Conflict and Political Violence*, edited by Caroline O. N. Moser and Fiona C. Clark, 69–82. London, UK and New York, NY: Zed Books, 2001.

Zarkov, Dubravka. "War Rapes in Bosnia: On Masculinity, Femininity and Power of the Rape Victim Identity." *Tijdschrift voor Criminologie* 39, no. 2 (1997): 140–51.

Zawait, Hilmi. "Impunity or Immunity: Wartime Male Rape and Sexual Torture as a Crime against Humanity." *Torture* 7 (2007): 27–47.

Živak, Strahinja. *Logor Čelebići 1992–4.* Edicija Srpske, 1997.

Zongwe, Dunia Prince. "The New Sexual Violence Legislation in the Congo: Dressing Indelible Scars on Human Dignity." *African Studies Review* 55 (2012): 37–57.

Zraly, Maggie A. *Bearing: Resilience Among Genocide-Rape Survivors in Rwanda.* PhD diss., Case Western Reserve, 2008.

Zraly, Maggie, and Laetitia Nyirazinyoye. "Don't Let the Suffering Make You Fade Away: An Ethnographic Study of Resilience Among Survivors of Genocide-Rape in Southern Rwanda." *Social Science & Medicine* 70, no. 10 (2010): 1656–64.

Zur, Judith. "Remembering and Forgetting: Guatemalan War Widows' Forbidden Memories." In *Trauma and Life Stories: International Perspectives (Routledge Studies in Memory and Narrative)*, edited by Kim Lacy Rogers, Selma Leydesdorff, and Graham Dawson. London, UK and New York, NY: Routledge, 1999.

Zwaan, Ton. *Civilisering en decivilisering: Studies over staatsvorming en geweld, nationalisme en vervolging.* Amsterdam, Netherlands: Boom, 2001.

INDEX

dissociation 260
Dolan, Chris 71
Donia, Robert 285
Dowd, Nancy 240
Drakulic, Slavenka 15
Drumbl, Mark 19, 189, 205, *see also*
women as perpetrators, in
Rwandan genocide
Drumond, Paula 68

East Pakistan/Bangladesh, genocide
in 11, 17, 28nn. 54, 55, 32n. 84,
121, 137n. 35, 225, 306
Eichmann, Adolf 9
Eicke, Theodor 169–70
Ekmekcioglu, Lerna 20, 215, *see also*
Armenian rescue efforts
enslavement and forced
assimilation 17–18, 88–9, 95,
97–9, 101, 287
Ensler, Eve
Vagina Monologues 135
Enver, Ishmail 93
extermination 6, 8–10, 64–6, 69,
79n. 6, 95, 171, 199, 217

Fearon, James 122
forced impregnation and maternity
2, 18, 107, 115, 121, 123–7,
299, 301
Serbian policies of 15, 108, 113,
121, 127–32, 134–5, 137n. 27
wartime sexual violence, case of
Bosnia 127–32
forced labor of children 73–6
in Congolese wars 74–5
and exposure to pervasive sexual
predation and servitude 75
humanitarian intervention
into 78
Human Rights Watch report 74
forced marriages 2–3, 81n. 28,
89, 95, 145–6, 153, 205,
252n. 44, 287
forced sterilization 2, 33n. 86, 48,
107, 112, 118n. 24, 127
Frankl, Victor 42–3, 56
Fraser, Nancy 269
Free the Slaves 75–6, 83n. 45

gacaca courts 191, 193, 195, 197,
201–4, 278
Gacaca Law 190, 193–5, 197
Gafishi, Philippe 143
Gaudillière, Jean Max 259
Gelissen, Rena 45–6, 48–50, 52
gendercidal institutions 63
intervention into 77
against men and boys 71–3
gendercide(s) 64, 95–7
gendered dimensions of genocide 1–4,
7, 17–22, 37–9, 280, 286,
298–301, 305–7
in Argentina 307–8
Armenian genocide 18, 20, 87–9,
94–100, *see also* Armenian rescue
efforts
Bosnia-Herzegovina genocide
15, 20–1, 79n. 6, 108, 125–6,
238–9, 242–9, 280, 306, 309,
313–15
contribution to genocide
prevention 4, 21, 66–9, 300,
306, 309, 311
in Darfur 306, 309–13
genocide determinations 21, 307–9
in Holocaust studies 1, 14–15,
18–19, 38, 40–51, 108–13, 125,
167–9, 182–3
justice 3, 21, 289–91
leaders and perpetrators of
genocide 2, 19, 13–14,
19–21, 37, 63, 70–1, 76,
78, 87, 89, 92, 94–8, 100–1,
113, 127, 131, 140–1, 146–9,
152, 169–74, 176, 179–81,
190–8, 285, 287–8, 290,
299–312
in postgenocidal Bosnia-
Herzegovina 3, 124–7,
134, 205
pronatalism of Bosnian Muslim
women, postwar 123, 134
role in memory and
commemoration 4, 9–10, 15,
26n. 38, 27n. 50, 39, 132–3, 154,
260–3, 267
in Rwandan genocide 2, 17–19,
21, 141–8, 306

Sendashonga, Seth 66
Serbian policies against Bosniak
    women
    of mass rape, forced impregnation,
        and forced maternity 18,
        127–32, 137n. 27
    pronatalism, postwar 123, 134
Sereny, Gitta 171–2
Sèvres Treaty 218
sexual identity and behavior, in context
        of Auschwitz 51–4
    concealment of pregnancies 54
    fight for survival and women's
        sexual conduct 53
    killing of newborn children 54
    lesbianism 52, 55
    moral choice 55
    Puffkommando (brothel), existence
        of 53–4
    women as a position of "double
        jeopardy" 56
sexualized killings 99–100
    eyewitness account of 99–100
    interlinked with ideas of femininity
        and masculinity 100
sexual mutilation and torture 7, 15,
        17–18, 20, 70, 89, 95, 109, 128,
        140, 146, 191, 239–40, 243–4,
        246–7, 249, 299, 301–5
sexual violence 305, *see also* forced
        impregnation and maternity;
        forced sterilization; genocidal
        sexual violence; mass rape; sexual
        mutilation and torture; wartime
        sexual violence, case of
    aftermath of 132–4, 149–52
    based on ascribed identities 147
    in Bosnia-Herzegovina 15, 108,
        113, 121–2, 238–9, 242–8
    in concentration camps 42–51,
        110–12
    conceptual approach 88–9
    in conflict zones 63, 67, 70–1, 73,
        75–6, 145
    defined 81n. 28
    during the 1994 genocide in
        Rwanda 146–9
    escalation during civil war 146
    ethnographic research 153–4

Human Rights Watch report
        149–50
    impact of 113–14
    Meredeth Turshen's comparative
        analysis, in Rwanda and
        Mozambique 141–2
    and Nazi prohibition on sexual
        relations between "Aryans" and
        Jews 47, 109, 112, 127
    rape survivors, status of 152–5
    survivors of 114–16
    Tutsi women, case of 147–8
sexual violence on males 69–71,
        see also male/masculine
        vulnerabilities in genocide;
        women and genocide, study of
    conflict-associated sexual
        violence 71
    in contemporary instances of
        genocide and war-unto-
        genocide 70
    in detention camps and other
        detention facilities 242–9
    male-on-male sexual abuse 69–71,
        240–2, 244
    male rape 7, 69–71, 78, 237–42
    male survivors of rape 246–9, 305
    reports of mutilation and
        subsequent public display of male
        genitalia 15, 20, 22, 70, 88,
        114, 140, 146, 240, 242–3, 282,
        301, 303–4
    testimonies 244–5
    victims seeking assistance 248
Shaw, Martin 304
Shik, Na'ama 114
Simić, Olivera 20, 237, *see also* sexual
        violence on males
Sinnreich, Helene 114
Sivakumaran, Sandesh 70
Smart, Carol 289–90
Smith, Valerie 154
Soh, C. Sarah 141, 155
Srebrenica genocide, survivors
        of 313–14
    Bosniaks, experiences of 238–9,
        242–5, 261
    confusion and betrayal, state
        of 264–6

survivors of sexual violence 215,
226–29, 232n. 18
Turkification process and 99
women and Bosnian genocide 14–15,
18, 21, 88, 107–8, 112–14, 121,
123–4, 137n. 27, 153, 226, 238
forced impregnation and
maternity 121, 127–32
marginalization of children born of
rape 132–4
rape and sexual violence 108, 114,
280–2, 286, 298, 301–2
social status of women 126–7
testimonies in international criminal
prosecutions 3, 260–70
women survivors 259–70, 289
Yugoslavian women, mass rape
of 280
women and Holocaust, study of
Auschwitz, privations and
experiences of at 42–5, 48–9
enslavement of women and
children 17, 88–9, 95, 97–9,
109, 111, 113–14, 140, 153, 240,
282, 287
Holocaust studies 14–15, 18, 39–42,
45–51, 166–8, 175–6, 179–81
mass rape 14, 70, 88, 108,
129–32, 199, 304–5
Nazi persecution, testimonies of
women 41–2
rape against Jewish women 18, 47,
109–11
women and Rwandan genocide 14–15,
18, 20, 67–73, 80n. 8, 92, 107–8,
112–15, 226, see also Rwanda;
Rwandan genocide; women as
perpetrators, in Rwandan
genocide

mass killings 69, 108
rape and sexual violence 69–70,
88, 114, 121, 146–9, 286, 298,
301–2
survivors of sexual violence 77, 115,
141, 148–55, 194, 196–7, 226
testimonies in international criminal
prosecutions 3, 260–70
women as perpetrators, in Rwandan
genocide
as authority figures 198–204
exposing victims
to the killers 192–4
female killers 190–2
to gain US citizenship 202–3
in property crimes 194–5
women's Holocaust studies 14–15,
18, 20, 39–42 , 45–54,
166–8, 175–6
women, views about
abortion-seeking 224
patriarchal beliefs about role and
status 123–4
in policy of rape warfare, forced
impregnation, and forced
maternity 131–2
sterilization 2, 33n. 86, 48, 112,
118n. 24, 127
as vessels of the state 134
Wood, Elisabeth Jean 88, 287

Yaghoubian, Dr. 224–6
Yugoslavia (former), war in 128

Zarkov, Dubravka 238, 240,
242, 318n. 23
Zawati, Hilmi 241
Zraly, Maggie A. 152
Zulu, Shaka 80n. 8